European Community Labour Law:
Principles and Perspectives

European Community Labour Law: Principles and Perspectives

Liber Amicorum
Lord Wedderburn of Charlton

PAUL DAVIES
ANTOINE LYON-CAEN
SILVANA SCIARRA
and
SPIROS SIMITIS

CLARENDON PRESS · OXFORD

This book has been printed digitally and produced in a standard specification
in order to ensure its continuing availability

OXFORD
UNIVERSITY PRESS

Great Clarendon Street, Oxford OX2 6DP

Oxford University Press is a department of the University of Oxford.
It furthers the University's objective of excellence in research, scholarship,
and education by publishing worldwide in

Oxford New York

Auckland Cape Town Dar es Salaam Hong Kong Karachi
Kuala Lumpur Madrid Melbourne Mexico City Nairobi
New Delhi Shanghai Taipei Toronto
With offices in
Argentina Austria Brazil Chile Czech Republic France Greece
Guatemala Hungary Italy Japan South Korea Poland Portugal
Singapore Switzerland Thailand Turkey Ukraine Vietnam

Oxford is a registered trade mark of Oxford University Press
in the UK and in certain other countries

Published in the United States
by Oxford University Press Inc., New York

Oxford is a registered trade mark of Oxford University Press
in the UK and in certain other countries

Published in the United States
by Oxford University Press Inc., New York

© The Authors and Contributors 1996

The moral rights of the author have been asserted

Database right Oxford University Press (maker)

Reprinted 2005

ISBN 0-19-826010-5

Dedication

This volume is neither a collection of random contributions from a few authors simply wishing to thank Lord Wedderburn for years of friendship, in other words a *Festschrift* in the traditional sense, nor yet does it include offerings from all those who feel, on whatever grounds, in his intellectual debt. It is, instead, an attempt to present a tribute to the man, the teacher and the author by elaborating a theme befitting his own very special and exacting set of values.

In all his intellectual work Lord Wedderburn combines a number of cardinal qualities which this volume strives to echo. First and foremost, he possesses an awareness of diversity in all its wealth of importance, which, as this century draws to a close, is sadly wanting in so many of his contemporaries. Without that perspective he would never have become the discerning comparatist that he is, uniting an intimate knowledge of institutions with a meticulous observation and thorough understanding of the circumstances under which they have originated and must function. And without that perspective he would not have been so quickly alive to the construction of Europe, to the hopes it inspired and to the frustrations and illusions it engendered. Neither optimistic in the logic of his thinking nor pessimistic in the clarity of his observation, he recognises only that all people everywhere have a history which it would be futile to deny but which they can, with enlightenment, learn to shape.

Europe is a concept in which there is no place for certainties. On that score Lord Wedderburn will be one of those who have served its cause best, for the innumerable articles, lectures and seminars which he has devoted to the Europe of employment and workers have all been marked by his resolute rejection of any unquestioning acceptance of ostensible certainties. It is from this, undoubtedly, that there stems the impression conveyed by all his utterances. They reveal a tirelessly questioning attitude and a critical approach which uncompromisingly urges those responsible for formulating projects and programmes and for planning action on the part of authorities and organisations to analyse and to explain and to abjure all false pretence. These are the obsessions of a man who is, in essence, a far more truly ardent European than the many who profess the pro-European dogma.

For Lord Wedderburn is an enthusiast, but one whose enthusiasm is visited by rigour. This quality is perhaps less apparent to his British colleagues than to others, who are constantly amazed to read from his pen more pertinent analyses of their own national systems than they themselves could offer. Legal texts and national processes are dissected with scalpel-like precision; their contexts, and the commentaries of the host of legal experts who vie in their attempts to derive interpretations and guidance on practice, are always described in knowledgeable detail; and lines of reasoning and logical positions are explained or suggested, with gentle irony.

It is not for the writer of these lines to judge whether the present volume succeeds in embodying the qualities of the man in whose honour it has been conceived. Our earnest wish was no more than that, forty years on from the signing of the Treaty of Rome, Community social policy should be analysed by authors from a number of different Member States who are all acutely conscious of the exacting set of values exhibited by Lord Wedderburn throughout his scholarly work.

The Editors.

Acknowledgements

The editors wish to thank the *Consiglio Nazionale delle Ricerche* for financial help to defray the inevitable additional costs associated with the transnational nature of this book. It is fitting that the source of this help should be an Italian one, for Lord Wedderburn both made a major contribution to understanding by English speakers of the values and principles of Italian labour law and industrial relations and drew inspiration from them in his approach to comparative labour law and the social law of the Community, the latter aspect of this interaction being perhaps particularly associated with his attendance over the years at the annual week-long 'Pontignano' seminars.

We also wish to pay a heartfelt public tribute to the translation skills of Rita Inston, only a small area of whose linguistic competence we needed to tap for the purposes of this book. Her cheerful good humour never failed, even under the strongest pressure, nor did her inventiveness in the face of even the most apparently intractable piece of prose ever fall short of delivering a wholly appropriate solution.

Finally, we wish to thank Oxford University Press for their support for this project. Until the very final days of the production process that support was expressed above all through the person of Richard Hart, who has now gone to pastures new but of whose perceptive, cultured but also hard-headed support for academic legal publishing the editors are privileged to have had the benefit.

List of Contributors

Emilia Casas, Professor of Law at the University of Carlos III, Madrid.

Wolfgang Däubler, Professor of Labour and Civil Law, University of Bremen.

Paul Davies, Professor of the Law of the Enterprise and Fellow of Balliol College, Oxford University.

Simon Deakin, Lecturer in the Faculty of Law and Assistant Director, ESRC Centre for Business Research, University of Cambridge.

Mark Freedland, Professor of Employment Law and Fellow of St. John's College, University of Oxford.

Bob Hepple, Professor of Law and Master of Clare College, University of Cambridge.

Antoine Lyon-Caen, Professor of Law at the University of Paris-X.

Gérard Lyon-Caen, Professor Emeritus at the University of Paris-I.

Federico Mancini, Judge of the European Court of Justice.

Miguel Rodriguez-Piñero y Bravo-Ferrer, Consejero Permanente de Estado, Professor of Labour Law at the University of Alcalá de Henares.

Silvana Sciarra, Professor of European Social Law, European University Institute, Florence and Professor of Labour Law at the University of Florence.

Spiros Simitis, Professor of Law, Centre for Labour and Information Technology Law, Johann Wolfgang Goethe-University, Frankfurt am Main.

Tiziano Treu, Minister of Labour and Social Security, Professor of Labour Law, University of Milan.

Fernando Valdés Dal-Ré, Professor of Labour Law, Complutense University of Madrid.

Professor Manfred Weiss, Professor of Law, Centre for Labour Law, Johann Wolfgang Goethe-University, Frankfurt am Main.

Table of Contents

TABLE OF CASES

Table of Cases before the European Court of Justice and the Court of First Instance

(Alphabetical)

Table of Cases before the European Court of Justice and the Court of First Instance

(Numerical)

Table of Cases before National Courts and Authorities

France

Germany

United Kingdom

United States

European Community Legislation, Treaties, and Rules of Procedure

Regulations

Treaties

Rules of Procedure

European Community Decisions and Communications

Table of National Legislation

France

Germany

Italy

1

Community Labour Law:
A Critical Introduction to its History

SPIROS SIMITIS AND ANTOINE LYON-CAEN

I. Starting-points

1. On 31 May 1995 the European Court of Justice delivered its judgment in a case between the Danish Union of Semi-Skilled Workers (*Special-arbejderforbundet i Danmark*) and the Confederation of Danish Industry (*Dansk Industri*) acting for Denmark's leading porcelain manufacturer, the Royal Copenhagen company.[1] About 70 per cent of the 1,150 workers employed in the production process were paid on a piecework basis. However, the rates for one group of employees, the 'blue-pattern painters', entrusted with the decoration of the porcelain and consisting almost entirely of women (155 out of 156), were substantially lower than, in particular, those of their fellow-workers employed in the exclusively male group of automatic-machine operators, i.e. 'throwers'. In the union's opinion this was a blatant infringement of the equal pay principle, an assumption rejected by Royal Copenhagen mainly, in view of the fact that the rates had been fixed by collective agreement. The Court held that the company's argument was untenable, on the grounds that Article 119 of the EC Treaty establishes a mandatory duty and that discrimination against female employees is therefore strictly prohibited irrespective of whether rates of pay are determined by a public authority, an individual contract or a collective agreement.

Some seven months earlier, on 5 October 1994, the Court annulled the Commission's refusal to engage a particular individual as a temporary employee because of lack of physical capacity.[2] The appellant had already worked for the Commission on several occasions between 1985 and 1988. In February 1989, with a view to a further spell of temporary employment, he was asked to undergo a medical examination that was duly performed a month later, but refused to comply with the demand of the Commission's medical service that he should take an Aids test. His refusal was, however, circumvented. According to the Commission's assertions, the test was carried out on the occasion of another perfectly usual and necessary procedure

---

[1] Case C–400/93, *Royal Copenhagen* [1995] ECR I–1275.
[2] Case C–404/92, *X v. Commission* [1994] ECR I–4780.

(lymphocyte analysis) and the result was positive. In the Commission's view, moreover, the appellant's willingness to be examined implied tacit but unequivocal consent to all procedures necessary to proper fulfilment of the medical examiner's task. But neither the Commission's arguments nor the largely concurring position of the Court of First Instance[3] convinced the Court. Instead, it pointed to the appellant's right to demand that his privacy be respected, at the same time stressing that this right derives from the common constitutional tradition of the Member States, is explicitly recognized by Article 8 of the European Human Rights Convention and hence belongs to the fundamental rights guaranteed by the Community legal order. In the Court's view the appellant's refusal therefore excluded all ways, direct or indirect, of conducting a test that had been expressly rejected.

Both decisions address crucial questions of labour law. They also, however, illustrate the Community's two different roles in regard to employment relationships. Quite understandably, for some considerable length of time the Community was perceived exclusively in its regulatory capacity. In other words, attention was focused on the impact of its policies and demands on the rules governing labour relations in the Member States, which were regarded as not only the natural but also the sole addressees of whatever principles it enounced. The more, however, the Community consolidated and the more its institutions expanded, the more it grew to acquire an additional role. It acts increasingly both as regulator and as employer. Other international organizations have certainly had similar experiences, but no international body has ever possessed comparable power to establish a new supranational legal order where the institutions initiating and formulating the rules themselves form an integral part of that order. The credibility as well as the effectiveness of the Community's policies therefore have to be measured against both the reactions of Member States and its own behaviour. Decisions such as the judgment in *X* v. *Commission* demonstrate that the prolonged and laborious efforts to outline and enact a common body of rules force the Community institutions, no less than the Member States, to revise their attitudes. Consequently, a critical evaluation of the history of Community labour law cannot stop at the Community's regulatory activities, but must also consider the way in which it has structured its own employment relationships.

2. The history of Community labour law, or what might perhaps be better termed the history of the ongoing relations between the construction of Europe and labour law, has yet to be written.[4] Although certain aspects of these relations have been explored with some thoroughness, one example

---

[3] Cases T–121/89 and T–13/90, *X* v. *Commission* [1992] ECR II–2195.
[4] See the suggestions of P. Davies, 'The Emergence of European Labour Law', in W. McCarthy (ed.), *Legal Intervention in Industrial Relations: Gains and Losses* (Blackwell, Oxford, 1992), 313–59.

being the changes wrought in each national system by Community law,[5] their essence remains largely shrouded in mystery. The truth of the matter is that, in addition to the traditional difficulties presented by any historical analysis of the law, in which rhetorical application of the past to present-day issues only too often predominates over describing and attempting to understand a context, the nebulous nature of Community labour law means that the subject brings further difficulties all of its own. The prime requirement in the study of legal concepts and rules is to eschew all inclination to regard them as simple products. Products though they undoubtedly are, it is the processes of their production that constitute the real subject of any historical analysis. In pursuing such studies, some scholars concentrate on social forces, the ways in which they act, and their views of the world, while others focus more searchingly on the legal system itself, the representations of the world that it incorporates and the operational constraints upon it.

In the case of Community labour law there are weaknesses in both of these approaches. It is difficult to identify what social forces influence the legal activity of the Community; to a large extent, its authorities or institutions are free from social pressure. Nor is it easy or indeed really justifiable to present Community law as a system; it was conceived as a partial super-imposed order, and remains so.[6] All in all, it is better not to think of Community law either as a product of itself, envisaged as a legal system, or as a compromise of social forces. In essence, the difficulty is the same one that a historian has suggested with reference to cannibalism: 'If I say that a person who eats human flesh actually eats it, I am right; but I am also right in saying that the eater concerned becomes a cannibal only when viewed in the context of mores which perceive this form of nourishment as barbaric or, conversely, sacred'.[7] Cannibalism *per se* does not exist. The implication is obvious: what has to be studied is when and why a shared system of values emerged that lent such an interpretation to this form of nourishment.

Community labour law, while certainly not to be likened to cannibalism, has to be studied in the same manner. Introduced in the 1957 Treaty of Rome under the heading of social policy and again referred to in the same way in the Treaty on European Union, it initially consisted of a *model* (II) whose features need to be charted. This model has led to *impasses* (III) which can probably be resolved only through a *revision* of the initial model (IV).

---

[5] See Diritto del lavoro e diritto comunitario (1991) 5, *Quaderni di Diritto del Lavoro e delle Relazioni Industriali*; *Le relazioni industriali nella prospettiva europea* (CEDES, Rome, 1988). On the subject of unforeseen harmonization, see G. Lyon-Caen, 'Réflexions sur la politique sociale européenne ou les ruses de l'histoire', in *Miscellanea W. J. Ganshof Van der Meersch* (Bruylant, Brussels, 1972), 241.

[6] D. Simon, 'Y a-t-il des principes généraux du droit communautaire?', [1991] *Droits*, 73 (PUF Paris).

[7] Veyne, 'Foucault révolutionne l'histoire', in *Comment on écrit l'histoire*, (ed. du Seuil Paris, 1966).

II. The Initial Model

As set forth in Articles 117 ff. of the Treaty of Rome, the model comprised three clear elements. The first is given its colour by the word that denotes it: *harmonization*. This was used to describe the condition in which it was intended that the Community should accommodate social systems: the representation which the original Member States chose to place upon the relations that were to prevail between their various social systems (which were not further defined) bore the stamp of peace, with no hint of tension. Such harmony, moreover, was promised as the outcome of a natural process of development not entailing any form of constraint. The future was mapped out without there being any need to do violence to the present. And to lend full emphasis to their ironical approach, the founding fathers linked the promotion of 'improved working conditions and an improved standard of living for workers' directly to 'their harmonization while the improvement is being maintained', i.e. upward harmonization.

The choice of wording struck an immediate chord among legal authors, most of whom[8] echoed the ambition displayed in the Treaty: rejecting all notion of identical techniques, legal homogeneity, or unification in some form or other, it established a realistic vision of the coexistence of different social systems directed towards achieving identical results. Attempts were made to demonstrate the originality of such an aspiration. Harmonization, as carefully distinguished from either co-ordination or approximation, 'is not concerned with the expression of legal rules, only their teleology'.[9] First voiced almost forty years ago, these terminological niceties subsequently attended the fierce debates provoked by the concept of Community directives and the policy pursued by the Commission and the Council in their use, as well as the calmer discussions surrounding comparative studies. Directives cannot, it has been argued, be made excessively detailed nor invested with direct effect without betraying their fundamental function of harmonization. The comparative method, in its turn, is seen as the means of discovering whether, behind the differences in their techniques, institutions, and rules achieve identical results, and of mapping out their possible adjustment in order to bring about such results.

[8] e.g. M. Udina, 'L'armonizzazione delle legislazioni nazionali dei paesi membri della Comunità europa' [1957–8], *Annuario di diritto comparato e di studi legislativi*, 192; I. Seidl-Hoheelden, 'Harmonization of Legislation in the Common Market' and 'The Heritage of the Common Law' [1962] *Journal of Business Law*, 247 and 363; R. Lecourt and R. M. Chevalier, 'Chances et malchances de l'harmonisation des législations européennes' [1963] *Recueil Dalloz* Chronique, 273; W. Hallstein, 'Angleichung des Privat–und Prozessrechts in der Europäischen Wirtschaftsgemeinschaft' [1964] *Rabels Zeitschrift für Ausländisches und Internationales Privatrecht*, 211.

[9] R. Rodière, 'L'harmonisation des législations européennes dans le cadre de la CEE' [1965] *Revue trimestrielle de droit européen*, 336.

Does the loftiness of the term 'federalist' necessarily imply the notion of extensive Community intervention in social policy matters? Not at all. Which brings us to the second element of the initial model: the *justifications* for regulatory activity on the part of the Community were given restrictive definition. They were linked exclusively to the requirements of competition within the Common Market. Following the *Spaak Report*,[10] Article 117 of the Treaty presented the functioning of the common market itself as the principle vehicle of harmony in the sense of 'upward harmonization' that was attributed to it. Regulatory action by the Community was envisaged only where necessary to remedy specific distortions of competition. That is why the Treaty basis provided for Community legislation was the approximation of national laws as laid down by Article 100, where the establishment or functioning of the internal market so requires. In the initial model, the sole approach to rules on social policy matters that is legitimate or, rather, compatible with the Community legal order is their role as an integral part of the conditions of competition. This limitation introduces controversy.[11] At its highest level of abstraction, the question is surely whether the objective of economic integration, as first pronounced in 1957 and subsequently reaffirmed, really requires an approximation of national provisions in the social sphere in particular, to the point where the regulatory structure of the Community resembles that of a single State. In fact, Community experience to date supports the thesis that no such approximation is necessary. If we look first at freedom of movement for workers, all the indications are that it has not imposed any real alteration of national labour laws and social security systems. The logic of unifying the rules on the conflict of laws that was adopted in the Rome Convention of 19 June 1980 would seem to confirm that differential provisions under national substantive laws were regarded as vested and virtually untouchable. And policy in regard to social protection, in its turn, has consisted in the co-ordination of national laws, with the guaranteed integrity of each national system constituting the very rationale for organizing continuity of the migrant worker's rights. No spatial homogeneity over Community territory, simply temporal continuity built into each personal situation: that is the clear message delivered by the action taken in implementation of Article 51 of the Treaty. Given that such experience offers little evidence of any need for approximation, the Community's position is a highly uncertain one when it proposes taking regulatory action in the social policy field in order to remedy a distortion of competition. How is a difference that allows selfish or opportunist action by

[10] *Rapport des chefs de délégations*, Intergovernmental Committee set up by the Messina Conference, Apr. 1956, Part I, 65.
[11] See the comments of Lord Wedderburn in 'European Community Law and Workers' Rights after 1992: Fact or Fake?' in *Labour Law and Freedom, Further Essays on Labour Law* (Lawrence & Wishart, London, 1995), 247.

enterprises to be distinguished from a genuine distortion? What argument will demonstrate convincingly that some particular disparity is likely to affect the functioning of the Common Market? These tricky questions were levelled against the Commission each time it used Article 100 of the Treaty as its basis for adopting an initiative with a view to approximating national laws in the social field. And nowadays they are raised when the case for intervention is based on 'social dumping' between Member States. At all events, the close tie between Community social policy and the requirements of competition lends all its weight to a severe diagnosis which has lost none of its relevance: 'the Treaty of Rome did not go as far as the 1919 Treaty of Versailles went'.[12]

The initial model included a third element which may perhaps be termed a kind of *statist or public syndrome*.[13] The absence of any stated intention to modify national labour law systems is, without doubt, evidence in itself not just of caution but of the conviction that each has developed in the wake of a history of the formation of the State, drawing from it characteristics that are irreducibly its own. But this conviction remains implicit. By contrast, there is explicit affirmation of the conferment on the Community authorities, and on them alone, of the capacities or powers to construct a form of Community labour law, however limited its justifications and its stated scope. Such action as is envisaged is confined to action on their part, and addressed solely to the Member States viewed in terms of their public prerogatives, notably of legislation. The purpose of the directives which the Council is empowered to issue on the basis of Article 100 is to approximate State provisions; and the task of promoting co-operation with which the Commission is charged under Article 118 relates exclusively to co-operation between Member States. The world of labour law as it is featured in the Treaty is peopled entirely by public entities, at either Community or national level.

This initial model, with social harmonization as its perceived principle, competition as its dynamic, and an institutional view of labour law as law associated with the State, was given formal endorsement by the Court of Justice.[14] According to the Court, the task entrusted to the Commission by Article 118 in no way affected the regulatory competence of individual Member States in the social field.[15] What is more, in its view there was no question of regulatory provisions in Member States, or the absence of such provisions, being subject to control under Article 117: 'Article 117 of the EEC

[12] G. Lyon-Caen, *loc. cit.*

[13] See, on the nationalist and formalist syndrome of legal experts, T. Treu, 'L'Europa sociale: dall'Atto Unico a Maastricht' (1991) 5 *Quaderni di Diritto del Lavoro e delle Relazioni Industriali* 16; 'Divergences ou convergences', in *Convergence des modèles sociaux européens* (Ministère du Travail, de l'Emploi et de la Formation Professionnelle, Paris, 1992), 33.

[14] The co-ordination of national social security laws preserves the fundamental differences between them. See, e.g., Cases 1/78, *Kenny* [1978] ECR L496; C–227/87, *Ronfeldt* [1991] ECR I–323; C–349/87, *Paraschi* [1991] ECR I–4501.

[15] See Case 126/86, *Gimenez Zaera* [1987] ECR 8697.

Treaty is essentially in the nature of a programme. It relates only to social objectives the attainment of which must be the result of Community action, close co-operation between Member States and the operation of the common market.[16]

III. *Impasses*

The history of Community labour law is the history of the *impasses* to which each of the elements of the original model has led. Many observers impute these *impasses* to defective functioning of the Community institutions, to diversity between Member States, and, when it comes to their intractability, to shortcomings in decision-making procedures when political disagreement persists. Although explanations of this kind may well be of some relevance, surely they mask the nub of the matter. The situation underlying these *impasses* is essentially one of rationale.

The Treaty of Rome harbours a *representation of the relations between national social systems* that it presents as a plan: harmonization. What, then, is to be the reaction when that harmonization fails to materialize, or, possibly worse, when the thesis gains ground that it no longer is or can be on the agenda? The Commission's official documents were quick to take note of this thesis, presented as a kind of indisputable diagnosis. In 1975, for instance, in its Green Paper on employee participation the Commission stated candidly: 'A sufficient convergence of social and economic policies and structures in these areas will not happen automatically as a consequence of the integration of Community markets'[17] (the case in point being the role of employees in the decision-making process within companies).

In 1975 the conclusion was still leavened with hope: 'The objective is gradual removal of unacceptable degrees of divergence between the structures and policies of the Member States.' A conclusion that was voluntarist in tone, although limited in its sights: it extended only to the reduction of degrees of divergence that were unacceptable, without being able to specify in any detail what measures would be useful instruments to that end.

Subsequently, all such hope drained away into the observation that the confrontation between different social systems that was entailed by the economic integration of markets did not nurture harmonization. Indeed, under the effect of the uneven but lively opportunism of individual Member States this confrontation even accentuated existing disparities. As a consequence, the initial plan lost all credibility. But in that case could it, or

[16] See Case C–72/91, *Sloman Neptune* [1993] ECR I–887. The point that Art. 117 was essentially in the nature of a programme had already been emphasized in Case 149/77, *Defrenne* [1978] ECR 1365.

[17] Employee Participation and Company Structure, Green Paper of the Commission of the European Communities, EC Bull., Su 8/75, 10.

should it, be stated in different terms? How, ultimately, could it still be claimed that the construction of a unified Europe has a social ambition, that it includes a bold conception of the relations that are to prevail between individual social systems while at the same time accommodating what it recognizes as their virtually irreversible differences? Although no such explicit questioning is recorded in the Community's official documents, it prompted a search for a new vocabulary: the appearance of the word 'convergence', for example, expressed the sense of this quandary. The vocabulary used exhibited growing uncertainty. But it was not just the vocabulary: the very conception of Community social policy was likewise affected, as witness the manner in which it was partially recast in the Single European Act.

Whilst underlining the special importance attached to the protection of workers' health and safety and establishing the possibility, to that end, of adopting directives by a qualified majority, the Single European Act introduced a new conception of the rules to be adopted on this basis. According to the literal wording of Article 118A of the Treaty resulting from the 1986 revision, these rules are to consist of *minimum requirements*. In fact, the text retained the pre-existing reference to the notion of 'upward harmonization' while at the same time introducing a view of the associated action as conceived in terms of minimum requirements. Such a combination would appear, at the very least, to defy all logic.

Upward harmonization and minimum requirements do not belong to the same philosophy. What is more, the expression 'minimum requirements' can be reasonably applied only to a narrow view of work: the setting of minimum standards is axiomatically confined to working conditions. By the same token the sudden appearance of this reference to minimum requirements, and its subsequent generalization in 1992, postulate an indifference (albeit one not stated explicitly) to everything lying beyond the confines of working conditions as such, whether it be the legal position of workers as individuals or the law governing industrial relations. This is something of a paradox at the very time when the Community is seeking to take on a political dimension. And the reference to minimum requirements embodies yet another paradox: such requirements are hardly compatible with the doctrine of subsidiarity that has been acquiring growing emphasis since 1986.

As it turned out, the incomprehension and tensions inevitably entailed by the reference to upward harmonization were removed when it was omitted from the Agreement on Social Policy of 7 February 1992 concluded on the basis of the Protocol of the same date.[18] Its omission, however, also signified

[18] It is noteworthy that, had the United Kingdom been willing to sign it along with the other Member States, the Agreement's provisions would have simply replaced outright the existing provisions of Arts. 117,118, and 118A of the Treaty. It is due to the United Kingdom's refusal that upward harmonization remains an element of the Community plan to this day, since Arts. 117,118, and 118A are still binding on the Member States.

the disappearance of one of the elements of the initial Community plan, namely, its view of the relations between different social systems. This could not help but give more prominence to the elaborate acknowledgement of 'the diverse forms of national practices, in particular in the field of contractual relations' and the pressing exhortation to take account of 'the conditions and technical rules existing in each of the Member States'.[19] It would, however, be wrong to regard the Agreement on Social Policy as no more than the completion of a process of elimination. It also illustrates the development that had taken place in the second element of the initial model, relating to the *justifications for regulatory action* on the part of the Community. At the start, such action had been envisaged as a means of remedying distortions of competition. No matter that not everyone found this credo convincing, or that there was no yardstick for distinguishing between differences that were acceptable and differences that amounted to a distortion. Economic growth was strong and it was easy to dismiss the doubts raised by such a credo and the manner of its application. Naïve though it might be, the belief that economic integration and Community-level regulation in the social field were complementary caused no problems for anyone, or virtually none.

However, as soon as serious disruptions appeared on the scene, and in particular soaring unemployment, this naïve belief ceased to hold firm. How, in such circumstances, should the justifications for Community regulatory action be reconsidered? There is no doubt that the Single European Act of 1986 marked a departure from the presumption of complementarity between competition and Community social policy. When it entrusted the task of promoting workers' health and safety to action at Community level it did not treat such action purely as a complement of economic integration;   the justifications provided extend beyond just the preconditions for healthy competition. But could the same be applied to matters other than workers' health and safety?

The Agreement on Social Policy of 7 February 1992 certainly reflects this concern. Indeed, it expresses a vigorous attempt to dispel the notion that Community action is confined to remedying distortions of competition, as is clear from the fact that it sets out a list of objectives encompassing improved living and working conditions, proper social protection, dialogue between management and labour, the promotion of employment, etc. The real implications of this attempt are, however, far from clear. The relevant point to note here is the structure of the Agreement: it is presented as a *programme* defined by its underlying *objectives* and the forms of action that it announces, perceived as *means* to that end.[20] Such a presentation is strongly imbued with a very instrumental view of Community regulatory measures: they are a

---

[19] Arts. 1 and 2(2) of the Agreement on Social Policy of 7 Feb. 1992.
[20] These forms of action are divided into particular areas.

means to an end and justified purely in terms of their contribution to the attainment of particular social results, however vaguely the objectives concerned are stated. What the Agreement illustrates is a way of thinking that disregards principles and gives concrete expression only to policies, and it is primarily the logical consequences of this way of thinking that need to be understood. Two possible versions are conceivable.

The first is a perpetuation of the *status quo ante*: if the justifications for Community rules are to lie in their likely effects on 'the promotion of employment . . . the development of human resources with a view to lasting high employment and the combating of exclusion', this leaves the way open for rules to be denounced as sources of rigidities and difficulties of adjustment in national labour markets. There is no certainty that such denunciation will always be heeded, but some support for it is provided in the programme outlined by the Agreement. It is also true that this scenario of the denunciation of rules is not one that could apply across the board, given that other objectives are stated that are less amenable to it, such as 'improved living and working conditions, proper social protection, dialogue between management and labour'. Hence the second version, which accommodates the range of different objectives stated. In this case the Agreement is seen as embodying several possible views of Community rules; the possible outcome is not only their denunciation as sources of rigidities but also their promotion as essential resources for balanced development and as requirements for a democratic society. But surely this 'pluralist' version, in its turn, condemns Community intervention to paralysis? Do the Community institutions, distant as they are from specific practical situations, possess the capacity to make wise decisions between these differing views of regulation—particularly since the Agreement expressly exhorts them to take account of the diversity of national practices? Doubt is not only permitted; it is a requirement.

To grasp the implications of the Agreement of 7 February 1992, another question needs to be asked which introduces a digression. Although little is known of what changes in each social system[21] may be imputable to its confrontation with the others within an integrated market, certain changes are imposed beforehand by Community law itself. The common rules relating to the establishment of the common market and its operation have a direct effect on national social policies. Although it was, and still is, proclaimed, the autonomy of these policies is no more than relative given that they are made subject to the rules of the market. For instance, in one case a national agency operating in the labour market was ruled to be an undertaking guilty of abuse of a dominant position,[22] while in another case national regulations instituting a retirement scheme for the self-employed

---

[21] 'Social system' is the term used in Art. 117 of the Treaty.
[22] Case C–41/90, *Höfner* [1991] ECR I–1979.

were ruled to be a restraint on the requirements of the market.[23] In short, national social laws are being eroded in the name of the demands of competition. The erosion is visible and disturbing, and as yet there is no knowing where it will end.[24]

The third element of the initial model, which confines labour law to what is produced by *public authorities* at either national or Community level, is the one that has been studied the most searchingly. There has been analysis of the Commission, the relative opacity of its operation, and, despite the central position it occupies with its monopoly of action, the virtual restriction of its legitimacy to that of resources of expertise; analysis of the combination of the Commission and the Council as the co-producers of regulatory provisions but nonetheless largely subject to social pressure and all kinds of procedures of political control; and analysis of the Court of Justice, mainly concentrated on its case-law, methods of interpretation and varying degrees of inventiveness in different areas.

Fairly quickly, however, a kind of imbalance becomes discernible in the Community edifice. Europe presents enterprises with a broad area of mobility and opens up to them new margins for manœuvre and new resources. But what is there to confront these collective actors with their growing power? Nothing, or virtually nothing. A call for a counterbalance to the free movement of capital, in the shape of a right to international industrial action, was voiced as long ago as 1972,[25] but has met with little response.[26] What has, by contrast, given rise to Community initiatives, with results now being written into Community law, is the formal creation of a European dimension in industrial relations. The objectives of the Agreement on Social Policy of 7 February 1992 also included support for European-level trade-union and employers' structures and the promotion of their activities. And the guiding principle behind the European Works Council Directive of 22 September 1994 was to encourage the establishment of multinational companies operating across the Community as centres or sites of industrial relations. These initiatives each have their own history, and this is not the place to recount them. The important thing to note is the official entry of the social partners onto the Community scene. This is no commonplace development simply correcting the excessive emphasis originally placed on the Member States and Community institutions. It comes at a time

[23] Case C–244/94, *Coreva* [1995] ECR I–4013.
[24] See Lord Wedderburn, 'Competition Law and Labour Law', in *Labour Law and Freedom*, n. 11 above, 370; A. Lyon-Caen, 'Droit du travail et droit de la concurrence', in *Ecrits en l'honneur à J. Savatier* (PUF, Paris 1992), 331; G. Lyon-Caen, 'L'infiltration du droit du travail par le droit de la concurrence' [1992] *Droit ouvrier* 313; S. Simitis, 'Dismantling or Strengthening Labour Law: The Case of the European Court of Justice' [1996] 2 *ELJ* 156, at 165,
[25] K. W. Wedderburn, 'Multinational Enterprise and National Labour Law, *Industrial Law Journal*, Mar. 1972, 19.
[26] The Agreement on Social Policy of 7 Feb. 1992 records the common reservation of the signatory Member States regarding the right to strike and the right of association, in respect of which they agree to take no action.

when a growing number of questions are being asked on the problematic issue of complementarity between individual rights established by law and collective rights (as the outcome of collective bargaining). No longer can it safely be assumed that the two will dovetail neatly and conveniently. Questions about levels of bargaining and their interlinked co-ordination are likewise on the increase. Is there not a danger of crediting forms of centralized negotiation with an illusory importance and, at the same time, weakening the actors and structures of collective bargaining which have come to be a feature, hard won at that, of each national system?[27] One thing that is quite certain is that the increasingly marked recognition of collective bargaining as a way of transposing directives[28] offers no kind of answer to these questions.

Although the sudden new prominence of the social partners and collective bargaining signifies a real change, it is clearly accompanied by problems that need to be addressed.

IV. Revision

Community experience in the social policy field, stretching back over more than thirty years, has been marked by a succession of *impasses* or, as they are often more prosaically called, challenges.

Things have now reached the point where the rules of the market clearly cannot continue to prevail without restriction. Indisputable recognized bases for public action have to be established. Within each national system, public action was originally preserved by the Treaty, with the Member States even regarded as exercising control over their own social policy. Today, under the powerful effect of the economic freedoms guaranteed by Community law and in the absence of any Community provisions on its justifications, public action at national level has a fragile and precarious position. And at Community level, if public action is to exist at all it must have more than the lofty but vague objectives with which it has been entrusted. Europe therefore needs to give its formal sanction to public action and thereby demonstrate that its sole creed is not that of the market. The market, in the form of its principal actors, caters for consumers and their needs, or at least some of them, but does nothing for the individual and the freedom and dignity of the individual, which in their various aspects require forms of organization that are independent of market considerations. The more firmly the political

[27] See A. Calon, L. Frey, R. Lindley, A. Lyon-Caen, H. Markmann, V. Perez Diaz, and S. Simitis, *The Social Aspects of Economic and Monetary Union* (Commission of the European Communities, Social Papers), Brussels, Apr. 1992.

[28] See Dir. 91/553 of 14 Oct. [1991] OJ L288; Agreement on Social Policy of 7 Feb. 1992, Art. 2(4).

dimension of European integration is established, the more pressing this latter requirement becomes.

Another need that cannot continue to be ignored is that of avoiding the harmful effects of an almost head-on confrontation between different national social systems. Such a confrontation threatens to become increasingly unmanageable as the effects of economic and monetary union start to make themselves felt. Whatever the accumulating evidence of this or that form of co-ordination between national social policies, the central paradox represented by the Community remains and is increasing: it has no guiding principle and lacks any reference framework. Harmonization remains no more than a fine idea, usually mentioned with nostalgia; it does not represent a reference framework for action nowadays. The allocation of roles and powers within the Community system can no longer be felt to follow a satisfactory architecture. Necessary though it may be to prescribe voting conditions for the adoption of a directive, and possibly useful to establish differences according to particular areas of regulation, these do not constitute lines of division between Community competence and the competence of Member States. And subsidiarity is no more than a mirage when it comes to laying the foundations of an edifice which aspires to being more than the construction of an area for trade in goods and mobility of economic agents. Action by the social partners, for which the Community has quite rightly recognized a growing role, is being encouraged against a background of doubts regarding the conditions of its legitimacy and its effects on national collective bargaining practices.

The logical conclusion to be drawn from all this should be obvious to everyone: Europe needs to find the *reference points* that it lacks at present. And those reference points should be the *fundamental rights of the individual*, with all that expression's wealth of meaning:[29] rights which are fundamental in the hierarchical sense that they would have to be ranked highest, fundamental by virtue of the coherence they would give to the forms of regulation over which they would hold sway, fundamental in the sense of the unique dignity of the holders of these rights, i.e. human individuals, and fundamental because they are common to the majority of Member State systems.

The Court of Justice, it must of course be pointed out, has already been integrating these fundamental rights into Community law for more than twenty years, by applying them as general principles. This work by the Court of Justice attests to the existence of gaps in the Community system of which the Community judges themselves are aware and demonstrates the Court's receptiveness to fundamental rights. Nevertheless, its work is not enough, for a number of reasons. Intervention by the Court in this respect is

[29] See V. Champeils-Desplats, 'La notion de droit fondamental et le droit constitutionnel français' [1995], *Recueil Dalloz* Chronique, 323.

circumscribed by the particular cases brought before it. Also, the use it makes of fundamental rights is restricted to invoking them against Community acts and national acts adopted in implementation: hence they serve only to limit regulatory activity, not to justify it and inspire its development. Furthermore, the Court's interpretations and its conclusions are not readily predictable and the formulas that it applies are abstract ones. Within the context of the cases brought before it and the powers it possesses, it concerns itself with stating fundamental rights, and even that with caution; it does not concern itself with the guarantees of their exercise, prisoner that it is of a tradition which identifies the guarantee of a right with its jurisdictional formulation. And lastly, it has to be remembered that the Court, however elevated its status in the Community's institutional edifice, does not actually possess the necessary legitimacy to establish underlying principles on its sole authority.

What the Europe of the Community needs is a new foundation, with the fundamental rights of the individual and the guarantees of their exercise as its pillars.[30] Provision should be made for the formal statement of a list of fundamental rights including not only the conventional rights to freedoms but also rights to dignity and rights that ensure the secure self-fulfilment of the individual (right to education, right to social protection, etc.). Explicit inclusion of guarantees of their exercise would have the twofold advantage of underlining the importance attached to the true effectiveness of these fundamental rights and avoiding the never-ending debates on economic and social principles, their formulation, and the extent to which they are justifiable. This enshrinement of fundamental rights would make it possible to give collective autonomy a genuine basis and define what it signifies. It would demonstrate that collective bargaining is not without its limits, since it must respect fundamental rights and the law plays a part in organizing the guaranteed exercise of those rights. It would also emphasize that labour cannot be viewed in abstraction purely as a factor of production and that behind it there lies the worker as a human individual.

More important still, a proclamation of fundamental rights would furnish Community labour law with the framework that it lacks at present. It would smooth the profile of relations between the various national social systems: no confrontation, since they would all be subject to common requirements, nor on the other hand the uncertainties of harmonization, since guarantees of the exercise of fundamental rights would in principle fall within the competence of the public authorities and social partners at national level. Community action would not necessarily be negligible, however. In the final

---

[30] As the Intergovernmental Conference commences, the Commission has resolutely opened up this prospect, starting from the concept of European citizenship. It stated that this concept, which is to be developed, rests on a European model of society that includes the guarantee of fundamental rights recognized by everyone and a commitment to solidarity between its members (*Commission Opinion on the Intergovernmental Conference*, 28 Feb. 1996).

analysis it would fall to the Community institutions to supervise proper observance of the common underlying principles, and action on the part of the Community authorities could be required in analysing, evaluating, and approximating the guarantees provided at national level for the exercise of these rights.

In addition, this formal enshrinement of fundamental rights and their guaranteed exercise could, surely, serve as a benchmark for what the Community will commit itself to in international negotiations and what it is entitled to impose as a condition during enlargement.

Is this pure Utopia? There are moments in history when Utopia becomes the very condition of survival for a grand scheme.

However, irrespective of whether fundamental rights are explicitly listed and acknowledged in a particular document or the *status quo* is maintained, the fact of the Union's commitment both in the Maastricht Treaty (Article F(2)) and in the Court of Justice's decisions to respect for and application of these rights directly affects future Community regulatory activity. It may not create a genuine new task of the union covered by Article 235 of the EC-Treaty.[31] Fundamental rights, nevertheless, not only set standards against which the Union's policies must be constantly measured but also define binding objectives for Community action.

The Union is hence more than ever compelled to continue and intensify, for instance, its efforts to implement terms and conditions of employment that secure the equal treatment of men and women. It is certainly true that in the past the Community has played a key role in the attempts to promote and achieve *de facto* equality,[32] not least because of the corrective intervention by the Court that forced the Member States, time and again, to review their hesitant, not to say reluctant, response to Community directives.[33] It is equally true that the aim to provide women with equal opportunities is far from being achieved; on the contrary, the still 'yawning gaps in pay between men and women' referred to in the already mentioned proposals for a fourth medium-term Community action programme are an alarming sign just as much of the deficiencies of actual policies as of the obvious tendency in the Member States to revert to practices that openly contravene the quest for equal access to employment by deliberately restoring the preferential selection of men for

[31] See Opinion 2/94 of the ECJ *Adhésion de la Communauté à la convention de sauregarde des droits de l'homme et des libertés fondamentales*, of 28 Mar. 1996.

[32] It has, in its own words, been 'a prime mover in changing the status of women in society' (Commission Proposal for a Council Decision on the fourth medium-term action programme on equal opportunities for women and men (1996–2000), COM(95)381 Final of 19 July 1995 A–13.

[33] The complicated legislative history of §611a of the German Civil Code prohibiting discrimination with especial respect to the conditions of access to regulation is still not really compatible with Community law, at least so far as the provisions on compensation are concerned. For a history of the various reforms and a discussion of the shortcomings of the present regulation, see especially W. Däubler, *Arbeitsrecht* (10th edn., Rowohlt, Hamburg 1995), 730 D. Schieck, *Zweites Gleichberechtigungsgesetz für die Privatwirtschaft* (Bund-Verlag, Cologne 1995), §611a, n. 91 ff.

particular posts and occupations.[34] Moreover, although judgments such as the Court's decision in the *Kalanke* case[35] may specifically address the legislation of a given Member State, they contain statements that are relevant to all attempts to correct existing discrimination through forms of positive action.

The Union can therefore neither rely on its past activities and their merits nor ignore the need to place the emphasis on a series of distinctly positive measures counteracting the negative experiences in Member States and improving conditions for the removal of obstacles to *de facto* equality. For example, the provisions regulating leave for parental or other family reasons have proved to be counter-productive, at least in their present form:[36] they offer a short-term benefit at the cost of the potential exclusion of women from the labour market. Future policies must consequently review traditional leave schemes and supplement them with conditions ensuring a realistic chance of reintegration into employment. Similarly, the still prevailing approach to the correction of discrimination in social security systems has to be abandoned: contrary to what has long been argued, equal opportunities are not guaranteed by simply eliminating existing forms of discrimination. What is really needed, particularly in view of the fact that women are especially threatened by unemployment, is an individualization of rights.[37]

Whilst equality has long been a major, if not predominant, theme of Community regulatory activities, other fundamental rights such as privacy have only recently been addressed. However, both the Commission and the Council have stressed that the Directive on the protection of personal data[38] is just a first step.[39] Rules as abstract as those stipulated in the Directive may indicate the principles to be applied, but they cannot deal in a really satisfactory manner with the specific problems arising out of a particular processing context. Whether, for instance, the right to know effectively grants access to all the data gathered by a given user, exactly where the limits of transmission to third parties should be drawn, or to what extent the consent of data subjects is a reliable barrier to retrieval, are all questions the

[34] See, for instance, the report on research into newspaper advertisements for managerial posts conducted by the Hamburger Institut für Personalwesen und Arbeitswissenschaft, in *Frankfurter Allgemeine Zeitung* of 9 Sept. 1995, 49.

[35] Case C–450/93 [1995] ECR I–3051.

[36] See S. Simitis, 'Welche Maßnahmen empfehlen sich, um die Vereinbarkeit von Berufstätigkeit und Familie zu verbessern?', in *Verhandlungen des 60. Deutschen Juristentages*, Münster 1994, ii, O 20 (C. H. Beck, Munich, 1994).

[37] See also the Commission's proposals for a fourth medium-term Community action programme, n. 31 above, B-21 ff.

[38] Council Dir. 95/46/EC on the Protection of Individuals with regard to the Processing of Personal Data and the Free Movement of Such Data, of 24 Oct. 1995.

[39] See para. 68 of the Dir.'s recitals, and also S. Simitis, 'From the Market to the Polis: The EU Directive on the Protection of Personal Data', *(1955) 80 Iowa Law Review* 445, at 466-7.

answers to which will necessarily differ according to whether the data are processed by banks, hospitals, employers, police authorities, insurance companies, marketing enterprises or health agencies. Hence, both the processing conditions and the scope of the data subject's rights can, ultimately, be convincingly determined only against the background of the given processing context. Whereas, for example, a data subject's claim to have access to all data concerning his or her person cannot seriously be challenged in cases where they are collected and stored by a credit agency, the same expectation is obviously untenable in the case of police databases. And natural though it may seem to regard the consent of a travel agency's customer as sufficient to legitimize transmission of the data needed for booking a flight, reserving a hotel room, or hiring a car, the data subject's consent must, to say the least, be viewed in a far more critical light in the case of insurance policies or employment contracts.

In short, omnibus rules expose data subjects to the risks of an uncertain process of interpretation; at best, they are able to make only an approximate assessment both of the implications of the use of their data and of the extent to which their rights must be respected. If really effective protection is to be achieved, the Directive will therefore need to be supplemented by sectoral rules adapting its omnibus provisions to the issues characteristic of particular processing contexts. The priorities are likewise clear. In no other case are personal data so systematically gathered and processed as in that of employees. And nowhere else are the dangers of multifunctional use so evident, as well as the importance of accurate, transparent, and controllable processing. The growing mobility of employees and the increasing centralization of processing within multinational companies are additional and by no means negligible arguments supporting the necessity of Union-wide rules. Significantly enough, as long ago as 1989 the Council of Europe supplemented its 1981 Data Protection Convention[40] with a Recommendation specifically on the use of employee data.[41] In the meantime, other international organizations such as the ILO, for instance, have also placed the processing of employee data on their agenda.[42]

Privacy is, however, also a good example of the dual aspect of Community regulatory action in regard to employment relationships that was mentioned earlier. Commitment to fundamental rights in general and respect for privacy in particular does not cease at the entrance to the Community's own offices.

[40] Convention for the Protection of Individuals with regard to Automatic Processing of Personal Data, 28 Jan. 1981.

[41] Recommendation No. R(89)2 of the Committee of Ministers to Member States on the Protection of Personal Data Used for Employment Purposes.

[42] See International Labour Office, Draft Code of Practice on the Protection of Workers' Personal Data, MEWP/1995/1; S. Simitis, 'Developments in the Protection of Workers' Personal Data' (1991) 10/2 *Conditions of Work Digest, Workers' Privacy, Part I: Protection of Personal Data* (International Labour Office, Geneva 1992).

The Court of Justice's decision in the X case[43] made it clear that in its capacity as an employer the Community itself is not exempted from the duty to observe employees' fundamental rights. Rules dealing specifically with the processing of employee data would define its duties further and, for instance, exclude all attempts to bypass employees' right to know by keeping a second file both unknown and inaccessible to them or to use security checks as virtually unlimited authorization for a continuous and unverifiable exchange of information with the national authorities.

The Union's explicit commitment to fundamental rights not only constrains it to enact rules securing their respect but also predetermines both the form and scope of such regulation. It is neither admissible to leave the acknowledgement of fundamental rights to the discretion of the Member States nor possible to allow their content to vary according to where they are applied. Equal opportunities are no more an exclusive feature of British or French law than privacy is a privilege of German employees. Just as the Court has made certain in judgment after judgment that fundamental rights are observed throughout the Community[44] irrespective of whether equal pay,[45] part-time work,[46] indirect discrimination,[47] or the prohibition of night work[48] was at stake, so it is the Union's foremost task to establish a closely knit system of rules preventing the infringement of fundamental rights and promoting their implementation.

In fact, what the Union must do is to lay down binding minimum requirements, a by no means unusual expectation although the number of directives prescribing such standards is, admittedly, still remarkably small.[49] Both the EC Treaty as amended by the Single European Act (Article 118A) and the Agreement on Social Policy (Article 2) treat minimum requirements as a perfectly normal form of regulation. It is nonetheless true that the term is, for the reasons already mentioned, ambivalent.[50] Moreover, far from being seen merely as a means of enabling the Community to express and impose regulatory aspirations the purpose of which is to improve working conditions, the setting of minimum standards is also perceived as a deliberate restriction of Community expectations to the minimum already contained in existing

[43] Case C–404/92, *X v. Commission* [1994] ECR I–4780.

[44] See especially M. Zuleeg, 'Der Schutz sozialer Rechte in der Rechtsordnung der Europäischen Gemeinschaft' [1992] *Europäische Grundrechte Zeitschrift* 329.

[45] See, for instance, Cases 43/75, *Defrenne* [1976] ECR 455; C–262/88, *Barber* [1986] ECR 1607; C–400/93, *Royal Copenhagen* [1995] ECR I–1275.

[46] See especially Cases 170/84, *Bilka Kaufhaus* [1993] ECR I–5535; C–360/90, *Bötel* [1992] ECR I–3589.

[47] See, e.g., Case C–127/92, *Enderby* [1991] ECR I–4062.

[48] See Case C–345/89, *Stoeckel*.

[49] Among the few examples are Dir. 75/129 (as amended by Dir. 92/56) on collective redundancies: Dir. 80/987 on insolvency protection; and Dir. 91/533 on employment information.

[50] See above, p. 8, but also G. Lyon-Caen and A. Lyon-Caen, *Droit social international et européen* (8th edn., Dalloz, Paris, 1993), 312.

regulations, a clearly reductionist interpretation that spares Member States the otherwise unavoidable revision of their systems.[51]

Both the Commission and the Council have, however, acknowledged that fundamental rights especially can be guaranteed only by regulations aiming at a 'high level' of protection.[52] Moreover, the Council's deliberations on the Data Protection Directive in particular confirmed that if this purpose is to be fulfilled the intended regulation has to be seen as an open-ended process. The Community must hence adopt rules that establish a regulatory content ensuring high standards, but not prevent the Member States from further developing and improving them. Thus, the very subject of this regulatory intervention, the protection of fundamental rights, compels the Community to accept the risk of divergent national laws and, consequently, of at least temporary obstacles to the unrestrained functioning of a common market.[53] In sum, the Member States are not exonerated from the duty to improve the standards, nor is the Community freed from the obligation to review its own demands against the background of national experiences. The regulatory concept is therefore, in the words of Lord Wedderburn, 'diversity built on a common floor of standards'.[54]

But instead of seizing the opportunity offered by the commitment to fundamental rights and the ensuing need for minimum requirements, the Community retreated into regulatory minimalism. Persistent references to the subsidiarity principle and repeated praises of the merits of soft law are clear signs of a deliberate passivity. It is certainly true that the Community's role has been defined by the Agreement on Social Policy (Article 2(1)) as 'supportive' and 'complementary'. It is, however, equally true that since its earliest days the Community has painstakingly resorted to subsidiarity whenever a possible intervention was discussed. Small wonder therefore that, for instance, efforts to amend the Agreement by explicitly inserting the subsidiarity principle into Article 1,[55] or by at least reaching an understanding that it should be regarded as a tacit premiss,[56] met with failure. There is hence no 'qualitative' change forcing the Community to review its policies and to adopt a stance essentially aiming at the preservation of the *status quo*.[57] Even leaving aside these considerations, however, the subsidiarity principle cannot justify passivity in the case of fundamental rights. For the reasons already mentioned, both their implementation and their protection depend on regulatory intervention by the Community clearly predetermining the measures to be taken by the Member States.

[51] See especially M. Heinze, 'Europarecht im Spannungsverhältnis zum nationalen Arbeitsrecht' (1992) 23 *Zeitschrift für Arbeitsrecht* 331, at 340–1.

[52] See, for instance, para. 10 of the recitals to the Data Protection Dir. and S. Simitis, 'From the Market to the Polis', n. 39 above, 448.

[53] See para. 9 of the recitals to the Data Protection Dir. and S. Simitis, n. 39 above, 463–5.

[54] N. 11 above, 273; see also Calon *et al.*, n. 27 above, 30.

[55] See *Agence Europe* No. 5632, 12 Dec. 1991, 6, and No. 5634, 20 Dec. 1991, 7.

[56] See, e.g., Heinze, n. 51 above, 340.   [57] See, however, Treu, n. 13 above, 16.

The Community is, however, ostensibly reluctant. Thus, the Medium-Term Social Action Programme 1995–7 speaks of 'an additional type of response', stresses the Community's role to promote joint discussions, exchanges of experience, and concerted actions, in sum to 'encourage high labour standards as part of a competitive Europe', and explicitly lists the protection of workers' privacy among the subjects for 'debates' to be 'launched'.[58] Similarly, in its proposals for the Fourth Medium-Term Community Action Programme on Equal Opportunities the Commission announces a 'sustained effort' in order, in particular, to further the adoption 'of outstanding proposals in the most suitable way', but at the same time visibly shifts the emphasis to advisory structures, consultation procedures, and communication on central issues.[59] In fact, both documents operate along the lines already drawn by the 1993 Green Paper[60] and 1994 White Paper on Social Policy.[61] The first emphasized the importance of soft law by meticulously detailing no fewer than fifty examples. The second questioned the need for legislative intervention, particularly with regard to regulatory aims addressed in the Agreement on Social Policy. Thus, priority is more or less openly given to the classic ingredients of soft law, i.e. resolutions, recommendations, memoranda, and codes of practice. Binding intervention is pushed into the background. Legislative action is featured as the *ultima ratio* or, in the Commission's own words, a 'last resort'.[62] In the same spirit, at its Edinburgh meeting the European Council urged the Community to 'legislate only to the extent necessary'.[63]

The importance accorded to soft law may[64] to some extent reflect concerns regarding the unquestionable difficulty of striking a balance between the Community's demands and the scope left for decisions by national legislators. In the main, however, it expresses a purely strategic move. As the experience of other international bodies[65] shows only too well, consideration of a shift of instruments usually arises when the policies and reactions of Member States impose compromises that substantially reduce the impact of forms of regulation carrying binding force. The switch from conventions to

---

[58] *Social Europe* 1/95, 9, 18, 19.

[59] N. 31 above, B–5, B–12 ff.

[60] *European Social Policy: Options for the Union*, COM(93)551 of 17 Nov. 1993, Annex II.

[61] *European Social Policy: A Way Forward for the Union*, COM(94)333, 27 July 1994, II.Guidelines, para. 3, points 5 and 6.

[62] *Report to the Council on the Principle of Subsidiarity*, SEC(92)1990 Final, 27 Oct. 1992, 4–5, 14.

[63] *European Council, Edinburgh, 11–12 Dec. 1995*, Conclusions for the Presidency, II, Guidelines, para. 3, points 5 and 6.

[64] For an analysis see also F. Snyder, *Soft Law and Institutional Practice in the European Community* in S. Martin (ed.), *The Construction of Europe—Essays in Honour of E. Noël* (Kluwer, Deventer, 1994), 194; J. Kenner, 'EC Labour Law: The Softly, Softly Approach' (1995) 11 *Int J Comp LL & Ind. Rel.* 307.

[65] See especially M. Bothe, 'Legal and Non-Legal Norms—A Meaningful Distinction in International Relations' (1980) 11 *Netherlands Yearbook of International Law* 65.

recommendations is a classic example of the gradual replacement of hard law by soft law.

In other words, and more precisely, soft law offers an alternative wherever the risk of a 'race to the bottom' appears to be too large. Hence, where conflict is as keen as it is in the case of most regulations affecting employment relationships, and the Community is not only increasingly manœuvred into a regulatory *impasse* by concessions minimizing the effect of its intervention but also split in an unprecedented manner by documents such as the Agreement on Social Policy,[66] a change of instruments is, seemingly, the only way out.[67] Soft law offers the chance of a form of regulation fully expressing the Community's views without preventing the Member States from applying their own concepts to whatever extent they wish. Thus, neither the Community nor the Member States need engage in laborious and endless negotiations that might ultimately force them to abandon the basic principles of their particular policies.

Soft law may mitigate conflicts, but it cannot eliminate them, as least as far as the implementation of fundamental rights is concerned. In fact, in the final analysis a change of instruments merely shifts responsibility for safeguarding and enforcing the fundamental rights assumed in the Maastricht treaty to the Court of Justice. And as experience shows, the Court will in fact attempt to ensure the protection that both the Commission and the Council avoided granting, and at the same time upgrade soft law, the better to justify its own decisions. For instance, in the *Defrenne* case[68] the Court acknowledged that a resolution concerning Article 119 of the Treaty could definitely have legal effects as long as its purpose was to encourage and accelerate full implementation of the equality principle. And in the *Grimaldi* case[69] it not only held that recommendations could be the subject of a reference to itself for a ruling under Article 177 of the EC Treaty but also confirmed that non-binding measures cannot be 'regarded as having no legal effect'. On the contrary, national courts must 'take Recommendations into consideration in order to decide disputes submitted to them, in particular where they cast light on the interpretation of national measures adopted in order to implement them'.

In short, an experience typical of the application of directives is repeated: the Court disregards the form and focuses on the content of the particular instrument concerned.[70] Soft law can and will, therefore, develop unobtrusively

[66] See *Commission Communication concerning the Application of the Agreement on Social Policy, presented to the Council and to the European Parliament*, COM(93)600 Final, 14 Dec. 1993, Summary para. 3.

[67] See also Snyder, n. 64 above, 3 ff.; Kenner, n. 64 above.

[68] Case 43/75, *Defrenne*, n. 45 above.

[69] Case C–322/88, *Grimaldi* v. *Fonds des Maladies Professionnelles* [1989] ECR 4407.

[70] See especially Case C–106/89, *Marleasing* [1990] ECR I–4135; J. Klabbers, 'Informal Instruments before the European Court of Justice' (1994) 31 *CML Rev.* 997; Kenner, n. 64 above, 310.

but steadily into quasi-hard law. Welcome as this may at first seem, however, the price is far too high: an insidious redistribution of powers within the Union that ultimately de-legitimizes the Court as well as the Commission and the Council. If, therefore, both the credibility of the Union and the readiness of its citizens to accept the unification process are really to be furthered, all efforts should be concentrated on the consequent enactment and application of hard law, not an escape into soft law.

2

In Support of a European Social Constitution

MIGUEL RODRÍGUEZ-PIÑERO
AND
EMILIA CASAS

I. The Difficult Situation of Labour Law within the European Union and the Constitutionalization of Fundamental Social Rights

Following the wide-ranging debate which it initiated in late 1993 with its Green Paper on *European Social Policy: Options for the Union,*[1] on 27 July 1994 the Commission adopted the White Paper on *European Social Policy: A Way Forward for the Union.*[2] In this document, 'preserving and developing the European social model' based on the Welfare State is singled out as an objective for the Union. In the face of views which hold that free competition of social systems and working conditions in Community countries is an element of the competitiveness and economic progress of the Community itself and of its less developed countries, the European Commission unhesitatingly asserts that the social dimension and the existence of a high level of social protection in Europe not only should not be seen as 'a cost' in terms of competitiveness, but actually constitutes 'a key element' in the economic competitiveness of the Union and its Member States. Competitiveness and social progress are, the White Paper affirms, 'two sides of the same coin'. Competitiveness is to be sought 'not through a dilution of the European model of social protection, but through the adaptation, rationalization and simplification of regulations, so as to establish a better balance between social protection, competitiveness and employment creation'.

The White Paper sets out the main lines of European social policy in the closing years of the century for the purposes of drawing up a new action programme for the Union in the light of its territorial enlargement, the revision of the Treaties, and the attainment of economic and monetary union. Does this entail a new European social model, which shifts the focus

---

[1] Communication by Mr Flynn, 17 Nov. 1993, COM(93)551.
[2] COM(94)333.

of social objectives away from labour law and its central themes to the less clearly defined area of social policy? The White Paper states that the Union's priorities in the social field are 'equal treatment of men and women, free movement of workers, health and safety, and—*to a limited extent*—labour law'. With the end of the period of the 'corporate restructuring' directives (resulting from the 1974 social action programme) and that of the harmonizing directives, and with the shift of emphasis, since the adoption of the Single European Act and the Community Charter of the Fundamental Social Rights of Workers, away from harmonization to convergence and from these harmonizing directives to the new directives on 'minimum standards' acceptable *for all*, the Commission makes two statements of the utmost importance in this document.

With reference to the diversity of the labour and social protection systems of the Member States, it declares that 'total harmonization of social policies is not an objective of the Union'. Rather, the goal is the free and harmonious coexistence of the different national systems through the convergence of these social policies in regard to the fundamental objectives of the Union, especially in the field of employment, the 'number one' priority among the principles fixed in the Commission's other White Paper on *Growth, Competitiveness and Employment*, and social protection.

Secondly, and in the face of the lack of consensus on the part of Member States 'about the need for further legislative action on labour standards at European level', the Commission considers that there is no need for a new programme of 'legislative proposals' and states that it will have recourse to legislation only when it is strictly necessary to achieve these objectives, which include completing the implementation of the second social action programme of 1989, which resulted from the Community Charter of the Fundamental Rights of Workers. Without prejudice to the use of collective bargaining mechanisms derived from or enshrined in the social dialogue, this legislation will take the form of directives on minimum standards whose purpose will be to prevent unfair competition (the infamous *social dumping*) and obstacles to the free movement of persons within the single market. In the field of social security, the White Paper considers that normative *co-ordination* of the national systems is the Community procedure best suited to the rapid evolution of these systems and people's endlessly changing requirements.

More generally, the Commission believes that consolidation and implementation 'of the existing corpus of law' are at least equally as important as any extension of Community labour and social security law, without prejudice to its amendment or even repeal where necessary. The White Paper also tackles the important subject of the effectiveness of Community labour law, reminding Member States of their Community obligations and the need to establish appropriate systems of control or effective and deterrent sanctions in a framework of co-operation between their respective administrations and between the latter and the Commission. The observance and proper and effective application of European-level provisions are essential if Community law in the social field 'is to have a real impact' on the situation of workers in Europe. Here, the Commission considers that 'the current level of compliance with and transposition of Union legislation . . . needs to be improved' and that a knowledge of it should be within the reach of all citizens. In order to improve the accessibility and transparency of this legislation, the Commission is to undertake the codification and consolidation of certain existing regulations and directives (the regulations relating to social security for migrant workers and the directives on collective dismissals).

Thus, labour law is, as the Commission states, 'at the heart of the debate about the relationship between competitiveness, growth and job creation' as well as in the centre of the controversy concerning the instruments which should ensure the economic and social convergence of Member States. Its development carries problems whose solution requires the adoption by the Community of policy decisions with important consequences for the future: from those concerning the rights of third-country nationals legally resident and working within the Community relative to the rights of workers who are citizens of Member States, to the effect of labour legislation on non-workers, the unemployed, and those excluded from social and economic life, and including the difficulty of constructing a European-level system of collective autonomy and collective bargaining. Even so, the key question at the present time, and one which can no longer be deferred, concerns the definition of the fundamental social rights of workers as an indispensable part of the constitutional basis of the political union which is awaited (either with eagerness or with apprehension).

Among the topics to be examined by the 1996 Intergovernmental Conference on the revision of the Treaties, in the field of social policy crucial are those issues relating to the establishment of social rights as a constitutional element and to the technical measures or instruments for achieving this objective, in addition to the political and legal fate of the Maastricht Agreement on Social Policy. As regards the latter, the White Paper expresses the hope that the anomaly of the existence of a Community labour law 'for eleven' will be surmounted in the future, something which it considers 'vital' if the principles of integrity of the law and equal opportunities for all are to be a reality in the Union. With reference to the incorporation of social rights in the Treaties, the Commission considers that this is a key issue which has to be examined in the context of the revision of the Treaties, since 'Certainly, there is a need to ensure that all people in Europe are aware of, and are able to exercise, their fundamental rights.'

II. Significance of a Constitutional Proclamation of
Social Rights at the Present Stage in the Process of
Construction of the European Union

The need for a constitutional proclamation of social rights is neither new nor separable from the European constitutionalist movement and the numerous initiatives aimed at furnishing the Community with a genuine Constitution.

The case law of the European Court of Justice (ECJ) has tended to confer the status of '*constitutional charter*' on the Treaties by affirming the direct primacy and effectiveness and binding force, both active and passive, of the Treaty provisions and their higher or supralegal ranking in the regulatory hierarchy of the Community legal order as a distinct, autonomous, and complete system which is European and superimposed on that of Member States (Case 294/83, *Les Verts—Party Ecologiste* v. *European Parliament* of 23 April 1986 and Opinion 1/91 of 14 December 1991 on the *Draft Agreement on a European Economic Area*).[3] Also, there are numerous doctrinal interpretations which, albeit from different standpoints, have supplied clear agreements to support the idea that a European Constitution or European constitutional law exists (identifying features, existence of a control of constitutionality by the ECJ). Nevertheless, the absence of a declaration of rights in the Treaties and the Community's lack of democracy are serious shortcomings which make it impossible to speak of a Community constitution.

Apart from this, the issue at present is to go beyond the conception and operation of the Treaties as a formal or procedural constitution, confined to the allocation of powers and competences, and to convert this into a genuine Constitution as a supreme set of rules, endowed with material content and substantive values. An essential part of this content would necessarily be the fundamental rights of workers, extending beyond the basic Community values (of an eminently economic nature) and the general principles of Community law developed by the ECJ with the status or identity of fundamental rights. If it is true that 'economic union alone is not a sufficient basis for a European Constitution',[4] it is equally true that the continued lack of a Constitution will mean that the European Union born at Maastricht remains no more than a free trade area.

The reasons for this renewed and growing interest in a European Act to establish rights correspond to a dual set of needs. First, in the context of

---

[3] Case 294/83 [1986] ECR 1339 and Opinion 1/91, [1991] ECR 6079.

[4] L. M. Diez-Picazo, 'Reflexiones sobre la idea de Constitución Europea', (1993) 7 *Revista de Instituciones Europeas*, 553; idem., '¿Una Constitucion sin declaración de derechos?' (1991) 32 *Revista Española de Derecho Constitucional* 155 ff.

general considerations, the constitutional guarantee of fundamental rights has become essential since the Treaty on European Union, which has extended the Community's powers over European citizens beyond their capacity as purely economic agents, such that these powers now influence 'situations which are recognized by national Constitutions as the subject of fundamental guarantees'.[5] Union policy is at a watershed, undeniable at this stage in the process of European integration and essential in its evolution towards a deeper European integration, and the need to link this more closely to its citizens demands a democratic basis. A 'Europe of citizens' would be meaningless without a constitutionalization of their rights.

Secondly, this time in the specific field of labour law, the constitutional operation of a declaration of fundamental social rights is essential in order to guarantee the maintenance and future course of the European social model which the Commission states that it wishes to preserve and develop. Maastricht strengthened economic freedom and integration without balancing and accompanying this reinforcement with recognition of the principle of the social State.

Thus, the enshrinement of social rights would form the foundation of the Union's social policy and law, the 'unitary base for a European labour law',[6] which would give the Union a fundamental and irreversible degree of legitimation and would be the necessary precondition for its Constitution. Without any shadow of doubt, this act of defining social rights in the Community legal order would be key to the realization of economic and social cohesion, one of the main objectives of the Union (Articles B and 2 of the Treaty). Without this legislative affirmation of rights, labour law would not only see its future evolution jeopardized, but would very probably pass into processes of re-nationalization.[7]

For these reasons, the social problems of the European Union are today posed in legal and constitutional terms. Social objectives have turned towards 'a strategy of constitutional policy'.[8]

The preoccupation with the recognition of fundamental rights in the field of European law, and the voices heard in support of this recognition, have grown more insistent and forceful in recent times. 'With no possible alternatives, labour law must be linked to clear constitutional principles', states Simitis;[9] and 'the path towards European integration necessarily includes stronger recognition, in the form of a constitutional act, of fundamental rights' repeats this author with A. Lyon-Caen.[10]

The constitutional Act which is being demanded would presuppose a

---

[5] M. D'Antona, 'Qui ha paura della sussidiarieta?' (1944) 4 *Lavoro e Diritto* 570.
[6] S. Simitis, 'Europeizzazione o rinazionalizzazione del diritto del lavoro?' (1994) 64 *GDLRI* 653.
[7] Ibid., 639 ff.   [8] Ibid., 654.   [9] Ibid., 661.
[10] A. Lyon-Caen and S. Simitis, 'L'Europe sociale à la recherche de ses références' (1993) 4 *Rev. du Marché Unique Europeen* 109.

qualitative leap in terms of legal policy relative to the present state of Community treaty law and derived law. The essential difference lies in the fact that a Constitution does not admit of a unilateral act of secession or denouncement. This is what distinguishes the binding effect generated by an international convention or agreement between States (in the form of a treaty and readily visible in the procedural regulation recorded in Article 8c of the Treaty on European Union) and the constitutional binding effect which results from a genuine Constitution or a Treaty-Constitution, as a legitimation of and limit on the legislative powers of the Union and the Member States and as a source of individual rights of citizens and a basis of petitions which may be the subject of legal enforcement.

III. Recognition of Social Rights in the Community Legal Order

1. The Treaties and the 'Creation of Rights' Function of the
European Court of Justice: Their Limits

What has been said above does not mean that the Community system of law has been operating empty of fundamental rights. Everyone knows of the important work of the European Court of Justice (from Case 29/69, *Stauder* and Case 11/70, *Internationale Handelgesellschaft*,[11] in the face of rebellion by the German and Italian constitutional courts) in the protection of fundamental rights recognized by the Constitutions or 'constitutional traditions' of the Member States and in the use and development by its decisions of the methods of interpretation of the national constitutional courts rather than the international courts. The Community Court takes the view that these fundamental rights, which are common to the national legal systems, and interpreted in accordance with international treaties which Member States have signed, most notably the European Convention on Human Rights, are *general principles of Community law* (Case 4/73, *Nold*, Case 36/75, *Rutili* and Case 44/79, *Mauer*[12]). The Court has imported into Community law rights and principles which are external or foreign to this law, inferred from the Constitutions of the Member States, and at the same time has developed specifically Community principles deduced from its own Treaties: rules against discrimination on grounds of nationality or sex, free movement, free exercise of an occupation, free enterprise, etc.

In this way the European Court of Justice has made up for the non-existence of an enumeration of rights in the Treaties or, at the very least, mitigated the more disturbing consequences resulting from this lack.

---

[11] Case 29/69 [1969] ECR 419; Case 11/70 [1970] ECR 1125, 1134.
[12] Case 4/73 [1974] ECR 491; Case 36/75 [1975] ECR 1219; Case 44/79 [1979] ECR 3727, 3744–50.

The Single European Act put an end to more wide-ranging debates and plans on the institutional reform of the Community, stopping short at ambitions aroused and without going so far as formally to proclaim the 'common civilized values' which the reports prepared within the Dooge Committee had called for.[13] The Preamble to the Single European Act based the joint promotion by the Member States and reaffirmation of 'the principles of democracy and compliance with the law and with human rights' in 'the fundamental rights recognized in the Constitutions and laws of the Member States, in the European Convention for the Protection of Human Rights and Fundamental Freedoms and the European Social Charter, notably freedom, equality and social justice'.

The Maastricht Treaty, for its part, confined itself to the European Court's interpretation, proclaiming respect by the Union for 'fundamental rights as guaranteed by the European Convention for the Protection of Human Rights and Fundamental Freedoms signed in Rome on 4 November 1950 and as they result from the constitutional traditions common to the Member States, as general principles of Community law' (Article F(2)). The European Convention is cited again in Article K.2 of the Treaty in relation to co-operation in the fields of justice and home affairs, in particular as regards free movement of persons, including immigration policy. The mention of compliance with the Convention in this provision, covering its systematic use in the body of the Treaty, 'limits its force but allows compliance with its principles to be extended to non-Community citizens'.[14] Nevertheless, the references to the European Convention are insufficient; and, obviously, the European Court does not have responsibility for the interpretation and observance of the European Convention.

All in all, from another perspective it may even be said that the Maastricht Treaty has introduced a step backwards in specifically Community 'constitutional' language. The four basic Community freedoms—free movement of workers, capital, goods, and services—are expressly called 'foundations of the Community' in the Treaty of Rome (Part Two, Titles I and III). Since the Maastricht reform, these 'fundamental' freedoms have been 'toned down' in favour of the 'strategic prominence' afforded to citizenship of the Union,[15] and are grouped together under the heading 'Community Policies', as its 'Part Three' is now entitled. Yet in 'Part Two', now entitled 'Citizenship of the Union' as based on possession of the nationality of a Member

---

[13] Text in (1985) 1 *Rev. de Instituciones Europeas* 347 ff. and (1985) 3, 1007 ff. See F. Pérez de los Cobos, *El Derecho comunitario en el Tratado de la Unión Europea* (Civitas, Madrid, 1994), 45 ff.

[14] M. A. Moreau, 'Tendances du droit social communautaire: des droits sociaux en quête de reconnaissance' (1994) 6 *Droit Social* 613.

[15] A. Mangas, 'La ciudadania de la Unión Europea', in *El Defensor del Pueblo en el Tratado de la Unión Europea*, Catédra J. Ruiz-Giménez de estudios sobre el Defensor del Pueblo, Universidad Carlos III de Madrid, Madrid, 1993, 33.

State (Articles 8 and 8e), nothing is said about the fundamental rights of European citizens, despite the fact that recognition of such European citizenship must have been intended to include certain fundamental rights for its holders, individual in scope and economic and political in nature.[16]

In the face of so scant a basis in the Treaties, the European Court of Justice has gone as far as has been possible for it in drawing its principles from common constitutional traditions, which, in general, correspond to the Social State model. In the view of some authors, affirmation of the fundamental rights and principles of the Community legal order via court decisions, a task fulfilled in exemplary fashion by the European Court of Justice 'as an instrument of democracy in the Community',[17] also has the advantage of flexibility and the adaptability of the Community legal order to particular cases (e.g. a ban on age discrimination), advantages which would be lost if there were central regulatory intervention. However, the more widespread view among authors today emphasizes the limitations of the European Court's capacity as regards declaring fundamental rights with binding effect on the Member States, pointing to the technical difficulties involved in performing a function similar to that of the U.S. Supreme Court (incorporation of Community fundamental rights in national legal orders), a model whose evolution is customarily compared with that of the European Union.

A wide variety of arguments are put forward to demonstrate the inadequacies, and even disadvantages, which result from this reliance on the European Court to establish rights. Fundamental rights declared to be such by the European Court are rights which are 'created on an *ad hoc* basis and amended on an *ad hoc* basis',[18] subject to the random influence of court judgments and lacking the necessary universality and stability. They do not enjoy secure identification and their scope is imprecise, since neither this identification nor this scope is common to the constitutional traditions of individual Member States, however much the European Court may assert it. A single example will suffice to demonstrate European constitutional diversity: the right to strike and to impose lock-outs. The mention of the latter in Article 2(6) of the Maastricht Agreement on Social Policy has generated vigorous controversy among French legal scholars as regards its implications: since Article 2(6), although it sets out rules allocating powers to Member States, does not proclaim any right at Community level capable of being binding on them, Verdier and Lyon-Caen state categorically, in

---

[16] C. Blumann, 'L'Europe des citoyens' (1991) 345 *Rev. du Marché Commun* 283 ff.

[17] G. F. Mancini, *La Corte di Giustizia: uno strumento di democrazia nella Comunità Europea* (Il Mulino, 1993), No. 3, pp. 604 ff.; also, 'The Making of a Constitution for Europe' (1989) *Common Market Law Review* 595 ff.

[18] S. Simitis, n. 6 above, 655.

response to Teyssié,[19] that the constitutional position on rights as laid down in French law remains unchanged. Furthermore, in terms of the division of powers the European Court is not a source of the creation of rights, and cannot take on functions properly belonging to the policy-making bodies of the Community (the Council, Commission, and Parliament), in spite of the Community's lack of democracy, nor can these bodies abdicate such functions. Apart from this, a situation where the constitutionalization of rights at supranational level is left to court decisions will always leave the way open for possible divergences of opinion and conflicts of competence between the ECJ and the national constitutional jurisdictions, since constitutional logic is not only not identical with but may sometimes cause a conflict of laws with Community logic. In short, opinions abound which openly proclaim the need for *judicial self-restraint*.

The situation is therefore far from satisfactory. Hence the calls for a Community declaration of rights or, at the very least, an express commitment on the part of the Community, as such, to the European Convention,[20] a proposal which entails a good many disadvantages (not the least among them would be relations between the Council of Europe's Court of Human Rights and the ECJ). This dissatisfaction becomes all the greater in the face of the absence of social rights both in Community case law (the ECJ has done less work in the field of social policy) and in the 1950 European Convention. The Treaty on European Union makes no reference to the 1961 European Social Charter nor, as is well known, to the Community Charter of the Fundamental Social Rights of Workers—the basis of the Protocol on Social Policy agreed between the 'Twelve' which authorized the conclusion of the Agreement on Social Policy between the 'Eleven'—which remains 'at the frontiers of Community law'.[21]

Lastly, ratification by the Community of International Labour Organization (ILO) Conventions, a source which is generally regarded as valuable, encounters serious obstacles both in the Community's own legal order and in that of the ILO, and could never satisfactorily replace a specifically European declaration of social rights.

To conclude, at the present stage of the Union the proclamation of fundamental rights via 'constitutional' interpretation on the part of the

[19] J. M. Verdier and A. Lyon-Caen, 'Sur le lock-out et l'accord européen relatif à la politique sociale du 7 février 1992' (1995) 1 *Droit Social* 49-50. And B. Teyssie, 'Le droit de lock-out' (1994) 9/10 *Droit Social* 795 ff.

[20] On this point, see M. A. Dauses, 'La protection des droits fondamentaux dans l'ordre juridique des Communautes Européennes. Position du problème, état actual et tendances' (1992) 4 *Rev. des Affaires Europeennes* 9 ff.; E. Perez Vera, 'El Tratado de la Union Europea y los derechos humanos' (1993) 2 *Rev. de Instituciones Europeas* 459 ff.; R. Alonso Garcia, *Derecho comunitario. Sistema constitucional y administrativo de la Comunidad Europea,* (Centro de Estudios Ramon Arèces, Madrid ,1994), 600 ff.

[21] A. Lyon-Caen and S. Simitis, n. 10 above, 116.

European Court of Justice is not sufficient. What is needed is a Community Act of a constitutional nature, which, in the social field, would provide a binding basis for Community social policy and law and would be the 'unifying' foundation of the labour law systems of the various Member States.

2. The Community Charter of the Fundamental Social Rights of Workers

2.1. *The Contradictory Objectives of the Charter*

From the very moment of its adoption through 'solemn declaration' by eleven Heads of State or Government meeting at Strasbourg on 9 December 1989, the Community Charter of the Fundamental Social Rights of Workers has aroused doubts and reservations as regards both its content and its legal relevance, whether in the Community legal order or in the internal legal order of the signatory States. Leaving aside the varying opinions on the Charter, expressing differing degrees of criticism,[22] what is quite certain is that its existence neither has been nor is irrelevant and that, were there no such Charter, the situation regarding social rights in their Community dimension would be far less favourable.

The difficulty surrounding the origins and genesis of the Charter are more than familiar to everybody.[23] Nevertheless, it is useful to note that the Charter embodies the confluence of three ideas, not to be confused with each other, which are connected with the problems that arose in the 1980s concerning the social dimension of the internal market and also with the trends towards deregulation and flexibilization of the labour market which commenced in the various Member States of the Union during those years. The first is the idea of the approximation of the national labour law systems, nowadays viewed from the perspective of equivalence of results; the second is the idea of the establishment of a minimum Community labour standard which ensures, by a process of adjustment from below, the maintenance of minimum social levels, accepted in all Member States, to overcome forms of *social dumping* and market imbalances; and the third is the idea of the

---

[22] See B. Bercusson, 'La Carta comunitaria dei diritti sociali fondamentali. Obiettivi strumenti' (1991) 3 *Lavoro e Diritto*; Lord Wedderburn, *The Social Charter, European Company and Employment Rights: An Outline Agenda* (Institute of Employment Rights, London, 1990); J. Addision and S. Siebert, 'The Social Charter of the European Community: Evolution and Controversies' [1991] *ILRR* 957 ff.; C. La Macchia, 'La Carta comunitaria dei diritti sociali' [1990] *DLR* 769 ff.; J. L. Monereo Pérez, 'Carta comunitaria de Dereches Sociales Fondamentales de los Trabajadores' (1992–3) 56–57 *Rev. Española de Derecho del Trabajo*; M. Rodriguez-Piñero, 'La declaración de derechos sociales comunitarios' (1989) *RL*; andC. Pettiti, 'La Charte communautaire des droits sociaux fondamentaux des travailleurs: un progrès?' [1990] *DS* 387 ff.

[23] See E. Vogel-Polsky and J. Vogel, *L'Europe Sociale 1993: illusion, alibi ou realité?* (Presses Universitaires, Brussels, 1991), 153 ff.

recognition at Community level of a number of fundamental rights of a social nature.

These three ideas imply a triple objective and signify in themselves an alternative to the former Community conception of upward social harmonization of the national systems, including the form of minimum harmonization which had been discussed by the European Parliament in 1986. Nowadays, the objective set is a less ambitious one, involving also a change of method, in the form of basic social guarantees or minimum social provisions. It consists in establishing a minimum common form of regulation in the social field, which also takes account of those aspects that influence the competitiveness of enterprises, in order to contribute towards the objective of completion of the common market but also to apply a common brake on the trends towards deregulation and flexibilization discernible in the various national systems.

This is the context surrounding the idea of a Community instrument such as a Charter or Declaration of social rights drafted with the aim of drawing together the main lines of this Community social minimum. Accordingly, the Charter adopts a defensive stance, which is to prevent policies of deregulation, without purporting to innovate or create new rights but only to identify the common minimum of social rights commonly recognized in the various national systems. Nor does it seek to extend the powers of the Community bodies; it merely facilitates, by giving principles and guidelines for action, the establishment of subsequent Community or national instruments which give effect to the declarations contained in the Charter.[24]

2.2 *The Inadequacy of the Charter*

From the outset, the Charter was manifestly a part of a system that had to be completed, with its final usefulness depending in large measure on its implementation through the other parts of the system which were necessary to pursue its objectives. The passing of time has justified the reservations expressed by the European Parliament in 1989, when it stated the need to establish Community legislation defining a floor of fundamental rights of workers linked to the completion of the internal market and requested the urgent adoption of a directive for the implementation of fundamental social rights in all Member States of the Community, and also envisaging a 'solemn Charter' in which Member States affirmed their commitment to ensuring other social rights, all those involving services (such as the right to education, to housing, to health care, to social protection, etc.[25]). The Parliament's opinion was that the instrument of a Charter or Declaration should be reserved purely for certain social rights which required public services and

[24] See T. Treu, 'L'Europa Sociale: Dall' Atto Unico a Maastricht' (1992) 11 *QDLR* 12; and M. Rodriguez-Piñero, n. 22 above, 3.
[25] Doc. A 2–399/88.

the availability of public funds, and in which the 'legal density' is less not only because of their vagueness of definition but also because they depend on the existence of financial and material means.

To the Parliament, a solemn declaration by the Council on the basic social rights of workers (slightly more accurate terminology than that subsequently adopted) was inadequate; it took the view, unreservedly, that such rights needed to be formulated as rights that could be pursued by judicial process under Community legislation.[26]

However, the Parliament's wishes were not taken into account. The Charter adopted by eleven members of the European Council turned into a solemn political declaration which neither is a Community instrument nor carries any binding legal force. The words 'proclamation' and 'declaration' demonstrate that it is a document of fundamentally political content and meaning, with no legal effectiveness, at Community or national level, either to limit the legislative powers of the Community or the Member States or to ensure a specific guarantee of enforcement, direct or indirect, of the rights it states to be proclaimed.

As a solemn declaration in which certain rights are proclaimed and particular objectives in the social field are recognized, the Charter falls within the pattern of other declarations of rights which, both at national and international level, have historically proved to be the precursors of instruments with greater legal relevance and binding force.[27] The special nature of the European Council, particularly prior to the Maastricht Treaty, coupled with the fact that it was adopted by only eleven of the twelve members, implies that the Charter is not a Community instrument and that its effectiveness lies at the level of political co-operation, even as regards guaranteeing the effectiveness of the 'rights' that are pronounced, whether this is through the action programme and common policies or through 'enforceable norms' at national or Community level. The Charter's political importance is considerable, because the solemn proclamation of social rights and principles from a common position of the signatory States paves the way for the collaboration of these States in the social field, as a blueprint for future Community action in this field.[28] Even if it does not embody binding legal undertakings with guaranteed judicial remedies, the Charter implies a political commitment to the achievement of the goals and objectives stated and specified in the Charter itself. Without being a binding legal norm at the traditional level of the law, it is a fundamental instrument of policy on law which establishes goals to be attained and legal ways and means of achieving this, as a guideline for action by the Member States and

[26] Doc. B 344/89.   [27] J. L. Monero Peréz, n. 22 above, 260 ff.
[28] F. Valdes Dal-Re, 'La Carta Comunitaria de los Derechos Sociales Fundamentales de los Trabajadores' in *El Espacio Social Europeo*, (Lex Nova, Valladolid, 1991), 22; and F. Perez de los Cobos, n. 13 above, 67.

Community bodies. Although not a legal instrument capable of guaranteeing the rights contained in it, the Charter is an instrument for the promotion of social action by the Member States and in particular by the Community, via means which include the social action programmes which it invites the Commission to draw up and also the annual report on progress in implementing the Charter which the Commission is required to submit. The Charter is therefore, it may be stressed, an important instrument for the furtherance of Community social objectives and for the future development of Community labour law.[29]

2.3. *The Rights Proclaimed in the Charter*

The special nature of the Charter lies in the fact that it attempted to define and specify its purpose and objectives in the form of a proclamation of individual rights. However, examination of the Charter shows that it is far from being a list of basic or fundamental social rights of workers which can be directly invoked or asserted by the latter against national and Community authorities and in relations between private individuals. The Charter does not create individual rights which operate as an objective limit on the Community legislators (although this criticism can be levelled beyond the Charter, given that the lack of recognition of rights in the Treaties means that no genuine individual fundamental rights exist in the Community sphere). As regards its content, the Charter includes both pronounced rights and a series of social-policy objectives or principles, combining what may be described as social rights proper, irrespective of the degree of precision in their definition, and what are not, strictly speaking, social rights but simply recommendations or objectives for social policy (including some named from the perspective of what is 'appropriate'). Scrutiny of the text reveals a surprising variation in the degree of specifically binding and concrete definition of its different provisions, reflecting a calculated legal imprecision which allows, through ambiguity and vagueness, a very wide margin for interpretation and regulatory development.

Thus, the Charter expresses a political will to give support and impetus to action in the social field, to back new initiatives by the Member States (and here express mention is made of the principle of subsidiarity) and by the Community itself, including action programmes, for which the Charter is nowadays an important political support. This is not all, however, because its proclamation in the form of fundamental social rights also implies the recognition, as a common element of the signatory States, of a number of higher values in the social field which are to be incorporated into Com-

---

[29] M. Roccella and T. Treu, *Diritto del lavoro della Comunità Europea* (Cedam, Milan, 1992), 22 ff.; Steindorff, 'Quo Vadis Europa?' in: *Weiterentwicklung der Europaischen Gemeinschaft und der Marktwirtschaft* (Heymanns, Colonia), 37; and M. A. Moreau, n. 14 above, 614.

munity social policy. The formulation of these social rights as higher values gives them a significance as principles which allows them to be incorporated into Community law, both in interpreting rules emerging from execution of the Charter and, in a more general sense, in serving as a source of guidance and direction in interpreting the rest of the Community legal order. This means above all through the work of the courts, and more particularly that of the European Court of Justice, which can draw from the Charter axiological values for deducing general principles of Community law. Hence it has been said that the Community Charter, despite being an external source, may be a source of guidance for Community law.[30]

Declarations of rights, particularly at international level, have frequently been the direct precursors of instruments of binding legal force. For this reason such declarations have been referred to as 'pre-law', inasmuch as they may precede or evolve towards a progressive recognition of a more legal binding force. The question we need to ask ourselves at the present stage of the Union, and within the horizon of the revision of the Treaties that the Intergovernmental Conference has to tackle next year, is how it would be best to achieve phase two in the protection of social rights at European Union level, which will necessarily require a legislative creation of rights. Following phase one as represented by the Charter, which, despite its limitations, has marked a major step forward, the time has come to say that new steps must be taken in order to achieve greater effectiveness in the objectives and to ensure that recognition of social rights cannot be dismissed as platonic in the European Union. Should the Charter be incorporated in the Treaty?

The Community Charter of the Social Rights of Workers is not legally binding on the Member States and does not confer on the citizens of these States individual rights that can be asserted judicially against the national and Community authorities.

2.4. *The 'Implementation' of the Charter and the Role of the Commission*

Nevertheless, the Charter itself exhibits some measure of concern for the protection of the rights proclaimed in it, and an intention to endow them with a legal significance and effectiveness greater than that of purely political principles. To this end, it assigns the realization of the rights proclaimed in it to the Member States and to the Community itself, although without delimiting their respective fields of powers and responsibilities (other than that it makes express mention of the principle of subsidiarity) or directly shaping the social and labour policy of the States concerned or of the Community.

The instrument used to attempt to give effectiveness to the Charter is extremely slight. The Charter assigns a dual task to Commission, and it is in

[30] J. L. Monereo Perez, n. 22 above, 878 ff.

this dual responsibility that its relevance as an instrument of policy on law really lies.[31]

First, the Charter invites the Commission to submit initiatives for the possible adoption of legal instruments directed at implementing the social rights it recognizes, within the Community's area of competence and with a view to completion of the internal market. The invitation is adjusted in this way to the legal framework of the Treaty because, except within the narrow scope of Article 118a of the Treaty, the unanimity rule is still the unavoidable requirement for instruments for the protection and enforcement of social rights to be viable in the sphere of the Community's limited powers. This reflects the marked mismatch existing between the objectives or principles set out in the Charter and the limited powers in the social field that are recognized in the Treaty and, consequently, the difficulties inevitably confronting the effective realization through Community instruments of the common will expressed in the Charter to establish and develop a fundamental social base common to the Community and to the Member States.

This first task made it legitimate for the Commission to draw up a Social Action Programme,[32] which it did contemporaneously with the adoption of the Charter. This lent the Programme increased political legitimation, but at the same time caused elements of confusion between implementation of the Charter and implementation of the Programme. Not all of the Charter was, as some have said, guaranteed through this Community action, nor did the whole of the Programme have its justification in the Charter, and there was no legal link between the Programme and the Charter. In other words, the Programme could have existed without the Charter (and would not be the first), and the implementation of the Charter at Community level could have been realized without the Programme as an intermediate instrument. All this, of course, is quite apart from the importance that the existence of the Programme has had.

Secondly, the Charter instructs the Commission to draw up an annual report on progress in its implementation by the Member States and by the European Community, to be forwarded to the European Council, the European Parliament and the Economic and Social Committee. Responsibility rests on the Commission, and this is very different from a model of control through requirements imposed on the Member States, such as exists in other international bodies with regard to the European Social Charter, to verify the degree of compliance with the commitments undertaken. In spite of this, the dual content of the report, i.e. application of the Charter

---

[31] See B. Hepple, 'The Implementation of the Community Charter of Fundamental Social Rights' (1990) 53 *Modern Law Review* 643; T. Pérez Del Rio, 'La dimensión social del Mercado Unico Europeo' (1991) 47 *Rev. Espanola de Derecho del Trabajo.*

[32] M. Rodriguez-Piñero, 'Programa de Acción Social de la Comunidad para la aplicación de la Carta Social'(1989) 24 *RL* 1 ff.; J. P. Landa Zapirain, 'La ejecución del nuevo programa de acción social de la CEE' (1991) 3 *RIE.*

at Community level within the Commission's areas of competence and application of the Charter by Member States, implies, by virtue of its transparency and political importance, a first step towards guaranteeing, in an indirect manner, the Charter's effectiveness. These reports on the Charter have focused more on aspects of social or labour policy than on the situation regarding social rights, and from the outset have devoted more attention to the Action Programme than to the implementation of the rights recognized in the Charter.[33]

It is, therefore, clear that as a 'constitutional protection of social rights' at Community level the Charter is inadequate, since it neither recognizes effective rights nor imposes binding limits on the national authorities or the Community authorities.

These shortcomings were recognized as long ago as at the European Council of Luxembourg, which pointed out the inadequacy of progress in the field of social policy from the point of view of completion of the internal market and stressed the proper role to be undertaken by the Community, the Member States and the social partners 'in the application of the principles contained in the Social Charter, according to their respective responsibilities', requesting that work on the Action Programme should be intensified. An eminently functional preoccupation is readily discernible in this critical approach, as witness the fact that it talks of 'principles', not rights, and equates implementation of the Charter with the Action Programme. In other words, the European Council exhibited greater concern with the difficulties encountered in the adoption of new Community legislative instruments in the social field than with the need to improve the legal protection of social rights.

The focus of attention then shifted to criticism of the unanimity requirement for the adoption of Community instruments connected with a Charter 'for eleven' not signed by one Member State which nevertheless has to accept specific Community directives implementing it. This explains why, among its proposals to the Intergovernmental Conference on 'political union', the Commission will point out the inadequacy of the Treaty's provisions on social matters and propose that they should be remodelled to broaden Community powers and facilitate the adoption of instruments by qualified majority voting.

3. The Maastricht Protocol and Agreement on Social Policy

It is only too well-known that the Intergovernmental Conference which met at Maastricht did not succeed in getting the United Kingdom to accept the proposals on reform of the Treaty's provisions on social matters. These

---

[33] P. Pochet, 'L'actualité du droit du travail communautaire: la mise en œuvre de la charte de 1989' (1993) 7/8 *Droit Social*.

were kept separate from the important institutional reforms that were included in the Maastricht Treaty and, instead, there was an Agreement on Social Policy, concluded between the Member States of the Community with the exception of the United Kingdom and annexed to a Protocol with the same title, annexed in its turn to the Treaty. This Agreement provided for a significant extension of Community competence in the social area, replacement of the unanimity requirement by the possibility of qualified majority voting for certain topics, and legal institutionalization of social dialogue in the form of compulsory consultation and collective bargaining on a European scale.[34]

The Protocol on Social Policy represents an important step in the evolution of social Europe, and there is no doubt that it continues along the same path laid down by the Social Charter, to which it makes express and explicit reference, noting in its Preamble that the eleven Member States concerned wish to 'continue along the path laid down by the 1989 Social Charter' and accordingly 'have adopted among themselves an Agreement to this end', and authorizing these eleven Member States to have recourse to 'the institutions, procedures and mechanisms of the Treaty for the purposes of taking among themselves and applying as far as they are concerned the acts and decisions required for giving effect to the above-mentioned Agreement'. Nevertheless, this Agreement on Social Policy, in then proceeding to set objectives in social matters, makes no reference to rights but solely to principles of social policy (promotion of employment, improvement of living and working conditions, proper social protection, dialogue between management and labour, achievement of lasting high employment and the combating of exclusion: Article 1), although they are now not linked strictly to the objectives of market integration.[35] In addition, the Agreement establishes several self-limiting principles for its application which will, undoubtedly, be imposed on the Charter by transference: the principle of subsidiarity as a corrective of 'regulatory hypertrophy of the Community', the principle of taking account of the diversity of national systems and practices, and the criterion of preserving the competitiveness of enterprises by seeking to reconcile the economic with the social, a criterion which normally implies that the latter is governed by the former. Despite the difference in their legal nature,[36] there is, in any event, a discernible

[34] F. Guarriello, 'L'Europa Sociale dopo Maastricht' (1992) 2 *Lavoro e Diritto*; G. Guery, *La dynamique de l'Europe sociale*, (Paris, 1991); M. A. Moreau, 'Tendances du droit social communautaire: ombres et brouillard à Maastricht' (1994) 1 *Droit Social*; B. Bercusson, 'Maastricht: A Fundamental Change in European Labour Law' [1992] *Industrial Relations Journal* 176 ff.; *Maastricht Social Protocol: Reality and Perspectives* (Assicredito, Rome 1995).

[35] B. Bercusson, 'Maastricht: A Fundamental Change in European Labour Law', n. 34 above, 188.

[36] G. Arrigo, 'Unione europea: diritto del lavoro tra integrazione e frammentazione' (1994) 2 *Lavoro e Diritto* 268; G. Lyon-Caen, 'Le droit social de la CEE après le traité de

parallelism between the Charter and the Agreement on Social Policy which is reflected, notably, in the fact that the latter requires an annual report by the Commission on progress in achieving its objectives (Article 7), which the Commission itself, in its Communication on the implementation of the Protocol on Social Policy,[37] decided to re-cast into a single report combined with that on the implementation of the Charter.

The Protocol on Social Policy is one step more, but it is also a different step from the Community Charter.[38] For example, parallel examination of the matters referred to in the Maastricht Agreement on Social Policy and in the Community Charter reveals that topics as substantively germane to the social rights of workers as the right of association, the right to strike and the employer's right to impose lock-outs are excluded from the Agreement (Article 2(6)),[39] and topics as important as protection against dismissal, social protection, representation and consultation of workers and conditions of employment for third-country nationals are still subject to the unanimity requirement (Article 2(3)). The Agreement unquestionably possesses considerable institutional significance in extending Community powers and increasing the possibility of Community-level instruments, both legislative and collectively agreed, in the social field. However, it certainly does not introduce a radically new approach capable of correcting the secondary nature of the social dimension in the Community, and can therefore not be seen as a significant advance nor as an adjustment of attitude in the process of protection of the social rights of workers at Community level. Not even the broadening of the role of social dialogue and the institutionalization of collective bargaining represent, *per se*, a recognition of fundamental social rights in a European dimension.[40]

Practical implementation of the Protocol on Social Policy has made it quite clear that the pre-existing difficulties for the development of social instruments at Community level have not been removed. In essence, the obstacles did not lie only in the decision-making process, the unanimity requirement or the opposition of the United Kingdom. The co-existence of two 'autonomous and complementary' legal frameworks for the adoption of provisions in the social field, i.e. the Treaty and the Agreement, is an additional complicating factor which the 1996 Intergovernmental

Maastricht' [1993] *CHR* 149; T. Treu, 'La Europa Sociale: Dall' Atto Unico a Maastricht' (1991) 10 *QDLRI* 22 ff.

[37] COM(93)600 final, of 14 Dec. 1993.

[38] See B. Veneziani, 'La politica sociale comunitaria dopo Maastricht' (1992) *LI* 6.

[39] On this exclusion, see the critical analysis of Lord Wedderburn, 'Freedom and Frontiers of Labour Law', in: *Labour Law and Freedom* (Lawrence Wishart, London, 1995), 405 ff.

[40] See M. Rodriguez-Piñero, 'The Agreement on Social Policy'; S. Sciarra, 'Il dialogo tra ordinamento comunitario e nazionale del lavoro: la contrattazione collettiva' [1992] *DLRI* 749; F. Guarriello, 'Autonomia collettiva e dimensione europea. Profili organizativi e funcionali' (1992) 11 *QDLRI*; idem., *Ordinamento comunitario e autonomia collettiva. Il dialogo sociale* (Giuffré, Milan, 1992); 62 ff.

Conference will have to overcome. The wish to do so has been expressed by the Commission, and by the Economic and Social Committee in the latter's Resolution in support of a European Union that is strong, democratic, open, and founded in solidarity, which was adopted at their last conference[41] and which also proposed the constitutional incorporation of the Community Charter in the Treaty. Social dialogue and collective bargaining on a European scale have proved much less feasible than was originally thought, and a longer running-in time may possibly have to be anticipated,[42] apart from the need for a better definition of the legal framework of the system which settles, among other extreme aspects of relevance, the key problem of the representativeness of trade-union and employer organizations, 'a subject not properly covered at European level'.[43] Lastly, the new flexibilization approaches that are becoming officially entrenched in the Union, as evidenced by the two important White Papers by Delors and Flynn, do not favour any steps towards an extension of Community regulation in the social field.

This may explain why application of the Agreement on Social Policy has resulted only in the adoption of Directive 94/45/EC of 22 September 1994 on the establishment of a European Works Council or a procedure in Community-scale undertakings and Community-scale groups of undertakings for the purposes of informing and consulting employees, the first Community rule 'for eleven' to be based on Article 2(2) of the Agreement. Without denying the Directive's importance, the *de facto* presupposition for its application is the element of transnationality, i.e. the existence of at least two establishments located in two different Member States. The Directive does not apply where this condition is not fulfilled, a fact which proves, indirectly, that the protection of a right to consultation and information of workers as such was not a predominant factor in its adoption.

IV. Fundamental Social Rights and European Social Identity

The new restrictive approach to Community action in the social field, which entails a renunciation of the upward harmonization of the laws of Member States and accepts and respects the diversity of existing national systems, also demands, if possible, developments towards the involution and re-nationalization of what little Community labour law exists are to be kept in check, not only a Community social minimum but also an effective guarantee of social rights at Community level. Although the regulatory

[41] Brussels, 9–12 May 1995.
[42] See Lord Wedderburn, 'Labour law and the individual', 298 ff.
[43] M. A. Moreau, n. 34 above, 615; See L. Pelaggi, 'Business Categories, Representativeness and the Social Protocol', in *Maastricht Social Protocol*, 118 ff.

harmonization of national labour systems may not be a realistic objective nowadays, that does not exclude the need for a supranational framework encompassing national labour laws from a common basic floor of rights, something quite different from a political basis for overloaded, ambitious, and ineffective action programmes. The point here is to reinforce European social identity through the effective legal recognition of social rights.

In the course of the debates stimulated and suggested by the Green Paper on   that was cited earlier, many calls were voiced for an institutionalization of the protection of social rights at Community level. It is true that this view incorporated the idea of minimum requirements to be implemented gradually as derived from the second paragraph of Article 118a of the Treaty, minimum social standards that would be extended and transferred from the area of working conditions to other labour matters. However, this approach is not appropriate in a context where the extension of Community provisions in the social field is being called into question.

The subsequent White Paper on Social Policy, which opts decisively for flexibility of the labour market, does not propose any notable advances in labour matters by way of Community instruments—its proposals are concerned more with preserving than innovating—and it states at the outset that total harmonization of social policies is not an objective of the Union. However, it indicates that a framework of basic minimum standards should be established as a bulwark against the use of social deregulation as an instrument of unfair competition or to gain competitiveness. The document stresses the priority of consolidation and implementation of the existing body of law, rather than the presentation of new proposals. In connection with this, it identifies various topics relating to social rights as subjects for further study (prohibition of discrimination, equal treatment, personal privacy, protection against dismissal, paid time off, and information and consultation) and announces a joint hearing with the European Parliament in 1995 to assess the achievements, problems, and perspectives following the Community Social Charter, five years on from its adoption.

In practice, the Social Charter has been a document directed more at the Commission than at the Member States, its link with the Protocol and Agreement on Social Policy has not been clear and it is unlikely that it could now be transformed into the motive instrument of social policy in the Union Treaty. The immediate objective should therefore consist in focusing not so much on the future of the Social Charter and its incorporation into the Treaty as on the constitutionalization of social rights in the European Union within or in addition to the Charter, at a stage when, apart from this, the need for their recognition and protection is all the greater because labour law regulation in the various fields is being called into question, so that the problem cannot be left solely to national levels. There must be a shift from exhortatory rules to legal rules, which requires a 'creation of rights' act in the process of the construction of Europe.

V. Constitutionalization of Rights, European Constitution and Citizenship of the Union: The Bases of a Supranational Labour Law

1. The 1996 Intergovernmental Conference

The occasion for such an act should be the Intergovernmental Conference planned for 1996 for the purpose of revising the Treaties.

The Intergovernmental Conference has its direct origin in the impossibility of reaching agreement on certain topics at the Maastricht Intergovernmental Conference. In order to make agreement possible at the time, the Treaty on European Union stipulated, in its Article N(2), that an Intergovernmental Conference should be convened in 1996 to examine those provisions in the Treaty 'for which revision is provided'. The list of topics for this Conference contained in the Union Treaty itself has been enlarged in successive stages, but this pre-set agenda, which does not include topics of a social nature, will not prevent other subjects from being dealt with at the conference, including those connected with social policy and with the protection of fundamental rights.

The change in circumstances between Maastricht and the present day is not, of course, favourable to a substantial or in-depth alteration—a 'major or radical reform'—of the European Union at the 1996 Conference. The climate is not yet propitious for the germination of the proposals for the adoption of a Constitution of the European Union (Draft Constitution by the European Parliament's Committee on Institutional Affairs, of 9 February 1994, which incorporates the 'Oreja Report' of 1993). However, this debate, which is largely political (its extremes are well-known: federalism vs. European nationalisms), must not engender the mistake of perceiving the problem of fundamental rights as a variable which is necessarily dependent on the existence or otherwise of a European Constitution. Even if the European Union is not consolidated in the near future as a genuine Federation of States, and even if it is not formally endowed with a Constitution and remains regulated by a Treaty (or by a Treaty-Charter, according to other proposals planned for the Intergovernmental Conference), recognition of constitutional rights or principles in the reform of the Treaty is possible and desirable.

Quite apart from the political model and pronouncements on structural aspects relating to the nature and evolution of the Union towards a genuine federal State, the vertical and horizontal division of power, and the maintenance of intergovernmental processes for adopting rules and decisions, and also quite apart from the principle of subsidiarity, and even if Community law continues to be 'a law without a State',[44] the imperative need to reduce the Union's deficit in respect of the social dimension and in respect of democracy makes recognition of the fundamental social rights of citizens 'as a constitutional element of the European Union', to quote the Commission's words in its White Paper on Social Policy, an essential step.

Such recognition would make it possible to pursue the process of European legal integration, both normative and jurisdictional, without prejudging the political model for the construction of the European Union or its deepening and enlargement ('variable geometry' option and its different interpretations and variants), just as the principle of subsidiarity and the major principles that ensure the primacy of Community law, of federalist tradition, likewise do not prejudge the Union's federal nature, which is why it constitutes a perfectly possible alternative.

2. A Proclamation of Fundamental Rights without a Constitution

This is the direction taken by the Franco-German proposal of Lyon-Caen and Simitis[45] advocating a proclamation of fundamental and objective rights of constitutional value (although the latter author, writing alone, recommends the recognition of 'binding constitutional principles which define the functions and limits of Community action clearly' and of their relationship to collective autonomy, not solely to the 'corporatist' social dialogue[46]). The proposal encompasses the set of rights and principles which define a material or social Constitution for the Community area. These constitutional rights and principles accommodate differing distributions of competence between the Union and its Member States in accordance with previous balances or with 'new balances'; they also have to accommodate varying options for the development of Community social legislation, either those emphasizing harmonization or those focused more on competition and particular national features, differing priorities, and objectives and standards of protection: ultimately, different political options. 'A Constitution lays down a framework, it does not exclude'.[47]

The central aspect of constitutionalization is its 'unifying value', both legal and political, and its value in delimiting the respective spheres of the market and the public authorities. Supranational constitutional rights would be individual fundamental rights, enjoying the necessary jurisdictional protection, which would signify a limit for activity on the part of the Com-

[44] M. D'Antona, n. 5 above, 567 ff.
[45] A. Lyon-Caen and S. Simitis, n. 10 above, 119 ff.
[46] S. Simitis, 'Europeizzazione o rinazionalizzazione . . .', op. cit., 653 and 658.
[47] A. Lyon-Caen and S. Simitis, n. 10 above, 121.

munity and national authorities as well as individuals and groups, while at the same time identifying the objectives to be attained by the Union's social policy. This list or charter of rights would determine developments in Community law in the social field.

3. European Citizenship and Proclamation of Fundamental Individual Rights: A Unitary Proclamation of Fundamental Rights beyond Citizenship of the Union

However, having arrived at this conclusion it is necessary to take a step forwards, or backwards, in deciding whether it makes sense at the present stage to maintain separate treatment of fundamental social rights, as is the case at international level (both in the United Nations and in the Council of Europe), although this has been superseded in national constitutional systems. The evolution of constitutionalization has led to the incorporation of social rights in the list of constitutional rights, despite the special nature of some of them as regards their specific definition and binding force. At European level the perceived lack of democracy demands the recognition of rights of citizenship, and in this context separate recognition of rights which are granted neither as a function of citizenship nor as a function of occupational status loses its significance.

The integral unitary view of fundamental rights that is imperative today, with a necessary interdependence of all human rights at the civil, political, or social level, makes any instrumental separation between fundamental rights and social rights inadvisable. In 1991 Mancini declared that the Treaty of Rome neither safeguards the fundamental rights of individuals nor recognizes, even in embryonic form, the existence of a constitutional right of European citizenship, since individual rights under the Treaty had been deduced via the work of the ECJ and as a function of the operational requirements of the Common Market.[48] There was, in fact, an initial correction of this situation in the form of the recognition of European citizenship by the Maastricht Treaty. However, this recognition proved to be mainly symbolic, with only limited consequences (right to move and reside freely within the territory of Member States; right to vote and to stand as a candidate in municipal elections and elections to the European Parliament; possible diplomatic and consular protection; and right of petition), despite the evolutive clause contained in Article 8e of the Treaty, which states that 'the Council, acting unanimously on a proposal from the Commission and after consulting the European Parliament, may adopt provisions to strengthen or to add to the rights laid down in this Part, which it shall recommend to the Member States for adoption in accordance with their

[48] G. F. Mancini, 'Principi fondamentali di diritto del lavoro nell'ordinamento delle Comunità europee', *Il lavoro nel diritto comunitario e l'ordonamento italiano* (Cedem, Padua 1988), papers of the Conference at Parma, 30–1 October 1995.

respective constitutional requirements'. As part of the preparatory work leading up to next year's Intergovernmental Conference, various proposals have been formulated for extending the rights of citizenship of the Union, which will necessarily also imply consequences for general rights of citizenship.

Thus, the *Resolution of the European Parliament on the functioning of the Treaty in the perspective of the 1996 Intergovernmental Conference— Realization and development of the Union*,[49] adopted on 17 May last in response to the invitation addressed to the Community institutions by the Corfu European Council with a view to the preparation of the Conference, proposes that greater content should be given to the concept of citizenship of the Union through the development of constitutional rights linked to this citizenship, including topics such as the principle of equality and non-discrimination, the prohibition of capital punishment, the right to information and political participation, the protection of minorities, etc.

The same approach of enriching the rights associated with European citizenship was advocated by the *Report of the Commission on the functioning of the Treaty on European Union*[50] which was adopted on 10 May, likewise in connection with the preparatory work leading up to the Intergovernmental Conference. The Commission states that the concept of European citizenship introduced by Maastricht carries an added value whose potentialities have not been fully used and should be, in particular through the drafting of a fundamental text which includes the fundamental rights and duties which such citizenship confers. This, in the Commission's view, will allow citizenship to acquire a sense of pertinence to the Union which is not possible with the present recognition of scattered or incomplete rights that are, furthermore, subject to restrictive conditions.

However, the subject transcends the actual conception of European citizenship. If we wish to go beyond a purely economic approach to the Union, if European legitimacy is to have a democratic foundation, the idea also has to be accepted that the Union and the Member States are subject to a common set of values and rules. To express this in the words used by the European Court of Justice in its *Report on certain aspects of the application of the Treaty on European Union*,[51] the Intergovernmental Conference will have to resolve problems of a constitutional nature such as 'the insertion into the Treaty of a list of fundamental rights, in accordance with the democratic character of the Union, which makes the protection of human rights an essential element of the construction of Europe'. The Court itself mentions the subject of its competence to exercise judicial control of respect for fundamental rights inserted into the Treaty by normative or individual acts which are adopted within the framework of Community law, pointing

---

[49] Doc. A 4–102/95.   [50] SEC(95)731 final.   [51] Luxembourg, May 1955.

out that this 'would not constitute a new function for the Court of Justice'. This statement makes it clear, however, that it is now referring to rights, not political declarations.

The insertion of such a declaration or list of fundamental rights into the Treaty on European Union is the only way of establishing a legal guarantee of these fundamental rights. The avoidance implied by Article F(2) of the Treaty—in affirming respect for fundamental rights as guaranteed by the Rome Convention on Human Rights and as they result from the constitutional traditions common to the Member States, as general principles of Community law—and its inclusion among the common provisions of a purely declaratory value meant that this declaration lacked any legal value or, at least, was not justiciable, and that enforcement of these rights by the ECJ was excluded from the outset (Article L).

The Union's lack of democracy cannot be overcome simply by means of increased transparency (a watchword in the Community institutions) to bring the process of European construction closer to its citizens, or by an improved distribution of functions between the Union's bodies: it also requires a democratic legitimacy achieved through the guarantee of fundamental rights, because only then can it be said that 'democratic principles' are the basis and foundation of the Union. Hence the proposals to include in the enacting provisions of the new Treaty a Charter of fundamental rights and freedoms which, as suggested in the Spanish Government's document on the Intergovernmental Conference, 'would include all those rights regarded as basic in the *acquis communautaire*, which would then be protected both by the institutions of the Union and by those of the Member States, and specifically through close co-operation between the Luxembourg Court and the national courts'.[52]

This declaration of rights would need to include, obviously, not only traditional fundamental rights but also social rights. It would be desirable for both to be included in one common instrument which ensures and protects the rights both of the human individual and of the citizen; this means, of course, that some of the rights, depending on their nature and status, would need to be recognized independently of status as a citizen of the Union—or of the European Economic Area countries or of those countries with which the Union has concluded an agreement.[53] It should be noted that one of the major confrontations which may occur (and in fact already occurs) in the present panorama of Community social policy is that which brings Community labour law face to face with intergovernmental

---

[52] *La Conferencia Intergubernamental: Bases para una reflexion*, 2 Mar. 1995, 86.
[53] See B. Von Maydell, 'Le traitement des ressortissants d'Etats tiers en matière de droits sociaux dans les Etats de la CE et de l'EEE', in *La Securite Sociale en Europe. Egalité entre nationaux et non nationaux*, Actes du Colloque Européen, Porto 10-12 Nov. 1994 (Lisbon, 1995), 139 ff.

Community policy on immigration. The ECJ has already ruled against discriminatory treatment of third-country nationals, the Court designating the place where work is performed (and not the nationality or place of residence of the worker) as the point of connection for application of Community labour and social protection laws. The opposite tendency is exhibited by the Schengen Agreement and by the Maastricht Treaty (Article 100c), which affirms a restrictive immigration policy in spite of the integration of the matter in the Union through the creation of the so-called 'Third Pillar' (Articles B and K.1 to K.9). Labour law is not an instrument of immigration policy. However, 'the employment opportunities of third-country nationals should be linked to constitutional principles which prevent a reduction of their fundamental rights applied in the name of a "flexible" migration policy'.[54] Moreover, the Commission recognizes in the second of its White Papers that: 'An internal market without frontiers in which the free movement of persons is ensured logically implies the free movement of all legally resident third-country nationals for the purpose of engaging in economic activities. This objective should be realized progressively'.

The recognition of social rights will, unquestionably, have to take account of the present text of the Community Social Charter, which is relatively complete, but correct some of its imprecisions and ambiguities. A better distinction will need to be made between plans, which are so intermingled in the present document, and the recognition of rights in the strict sense and setting of clear objectives of social policy. In this respect, it is always preferable to adopt, realistically but rigorously, a list of rights that are effectively recognized, such as the right to freedom of movement, the right to freedom of association and of collective bargaining, and the right to strike, rights to information and consultation, the right to non-discrimination, etc., rather than attempt to include everything and draw up a very extensive list which will merely be reduced to a list of well-meaning aspirations. The important thing is to enshrine fundamental social rights as Community law,[55] and to entrust the function of giving them practical effect in some cases to the Member States and in others to Community instruments. The European constitutionalization of fundamental rights, including social rights, represents the most important challenge and objective at the present stage of the European Union. Only in this way will it be possible for a genuine supranational regulatory framework to exist.

[54] S. Simitis, n. 6 above, 661.

[55] See W. Däubler, *Market and Social Justice in the EC: The Other Side of the Internal Market* (Gütersloh, 1991),; S. Sciarra, 'Uno "strabismo di Venere": le politiche socialé comunitarie verso il completamento del mercato interno' [1991] *PS* 33; ead, Social Values and the Multiple Sources of European Social Law, [1995] ECJ, 60.

3

Subsidiarity

GÉRARD LYON-CAEN

We must start by coming to grips with the concept itself, one which before the Maastricht Treaty was not in what might be termed widespread use (Part I).

Next, the subsidiarity principle needs to be examined in the light of the division of powers between Member States and the Community, within the European legal system (Part II).

Lastly, for enthusiasts of social policy law (if any such remain) an evaluation has to be made of the repercussions of subsidiarity on a social policy which already had problems enough of its own without the introduction of this added consideration (Part III).

I. A More than Ambiguous Concept

As a word, *subsidiarity* is lacking in both elegance and exactness. And it is always dangerous when a legal principle is framed in words which fail to match up to the rules underlying the aesthetics or essence of language. Sooner or later it pays the price. This is, perhaps, beginning to befall the terms 'Community' and 'Union'. With 'subsidiarity', we are floundering in the muddy waters of inexactitude from the outset.

Tracing the source of its derivation is easy enough; its etymology lies directly in the word *subsidy*, a sum of money paid by way of help or assistance. The Latin word (*subsidium*) had one meaning which was little different from our present meaning of a tax or contribution. However, it was also used in the sense of auxiliary troops. The idea of voting a subsidy covered approval of the levy either of a tax or, equally well, of soldiers. In French, the term ('*subside*') is long-established in both private and public law. In private law, in family relationships, it denotes a form of fulfilment of the obligation to provide maintenance, and the expression '*action à fin de subsides*' (application for maintenance) is used in civil law; in public law, in the relationship between the individual citizen and the State and relationships between public bodies, it denotes financial assistance, either granted or levied. To pay a subsidy is thus to subsidize or, alternatively, to assist.

There is some relevance in pausing to reflect on this derivation of the concept, since legal relationships inside the Community are axiomatically rooted in financial relations. Within the entity that the Community constitutes, subsidies are paid by Member States to the Community (Article 200 of the Treaty) and by the Community to Member States (Article 125). The first of these situations consists in the contributions by Member States to the Community budget on a proportional scale laid down in the Treaty, contributions which are made regularly and on a differentiated basis. In the second situation we have the contributions made by the Community, through its various Funds, to the activities of individual Member States. Financial assistance takes place *in both directions*, a fact to which it is worth drawing attention at the start of our analysis: it is not an instrument of *unidirectional* subsidiarity.

The noun 'subsidy' gives rise to the derivative formation of the adjective *subsidiary* (and the adverb *subsidiarily*). Here, the scholar of semantics is in for something of a surprise, because 'subsidiary' does not have the meaning of something which pertains to subsidies or which qualifies a sum paid by way of a subsidy. The derived meaning is far removed from the source meaning. There is a presumption that the intended recipients to whom a subsidy is paid already possess resources of their own. A subsidy serves merely to make up or add to a main source of financing. A king possesses money derived from his Crown property, and his loyal subjects then pay him subsidies to make up the shortfall in these existing resources of his own for the purposes of meeting urgent occasions such as a war.

If we generalize these premises, something which is subsidiary is something accessory. The adjective presupposes the existence of some other, main element; once beyond that, however, it may be used in all kinds of senses which have no financial connotation. It is much employed, in particular, by practising lawyers, who speak of a subsidiary issue, subsidiary argument, or subsidiary claim; it denotes an issue which is raised secondarily to the main issue, or an argument which is advanced only in the second instance. A subsidiary point is raised in circumstances where the main argument or main claim is judged not to be pertinent and therefore rejected. If a first point fails to carry the day, a line of argument which is deemed to be secondary is invoked subsidiarily. It is part of the jargon of the courts.

Internal relations within the Community provide a perfect illustration of the subtle interplay between the main and the subsidiary. The moment a 'common policy' exists, the questioning starts: is national policy the main policy, with Community measures intervening in a subsidiary capacity? Or is Community policy the main element, with national policy fulfilling only a subsidiary role? The whole of Community law, from the outset, has been dominated by this never-ending question. In the case of agricultural policy, Article 45 of the Treaty makes explicit mention of the replacement of national organizations, which are to be confined to a subsidiary role, by forms of common organization.

Just as the adjective 'subsidiary' carries a meaning far removed from the word 'subsidy', so the noun *subsidiarity* obliges us to make an even more unexpected leap. Subsidy and subsidiary are words long-established in traditional usage; subsidiarity comes to us from a vocabulary created by scholars, relatively modern and with more than a hint of pedantry.

The concept has probably featured in internal relations within the Catholic Church (relations between Rome and local dioceses), territory into which it does not do to venture too far. But its famous use has been in the major encyclicals expressing what is known as 'Catholic social doctrine'. In its wish to mark out a path distinguishable both from 'Statesocialism' and from pure 'liberal individualism', the Catholic Church developed the criterion that the intermediate authorities standing between the individual member of the social body and sovereign power should function in accordance with a principle given the name of the principle of subsidiarity: the public authority which is most immediately close to the individual citizen should be the one which comes to his assistance, with the next higher authority intervening only in a supplementary capacity and in the event of default, and the central authority or State itself fulfilling only a function of last resort. The principle is applicable to services as essential as hospitals and schools; the State should encourage private initiative, if necessary helping things to get done by subsidizing them, rather than do things itself. The same principle applies even to the family as an institution, which the public authority in its multiple role should not replace, but merely foster or subsidize. It governs relations between the State and local government bodies, which, as the level most immediately close to the individual, should be chosen as the context for the services which are essential to modern life, in preference to the central authority. The latter has a function which is, ultimately, unique: supplying what is lacking and intervening only in a subsidiary capacity. Family, enterprise, commune, region, and all lower-level authorities come into play before the State does.

Since the Community is, in the legal construct, a higher-level authority than its individual Member States, it is logical to conclude from the above that talk of subsidiarity in connection with the Community can mean only one thing: its function is merely *to fill the gaps in national action*; its role is confined to taking on those functions which individual Member States cannot perform. Just as the Stateshould feature only in those areas of social life where private initiative, local initiative, and intermediate bodies are unable to perform an essential task appropriately, so the proper function of the Community authorities is confined to taking measures in those matters where national authorities have taken no action or are unable to act effectively. But expressing it this way takes us into the realms of political science.

Stated in terms of the law it signifies, rather, that a Community rule is supplementary in nature or that action at Community level is a substitute for national action.

Does the concept necessarily go hand in hand with the Community's evolution towards some form or other of federation, or perhaps confederation? It would not appear so: a federation or confederation does not supplement inaction on the part of its Member States, nor does it act as a substitute for them if the task in hand is beyond them. It is vested with powers of some specified scope and may act only within the limits of those powers. The situation is therefore very different, even if the results may sometimes seem similar.

Thus, in attempting to determine the relations between subsidiarity and competence it has to be accepted that the principle of subsidiarity, in the sense outlined above, *presupposes that powers are not properly divided or not clearly allocated* (and hence do not confer exclusive competence), either overall or as regards their various elements, a situation which is expressed by saying that powers are undifferentiated, joint, combined, or (as some would put it) concurrent, the latter being a not altogether felicitous choice of word since there is no competition here.

II. Member States and Community: The Opposite of Subsidiary

This is how relations between the Community and its Member States are envisaged by the new Article 3b, in the wording of the Maastricht Treaty: 'in areas which *do not fall within its exclusive competence*, the Community shall take action, *in accordance with the principle of subsidiarity*, only if and in so far as the objectives of the proposed action *cannot be sufficiently achieved* by the Member States and can therefore, by reason of the scale or effects of the proposed action, be *better achieved* by the Community'.

Interpretation of this text has been engendering somewhat panic-stricken reactions,[1] because: (1) it excludes all matters falling within the Community's exclusive competence from application of the principle of subsidiarity, yet makes no mention whatever of those which fall within the *exclusive* competence of the Member States, which would have been the logical thing to do; (2) it makes application of the principle conditional on the impossibility of a proposed action being carried out *sufficiently* by individual Member States, leaving the evaluation of what constitutes sufficiency wide open to uncertainty. 'Sufficiently' is not the same thing as 'better'; (3) it presents the

---

[1] Communication from the Commission to the Council (SEC(92)1990 final), [1992] *Rev. Trim. Droit Européen* 728. This extremely interesting document contains the suggestion that the provision has been diverted from its original purpose, which was to assign straightforward objectives to Member States, and nothing more. Could it be that all the Community's troubles stem from this?

mechanism of subsidiarity as tied both to the *scale* and to the *effects* of a proposed action, thereby inviting comparison with the objectives set for the Community; and (4) it enshrines, subject to these reservations and conditions, the idea that the Community has only a subsidiary function: it takes action *only if* and *in so far as*. The principle is thus affirmed that everything is dealt with at the level of the individual Member States. By way of exception only, the Community may act in their stead provided that some insufficiency can be imputed to them. And even then within prescribed limits.

Unfortunately, history neither begins nor ends with Maastricht. Commentators cannot avoid asking themselves certain questions. What were the precise implications of the Treaty of Rome in this respect? What have been the implications of its successive amendments, and of the manner in which it has been ultimately applied at the instigation of the Court of Justice? Does what is spelled out in the Maastricht Treaty mark a real change of direction? Is subsidiarity a new organizational mechanism, to be viewed by some as a return to good sense but by others as a setback to the construction of Europe?

The fact that the word 'subsidiarity' appears for the first time in the Maastricht Treaty and was not previously used as such[2] admits of two possible interpretations: (1) either the principle is an entirely new one, or (2) the principle was in fact already being applied albeit by way of different forms of wording, and the change in vocabulary is purely superficial and in any event less radical than might initially be assumed from reading the new Article 3b.

We need to re-read the treaties, and possibly also the Court judgments delivered, in the light of the wording which was adopted at Maastricht. And this may hold a number of surprises. The language of the European treaties (and behind it, the fundamental concepts and, as the very basis of the construction of Europe, the system itself) has always been enveloped in a smoke-screen, a deliberate ambiguity. When all is said and done, and quite apart from the question of application of the Maastricht Treaty, it is quite possible that Community law enshrines various legal principles which are so at variance with the principle of subsidiarity that the latter's appearance can be regarded only as an empty illusion. The mere fact of affirming something (particularly when this is incidental, as is the case in the Maastricht text) does not make it law.

---

[2] Curiously, the Single European Act (Art. 130r(4) of the Treaty) stated that: 'The Community shall take action relating to the environment to the extent to which the objectives referred to can be *attained better at Community level* than at the level of the individual Member States'. This embodied the notion of subsidiarity without using the word itself, but in the Maastricht Treaty the para. disappeared. Clearly, the *extension* of Community competence which it had carried did not find favour with the plenipotentiaries who met in Limburg province.

In more strictly legal terms, one might be forgiven for thinking that some kind of *incompatibility* is gradually emerging between Article 3b and the rest of the treaties. Such a supposition is in no way unlikely: it needs to be verified. Article 3b itself alludes to the hypothesis of an area in which the Community possesses exclusive competence. But the Treaty was founded on the notion (more legal than that of subsidiarity) of a *division of powers*. How can the two techniques be harmonized? If the Member State level and the Community level each have their precisely specified powers, what room is left for supplementary or subsidiary action? Or for a new emphasis intended to forestall unwarranted interventions by the Community, while the wording actually appears to regularize (in certain cases) an unforeseen assumption of powers? Surely Article 3b, whether intentionally or not, is simply one of a pair with Article 235? Article 235 stipulates that the Community shall take action *if*, and Article 3b that the Community shall take action *only if*. But the result is identical: an extension of competence. This amounts to saying that the delimitation of powers remains very fluid (and there are examples of this in social policy law), that areas exist in which powers are shared or concurrent—and here is where there is room for the principle of subsidiarity. But it has yet to be shown that it can be reconciled with a system founded on competence as such. The Community either *possesses* competence or *lacks* competence. For instance, the Court decided that the Commission lacked all competence in regard to the policies of Member States concerning immigration of people from non-member States.[3] Hence it could not possess 'subsidiary' powers. The notion is therefore, at the very least, confused.

The reasons for suspending judgment, i.e. for doubting the possibility of injecting a dose of subsidiarity into something which is governed by the concept of competence, are all the more numerous because the European Community system was in fact constructed on the basis of fundamentals which are the absolute opposite of subsidiarity. Nowhere is there any question of a Community which imposes limits on itself in favour of its individual Member States—quite the reverse. As long ago as 1950 (Declaration by the French Government of 9 May 1950), when it was a matter of the fusion of *particular* resources, the coal and steel sector was placed under a common authority to which the states that were to be signatories to the 1951 Treaty of Paris delegated *certain* specified powers, with a 'special' Council of Ministers created alongside it as an intergovernmental body. In 1957, in the Treaty of Rome, the technique was not greatly different. The text of the Treaty divides functions and tasks between the Community and its Member States and— something which is of considerable relevance to our present discussion— defines the powers of the various Community bodies.

[3] Cases 281, 283–5 and 287/85, [1987] ECR 3203 *Germany, France, Netherlands, Denmark and United Kingdom* v. *Commission*.

The Community's competence is normally a competence that is conferred *ratione materiae*, i.e. dominated by the principle of specialty: the Member States, which for their part possess *general* competence, transfer to the Community *certain* powers formerly belonging to themselves, with varying extent and scope. For instance, in the case of common policies the transfer is accompanied by an almost total restriction of a Member State's own competence. Even then, however, the Community possesses competence only if and to the extent that the Treaty expressly so provides. The whole mechanism operates in the opposite direction to the notion of subsidiarity: the 'lower' level restrictively relinquishes powers in favour of the 'higher' level. Here, it is not that the Community is required to limit itself to a supplementary role (subsidiarity) but that the Member States themselves entrust it with a task which has hitherto been reserved for them (transfer), and do so within clearly defined limits. The Community's competence consists in those powers which are conferred upon it by the Member States.

Furthermore, although the Commission possesses the right to put forward proposals, the right to take decisions rests with the Council, which is made up of representatives of the Member States. This being so, the fundamental question is and remains: does the Council decide on a particular matter by unanimity, qualified majority, or simple majority voting? This is a different question, and one on which the principle of subsidiarity manifestly has no bearing. The two things are not on the same wavelength. The manner in which the founding treaties broach the regulation of the 'common markets' (coal and steel market, then agricultural market, transport market, labour market, and global market in goods, services, and capital) is not that of creating an institution which supplements action by the Member States. The idea of joint exercise of previously defined powers, or delegation of power to an intergovernmental body, is closer to the reality.

Admittedly, the course of the past quarter of a century has seen the situation evolve, but certainly not towards minimizing the Community's role! The Court of Justice has consistently afforded the *Community's functions and powers a broad interpretation*; it has always given prevalence to a *purposive* conception of whichever rules it was interpreting, enabling them to produce their 'full effectiveness' in the light of their stated objectives. The result has been a development of the Community's *implicit powers*. This signalled a clear departure from the idea that the Community possessed only such special competence as had been conferred upon it. And affirmation of the supremacy of Community law over domestic law strengthened the impression of a kind of gradual dwindling of national powers, or their subordination to those wielded by the 'centre'. The emergence of 'concepts of Community law' represented a similar line of development. I shall refrain here from voicing an opinion either way, and merely comment that the initial strict division of powers is giving way to a real 'progressive

Communitization' of law which was not provided for by the treaties; or, to express it differently, that the Court imposes restrictions on action by Member States to the extent necessary to achievement of the Community's objectives. 'Subsidiary role of the individual member state?' The wording might seem a little extreme, but it gives the picture.

Who can fail to see that the Court of Justice has in this way restricted the field of action of Member States and enlarged that of the Community, that it has thereby consistently applied 'contra-subsidiarity'? Slowly, Member States have been divested of various powers because they belong to a collective whole which has its own requirements. A typical example is the Court's famous decision in the ERTA case[4] the essential passage of which reads as follows: 'In all cases where, for the purposes of implementing a common policy provided for by the Treaty, the Community has adopted measures, whatever their nature or form, which are intended to establish common rules, Member States *cease to possess the right* to enter into obligations towards non-member countries affecting those rules. . . . The Community *alone* possesses the capacity to undertake and fulfil, in regard to the entire scope of application of the Community legal order, commitments contracted towards non-member countries'.[5]

In any event, the Treaty of Rome's system itself contained a potential margin for or, as it were, virtual increase of Community intervention, as witness Article 235: if the Community has not been provided with the powers necessary to the attainment of one of the objectives of the Community, the Council, acting unanimously, 'shall' take the appropriate measures (i.e. is required to do so). What could possibly be more at odds with the notion of subsidiarity? It was this Article that was used as the base for the Court's decision in the ERTA case.

Article 3b can thus be identified for what it is: an *outburst of resentment* directed against the Court of Justice and, as a secondary target, the Commission. It cannot, in itself, modify the respective competences (whether exclusive or concurrent) of the Community and the Member States—modify the system of sources of law within the Community—or influence the decisions of the Court of Justice. Rather, at Maastricht itself (not without some contradiction) the field within which Community-level action is able to develop was not restricted but *extended*, with its limits pushed a long way outwards. Citizenship of the Union and the right to vote in municipal elections . . . monetary policy . . . education, culture and research . . . environment. . . . The list of new areas in which the individual Member State is *giving ground* to the Community is a long one. The Community is

---

[4] Case 27/70 *Commission* v. *Council* [1971] ECR 253.

[5] The Court's stance would appear to have been moderated in Case C–158/91, *Levy* [1993] ECR I–428 concerning denouncement of the ILO Convention on the prohibition of night work for women. See also Opinion 2/91 [1993] ECR I–1061.

no longer merely 'economic' and has been followed by its shadow: the Union. The principle of subsidiarity does not therefore, signify any definite or foreseeable redistribution of roles and functions. It is a reaction expressing impatience with the encroachments that have been permitted by the Court to the detriment of Member States.[6] But a superficial reaction no more than skin-deep, since at the very time when the principle was pronounced the erosion was being continued with the tolerance or somnolence of the Member States themselves.

If the new prescription in Article 3b consisted in conferring an exceptional capacity to act upon whichever of the two levels (national or Community) is the one at which a proposed action would have optimum effectiveness, the principle of subsidiarity could lead equally well to a strengthening either of the Community's powers or of the powers of Member States; the Court would again have to be called upon to decide. In all likelihood, judging from the precedents, this would be to the advantage of the Union rather than its individual members.

However, the fact remains that subsidiarity, which is not so much a principle of law as an incantation or myth, is directed against the encroachments of the Brussels 'bureaucracy'. Such a myth can have little effectiveness against a system which itself originally professed to be restrictive towards Community competence but which the course of events has since pulled in the opposite direction. And in the practical terms of a specific field like the law on social policy, it is even more difficult to see which powers would be subject to the subsidiarity rule.

III. A Cause of Confusion in Community Law on Social Policy

In the particular case of social policy law, the new subsidiarity rule would seem at first sight to be a matter of indifference. Surely things are perfectly clear, with social policy law falling *not within the competence of the Community authorities* but within the *exclusive* competence of Member States. Subsidiarity already existed in the absolute (without the word as such). There were indeed some exceptions: most notably, the free movement of persons (Article 48) and social security arrangements for migrant workers (Article 51), the operation of the European Social Fund (Article 125), equal pay for men and women (Article 119), and the general principles of a common vocational training policy (Article 128). But these exceptions were few in number, and all the Community measures to be taken on them had been completed long before Maastricht.

This pattern of the division of powers had, it is true, been slightly altered

---

[6] An interpretation borne out by statements made by Chancellor Kohl and Prime Minister Major.

by the Single European Act, which in introducing the new concept of *economic and social cohesion* 'seemed' to call for a more substantial degree of Community-level action; it also opened up to the Council the new possibility of acting by qualified majority in the (admittedly vaguely defined) field of the *work environment*. The Charter of Fundamental Social Rights, on the other hand (contrary to what might have been expected), stated categorically that it was not to entail any change in the division of powers between the Member States and the Community. Its own terms thus rendered it purely aspirational.

On their own, however, these facts give quite the wrong impression of the extent of Community intervention that was possible even before Maastricht. The boundary between the two levels of competence had been shifted as early as the 1970s, not so much on the basis of Articles 117 and 118 concerning social harmonization (on which agreement has never been reached) as on the basis of Article 100, i.e. by using the required approximation of national laws as a legal base. This was the base used to enable the three famous 'corporate restructuring directives' (Directive 75/129 on collective redundancies, Directive 77/187 on transfers of undertakings, and Directive 80/987 on the insolvency of employers) which, in the interpretation given them by the Court, have seriously curtailed the competence of Member States.

The rule of careful delimitation of Community-level intervention had therefore been bent not so much through any multiplication of the agreed circumstances in which such intervention was expressly encouraged as through broad interpretation (at one time emanating from the Council and relayed by the Court).

Was the intention of Maastricht to put a stop to this drift? Paradoxically, no. Leaving aside for the moment the famous Social Protocol annexed to it, the Treaty itself *again added to* the number of situations in which the Community possesses competence to intervene: the work environment (once more), health and safety protection for workers, economic and social cohesion, and, most notably, all forms of *education and training* ('the Community shall implement a common vocational training policy'). These various instances are not established as exclusive to the Community; it is clear that the competence of Member States remains in place, and that powers are therefore *concurrent*. Does this mean that the subsidiarity rule will be called into play? Nothing could seem less likely. In the field of health and safety, a multitude of detailed texts have already been issued, leaving Member States but a scant share. And as regards training, the Community is not restricted to taking action only where Member States neglect to do so; it is to implement a policy, the text states. This is manifestly *contra-subsidiarity* in operation.

Things are more difficult to interpret in the case of the new Article 118b, which was inserted by the Single European Act but remodelled and given enlarged scope at Maastricht. Does the European-level collective bargaining (social dialogue) which it provides for signify a broadening of Community competence or, conversely, its restriction? Some authors[7] have seen this provision as an actual expression of the subsidiarity principle, holding that the referral of an issue to joint decision by the social partners represents a form of curtailing the power of the authorities at both Brussels and national level. This is actually a way of evaluating an old-established principle (the autonomy of the social partners) using a new measurement technique (subsidiarity). Is it truly an instance of the notion of subsidiarity? It seems doubtful. In my view, it would be nearer the truth to say that, in authorizing collective bargaining to span the European arena—and no longer just the national arena—Article 118b extends Community-level 'competence' in the broad sense of the term (including that of the social partners), to the detriment of competence at national level. What is the subject at hand here? Collective bargaining. And what Maastricht permits is European-level collective bargaining. Instead of being dealt with through a central directive, an issue will be referred to the social partners, whose agreement will then be replicated in the form of a Council decision. This is a new method, and unquestionably a welcome one. But is it the mechanism of subsidiarity? Contrary to the view taken by Ph. Langlois (*loc.cit.*), it does not represent a 'second subsidiarity'. For this to be so, it would have to be the case that, when a national government refrains from fixing pay levels and establishes the principle that they are to be fixed through agreements between employers and employees, it is implementing the principle of subsidiarity. But this simply represents the operation of contractual freedom. And it is merely such contractual freedom which is now being recognized (still only within certain bounds) for European employers and unions. It cannot be interpreted as an instance of 'subsidiarity' because, quite on the contrary, such bargaining will take place far away from those concerned, not 'as closely as possible' to them. What we have here is a new application of contractual freedom: whether or not it represents progress is another matter. The idea of subsidiarity as a kind of deliberate diffidence on the part of the European Union (towards its Member States) is unlikely to enter into it. The debate is a quite different one: it concerns relations between the regulatory and the collectively agreed approach, not those between Member States and the Union.

It is indisputable that the Protocol and Agreement annexed to the Treaty go even farther in exemplifying *contra-subsidiarity*, since they extend the area in which powers are combined and intermingled well beyond its former limits. This may perhaps give serious cause for doubting that the Agreement

---

[7] Ph. Langlois, 'Europe sociale et subsidiarité', [1993] *Droit Social* 201.

will ever be applied. At all events, the drafters have allowed themselves a field-day in multiplying the instances of encroachment by the Community authorities into the hunting-grounds of individual Member States. Article 1 of the Agreement on social policy is an example of precisely what not to do: in virtually all areas of social policy law, ranging from employment to social protection, the Community *and* the Member States possess powers without the slightest hint being given of whether they should be classed as common, concurrent, or joint. Whereas before Maastricht there was some delimitation of Community action, the Protocol and Agreement have entangled everything together; both national authorities and the Community authorities may act in any area, whatever it may be. This accounts for the inclusion of subsidiarity as a corrective. But the method used previously would have been more effective. And no real attempt has been made to link the two levels of action in a co-ordinated manner. We are thus presented with systematized confusion. The Community *'shall support and complement'* *the activities of the Member States* (the respective powers therefore being complementary or concurrent) in the fields of working conditions, the information and consultation of workers, equality between men and women, and the integration of persons excluded from the labour market (all with the possibility of acting by a qualified majority) and social security, termination of the employment contract, the representation and collective defence of the interests of workers and employers, including codetermination, the employment of nationals of non-member countries, and the financing of the promotion of employment (all requiring that the Council should act unanimously). This is exactly what the text says: the Community's function is to support and complement, not to supplement if necessity so dictates.

What does this make of the pronouncement of the subsidiarity principle? It is possible that the Eleven, while greatly extending the areas of Community intervention, actually intended the subsidiarity rule to act as a curb; henceforth, the Community *may* address a problem that was formerly beyond its reach, but is to do so *only if necessary and even then within bounds*. This approach, if such it was, is not without its contradictions. If the intention was to prevent Community interference, it would surely have been simpler not to mention it in the first place. To put it more bluntly, could they not see that what they had just given with one hand they were taking away with the other? To increase the instances of Community intervention and then stipulate that such intervention should play only a subsidiary role is anything but consistent. It is reasonably safe to say that, particularly where unanimity is required, directives or decisions will be all the more easily blocked because opponents will be able to argue that the subsidiarity rule must be observed. One cannot help thinking that the drafters have landed themselves in an inextricable contradiction.

The result, in the final analysis, is that subsidiarity can really operate only in areas where the texts are silent or where they formally *prohibit* the Community from featuring (Article 2(6) of the Agreement), i.e. in regard to pay, the right of association, the right to strike, and the right to impose lock-outs. But in that case what point is there in mentioning subsidiarity at all? All that is needed is to apply the text. Should we, *a contrario*, see its logic in terms of what is not prohibited? That is, should we read Article 2(6) more as a list of straightforward examples of the subsidiarity rule, which would then be susceptible of other applications? It is impossible to tell. The subject of working hours is a case in point. Does it fall within an area where Community competence is prohibited (competence of the Member States), or within an area of concurrent competence, with the subsidiarity rule prescribing abstention? Nothing is certain, other than the fact that the subsidiarity rule is in no way *compatible* with a treaty system based on the allocation of specified powers. The result is muddle and disorder.

It is not impossible that there was some confusion with the idea that the Community lays down minimum rules, leaving Member States free to uphold more detailed and more protective provisions. But that is the notion of a *minimum Community public policy* from which Member States are able to derogate '*in melius*' (system of mandatory minimum social provisions). It does not embody the idea of subsidiarity. The mechanism is encountered in the field of workers' health and safety; it has no connection at all with the text of Article 3b. If this was what the drafters had in mind, they have confused two different ideas.

Nor is it impossible that what some had in mind was a different way of presenting subsidiarity in relation to the competence of Member States and that of the Community authorities. On this assumption, the instances where the Council may from now on act by a *qualified majority* are evidence of the wish to oblige Member States to bow to a decision by the supreme Community authority (e.g. Article 118a, work environment), while those where *unanimity* is stipulated represent straightforward application of the always underlying principle of subsidiarity (e.g. Article 100a(2), 'rights and interests of workers'). This interpretation likewise appears to confuse two quite separate things: on the one hand, voting procedures within the Council, which are intended to vary according to the gravity of the issues at stake; and on the other hand, the shaping of the European Union towards a grouping of Member States within which the decision-making process remains close to those concerned, and therefore normally within the national context. These ideas gain nothing from interfering with each other.

The dogmatically minded may assert that subsidiarity signifies the refusal of the authors of the Maastricht Treaty to commit themselves to the path of federalism. The higher authority is not to intervene unless a particular action is possible only at that level. This means, it may be asserted, that federal development is rejected.

Since the same Treaty is the source of the single European currency, however, this analysis is very likely to run into further contradiction. Maastricht, delightful town though it is, did not nurture the lucid expression of straightforward ideas.

It is safer to say that:

- the Treaty's drafters used an imprecise word without properly weighing up its implications and without verifying that it was compatible with a system based on the allocation of specified powers;
- in the social policy field, the drafters of the annexed Protocol and its accompanying Agreement failed to realize that the provisions they were adopting were logically inconsistent with the entire development of Community law on social policy between 1951 and 1992.

Nothing more, and nothing less.

4

Labour Law as Market Regulation: the Economic Foundations of European Social Policy

SIMON DEAKIN

1. Introduction

The principal influence over European Community social policy has been, and remains, the economic goal of market integration. Even the apparently fundamental social right to equal pay in Article 119 of the EC Treaty owes its existence to concerns over unfair competition.[1] The Ohlin Report of ILO experts cited sex discrimination as one of the few instances in which transnational labour standards would be needed to deal with a distortion of competition arising from the liberalization of trade; without some degree of harmonization, it was feared that low-cost producers located in States lacking effective laws on equal pay would enjoy an 'economically unsound' advantage.[2] But the ILO experts rejected arguments for a more general programme of harmonization of labour and social security law. They concluded that, for the most part, 'international differences in labour costs and especially in social charges . . . do not constitute an obstacle to the establishment of freer international markets',[3] and maintained that the Member States should largely retain their autonomy in the area of social policy. This view was cemented into place by the Treaty of Rome and continues to limit the competence of the Community to act in the social sphere. Even those social policy objectives which are contained in the Treaty itself, such as the protection of the working environment which is expressed in Article 118a, tend to be put forward alongside economic objectives when legislation is being formulated; it seems that European social policy can only proceed through what Lord Wedderburn has termed 'an almost Manichean counterpoint of competition and welfare'.[4]

[1] For further discussion of how far the right enunciated in Art. 119 is in fact 'fundamental', see Bob Hepple, 'Equality and discrimination', Chap. 10 below.

[2] International Labour Office, 'Social aspects of European Economic Co-operation' (1956) 74 *International Labour Review* 99, 105; see also Case 43/75 *Defrenne* v. *Sabena (No. 2)* [1976] ECR 455, at para. 12.　　　　　　　　　　　[3] ILO, n. 2 above, 99.

[4] Lord Wedderburn, 'Workers' Rights: Fact or Fake?' (1991) 13 *Dublin University Law Journal* 1, 17.

As the single market programme has advanced, the task of reconciling economic and social goals has become more difficult and the statements of Community organs on this question more contradictory. In its recent decisions interpreting the employment protection directives, the ECJ has referred to the need 'both to ensure comparable protection for workers' rights in the different Member States and to harmonize the costs which such protective rules entail for Community undertakings';[5] but at the same time, the Court has stepped back from attempts to impose a 'level playing field' in labour costs through the use of the free movement and competition policy Articles of the Treaty.[6] The Commission has also offered divergent views on these questions. The *White Paper on Social Policy* of July 1994 stated that 'the Union's social policy cannot be second string to economic development or to the functioning of the internal market',[7] but in September of the same year the Industrial Policy Directorate argued that Articles 101 and 102 of the Treaty be used to achieve 'further deregulation' in labour relations, amongst other areas, in order 'to ensure the smooth operation of the internal market'.[8]

This paper aims to locate the place of economic reasoning in the evolution of European social policy and to suggest ways in which it may shape its future development. It is necessary at the outset to distinguish between three inter-dependent but separate issues. The first concerns the relationship between social policy and market integration. Does the goal of market integration require a particular form of harmonization of social policy, and if so what does this involve: in particular, should intervention be aimed at achieving a 'parity of costs' or 'level playing field' between Member States? Moreover, should harmonization seek to raise standards with a view to improving living and working conditions ('positive harmonization'), or should the aim be their reduction to a new low but common level ('negative harmonization')? It will be suggested here that the aim of a 'level playing field' is, in itself, neither necessary nor desirable, and should not be confused with the entirely different concept of a transnational floor of rights in labour standards, which would aim to entrench certain irreducible levels of protection. There is a good economic argument for putting such a floor in place and for setting it at a more than minimal level.

The second issue may be referred to as that of 'economic competitiveness'. It is linked to the first, since one of the goals of market integration

---

[5] *Commission* v. *United Kingdom*, Case C–383/92 [1994] IRLR 392 and Case C–383/92 [1994] IRLR 412, at paras. 16 and 15 respectively.

[6] See below, Part 3.

[7] Commission of the European Communities, *European Social Policy: A Way Forward for the Union* COM(94)333, July 1994, 2.

[8] Commission of the European Communities, *An Industrial Competitiveness Policy for the European Union. Communication from the Commission to the Council and Parliament and to the Economic and Social Committee and the Committee of Regions*, COM. EN 8.DOC, 14 Sept. 1994, 7.

is economic development in a wider sense.[9] However, it raises a broader set of questions concerning the appropriateness of social regulation at a time of economic 'globalization'.[10] Is the European pattern of labour market regulation, coupled with the preservation of a high level of welfare state spending, compatible with the maintenance of competitive advantage in world markets? It will be suggested here that, contrary to the recent consensus in favour of deregulation in economic policy-making, a growing body of thought no longer sees social regulation as necessarily being a fetter on economic efficiency; on the contrary, the role of labour and social standards as necessary inputs into sustained and balanced economic development is being stressed. This body of thought should be taken into account at the level of policy-making.

The third set of issues relates to unemployment, labour-market participation rates, and the capacity of the Community to combat social exclusion. Again, this theme is linked to the other two, since economic development may be expected to contribute to the lowering of unemployment. But the possibility is also emerging that a high level of economic growth will not necessarily translate into an improved rate of job creation. Thus social policy also needs to address the issue of how best to achieve the reintegration of the long-term unemployed and the widening of economic opportunities in ways which are most compatible with broader economic and social objectives.

In this Chapter the themes outlined above are addressed as follows. Part 2 examines in more detail the economic reasoning of the Ohlin and Spaak reports in relation to transnational labour standards, and Parts 3 and 4 consider the extent of 'negative' and 'positive' harmonization respectively which has been achieved since the 1950s. Part 5 then develops the theme of economic competitiveness and Part 6 is concerned with social integration and issues of the regulatory design of standards. Part 7 concludes by suggesting that market regulation is one of the basic functions of labour law and that it should be seen as an essential mechanism for achieving wider, equity-related goals.

2. Labour Costs and Comparative Advantage

Bertil Ohlin, the Swedish politician who chaired the group of ILO experts which produced the 1956 report *Social Aspects of European Economic*

---

[9] Cf. EC Treaty, Art. 2.

[10] See Lord Wedderburn, 'Labour Standards, Global Markets and Labour Laws in Europe', in Werner Sengenberger and Duncan Campbell (eds.) *International Labour Standards and Economic Interdependence* (International Institute for Labour Studies, Geneva, 1994).

Co-operation, was also a practising economist who had been responsible for developing the modern international trade theory of *comparative advantage*.[11] This theory essentially holds that the freeing up of international trade between two nations will enable each one more fully to exploit its particular, comparative specializations; a more extensive division of labour and superior economies of scale will result, leading in turn to a virtuous circle of increased productive efficiency, higher productivity, and enhanced demand. This was adopted as the basic assumption of the Community policy of economic liberalization in the inter-governmental Spaak Report of 1956 which paved the way for the Treaty of Rome, and later in the Cecchini Report of 1988 on the completion of the internal market.

According to the Ohlin Report, differences in wage costs between States engaged in international trade do not, in themselves, pose a serious obstacle to the realization of efficiency gains from liberalization. This is because:

differences in the *general level* of wages and social charges between different countries broadly reflect differences in productivity. Where productivity is high because a country has rich natural resources, abundant capital, efficient entrepreneurs and well trained managers and workers, the general level of wages, as of other incomes, will tend also to be high.[12]

This basic point is often overlooked in debates about comparative labour costs within the EC: what matters is not the *nominal* level of wage costs in a given industry or firm but its *net unit labour costs*, that is to say the costs of labour for each unit of production after taking productivity into account. Higher wages tend to go hand in hand with higher productivity. Marsden and Silvestre show, for example, that in the late 1980s nominal labour costs per employee, including gross wages and salaries and social charges, were 122 per cent of the EC average in pre-unification Germany, compared to only 77 per cent in Britain.[13] However, unit labour costs in Germany were only 104 per cent of the EC average, compared to 107 per cent in Britain. In other words, 'Britain's labour costs [were] less than 80 per cent of the European average, yet unit labour costs [exceeded] those of Germany. The difference in costs structures is accounted for by the fact that Germany has sought to compete on the basis of high wages and high productivity, rather than emulate Britain's low-wage, low-productivity route.'[14]

---

[11] This is often referred to as the Hecksher–Ohlin theory of international trade. On the relative contributions of Hecksher and Ohlin, and on Samuelson's subsequent integration of their work into a general equilibrium framework, see Eli F. Hecksher and Bertil Ohlin, *Heckscher–Ohlin Trade Theory* (Harvard University Press, Cambridge, Massachusetts, 1991), edited with an introduction by Harry Flam and M. June Flanders.

[12] ILO, n. 2 above, 102.

[13] David Marsden and Jean-Jacques Silvestre, 'Pay and European Integration', in David Marsden (ed.), *Pay and Employment in the New Europe* (Edward Elgar, Aldershot, 1992).

[14] Peter Nolan, 'Labour Market Institutions, Industrial Restructuring and Unemployment

If a high-wage industry in a particular country finds that it cannot compete effectively once trade barriers are removed, this must be because it has
not attained the average level of productivity in *that* country: but as the
Ohlin report stressed, 'it is precisely the fact that there are such cases in
every country that makes international trade mutually advantageous: those
products which a country cannot produce competitively for itself can more
economically be imported and paid for by exports of other commodities in
the production of which the country has a comparative advantage'.[15] The
point can also be put slightly differently: the removal of barriers to international trade exposes inefficient industries which had previously been
sheltered by tariff walls or equivalent obstacles to the free flow of goods.
Liberalization, leading to greater competition, is a disciplinary force which
operates to enhance the productive efficiency of industry generally within
the states affected.

This does not mean that certain institutional mechanisms would not be
needed in order to cope with dislocations which might follow from the
liberalization of trade. However, Ohlin suggested that these could successfully operate at the level of individual nation states. Over the long term,
income and wage levels within nations would be kept in line with relative
productivity by the mechanism of equilibrium in a given country's balance
of payments; if this was disrupted in the short term, it should be restored by
measures aimed at switching investment into exports and/or by revising the
country's exchange rate downwards. Special assistance for industries forced
to undergo substantial restructuring would also best be dealt with at state
level. This meant that transnational institutions could be largely confined to
the role of ensuring freedom of movement for economic resources; but it
equally followed that the Community's policy of 'neoliberalism' at the
transnational level should not necessarily be translated into similar policies
at national level. On the contrary, Ohlin assumed that active economic
policy-making and government intervention at the level of the nation state
would not only continue, but would provide an essential mechanism of
adjustment as international barriers to mobility were removed. In particular,
the realization of economic gains from freer trade was seen as dependent on
the preservation of strong labour standards *within* states. The expected gains
in productivity would lead to improved living and working conditions, not
simply by virtue of 'the more efficient international division of labour', but
also because of 'the strength of the trade union movement' in European
countries and of the sympathy of European governments for social aspirations, to ensure that labour conditions would improve and not deteriorate'.[16]

in Europe', in Jonathan Michie and John Grieve Smith (eds.) *Unemployment in Europe*
(Academic Press, London, 1993), 69.

[15] ILO, n. 2 above, at 103.
[16] Ibid. 112.

The ILO experts also accepted that in some instances, transnational harmonization was needed to eliminate 'such discrepancies within each country as would substantially distort international trade by causing certain lines of production to be carried on in areas and by methods that are clearly less suitable than other areas or methods would otherwise be'. The problem arises not because the general level of wages in a given country might be low in comparison to that in another, for the reasons just outlined; but because, instead, an industry may enjoy an advantage in terms of wage levels and/or social charges which are exceptionally low in relation to the general level of costs in *that country*. If this advantage is unrelated to productivity, 'the whole situation is economically unsound' and workers and employers in other countries can justifiably complain about 'unfair competition'. The low-cost producer gets the benefit of what is in effect a subsidy, since differences in national exchange rates, which reflect *general* prices and productivity within States, will not be able to eliminate the advantage enjoyed by just one industry. In particular:

a certain distortion of international competition arises from differences in the extent to which the principle of equal pay for men and women applies in different countries. Countries in which there are large wage differentials by sex will pay relatively low wages in industries employing a large proportion of female labour and these industries will enjoy what might be considered a special advantage over their competitors abroad where differentials according to sex are smaller or non-existent.[17]

Similar considerations applied to working time: if, within a country, working hours in certain sectors were excessively long because of a lack of effective labour organization in those industries, the result would be a distortion of international competition, although in 1956 it was considered 'doubtful whether many instances of this nature exist' and it was suggested that the ILO itself represented the most effective means of ensuring compliance with basic standards.[18] In relation to social security contributions and employment taxation, the ILO experts argued that differences between States might lead to changes in the *composition* of international trade—the imposition of high social charges on industry might, for example, lead to a country to specialise in capital-intensive, high productivity industries for exports—but it would not alter the basic principle of mutual gains from free trade between nations. It was also thought that any significant intra-country differences in the charges levied on industries would often be offset by other economic factors, and that the difficulty in identifying distortions in this area ruled out any attempt at general harmonization.

In short, the Ohlin report provided strong support for using institutions

[17] ILO 1956: 107.　　[18] Ibid. 108.

at transnational level to achieve economic liberalization and rejected a *general* role for harmonization in social policy; but at the same time the Report stressed the importance of retaining national autonomy in economic policy-making and in the maintenance of effective labour standards. Free trade at transnational level neither implied nor required deregulation within nation States—just the opposite. *required regulation at national level*

Essentially the same approach was subsequently adopted by the inter-governmental Spaak Report which formed the basis for the Treaty of Rome.[19] While arguing that 'economic integration presupposes fair competition', Spaak also accepted that:

competition does not necessarily require a complete harmonization of the different elements in costs; indeed, it is only on the basis of certain differences—such as wage differences due to differences in productivity—that trade and competition can develop. . . . In addition, wage and interest rates tend to level up in a common market—a process which is hastened by the free circulation of the factors of production. This is a consequence rather than a condition of the common market's operation.[20]

This assertion of a natural tendency towards levelling-up was again derived from comparative-advantage theory, which predicts that international trade will lead over time to the equalization of the relative scarcity of national factors of production (including labour) and hence to the equalization of factor prices. However, in some accounts of the theory the conditions of equalization are strict, and it is clear that Ohlin, for one, did not regard them as being easily satisfied in practice: much depends on how far in-dustries combine different factors in roughly similar proportions. Ohlin thought that 'it is impossible to assess the likelihood of this occurring, and there is therefore no justification for assuming that it will'.[21] However, the notion of an automatic tendency towards convergence provided such a potent justification for the favoured policy of abstentionsm in social policy that it came to be embodied in Article 117 of the Treaty of Rome: im-provements in living standards were expected to 'ensue from the functioning of the common market'. While Article 117 did not rule out a role for harmonization, nor did it provide any specific legal authority for it. Article 119 on equal pay and Article 120 concerning annual paid leave represented

---

[19] Comité Intergouvernemental Créé par la Conférence de Messine, *Rapport des Chefs de Délégation aux Ministres des Affaires Etrangères*, (Brussels, 1956), summarized in English in Political and Economic Planning, *Planning* (1956), no. 405 (subsequent references are to this English text); see Paul Davies, 'The Emergence of European Labour Law', in W. E. J. McCarthy (ed.), *Legal Intervention in Industrial Relations: Gains and Losses* (Blackwell, Oxford, 1992), 323-325.   [20] Spaak, Report, n. 19 above, at 233.
[21] Ohlin, n. 11 above, at 94. Ohlin's own work is both more dynamic and empirical in orientation than the modern theory of comparative advantage which bears his name, which is predominantly static, equilbrium-based, and formal in character: see Flam and Flanders, n. 11 above. See also the modifications made to the basic theory by 'strategic trade' models: Paul Krugman and Aladair Smith (eds.), *Empirical Studies of Strategic Trade Policy* (University of Chicago Press, Chicago, 1994).

limited concessions to the possibility that inequalities within Member States could give rise to distortions of competition.

Yet notwithstanding the rationale offered by the Ohlin and Spaak reports, the balance struck in the Treaty of Rome between State action and Community competence in the conduct of economic and social policy was inherently precarious, and it has become increasingly difficult to maintain as the push for economic integration has intensified. It is open to attack on two opposing grounds. There is first an argument to the effect that the complete removal of barriers to international trade and mobility of economic resources is no longer compatible, if it ever was, with the preservation of substantial national autonomy in the area of social policy: this argument would lead to the widespread dismantling of social and labour legislation in the name of market integration. The second argument is that the Ohlin report's preconditions for confining the harmonization of social policy to a few isolated instances no longer hold, and that a more extensive degree of transnational regulation is needed, leading to a widening and deepening of the existing body of Community labour law.

3. Market Integration, Competition and Deregulation: Judicial Interventions

The single market is constructed on the 'four freedoms' which guarantee transnational mobility of economic resources in goods, persons, services, and capital.[22] In each case, Member States are required to remove formal barriers to movement and to observe the principle of equal treatment of EC nationals.[23] In addition, Article 3(g) of the EC Treaty specifies the aim of 'ensuring that competition in the internal market is not distorted'. More specifically, Article 85 prohibits agreements or associations between undertakings and other concerted practices 'which may affect trade between Member States and which have as their object or effect the prevention, restriction or distortion of competition within the common market',[24] and Article 86 prohibits abuses by undertakings of a dominant market position. Articles 85 and 86 are concerned with the activities of undertakings; under Article 90, their requirements, together with those of the other Treaty provisions, are also applied to state support for undertakings, with only a limited provision made for derogation.[25] Under Article 92, 'any aid granted by a Member State or through State resources in any form whatsoever which distorts or threatens to distort competition by favouring certain undertakings

---

[22] EC Treaty, Arts. 30, 48, 52, and 59 and 73b respectively.
[23] The principle of equal treatment is enshrined in Art. 6 of the EC Treaty.
[24] This is subject to the agreements or categories of agreements in question meeting the conditions listed in Art. 85(3): see Richard Whish, *Competition Law* (3rd edn., Butterworths, London, 1993), 227 ff.   [25] Art. 90(2).

or the production of certain goods' is deemed incompatible with the common market, subject again to some stated exceptions.[26] *free trade competition law etc.*

These provisions together provide the framework for the establishment and functioning of the common market. According to Kapteyn and VerLoren van Themaat, the common market is 'a market in which every participant within the Community in question is free to invest, produce, work, buy and sell, to supply or obtain services under conditions which have not been artificially distorted, wherever economic conditions are the most favourable. This definition means that a common market has a character analagous to that of the domestic market of a single State'.[27] In this context, the avoidance of distortions means that conditions of competition 'have not been rendered unequal'.[28] But this approach seems much too broad: the obvious difference between domestic markets and the single market is that the laws operating in the former will tend to possess a greater degree of uniformity and homogeneity. Does the goal of economic integration, as expressed in the EC Treaty, truly require a degree of uniformity of regulation approaching that which is to be found within individual Member States?[29]

One possibility is that the free-trade and competition policy provisions of the Treaty can be invoked to bring about a 'levelling-down' of national legislative standards, or 'negative harmonization' as it is sometimes called. It has been clear for some time that a large range of national regulations which might have an effect on inter-State trade fall within the scope of Article 30, which bans quantitative restrictions on imports 'and all measures having equivalent effect'. Article 30 catches measures which both directly and indirectly discriminate against imports from other Member States and was said, in the *Dassonville* case, to extend to 'all trading rules enacted by Member States, which are capable of hindering, directly or indirectly, actually or potentially, intra-Community trade'.[30] On the face of it, this approach could catch a range of labour law regulations which affect production costs, in particular those placing limits on working and/or operating time.

conflicts between the four freedoms & national law

Competition law, whether it operates at national or transnational level, has a variety of techniques for dealing with restrictions on or barriers to trade; some are subject to a rule of *per se* illegality, but many others fall under a 'rule of reason' test which requires the court (or similar body) to

---

[27] P. J. G. Kapteyn and P. VerLoren van Themaat, *An Introduction to the Law of the European Communities* (2nd edn. by L. Gormley, Kluwer, Deventer, 1989). 78.

[28] Ibid.

[29] See, for further discussion of this point, Gérard Lyon-Caen, 'L'infiltration du droit du travail par le droit de la concurrence', *Droit Ouvrier*, Sept. 1992, 314; A. Lyon-Caen, 'Droit social et droit de la concurrence. Observations sur une rencontre', in *Orientations Sociales du Droit Contemporain: Ecrits en l'honneur du Pr. Jean Savatier* (PUF, Paris 1992); Paul Davies, 'Market Integration and Social Policy in the Court of Justice' (1995) 24 *Industrial Law Journal* 49. Lord Wedderburn, *Labour Law and Freedom* (Lawrence & Wishart, London, 1996), 370–91.

[30] Case 8/74 *Procureur du Roi* v. *Dassonville* [1974] ECR 837, at para. 5.

weigh up the anti-competitive aspects of the rule or practice in question against other, countervailing benefits. So it is with Article 30; notwithstanding the broad scope of the *Dassonville* formula, both the Treaty, in Article 36, and the jurisprudence of the ECJ, through the concept of legitimate 'mandatory requirements' stemming from the *Cassis de Dijon*[31] case, allow for numerous exceptions to the principle of free movement of goods. One such mandatory requirement is constituted by the goal of social protection which underlies labour legislation.[32] However, the difficulty with any rule of reason test is that it gives the courts extensive discretion to engage in a weighing exercise, to the detriment of those goals or objectives which are seen to place a fetter on competition. This is essentially what happened in the early Sunday trading cases. In its ruling in the *Torfaen* case the Court appeared to conclude that laws of this kind fell under the scope of Article 30, but that they could be justified by the goal of social protection as long as their 'restrictive effects on Community trade . . . do not exceed the effects intrinsic to rules of that kind'.[33] This formula proved completely inadequate to the task of guiding national courts. While one English court considered that the Shops Act 1950 was founded on a view 'capable of forming a rational basis for legislation',[34] another thought that its principal aim was not the protection of employees but the preservation of Sunday observance and that it was not proportionate to this latter goal.[35]

At this point, the judicial review of labour and social legislation to test its compatibility with principles of market integration seemed a distinct possibility. Such a conclusion would have been at odds with the principle of national autonomy in the field of labour and social legislation which, as argued above, was not just a major plank of the Ohlin and Spaak reports, but was implicit in the structure of Treaty of Rome well before the principle of subsidiarity was introduced by the Treaty on European Union in 1992. Is this why the Court executed such a rapid volte face from the position it had adopted in *Torfaen*, choosing in *Stoke-on-Trent*[36] simply to declare that 'Article 30 of the EEC Treaty is to be interpreted as meaning that the prohibition which it lays down does not apply to national legislation prohibiting retailers from opening their premises on Sundays'? The Court's present approach, developed initially in *Keck* and *Mithouard*[37] in a non-

---

[31] Case 120/78 *Rewe-Zentral AG* v. *Bundesmonopolverwaltung für Branntwein* [1979] ECR 649.

[32] Case 155/80 *Oebel* [1981] ECR 1993; Case 279/80 *Webb* [1981] ECR 3305.

[33] Case C–145/88 *Torfaen Borough Council* v. *B. & Q. plc* [1989] ECR 3851, para. 17.

[34] *Stoke-on-Trent City Council* v. *B. & Q. plc* [1991] Ch. 48, 71 (Hoffman J).

[35] *B. & Q. Ltd* v. *Shrewsbury & Atcham Borough Council* [1990] 3 CMLR 535.

[36] Case C–169/91 *Stoke-on-Trent City Council* v. *B. & Q. plc* [1993] 2 AC 900 (ECJ and HL), affirming earlier rulings in Case–312/89 *Conforama* [1991] 1 ECR 997 and Case C–332/89 *Marchandise* [1991] 1 ECR 1027.

[37] Joined Cases C–267/91 and C–268/91 *Keck* and *Mithouard* [1993] ECR I–6097; see Catherine Barnard, 'Sunday Trading: A Drama in Five Acts' (1994) 57 *Modern Law Review* 449.

social policy context and then applied to opening hours in *Heukske*,[38] is that Article 30 has no application to national legislation which treats domestic and imported goods equally and does not impede or prevent access by foreign producers to the market in question. This is consonant not only with the preservation of national autonomy in social policy, but also with the economic philosophy underlying the Treaty of Rome, which stopped a long way short of identifying free competition with uniformity of national laws. As the Ohlin Report stressed, because labour standards applied by one Member State impose no impediment to access by goods produced in other Member States (as opposed to product requirements which may well do), there is simply no *economic* case for applying Article 30 to labour standards at all. It is beside the point that the *Cassis de Dijon* formula allows an extensive defence of legitimate mandatory requirements: the rule-of-reason test is sufficiently open-ended to leave a wide range of social legislation vulnerable to challenge on grounds which have nothing to do with economic efficiency, and everything to do with the private interests of those campaigning to undermine social protection.

Another area of potential conflicts is that of the free movement of labour and services, but here the principle of national autonomy appears to be firmly entrenched. All Member States operate a version of territoriality with regard to their own labour and social security legislation; almost invariably, such legislation applies to all workers lawfully employed on the territory of the Member State regardless of their nationality. As far as social security is concerned, resolution of the differences between the law of Member States is approached through the technique of co-ordination. Article 51 of the EC Treaty, which dates from the Treaty of Rome, makes provision for measures in two related areas: aggregation, whereby workers may accumulate social insurance contributions paid in different States, and 'deterritoriality', whereby they may receive social security benefits earned in one State while resident in another.[39] Co-ordination of social security is both an essential adjunct of freedom of movement and a means of preserving national diversity of provision; by seeking to resolve conflicts of laws and ensure that migrant workers are not discriminated against by virtue of their status, it aims to avoid the need for harmonization in this area.

National autonomy and territoriality have also been preserved in relation to the terms and conditions which are applicable to migrant workers while they are employed in another Member State. According to the Judgment of the Court in *Rush Portuguesa Ltda.* v. *Office Nationale d'Immigration*,[40]

[38] Joined Cases C–401/92 and C–402/92 *Criminal Proceedings against Tankstation 't Heuske vof and J. B. E. Boermans* [1994] ECR I–2199.
[39] The highly complex rules governing co-ordination are contained in Reg. 1408/71 and a number of related measures. See A. I. Ogus, E. M. Barendt, and N. J. Wikeley, *The Law of Social Security* (Butterworths, London, 1995), ch. 18.
[40] Case C–113/89 [1990] ECR 1417. In relation to the draft Dir. on the Posting of

States retain the right to apply their labour laws to the employees of subcontractors from another Member State while they are working on their territory. This does not amount to an infringement of Article 59, even though it may well entail a greater cost burden for the employer and could be seen as a disincentive to supply services in the Member State concerned. This is a strong reassertion of the rights of Member States to set labour standards which will give rise to differences in the level of costs within the common/internal market, the needs of economic integration notwithstanding.

Articles 85 and 86 provide a potentially much broader avenue of attack on competition-related grounds. Although the Court has said that these provisions are 'concerned only with the conduct of undertakings and not with national legislation of Member States', they also 'require Member States not to introduce or maintain in force measures, even of a legislative nature, which may render ineffective the competition rules applicable to undertakings'.[41] It is necessary to remember that Articles 85 and 86 are not about competition *in general*: they are specifically concerned with restrictive agreements between undertakings and with abuse of a dominant position by one or more undertakings, and they only apply where inter-state trade is affected (although this concept is widely interpreted to include measures with the potential effect of partitioning markets along national lines). At first sight, therefore, they would not appear to pose much of a threat to labour legislation. It is perhaps not impossible to argue, however, that multi-employer collective agreements and legislation governing wages and conditions may constitute an implicit barrier to entry to a given market. The U.S. Supreme Court arrived at this somewhat surprising conclusion in *United Mine Workers* v. *Pennington*.[42] It ruled that a labour union loses its immunity under the Sherman Antitrust Act where

it is clearly shown that it has agreed with one set of employers to impose a certain wage rate on other bargaining units. One group of employers may not conspire to eliminate competitors from the industry and the union is liable with the employers if it becomes a party to conspiracy. This is true even though the union's part in the scheme is an undertaking to secure the same wages, hours or other conditions of employment from the remaining employers in the industry.[43]

It remains to be seen whether a variation of this argument could be successfully invoked in the context of Community law. Aside from the unusual situation of a union being involved in a conspiracy of firms to exclude outsiders, it may be argued that it should not succeed, for the reasons considered above in the context of Article 30:[44] as long as undertakings

Workers (amended version [1993] OJ (187/93), a common position was adopted by the Council on 3 June 1996. See (1996) 270 *EIRR* 12, 15.

[41] Joined Cases C–401/92 and C–402/92 *Heukske*, at para. 16.

[42] 381 US 657 (1965); for discussion, see Oliver E. Williamson, *Antritrust Economics* (Blackwell, Oxford 1987), ch. 8.   [43] 381 US 657 (1965), 665–6.

[44] See above, pp. 71–3.

have equal access to the domestic market of the State in question, in the sense of the freedom to supply both goods and services, there is no reason to assume that differences in labour standards of themselves give rise to a distortion of competition.

Articles 85 and 86 are of more immediate relevance in relation to the rules governing State undertakings, of which they form a part.[45] Here the Court has adopted a highly interventionist position. In *Macrotron*[46] it held that the German Federal Employment Office was not entitled to maintain its statutory monopoly over employment placement services. The basis for this ruling was not the grant of the statutory monopoly as such; Article 86 is concerned not with a dominant position *per se*, but with its *abuse*. However, since in this case it was admitted that the statutory service could not meet demand and tolerated private 'headhunters' even though their activities were illegal, a breach of Article 86 was established.

In *Merci*[47] the Court was invited to consider an Italian dock labour scheme operating in the port of Genoa, which granted a monopoly to local companies consisting of dock workers who, by law, had to be Italian nationals. The company was found to be a State undertaking under Article 90. As in *Macrotron*, the mere existence of a statutory monopoly did not breach Article 86; however, as there was evidence that the company was abusing its monopoly to demand payment for unrequested services, offer selective reductions in prices, and 'refuse to have recourse to modern technology',[48] it was in a position where merely exercising the rights granted to it involved a breach of Article 86. The Court also found that the requirement that dock workers should be Italian nationals breached Article 48, and that a breach of Article 30 was made out on the grounds that the 'the unloading of goods could have been effected at a lesser cost by the ship's crew, so that compulsory recourse to the services of the two undertakings enjoying exclusive rights involved extra expense and was therefore capable, by reason of its effect on the prices the goods, of affecting imports'.[49]

The combination of circumstances in *Merci* may have been somewhat exceptional, but the most striking feature of the Court's Judgment is the almost complete disregard shown for the social arguments which could have been put in favour of the dock labour monopoly. The need to combat casualization was not referred to. The appellant in the main action, Merci, was being sued by a shipping company for delays arising from a strike of dock workers. However, Merci itself was an intermediary which was required by the Italian legislation to employ the services of the dock companies, consisting of the dock workers, whose monopoly was at issue. In

---

[45] Cf. Art. 90(1).

[46] Case C–41/90 *Höfner and Elser v. Macrotronm GmbH* [1991] ECR I–1979.

[47] Case C–179/90 *Merci Convenzionali Porto di Genova SpA v. Siderurgica Gabrielli SpA* [1991] ECR I–5889; see G. Lyon-Caen, n. 29 above.

[48] [1991] ECR I–5889, at para 19.   [49] Ibid., para. 22.

common with the respondents, Merci argued against the retention of the companies' monopoly, and helped to present a picture of inefficiency and abuse of position which appears to have gone largely unchallenged. The Court's ruling also indicates a general lack of concern for the right to strike. Can it really be the case, for example, that a strike of transport workers employed in a State undertaking which causes 'extra expense . . . affecting imports' will lead to a breach of Article 90?

In relation to Article 92, on the other hand, the Court has resisted arguments that the exemption of small and medium-sized enterprises from certain aspects of legislation governing working conditions and employment protection constitutes an illegitimate 'State aid' or subsidy to those firms.[50] In *Kirshammer-Hack* v. *Sidal*[51] the exclusion from German unfair dismissal law of enterprises employing fewer than six full-time employees was considered. The labour court which made the reference asserted that thanks to this exemption, small firms enjoyed 'a significant competitive advantage compared to other undertakings', but the Court confirmed a number of earlier rulings which took the view that Article 92 is only concerned with a transfer of *State resources* to an undertaking, and not with any action of the State which might lead to the provision of a competitive advantage: 'the exemption of a category of undertakings from the system of protection in question does not lead to any direct or indirect transfer of State resources to those undertakings'.[52]

Overall then, national systems of labour and social security law remain largely untouched by the requirements of transnational economic integration. The single market can, it seems, continue to coexist with a high level of national autonomy in the setting of labour and social standards, in keeping with the perspectives of the Ohlin Report. However, the potential for a much more serious clash between labour law and competition law (or the law of the single market) undoubtedly exists, in particular under Articles 85 and 86.[53] The Treaty itself is one cause of this difficulty. In contrast to the coherence of the provisions governing free movement and competition policy, social policy remains marginal and fragmented and, notwithstanding the jurisprudence which is developing from *Keck* and *Mithouard*, it is too soon to say that the Court has turned its back for good on arguments which see uniformity as an essential part of economic integration. For these reasons it may be that the threat of deregulation or 'negative harmonization' inspired by the free trade provisions of the Treaty can only be properly contained, in the longer run, by extending the 'positive harmonization' of

[50] The strict separation of Arts. 92–94 from labour and social issues goes back to the discussions which preceded the Treaty of Rome. See Davies, n. 19 above.

[51] Case C–181/91 [1994] IRLR 185.

[52] Ibid., para. 16; Case C–72/91 *Sloman Neptun*, Judgment of 17 Mar. 1993, not yet reported.

[53] Similar problems may also arise in relation to the interface between labour standards and public procurement rules, although they have yet to emerge clearly. See Lord Wedderburn, n. 29 above, 379–85, for analysis of the issues.

labour standards, so that national laws are effectively underpinned by a set of transnational norms within the corpus of Community law. However, such harmonization raises a further set of largely unresolved problems concerning the level at which standards should be set; the scope for States to set higher standards than those operating at the transnational level; and the need to find a clear economic rationale for social policy interventions.

4. Social Policy, Harmonization and Distortions of Competition

The goal of harmonization in social policy might seem to be a logical step towards making the single market more like the market of a domestic State. We saw earlier that in *Commission* v. *U.K.* the Court stated that in the Directives on Collective Redundancies and Acquired Rights[54] 'the Community legislature intended both to ensure comparable protection for workers' rights in the different Member States and to harmonize the costs which such protective rules entail for Community undertakings'.[55] What seems to be envisaged here is a transnational 'level playing field' in terms of social and labour costs. The Court made no attempt to argue, however, that the economic justification given for Article 119 and, by extension, for the equality directives—namely the persistence of structural inequality between groups *within* a Member State—could also apply to the employment protection directives. It is not clear what economic justification, if any, the Court thought it was relying on for its decision in these cases.

A more extended recent attempt to justify social policy interventions on the grounds of the harmonization of social costs is that offered by the Commission in its 1990 *Explanatory Memorandum on the Proposals Concerning Certain Employment Relationships*.[56] Consistently with Ohlin, the Commission noted the role of relative productivity in offsetting differences in wage levels between countries: 'these differences do not hamper the operation of healthy competition in the Community. The differences in productivity levels attenuate these differences in unit labour costs to a considerable degree'.[57] On the other hand:

Other cost differences are not offset by factors such as differences in productivity and do not help to improve the Community's social and economic cohesion. This is so in particular as regards the relative cost differences resulting from different kinds of rules on different types of employment relationships, which may provide comparative advantages which constitute veritable distortions of competition. Clearly [*sic*], if a Member State can produce with lower labour costs than the other

---

[54] Dirs. 75/129/EEC and 77/187/EEC.
[55] See n. 5, above.
[56] CVOM(90)228–SYN 280–SYN 281.
[57] Ibid., para. 22.

Member States—yet that difference does not result from factors such as those examined above, but is due to segmented labour markets having different costs for the same type of work, attributable solely to the different rules applicable to the different types of employment relationships—it will have a comparative advantage which cannot be considered permanent and runs counter to common interests.[58]

This formed the basis for the Commission's much-criticized distinction between regulations governing wages and salaries, which were not deemed appropriate for harmonization, and those governing indirect wage costs resulting from social charges and employment regulation, which were.[59] If the value of wages and terms and conditions enjoyed by part-time and temporary workers is low compared to their productivity, there is a strong case for social policy intervention to improve their position relative to full-time workers, and there is an economic case for establishing a set of minimum standards at transnational level. There is no economic logic in excluding wages and salaries from the scope of any harmonizing measure, however, not least since the distortions referred to by the Commission are not, in practice, attributable *solely* to the different legal rules which are applicable to different employment relationships.[60] Nor is there much legal logic in drawing a distinction which runs directly contrary to Article 119 and to the sex discrimination directives which require parity of both pay and non-pay aspects of terms and conditions of employment.[61]

There is also a more general objection to the approach adopted by the Commission in the 1990 *Explanatory Memorandum*, which is that the aim of achieving a 'parity of costs' between undertakings in different States is probably unattainable and in any event undesirable. To argue for a static parity of costs at transnational level is to misunderstand the economic purpose of labour standards. Their function is not to create uniformity either of costs or of regulation, but to set minimum levels of protection, or a 'floor of rights', from which there may be no downwards derogation but on which it is normally possible to improve.[62] Differences in the levels of costs are inevitable as long as Member States, through their own laws, and the

---

[58] Ibid. para. 25.

[59] See Wedderburn, n. 4 above, 22–3. The Commission's proposal for a dir. under Art. 100a, to which this discussion specifically related, failed to win wide support among the Member States and was eventually dropped.

[60] On the wider causes of such segmentation, see Frank Wilkinson, 'Equity, Efficiency and Economic Progress: The Case for Universally Applied Equitable Standards for Wages and Conditions of Work', in Werner Sengenberger and Duncan Campbell (eds.), *Creating Economic Opportunities: The Role of Labour Standards in Industrial Restructuring* (International Institute for Labour Studies, Geneva, 1994).   [61] Wedderburn, n. 4 above, 22.

[62] Lord Wedderburn, 'Inderogability, Collective Agreements, and Community Law' (1992) 21 *Industrial Law Journal* 245; Werner Sengenberger, 'Labour Standards: An Institutional Framework for Restructuring and Development', in Werner Sengenberger and Duncan Campbell (eds.), *Creating Economic Opportunities: The Role of Labour Standards in Industrial Restructuring* (International Institute for Labour Studies, Geneva, 1994); Simon Deakin and Frank Wilkinson, 'Rights vs. Efficiency? The Economic Case for Transnational Labour Standards' (1994) 23 *Industrial Law Journal* 289.

'social partners', through collective bargaining, retain the right to set standards above the basic floor set by any transnational regulations. In itself there is nothing wrong with this, and indeed it could be seen as a vital part of the process of 'automatic levelling up' of labour standards which the Spaak report argued would flow from liberalization of trade.

On the other hand, the argument that the 'harmonization of costs' is necessary in order to avoid distortions of competition can very quickly become an argument for a low level of basic provision which provides a ceiling rather than a floor of social protection. This was hinted at by the Industrial Policy Directorate, DG III, when it called for 'further deregulation, examining, for example, the expediency of invoking Articles 101 and 102 of the Treaty' as part of a competitiveness policy for the Union.[63] Articles 101 and 102 date back to the Treaty of Rome but 'have not gained the importance which the Spaak Report indicates that the framers of the Treaty intended'.[64] Under Article 101, the Council has a power to issue a directive on the basis of a qualified majority where 'a difference between the provisions laid down by law, regulation or administrative action in Member States is distorting the conditions of competition in the common market and . . . the resultant distortion needs to be eliminated'. There must first be consultation by the Commission and an attempt to reach agreement on the elimination of the distortion. Under Article 102, the Commission has the power to issue a recommendation to a Member State which is considering adopting new laws or amending existing ones in such a way as to cause a 'distortion of competition'. As elsewhere in the Treaty, the phrase 'distortion of competition' is not defined, but it is possible to argue here that its scope is a restricted one. The Spaak Report took the view that:

the degree of deliberate harmonization needed for the proper working of the common market is limited. It must combat only those specific distortions which favour or handicap certain branches of economic activity. . . . Distortion only arises when an industry is more heavily or less heavily burdened than the average of the national economy or of the common market as a whole: for example, an industry is not penalised if the corresponding industries in other countries are at a similar disadvantage. Finally, the same industry may be handicapped by one law and at the same time favoured by another.[65]

Certain 'specific distortions' which were considered appropriate for harmonizing measures included those caused by national laws on 'the financing of social security' and 'working conditions, such as equal or unequal pay for men and women, working hours, overtime and paid holidays',[66] but the Report also reiterated the view that 'working conditions . . . will tend to

---

[63] Commission of the European Communities, *An Industrial Competitiveness Policy for the Union* n. 8 above, 7.

[64] Kapteyn and VerLoren van Themaat, n. 27 above, 484.

[65] Spaak Report, n. 20 above, 233–4.   [66] Ibid., 234.

level up, particularly as a result of trade union pressure'.[67] In short, the Spaak Report does not provide much support for the use of Articles 101 and 102 as a means of achieving downwards harmonization of labour and social security law, whatever their potential might be in other areas.[68] However, in the changed circumstances of the 1990s they could be said to have acquired a more central role in the realization of the single market. This was the view pressed by the Industrial Policy Directorate:

The aim is no longer simply to endow the European Union with legislation removing the barriers to trade but to put into operation a 'market' in the true sense of the term. This will entail liberalization of financial services, sustained deregulation of certain sectors to allow effective access to the markets, greater flexibility on the labour market, reduction of the tax disparities which lead to fragmentation of markets and open, confident acceptance, by the Member States, of mutual recognition of standards.[69]

If the potential of Articles 101 and 102 is largely unexplored, there are already other areas in which harmonization is not only well-advanced but has also pre-empted the rights of States to higher standards than those operating at transnational level. Following the judgment of the Court of the *Cassis de Dijon* case,[70] the Commission announced that it would seek to introduce harmonizing measures principally in the areas where States retained the right to make exceptions to the principle of the free movement of goods under Article 36 and the concept of 'mandatory requirements'.[71] Once the harmonizing measure is put in place, it has the potential to 'occupy the field' and exclude any contrary State measure. The effect of this 'total harmonization' is that 'a national measure may be justified as protecting a mandatory requirement only if the matter at issue is not already regulated by Community law'.[72] The Single European Act of 1986, as amended in 1992, put two glosses on this: when proposing measures relating to the establishment and functioning of the internal market under Article 100a in the areas of health, safety, environmental protection, and consumer protection, the Commission must 'take as a base a high level of protection' (Article 100a(3)); and under Article 100a(4), if the measure concerned is passed by a qualified majority, a Member State may apply its own national provisions where they relate to one of the grounds established by Article 36 or to the protection of the environment or working environment.[73] But if

[67] Spaak Report, n. 20 above, 235.
[68] See generally the useful discussion of Kapteyn and VerLoren van Themaat, n. 27 above, 485–6.
[69] Commission, op. cit n. 8, 12.
[70] Case 120/78, n. 31 above.   [71] [1980] OJ C256/3.
[72] John Usher, 'Free Movement of Goods', in T. C. Hartley, N. Green and J. Usher, *The Law of the Single European Market* (Clarendon Press, Oxford, 1991), 71.
[73] It is not clear from the wording of Art. 100a(4) whether it entitles a State to introduce new legislation or simply to maintain existing legislation in the area in question. For discussion see Damien Geradin, 'Trade and Environmental Protection: Community

this last provision does not apply, a Member State may find that it has lost the right to apply superior standards, for example, in the area of technical specifications for products.[74]

This result is avoided in the case of most of the social policy directives by the specific inclusion of provisions allowing Member States to set higher levels of provision, thereby recognizing the 'floor of rights' character of this legislation.[75] This is clear, for example, in the employment protection directives of the 1970s which preserve 'the right of Member States to apply or to introduce laws, regulations and administrative provisions which are more favourable to employees'.[76] Similarly, Article 118a refers to directives laying down 'minimum requirements' and the Health and Safety Framework Directive is stated to be 'without prejudice to existing or future national and Community provisions which are more favourable to protection of the safety and health of workers at work'.[77] A different kind of provision is contained in the Directive on Working Time and the Directive on Protection of the Health and Safety of Pregnant Workers; these each provide that 'the Directive shall not have the effect of reducing the general level of protection of workers in comparison with the situation existing in each Member State at the time of its adoption'.[78] It is odd that these measures do not offer more positive encouragement for a further improvement in standards, even in Member States already applying standards on the whole superior to those laid down at EC level.[79]

Nonetheless, the labour law notion of a floor of rights offers a far more coherent basis for social policy interventions than the concept of 'parity of costs'. As the process of economic integration continues, the dangers of 'social dumping' become more intense; there may then be a need for a transnational floor of rights in order to avoid a 'race to the bottom' between states. Although 'social dumping' is a rather imprecise phrase, a

Harmonisation and National Environmental Standards' [1993] *Yearbook of European Law* 151, 184-5.

[74] See Case 278/85 *Commission* v. *Denmark* [1987] ECR 4069. This ruling concerned Dir. 79/831/EEC which preceded the procedure introduced by Art. 100a(4); however, Denmark may be able to invoke Art. 100a(4) in relation to later dirs. in the area of product packaging. See Ruth Nielson and Erika Szyszczak, *The Social Dimension of the European Community* (2nd edn., Handelshojskolens Forlag, Copenhagen, 1993), 255–6.

[75] This is not the same as the concept of 'optional harmonization' in, for example, environmental law, which refers to the right of a State to set *lower* standards than those applying at Community level. See Geradin, n. 73 above, 181.

[76] Dir. 75/129/EEC, Art. 5; Dir. 77/187/EEC, Art. 7; Dir. 80/987/EEC, Art. 9.

[77] Dir. 89/391, Art. 1(3).

[78] Dir. 93/104/EC, Art. 1(5); see also Dir. 92/85, Art. 1(3).

[79] However, their approach is at least preferable to that of the dirs. on equal pay and equal treatment, which do not formally rule out implementation by 'levelling down' the conditions of the previously advantaged group. Levelling down is also permitted under Art. 119, following the judgment of the Court in Case C–408/92 *Smith* v. *Avdel Systems Ltd* [1994] IRLR 602.

social dumping

clear enough meaning can be attributed to it if it is thought of as a process whereby differences in the forms and levels of labour law regulation between countries within a single trading bloc, such as the EC, encourage firms to seek out sources of under-valued labour within less highly-regulated systems. This in turn puts pressure on countries with more advanced systems of protection to reduce costs imposed on firms: as the OECD suggests, 'investment may indeed flow into countries where the cost of labour is lower and regulations more flexible, thereby provoking downward pressures on costs and conditions' in other countries inside the bloc.[80] In principle, firms will not relocate if the lower nominal wage costs incurred in less regulated system are simply a function of the lower productivity of the workforce there. However, it may be that there are greater opportunities for exploiting undervalued labour in a system which does not adequately respect the principle of equal pay for equal work between male and female workers, for example, or between 'atypical' workers and those 'regular employment'. It may also be that firms see greater advantage in a lower-wage, lower-productivity strategy to the management of labour than in maintaining a higher-wage, higher-productivity approach in a more highly regulated system.[81]

Two further features of increased economic integration make 'social dumping' a more realistic possibility. One is greater labour mobility: there is a higher likelihood of convergence around a lower standard once the migration rates of workers within the single market begin more closely to approximate those of a national market. In particular, 'large-scale migration flows could . . . lead to lower benefits in countries where provisions governing social protection are more generous'.[82] As yet there is little evidence of such a trend,[83] but this may be because the practical obstacles to free movement are still considerable. As they are reduced, the rate of migration may be expected to increase. A second factor arises from the gradual implementation of monetary union.[84] Even before the point is reached where exchange rates are irrevocably fixed prior to the establishment of the single currency, the need for convergence of national economies will limit the scope for autonomy in economic policy, not least on the question of exchange rates. As currency devaluation is ruled out and the scope for changes in taxation and public expenditure is implicitly limited by the convergence criteria agreed in the Treaty on European Union,[85] states may have resort to 'social devaluations', or cuts in social and labour protection, as a means of dealing with short-term economic fluctuations.[86] The Maastricht criteria,

---

[80] OECD, 'Labour Standards and Economic Integration', in *Employment Outlook 1994* (OECD, Paris, 1994), 155.

[81] Ibid, 155.   [82] Ibid.   [83] Ibid., 157.

[84] EC Treaty, Arts. 3a(2) and 109a–109m.

[85] See, in particular, EC Treaty, Protocols 5 (Excessive deficit procedure) and 6 (Convention Criteria).   [86] OECD, n. 80 above.

then, threaten the very freedom of action at the level of the nation State which the Ohlin Report considered essential if economic integration was to lead to improved living working conditions.

On the whole, the conclusion of the OECD that 'despite these pressures on labour standards, there is no compelling evidence that "social dumping" has occurred so far in OECD countries'[87] probably holds good for the EC. But this does not mean that transnational labour standards do not have an important preventive role in ensuring, as the *White Paper on Social Policy* puts it, 'that the creation of the single market [does] not result in a downward pressure on labour standards'.[88] Similarly, the *Green Paper on Social Policy* explicitly associates the need for agreement on 'common minimum labour standards' with the threat of a 'negative competitiveness between Member States', which 'would lead to social dumping, to the undermining of the consensus-making process identified in the Maastricht Social Agreement, and to danger for the acceptability of the Union'.[89]

From this point of view, labour standards are seen as a means of rendering economic integration legitimate. This is an important role: the ILO has long stressed the link between the expansion of free trade and the achievement of agreement on international labour standards.[90] There is nevertheless a sense in which it fails to address the problem of the marginal status of social policy within the wider framework of the EC. To see whether a more central role is available for social regulation, it is necessary to consider the wider links between social policy and economic competitiveness.

5. Social Policy, Labour Standards, and Economic Competitiveness

The Treaty on European Union authorised the Community to act in a new area, namely 'the strengthening of the competitiveness of Community industry'.[91] This addition to Article 3 implied that economic integration was only one aspect of competitiveness, and that further measures were needed in addition to those designed to establish and maintain the common market. Specifically, the amended Article 130 of the EC Treaty now authorizes Community action to speed up the adjustment of industry to structural change; encourage an environment favourable to the growth of firms, in particular small and medium-sized enterprises; encourage inter-firm co-operation; and foster the exploitation of policies of innovation and technological development. The Council's power to adopt measures in pursuit of these goals, which is subject to the need for unanimity,[92] has not

---

[87] OECD, n. 80 above, 138. [88] Commission, n. 7 above, 21.
[89] *European Social Policy: Options for the Union*, com (93) 551 final, 46.
[90] See generally Lord Wedderburn, n. 10 above. [91] EC Treaty, Art. 3(l).
[92] EC Treaty Art. 130(3), as amended by the Treaty on European Union. See also Arts. 130a–130e.

yet produced any legislation, but the 1993 Commission *White Paper on Growth, Competitiveness and Employment* spells out the goals of Community intervention in greater detail: these include the co-ordination of economic policies and exchange rates and the establishment of a 'stable macroeconomic framework as a basis for sustainable job-creating growth' and creating jobs,[93] aims which it is envisaged will be fulfilled by the achievement of economic and monetary union according to the timetable laid down at Maastricht.

What, if anything, has this to do with social policy? The traditional view of labour standards and social protection is that they are the fruits of economic progress which has been brought about by *other means*. The most often-cited justifications for social policy are ethical or moral rather than economic in nature; the protection of human rights at work, or the enhancement of equality of opportunity and reward, are seen as goals in their own right. If this view is taken, it is not inevitable, but nor is it difficult to portray social policy as a potential fetter on economic development. Social regulation, according to this point of view, involves a trade-off between protection and economic efficiency. The 'burden' of social regulation may not matter much during a period when the economy is enjoying a rapid rate of growth, as in the so-called 'golden age' in the western industrialized world from around 1950 to the early 1970s.[94] However, during a period of high unemployment and recurrent economic crises, those who might otherwise argue for social policy interventions on non-economic grounds could be dissuaded from doing so by the apparent economic cost; while the opponents of social policy are also able then to call on a range of efficiency-related arguments for removing protective measures which had been introduced under more favourable economic circumstances.

This perspective has dominated the debate over labour market 'flexibility' since the late 1970s: over-rigid labour laws and excessive social security provision in western Europe are identified as responsible for slowing down processes of labour market adjustment. The 1994 *White Paper on Social Policy* even commented that 'the need to alter fundamentally, and update, the structure of incentives which influence the labour market is still not adequately recognized'.[95] In itself this is a studiedly ambiguous statement, though. It can be regarded as offering support for deregulation but it must also be read against the *White Paper's* insistence, practically in the same breath, that 'long-run competitiveness is to be sought, not through a dilution of the European model of social protection, but through the adaptation, rationalization and simplification of regulations, so as to establish a better balance between social protection, competitiveness, and employment

[93] *Growth, Competitiveness and Employment: The Challenges and Ways forward into the 21st Century* (Luxembourg, OOPEC, 1993), 54.

[94] See generally Steven A. Marglin and Juliet B. Schorr (eds.), *The Golden Age of Capitalism: Reinterpreting the Postwar Experience* (Clarendon Press, Oxford, 1992).

[95] N. 7 above, 11.

creation'.[96] This seems to be a version of the trade-off theory, albeit one which appears to suggest that the negative impact of social standards can be minimized if the *form* of regulation is improved. But elsewhere the *White Paper* refers to a view which suggests that there is no *necessary* conflict between economic and social goals: 'the pursuit of high social standards should not be seen only as a cost but also as a key element in the competitive formula. It is for these essential reasons that the Union's social policy cannot be second string to economic development or to the functioning of the internal market'.[97]

The economic case for labour standards depends, in part, on seeing them as a response to market failures of the kind which are endemic in labour markets.[98] In particular, there can be no assumption that if the labour market is deregulated, the price mechanism is then released to allocate resources to their most efficient use. Even in an apparently 'unregulated' labour market, structural imperfections, in the form of uncertainty, limited information, and sunk costs, are likely to have the effect that labour of comparable productivity is available to employers at different wage rates. The availability of undervalued labour is a cause of productive inefficiency in its own right, compensating less efficient firms for their managerial and organizational inadequacies, enabling obsolete plant and equipment to remain in use, and encouraging low-wage competition among employers which makes workers increasingly dependent on social security. This is becoming a familiar picture of the effects of deregulation in systems, such as the United Kingdom, where that policy has been most vigorously pursued since the early 1980s.[99]

At the same time, labour standards offer more than just a response to market failure; they can be seen as important inputs into balanced and sustained economic development. It is only in the context of the flexibility debate, which focuses almost exclusively on the individual firm or enterprise as the appropriate level of decision-making, that labour standards are seen as undesirable rigidities. More recent work on this question has stressed the role of the general business environment in providing the context within which individual firms can pursue strategies based on technological advance and innovation in organization and design:

the very nature of competition has changed. In addition to factor costs and product prices, product quality, innovative capacity, flexibility, good design, and industrial organization, have assumed great importance as competitive dimensions. It has been recognized that for meeting these criteria an 'enabling' business environment is of the utmost importance. Ultimately, innovation and dynamism are not derived

---

[96] Ibid.   [97] Ibid., 2.

[98] See Giandomenico Majone, 'The European Community between Social Policy and Social Regulation' (1993) 31 *Journal of Common Market Studies* 153, 157.

[99] See Simon Deakin and Frank Wilkinson, 'Labour Law, Social Security and Economic Inequality' (1991) 15 *Cambridge Journal of Economics* 125.

from making labour resources cheaper, but for making labour more effective, productive and innovative. While enlightened firms may follow this advice independently, commonly agreed and shared standards are needed to diffuse the productive impact of good labour use on a wider scale. Instead of looking at institutions and regulation as mere straight-jackets, attention should be focused on the opportunities they provide.[100]

Labour standards, then, form one of the conditions which *both permit and require* firms to pursue a high-wage, high-productivity strategy, based on continuous improvements in labour quality. Training is supported, for example, not simply by formal entry requirements and by regulation of training processes and certification at national or industry level, but also by substantive labour standards of a more general nature, which by imposing certain fixed costs on firms essentially oblige them to invest in labour quality. More generally, long-term co-operation within and between firms may be enhanced by the presence of collective standards of both a substantive and a procedural kind. This is a consistent theme running through studies of industries, regions and countries which have successfully competed on the basis of high quality in production.[101]

But if this hypothesis is correct and firms can successfully compete on the basis of a high-wage, high-productivity strategy, and if countries with an extensive systems of labour protection are, for this reason, placed at a competitive advantage to those with lighter systems of regulation, why is there any need for transnational regulation? According to one point of view, the liberalization of inter-state trade and of the rules governing the movement of labour and capital, by implicitly placing different regulatory and welfare-state régimes in competition with each other, is sufficient to initiate a process of market discovery for the optimal framework of regulation.[102] Those systems with the most economically successful balance of competitive and regulatory forces could be expected to win out over time. *need of regulation*

This argument assumes away the existence of the market failures which most commentators are prepared to accept are endemic to a process of economic integration such as that now being undertaken in the European

[100] Sengenberger, n. 62 above, 10.

[101] See Frank Pike, Giacomo Beccattini and Werner Sengenberger (eds.), *Industrial Districts and Inter-Firm Co-operation in Italy* (International Institute of Labour Studies, Geneva, 1990); Wolfgang Streeck, *Social Institutions and Economic Efficiency* (Sage, London, 1992); Mari Sako, *Prices, Quality and Trust. Inter-Firm Relations in Britain and Japan* (CUP, Cambridge, 1993). These studies are linked to a wider debate about the role of the institutional environment in fostering the 'trust' on which co-operative contracting is said to depend: see John Kay, *The Foundations of National Competitive Advantage* 5th. ESRC Annual Lecture, 1994; Simon Deakin and Frank Wilkinson, 'Contracts, Co-operation and Trust: The Role of the Institutional Framework', in David Campbell and Peter Vincent-Jones (eds.) *Contract and Economic Organization: Socio-Legal Initiatives* (Dartmouth, Aldershot, 1996).

[102] Daniel Fischel, 'Labor Markets and Labor Law compared with Capital Markets and Corporate Law' 51 *University of Chicago Law Review* 1061 (1984).

Union.[103] There is also a sense in which more fundamental uncertainty about the economic implications of different regulatory régimes may undermine the potential success of systems designed to promote a high-wage, high-productivity cycle. The regulations, standards, and norms which provide these systems with an element of competitive advantage are costly to maintain, and there is the danger of free riding. Although 'social institutions which support trust relationships and the development of tacit knowledge have major advantages', it is also the case that 'it is easier to destroy trust relationships than to create them. So whatever the commercial advantages of these structures, they are under constant pressure from those who identify immediate gains from more opportunistic behaviour.'[104] States with an extensive system of regulation cannot be sure, in advance, that undertakings will not take advantage of differences in nominal wage costs to relocate all or part of their production. This can be seen as a form of opportunism, but is no easier to deal with for all that. Multinational firms are capable, for example, of outsourcing services to lower-cost regions both within and outside the territory of the European Union, a process which has been facilitated by developments in information technology.[105] The point here is not that transnational labour standards can prevent this happening, nor that they should nullify the effects of such movements by seeking to impose a strictly 'level playing field' on all nations engaging in trade. The role of transnational standards is a more limited but far from insignificant one: by seeking to build consensus on a minimum core of standards which can form the content of a floor of rights, they seek to discourage states, whether high-cost or low-cost, from pursuing a mutually destructive strategy of cutting labour protection with the aim of either attracting or retaining capital investments. In other words, the role of transnational standards is not to create a static end-point, once a parity or equivalence of costs has been achieved; their role is dynamic in the sense that they seek to guide the direction in which labour standards develop at state level and to promote a process whereby rising labour standards and rising labour productivity go hand in hand.

For this to be achieved, it is arguable that there must be some degree of congruence between the 'economic space' created by the rules of inter-state trade, and the 'social space' of labour standards and regulations. As long as labour regulations are confined to the level of the nation state, they remain vulnerable to the pressures of destructive competition at the transnational level. This is not to suggest that a 'race to the bottom' between states is inevitable. There are economic processes which could lead to a degree of

---

[103] e.g. Majone, n. 98 above.   [104] Kay, n. 101 above, 10.

[105] Michael J. Piore, 'Labour Standards and Business Strategies', in S. Herzenberg and J. Perez-Lopez (eds.), *Labor Standards and Development in the Global Economy* (US Department of Labor, Washington D.C., 1990). See also Katherine van Wezel Stone, 'Labor and the Global Economy: Four Approaches to Transnational Labor Regulation' (1995) 16 *Michigan Journal of International Law* 987.

convergence around a reasonably high level of labour and social protection, without transnational intervention. Indeed, if these autonomous economic processes did not exist, it would be impossible to make the case for labour standards made here. The function of labour standards is not to prevent economic development from taking place, but to foster economic development of a particular kind by increasing the costs of certain 'destructive' strategies or options for both undertakings and states: 'by obstructing downward-directed competition, and supporting dynamic modes of adjustment, the overall performance of the economy can be enhanced and the outcome of adjustment made more acceptable'.[106] In this respect, it is clear that a great deal depends on the precise form of labour standards and the degrees of protection which they embody. What is not acceptable, though, is a position that labour standards are harmful to economic development, at transnational level or otherwise.

6. Labour Standards, Social Integration, and Re-regulation

In making the case for a more extensive European social policy, it is important to acknowledge that labour standards may not in all circumstances constitute an unqualified public good. There is no doubt that the standards set in any given system in terms of wages, hours, and job security could be too demanding of certain firms or certain forms of employment, and hence give rise to widespread evasion or to 'dualism' of the kind sanctioned by legislation exempting temporary and part-time workers or workers on government make-work schemes from the scope of protection.[107] Labour standards, particularly national or transnational ones, should also allow for some degree of flexibility in their application, to take into account certain industry- or firm-specific conditions.

A more fundamental problem is that labour standards, even where they can be seen to enhance labour quality and hence competitiveness, do not necessarily provide a mechanism for ensuring that the resulting economic growth is translated into a growth in employment. They may offer no immediate solution, then, to the problem of social exclusion. Within the EU this takes the particular form of a high rate of long-term and youth unemployment, coupled with a low rate of employment participation by comparison with Japan or the USA.[108] For this reason the *White Paper on Social Policy* of 1994 stressed the need to combine 'increased competitiveness' with 'the search for more job creation with a high employment intensity of

---

[106] Sengenberger, n. 62 above, 39.

[107] For a critical discussion of labour regulation in Europe which refers to some of these points, see David Grubb and William Wells, 'Employment Regulation and Patterns of Work in EC Countries' (1993) 21 *OECD Economic Studies* 7.

[108] See Deakin and Wilkinson, n. 62 above, 296.

that growth',[109] even to the extent of seeking to create areas of lower-productivity employment: 'it is important to ensure that, as well as supporting high productivity jobs, the Union maximises its ability to generate and sustain jobs at other levels, particularly in the unskilled, semi-skilled and personal and local services fields'.[110]

At the same time, the principal solution canvassed by the *White Paper*—namely the creation of unskilled and semi-skilled jobs alongside higher productivity jobs, through a combination of wage subsidies for the lower paid and cuts in indirect wage costs in the form of reduced social charges—appears to be founded on a contradiction. How will economic competitiveness be maintained in those sectors which become heavily reliant on low-wage, low-productivity employment? While it might once have been possible for parts of the public sector or for sectors such as retailing, which have been insulated from international competition, to perform this function, it seems doubtful that they can continue to do so in the future, given the shrinkage of the public sector and the opening up of a wider range of services to international competitive pressures as economic integration increases. These sectors, in just the same way as manufacturing, are under constant and increasing pressure to improve their labour productivity rates. More generally, there is a danger that measures aimed at subsidising low-paid and low-skilled employment will create a 'disincentive to upgrade the productive system if this would involve the labour losing its subsidy . . . the economy may be diverted towards those low-skill, low-investment sectors that are subsidised by the policy'.[111]

The problem of unemployment is not one which can be solved by changes to labour law alone. There is a case for a more targeted use of macro-economic policy, together with economic measures to encourage investment in manufacturing capacity, in this area.[112] However, there is also a need for more effective regulation, or *re-regulation,* within labour law which will reflect the developing nature of the labour market and the new forms of inequality which have grown up over the past two decades, as well as seeking to ensure that differing forms and levels of standards operate effectively together.[113] From the point of view of regulatory design, there are certain principles to which labour standards could usefully conform. These are, first, that in any given system standards of differing kinds should be *complementary.* Both the social and economic cases for standards rest upon

[109] N. 2 above, 2.   [110] Ibid., 10.

[111] Jonathan Michie and Frank Wilkinson, 'Wages, Government Policy and Unemployment' (1995) 7 *Review of Political Economy* 133, 148.

[112] Ibid.

[113] See Ulrich Mückenberger and Simon Deakin, 'From Deregulation to a European Floor of Rights: Labour Law, Flexibilization and the European Single Market' (1989) 3 *Zeitschrift für ausländisches und internationales Arbeits- und Sozialrecht* 157; Duncan Campbell, 'The Rationale for Multi-level Labour Standards', in Werner Sengenberger and Duncan Campbell (eds.), n. 62 above.

them performing a number of mutually-supportive functions, so that if one element is missing the others may not produce the intended results. It is widely recognized that substantive standards governing, for example, the length of the working week, are not self-enforcing but depend for their implementation on procedural or participatory standards of various kinds which support collective institutions for the negotiation of terms and conditions and the monitoring and enforcement of employees' rights. In addition, Werner Sengenberger has stressed that a third form of standards, 'promotional' standards in the areas of training and active labour market policy, provides a vital mechanism for seeking to upgrade skills and integrate excluded groups into employment, in particular where substantive standards are pushing firms in the direction of a high-productivity strategy.[114]

A second principle of regulatory design identified by Sengenberger is that standards should be *universal* in their coverage.[115] What this means is that the formal exclusion of particular groups from protective coverage should be avoided: 'for it to have legitimacy, a system of labour law should be one which avoids discrimination itself and which also actively seeks to reduce discrimination within the labour market'.[116] This goal runs directly contrary to the open encouragement of dualism in employment protection, designed to facilitate the reintegration of the unemployed by making it less costly for employers to hire temporary or part-time workers. The latter policy is defended on the ground that it provides a route back to full-time employment for the employees who find jobs via this route.[117] However, there is a growing consensus that this is not the effect in practice, and that many employees are more likely to move from one precarious job to another than to find 'permanent', full-time work.[118] There may also be a considerable displacement effect, as a growing proportion of new hirings which would once have been on an indefinite and full-time basis take a casual form, thanks to the various incentives being offered to employers.

At the same time, if these effects are to be avoided and a core body of standards applied generally to full-time workers and others, they must be designed in such a way as to apply both to full-time, 'permanent' work and to other forms of work. A major difficulty with the substance of most employment protection régimes in western European countries is that they were designed for the so-called 'standard' employment relationship, and

[114] Sengenberger, n. 62 above, 32.   [115] Ibid.

[116] Mückenberger and Deakin, n. 113 above, 199.

[117] See Michael Emerson, 'Regulation or Deregulation of the Labour Market: Policy Régimes for the Recruitment and Dismissal of Employees in Industrialised Countries' (1988) 32 *European Economic Review* 775.

[118] Christoph Büchtemann, 'More Jobs through Less Employment Protection? Evidence for West Germany' (1990) 3 *Labour* 23; Christoph Büchtemann and Sigrid Quack, ' "Bridges" or "Traps"? Non-standard employment in the Federal Republic of Germany' in Gerry and Janine Rodgers (eds.), *Precarious Jobs in Labour Market Regulation* (International Institute for Labour Studies, Geneva, 1989).

cannot easily be applied to other forms.[119] The provisions which govern the rights of employees to compensation for lay-off, when considered together with the rules of social security relating to loss of benefit where the claimant is employed part-time or on short-time working, illustrate the kinds of regulatory failure which may arise for this reason: in the U.K. both sets of rules assume a clear division between full-time work, on the one hand, and unemployment, on the other, which as the courts have recognized does not reflect the experience of many employees.[120] Mainland European systems have attempted to address the problem, with varying degrees of success, via the concept of 'partial unemployment'.

The principle of universality has a particular application in the context of transnational standards. Given extensive differences of form and substance between the laws of different Member States even within a trading bloc as comparatively homogenous as the EC, it is clear that transnational standards have to be drafted in a particular way. They should respect diversity of approach as well as differences in the degree of protection which reflect the various levels of economic development which Member States have arrived at.[121] It need not be thought, however, that transnational labour instruments are incapable of being phrased in the necessary way. There is a long and active tradition to draw on here in the Conventions and Recommendations of the ILO and the Council of Europe's Social Charter, as well as EC directives and regulations themselves.

The third principle suggested by Werner Sengenberger is that of _adapt- ability_. This implies both that standards are capable of developing in response to changing economic circumstances and that the norms which they lay down are capable of adaptation to the requirements of particular industries and firms. In this sense, adaptability and universality are intrinsically linked. The development of techniques of 'controlled derogation', permitting substantive norms to be departed from on condition that there are compensating factors for employees affected and/or that derogations are agreed and monitored by collective representatives of the workforce, has been a major feature of changes in labour law in the Member States over the past decade and a half.[122] The issues raised by this form of 'flexibilization' of standards are not necessarily straightforward, and it is perhaps an open question whether in some cases the scope for derogation has become too wide. This is a complaint which could be made against some of the

---

[119] See generally Mückenberger and Deakin, n. 113 above.

[120] *Chief Adjudication Officer* v. *Brunt* [1988] AC 711.

[121] Cf. *White Paper on Social Policy*, n. 7 above, 5: standards 'should not over-stretch the economically weaker Member States, and they should not prevent the more developed Member States from implementing higher standards'.

[122] See Lord Wedderburn and Silvana Sciarra, 'Collective Bargaining as Agreement and as Law: Neo-contractualist and Neo-corporative Tendencies of our Age' in A. Pizzorusso (ed.), *Law in the Making* (Springer Verlag, Berlin, 1988).

derogations made in the EC Directive on Working Time. It seems illegitimate, for example, to grant an exemption in relation to 'the activities of
doctors in training', a derogation patently designed to permit the United
Kingdom to maintain its practice of employing junior hospital doctors on
contracts of employment requiring exceptionally long weekly hours.[123] Even
more dubious is the permission given to the United Kingdom, but to no
other Member State, to implement parts of the Directive on the Employment of Young Persons several years after the other Member States.[124] The
very purpose of standards is that, at some point, rigidities will be imposed
regardless of local conditions or short-term changes in market structure: 'if
standards are so "flexible" as to follow such vicissitudes, they cease to
be "standards." They lose their important function as a compass, and as
providers of certainty, predictability and stability in the labour market and
the product market'.[125]

7. Conclusions: Market Regulation and Fundamental Rights

The search for autonomy in European social policy continues, just as it does
within individual labour law systems.[126] In the European context, the development of a free-standing social policy is seemingly prevented by the need
to find economic justifications for interventions at Community level. The
close association of social policy with integrationist reasoning is, indeed,
fraught with dangers and difficulties for labour law. The notion that the
general harmonization of social policy is justified by reference to 'distortions of competition' brought about by differences between the labour law
régimes of Member States is a delusion, as the Ohlin Report acknowledged.
Not only is there no compelling economic case for such harmonization on
the grounds of 'parity of costs' or a 'level playing field'; such a development
could only harm labour law traditions at state level, by enabling the Community organs to impose a lowest common denominator of minimal standards on national legislatures. The use of European Community competition
law as a mechanism of deregulation has so far been avoided, thanks to a
combination of the Court's refusal, late in the day, to use Article 30 to
impose a rule of reason test on all national legislation affecting trade, and
the reluctance of the Commission to make use of Articles 101 and 102 of
the Treaty. However, the substantial potential for further developments in
this area cannot be ignored, which is one reason for considering a role for

[123] Dir. 93/104, Art. 17.
[124] Dir. 94/33, Art. 17.
[125] Sengenberger, n. 62 above, 38.
[126] Lord Wedderburn, 'Labour Law: From Here to Autonomy?' (1987) 16 *Industrial Law Journal* 1; 'Workers' Rights: Fact or Fake?', n. 4 above, in particular at 15.

the 'positive harmonization' of social policy which would place its status within the legal order of the Community beyond doubt. Another argument for positive harmonization is to discourage the Member States themselves from initiating a 'race to the bottom' in social policy, particularly given the limitations on national economic policy which are implied by the need to comply with the Maastricht convergence criteria. However, neither of these essentially defensive justifications offers a particularly positive outlook on the future of European social policy. At best, they might prove slightly more effective than existing arrangements in preserving the status quo against encroachment from deregulationary forces.

A better approach would be to explore the potential for stronger links between social and economic policy. If labour law has been weakened recently by attacks from European Community competition law, that is largely because of the particular conception of competition which the latter has come to embody. In the Sunday trading cases prior to *Heukske*, liberalization of trade was pursued as a goal in its own right to the point where the Court's interventions ceased to have any clear basis in economic welfare, not to mention their impact on national autonomy. There is an important distinction here between competition for its own sake and the *competitiveness* of firms and economic systems; the former can directly threaten the latter, as for example in the case where destructive competition over prices directly threatens the quality of inputs and products.

The addition of 'competitiveness' to the goals of the European Community is therefore a positive development for social policy, which can benefit from the argument that labour standards have a role to play as inputs into the competitiveness of the European economies. This 'dynamic' role of channelling economic development may be contrasted with the essentially 'static' view of harmonization as seeking to create a level playing field of regulation. To advance this 'economic' rationale for labour regulation is in no way to detract from the wider, equity-related goals which, historically, have formed most of the momentum for social policy interventions at both national and transnational level: equity no less than efficiency requires that means be found to ensure a more effective matching of labour supply and demand, and to reconcile the continuing need for high labour productivity with an expansion of job opportunities. It may be that a deeper appreciation of the economic functions of labour law, and of the role played by market regulation in realizing the goals articulated by fundamental social rights, will provide a more lasting basis for European social policy than has so far been achieved.

5

The European Court of Justice, National Courts, and the Member States

PAUL DAVIES

I. The Context of Judicial Activism

A. Introduction

In the writings of Bill Wedderburn there is reflected an approach to judicial activism which is shared by many labour lawyers in the United Kingdom and which to some extent sets them apart from other legal writers in the 'progressive' mould.[1] That approach can be characterized as one of suspicion of the driving forces behind, and the impact upon labour law of, such activism. This scepticism is not derived, of course, from any assertion of conscious bias on the part of the judges but is based rather on a three-stage analysis of, first, the fundamental and early training of practising lawyers[2] in Britain in the common law; secondly, the centrality, within the common law, of rights based upon property and contract which were, and are, incompatible in particular with the effective collective organization of workers; and, thirdly, the failure of British labour lawyers to establish the autonomy of their subject from common law concepts and modes of thought.

Should labour lawyers, whether in Britain or elsewhere within the European Union, be equally sceptical about the activism of the European Court of Justice? To be sure, whatever the activism of the British courts over the past decades, especially within the field of industrial conflict law, it pales into insignificance when compared with that of the European Court of Justice, which, with only some exaggeration, can be said to have created a new *system* of law. But, as the description of Wedderburn's analysis makes clear, it is not judicial activism *per se* which is the object of his criticism, but rather activism by judges trained in a particular manner and having a particular legal 'mind set' inimical to the tenets of an effective labour law.

[1] See, e.g., T. J. Christian and K. D. Ewing, 'Labouring under the Canadian Constitution' (1988) ILJ 73 for an expression of scepticism about the utility in the labour law field of the enactment in Britain of a 'Bill of Rights' because of the empowerment of the judiciary which that step would entail. It should be noted that Ewing is a distinguished writer on civil liberties as well as on labour law.

[2] British judges are drawn from the senior ranks of practising lawyers; the judiciary is not a separate profession for which young lawyers opt at the outset of their careers.

Consequently, activism on the part of the ECJ can be neither welcomed nor deplored by labour lawyers without an examination of the determinants of and constraints upon that activism and of its relationship with the goals of labour law.

It is the purpose of this essay to offer such an examination. It is a task which will require us to range quite broadly over the case law of the European Court and certainly to consider matters which may seem rather removed from the immediate interests of a labour lawyer. It will not be possible to focus too narrowly on the 'labour law' decisions of the Court and on its attitude towards labour law. This is because, as Mancini pointed out some years ago, 'the founding fathers of the Community—and the same applies to the Council and the Commission in Brussels—never sought, or at all events never sought as their first aim, to reform the lot of the man who sells his labour'.[3] The Treaty of Rome was more concerned with labour as a factor of production—see the strong free movement provisions contained in the part of the Treaty which, at that time, was labelled the 'Foundations of the Community'—than with mechanisms for redressing the asymmetrical relationship between employer and employee—see the weak provisions on social policy contained elsewhere in the original Treaty. Consequently, labour law, as such, has always been something of a side-show for the European Court, though it has now delivered a substantial number of judgments in the areas of equal treatment of men and women at work and of workers' rights in relation to transfers of businesses. However, it is my contention that an analysis which confines itself to the judgments in these labour law cases will miss crucial elements which help to explain the activism of the European Court. In this essay, accordingly, I will attempt to put the labour law decisions in a somewhat more rounded context.

It is hardly a secret that the principle which has had the greatest influence upon the European Court's general approach to the welter of cases which have come before it has been, in the words of a former judge of the Court, 'the principle of the progressive integration of the Member States in order to attain the objectives of the Treaty'.[4] It is proposed to look at the Court's application of this principle in three, not entirely separate, areas. The first, especially strong in the early years but still today a preoccupation of the Court, was its drive to ensure that the those parts of Community law which were intended to govern relations between and among legal persons in day-to-day life did in fact give rise to legal rights and obligations within the

---

[3] 'Labour Law and Community Law' (1985) 20 *Irish Jurist* 1. Post Maastricht, of course, such a statement, as a statement of the Community's current aims, would be incomplete, but cases arising out of the Social Protocol have yet to appear in the Court. See further Deakin in this volume at 77 ff.

[4] H. Kutscher, 'Modes of interpretation as seen by a judge at the Court of Justice' in Court of Justice of the European Communities, *Judicial and Academic Conference* (Luxembourg, 1976).

judicial systems of the Member States. Once this was established the Court began to generate a second, though obviously linked, area of interest, as it sought to ensure that the procedural and remedial laws of the Member States governing the enforcement of causes of action derived from Community law were effective.

This process has been characterized as one whereby the Court 'constitutionalized' the Treaty,[5] but, as Bermann has perceptively noted,[6] the Treaty of Rome does not score high marks as a federal, or potentially federal, constitution, because it did not address directly the question of the division of powers between the centre and the constituent States. On the one hand, its overriding concern with the creation of an effectively functioning internal market was capable, if not carefully controlled, of invading all aspects of domestic regulation of economic activities, as the 'Sunday Trading' cases revealed.[7] On the other hand, the concentration of the Treaty of Rome on the common market was too narrow a basis for a sensible overall division of powers between the centre and the constituent States, because it left so many functions of a modern State out of account. Even in the post-Keynesian State, the whole of the governmental function cannot be encapsulated within the idea of guaranteeing free trade in goods, services, capital, and other factors of production. It is not surprising, therefore, that the Maastricht Treaty, the first attempt to move the Community beyond its exclusive focus on the internal market, also contained devices, such as subsidiarity, which were designed to deal explicitly with the issue of an appropriate division of this now wider range of powers.

However, long before the Member States faced the matter at Maastricht, cases had arisen before the Court of Justice in Luxembourg which indirectly raised the issue of the division of powers, or of 'competences', between the centre and the Member States. Should the Court promote the integration of the Member States by giving a broad interpretation to the law of the Community, a course of action which would normally expand the powers of the centre while diminishing the freedom of action of the constituent States? This issue arose, no doubt, in many contexts. We will examine in this Chapter the impact of this choice upon the 'labour law' decisions of the Court, our third area of investigation.

B. The Constraints upon Activism

While it is tolerably clear what the European Court was trying to do, it is less clear what were the constraints upon the Court's achievement of its

---

[5] Eric Stein, 'Lawyers, Judges and the Making of a Transnational Constitution' (1981) 75 *Am Jo Int L* 1.

[6] G. Bermann, 'Taking Subsidiarity Seriously' (1994) 94 *Col . LR* 331.

[7] See P. Davies, 'Market Integration and Social Policy in the Court of Justice' (1995) 24 *ILJ* 49.

goals. It is suggested that there were, and are, two principal ones: the need to ensure that the Court's decisions were acceptable to the national courts, on the one hand, and the Member State governments, on the other.

1. *National judiciaries*

Of the two the European Court's reliance on the national courts is the more obvious. In this context it is crucial to remember that the Treaty of Rome established only one Community court, the Court of Justice in Luxembourg, to which the Court of First Instance was added some thirty years later. In the absence of a national or, better, local system of Community courts in which litigants could assert claims based on Community law, the European Court, wishing to break decisively with the inter-governmental model in its approach to the Treaty of Rome, was necessarily dependent upon the courts of the Member States accepting that Community law was part of the national legal systems and could give rise to rights and obligations enforceable in the national courts. The efforts of the European Court in developing to this end the doctrines of the direct effect and supremacy of Community law would be set at nought if the national courts were not prepared to accept and apply the Community rules in their domestic dispute settlement processes.

Equally, the ability of the European Court to develop the founding doctrines and to monitor and channel the use made by national courts of Community norms depends upon the willingness of the national courts to make preliminary references under Article 177, seeking the guidance of the European Court on the interpretation of Community law, and to abide by the rulings given. So, although notions of supremacy and direct effect appear to put the European Court in the driving seat in doctrinal terms, the practical results of Community law depend as much upon the wholehearted co-operation of the national courts as they do on the conceptual inventiveness of the European Court. Ultimately, that co-operation cannot be coerced; the national courts must be convinced of the utility of what the European Court is trying to do. Consequently, when considering the effectiveness of Community law, the European Court cannot confine itself to the question whether a particular development would make Community law *doctrinally* more secure; it must also ask itself whether such a development would be accepted and implemented in practice by the national courts.

Despite the potential for institutional misunderstanding and divergence of objectives, which is inherent in this way of implementing Community law at local level, it does have distinct advantages. First, as Weiler has pointed out, it means that the Community rules are applied by national courts and, if a defendant loses a law suit because of Community rules implementing a Community policy, it is likely to be less easy for the defendant, especially if it is the government of the State in question, to raise political objections to the decisions of its 'own courts' than if the condemnation had come from a foreign or international court.[8] Secondly, the doctrine of direct effect puts at the disposal of those with the greatest interest in enforcing the Community rules, i.e. particular litigants involved in particular controversies,[9] all the long-established and long-accepted apparatus of the Member State's judicial system to investigate, assess and enforce the plaintiff's Community rights. By co-opting the national civil justice systems for the enforcement of Community norms, the European Court acquired at a stroke a level of decentralized institutional support for Community law it which would have taken decades to create from scratch.[10]

Moreover, it should not be imagined that the national courts may not be attracted by the prospect of being involved with the European Court of Justice in the project of making Community law effective in the Member States' legal systems. It may provide a way for the national courts, especially the lower national courts, to escape from the constraints of their national laws by appealing to the superior force of Community law. Well-selected references to the European Court may enable those lower courts to mould the national system in ways which would not otherwise be available to them.[11] Further, Community law may result in a more systematic empowerment of the national courts as against the government of the State, especially in those Member States without strong traditions of judicial control of the executive.

[8] 'Here we are faced with a bald political fact: a member state—in our Western democracies—cannot disobey its own courts': J. H. H. Weiler, 'A Quiet Revolution—The ECJ and its Interlocutors' (1994) 26 *Comparative Political Studies* 510, 515.

[9] Indeed, so successful has the method become of enforcing Community law by way of litigation begun by plaintiffs in national courts that preliminary references under Art. 177 are a much more substantial part of the ECJ's workload than actions begun directly before it by the Commission or other Community institutions. Perhaps for this reason the issue of the direct effect of Community law in general and of dirs. in particular has come to be equated in some quarters with the protection of the rights of individuals. In labour law cases this may often be the situaion. And it is certainly true that a common loser in the national litigation is the national government, vainly trying to protect domestic policy agains the impact of some Community rule to which, in all likelihood, it had previously assented at the Council of Ministers. However, it is worthwhile to bear in mind Mancini's words that 'our [the ECJ's] most faithful customers are not blue and/or white collar workers but steelworks, large and small, multinational drug companies, meat or cereal importers and exporters, herring fishermen, cheese manufacturers and, above all, customs aurthorities' (n. 3 above at p ?). Direct effect has the potential to benefit not only individuals but all non-State litigants in national courts.

[10] Of course, reliance on national procedural systems, which vary from Member State to Member State, also involves acceptance of a certain diversity of procedural arrangements across the Community. The difficulties which this may cause are discussed in section III.

[11] The decision of the Court in Case 106/77 *Simmenthal II* [1978] ECR 629 is significant here, for it operated so as to preserve the freedom of all national courts to apply Community law to the issues before them and to prevent national systems from centralizing such questions (or a particular class of such questions) in a single national court, here the Italian Constitutional Court.

2. National governments

As befits a group of western democracies, committed to the sometimes exaggerated doctrine of the separation of judicial and executive power, the extent of the dependence of the Court upon the Member States is something which neither side talks about with complete freedom. In the early days the relationship seems to have been one of relative indifference on the part of the Member States. One of the most famous articles written on the Court begins with the memorable sentence: 'Tucked away in the fairyland Duchy of Luxembourg and blessed, until recently, with benign neglect by the powers that be and the mass media, the Court of Justice of the European Communities has fashioned a constitutional framework for a federal-type structure in Europe.'[12] As this sentence recognizes, by 1980 things were already beginning to change and by the 1990s the Court was well and truly part of the political concerns of the Member States. Even so *communautaire* a politician as Chancellor Kohl has attacked the Court for going too far;[13] and proposals have been floated to emasculate the Article 177 reference procedure by confining the power to refer to the court at the top of the national hierarchy and to give the Council a simple mechanism for over-ruling interpretations by the Court which it dislikes, even, it would seem, interpretations of the Treaty.

All this is rather different from the early days of the Court's activism. Although the Member States, intervening in the early cases, argued against the development of the doctrines of direct effect and supremacy, it seems that they were prepared to accept the contrary outcome, if only because it could be argued that the Court was doing no more than securing the effective implementation of what the Member States had clearly agreed to. One should not look at the Member States' interests too simplistically. As a defendant in the national courts a Member State may regret the development of direct effect and, even more, of State liability under the *Francovich*[14] doctrine, especially if the national legislation under challenge was adopted in pre-*Francovich* days when the national governments might have thought themselves to have in practice a greater freedom of action than has turned out to be the case. On the other hand, sitting around the table at the Council of Ministers, a Member State may have a strong interest in the development of legal doctrines which make it more likely that the agreements reached in Brussels will be translated into reality by the other Member States. Indeed, the judicial policy on effectiveness seems to be reflected on

---

[12] E. Stein, n. 5 above at 1.

[13] For some details see F. Mancini and D. Keeling, 'Democracy and the European Court of Justice' (1994) 57 *MLR* 175,185–6. See also the *Financial Times*, 3 Apr., 1995, 17, an article entitled 'In the Hot Seat of Judgment' and sub-titled 'The European Court is coming under fire, accused of pushing a political agenda'.

[14] Cases C–6 and C–9/90 [1991] ECR I–5357.

the legislative side in the additions to Article 171 agreed by the Member States at Maastricht. Under these amendments the Commission can now seek, and the Court can impose upon a Member State, monetary penalties if the State fails to remedy the situation after having been condemned in an infringement action brought by the Commission.[15]

When, however, the Court turns to the interpretation of the substantive law contained in the Treaty or in subordinate Community legislation, it is running a greater risk if it adopts a bold approach, especially if, as is increasingly likely to be the case, the secondary legislation was adopted on the basis of majority voting rather than unanimity. Member States are likely to be particularly sensitive to the loss of 'voice' involved in the extension of majority voting if they think that such legislation will form the basis of uncontemplated developments of the substantive law by the European Court which expand the sphere of Community control and diminish the discretion of the Member States. With Member States now regularly active in the process of Treaty revision, the danger that they might react to the Court's judgments with some changes adverse to the Court's interests cannot be regarded as negligible.

Nevertheless, as we shall see, the Court has not been afraid to take this risk. Sometimes one has the impression that the Court has simply blundered into a broad interpretation to which some of the Member States have subsequently taken objection. At other times, the Court seems to have acted with greater deliberation, with the intention of unblocking the Community's legislative process by taking as a matter of interpretation of the existing law the decision of principle over which the Member States could not reach agreement in their legislative capacities.

We shall now look at the three areas mentioned above in the light of these consideration.

II. Community Law and National Law: Rights and Obligations

Here one can see displayed both the overwhelming drive on the part of the Court to make Community law effective in national courts and its need to temper doctrinal development by considerations of what the national judiciaries would accept. The former is, no doubt, the dominant characteristic.

---

[15] This is not to say that the new version of Art. 171 is likely to be particularly effective in practice. For a critique see D. Curtin, 'The Constitutional Structure of the Union: A Europe of Bits and Pieces' (1993) 30 *CMLRev.* 17, 32–4. The key to Member State acceptance of the principle of State liability is probably that it should not catch good-faith attempts by Member States to transpose a dir. or render the State liable where the ECJ, subsequent to transposition, has given a provision of a dir. a meaning which is unexpected. The decision of the Court in Case C–392/93 *R.* v. *H. M. Treasury, ex p. British Telecommunications* [1996] IRLR 300 suggests that it is sensitive to this need. See below p. 111. State liability in national courts is likely to be more significant than liability before the ECJ.

To the doctrines of the direct effect and supremacy of Community law signalled in the early cases of *Van Gend en Loos*[16] (1963) and *Costa* v. *ENEL*[17] (1964) were added later the doctrines of indirect effect (the duty of national judges to interpret national law in the light of Community law) and, much more important, the principle of liability on the part of the State toward those harmed by the State's failure to transpose directives (the *Francovich* principle). Yet the story is by no means one of a smooth and unilinear progression; the sensitivities of the national judges blocked certain avenues of thought and forced the European Court to consider other possibilities.

A. Direct effect of Treaty Articles

The initial developments had a positive impact upon the scope of Community labour law, notably through the stunning decision in *Defrenne II*.[18] The European Court there gave a positive answer to a question from a Belgian court as to whether Article 119[19] provided a cause of action in the Belgian court to a female plaintiff claiming equal pay against her employer, the airline SABENA. It is important not to let hindsight and familiarity obscure the startling nature of this decision. Writing some sixteen years earlier, before the development of the doctrines of direct effect and supremacy, Otto Kahn-Freund reflected the understanding of the time in stating that such a claim was unsustainable.

Although it creates binding obligations among the Member States, Article 119 is very cautiously formulated. The principle of equal pay for equal work does not *ipso facto* become part of the legal systems of the members, and the Council has not even been given power to issue regulations enacting it into law. The Member States have gone no further than to accept an obligation to each other and to the Community to transform their systems of wage rates so as to ensure application of the principle in the course of the first stage of the transitional period. Article 119 does not, therefore, confer any rights or impose any obligations on any individual based on the principle of equality. It does no more than to create an obligation binding the Member States in international law.[20]

By 1976, however, the European Court was able to brush aside all the arguments against giving Article 119 full effect within the legal systems of

---

[16] Case 26/62 [1963] ECR 1.　　　　　　　　[17] Case 6/64 [1964] ECR 585.

[18] Case 43/75 [1976] ECR 455.

[19] 'Each Member State shall during the first stage ensure and subsequently maintain the application of the principle that men and women should receive equal pay for equal work.'

[20] O. Kahn-Freund, 'Labour Law and Social Security' in E. Stein and T. L. Nicholson (eds), *American Enterprise in the European Common Market* (University of Michigan Press, Ann Arbor, Mich., 1960), i. at 329. It should be noted that Kahn-Freund was clear that Art. 119 was wide enough to catch fringe benefits, including 'participation in pension schemes' (330).

the Member States. It did not matter (i.e. it was not a complete obstacle to the application of the doctrine of direct effect) that the obligation laid down in Article 119 was imposed upon the Member State (no doubt, *Van Gend* had said as much); nor that, unlike in *Van Gend*, the obligation was a positive one (i.e. to introduce the principle of equal pay into the national legal system, not simply to refrain from putting up tariffs); nor that the obligation was a very general one, stating a social policy objective in the implementation of which the Member States were clearly intended to have some discretion;[21] nor that, and this was perhaps the crucial development, the defendant in the case was not the Member State which had failed to discharge its obligation, but a private employer.[22]

1976 was undoubtedly an opportune time for the Court to proceed boldly with the application of Article 119. After years of neglecting their obligations under that Article, the Member States had adopted at the Paris summit of 1972 their first Social Action Programme, in which the promotion of equal opportunities for women featured large; the previous year the Member States had begun to live up to their commitments by adopting Directive 75/117 on equal pay; and earlier in the same year as *Defrenne* was decided had adopted Directive 76/207 on equal treatment. Thus, in deciding *Defrenne II* in the way it did, the Court was cutting with, not against, the grain of legislative developments in the Community at the time. Nevertheless, one should not underestimate the decisive shove which the Court gave to the promotion of equality for women in this decision. From now on, by virtue of *Defrenne II*, the principle of equal pay would cover all employment relationships and be enforceable in the national courts of the Member States, no matter what national governments and legislatures had said, or, rather, had failed to say, on the matter. It was a decision which had a profound impact upon the laws and practices of the Member States, even, perhaps especially,[23] those such as the UK and Germany, which had already taken some steps towards the domestic implementation of the principle.

[21] Direct effect was, however, confined to 'direct and overt discrimination which may be identified solely with the aid of the criteria based on equal work and equal pay referred to by the Art. in question' (judgment at point 18)

[22] This, at least, was the basis upon which the ECJ proceeded. In the light of subsequent decisions, it is to some extent unclear whether SABENA, a nationalized company, would be regarded as part of the State for these purposes or not: see Case C–188/89 *Foster* [1990] ECR I–3313, but cf. *Doughty v. Rolls-Royce* [1992] IRLR 126 (Eng. CA, applying *Foster*, holding a—then—nationalized aero-engine company not to be part of the State).

[23] It is an interesting question, which cannot be explored here, whether ECJ decisions on preliminary references have a greater impact in Member States where there is already in place a doctrinal substratum into which the national lawyers can integrate the new Community principle than in Member States where the Community norm is completely unsupported by the domestic law.

B. Direct Effect of Directives

Yet, from the point of view of a labour lawyer it could be said that at this moment the Court displayed a fatal hesitation in relation to the extension of the doctrine of direct effect to directives. To be sure, an extension was made, but, it eventually became clear, only 'vertically' (i.e. between State and citizen) and not 'horizontally' (i.e. between citizens). This reluctance to drive the doctrine to its ultimate conclusion hobbled Community law generally, but it was particularly problematic for Community labour law. As Deakin explains elsewhere in this volume, outside the areas of free movement and equal pay the drafters of the Rome Treaty saw little reason to include provisions on the position of workers. Consequently, in the pre-Social Agreement period Community labour law had to be built up slowly and painfully, mainly through the use of directives adopted under the 'gap-filling' provisions of Article 100.[24] If direct effect did not apply fully to directives, then it would not be applying fully to the bulk of Community legislation in the labour law area.

For some years the Court agonized about whether the doctrine of direct effect should be applied to its full extent to directives, in particular whether it should be applied 'horizontally'. Initially, the Court seemed likely to take a bolder course. Its early discussions of the application of the doctrine of direct effect to directives were couched in terms of the need to ensure the *effet utile* of Community law. While it is true that legal catch-phrases, whether couched in a dead foreign language, a living one, or in one's own vernacular, tend to obscure more than reveal the policy issues underlying the legal decisions, the implication of the use of the phrase was that direct effect should apply to directives in the same way and to the same extent as it applied to Treaty Articles or to regulations.[25]

However, these were cases where the defendant was in fact the State and so, without contradicting the outcomes of the previous decisions, the Court was able subsequently to make a significant shift in what it saw as the underlying rationale of the direct effect doctrine as it applied to directives. The scheme for directives, as set out in Article 189, envisages that the Member State is the primary addressee of the directive, whose duty it is to

---

[24] See P. Davies, 'The Emergence of European Labour Law' in McCarthy (ed.), *Legal Intervention in Industrial Relations* (Blackwell, Oxford, 1992). Note the continuing dominance of dirs. under the Agreement on Social Policy, which confines the law-making powers of the Council when acting by qualified majority vote under Art. 2(3) to dirs.

[25] Thus, in Case 9/70 *Grad* [1970] ECR 825 the ECJ said in relation to decisions that 'although the effects of a decision may not be identical with those of a provision contained in a regulation, this difference does not exclude the possibility that the end result, namely the right of the individual to invoke the measure before the courts, may be the same as that of a directly applicable provision of a regulation'. The same thing was said in Case 41/74 *Van Duyn* [1974] ECR 1137 in relation to dirs.

transpose the directive into national law, which national law would provide the cause of action for plaintiffs in the national courts.[26] The initial approach of the Court may be said to have been based on something like the English equity lawyer's maxim that the court should treat as having been done that which ought to have been done, so that, at least in relation to clear and unconditional obligations contained in directives, the national courts should proceed, for the benefit of all plaintiffs and no matter whom they were suing, as if those obligations had been transposed. In short, where it was possible to do so, the Court should dispense with the transposition requirement if the Member State had failed to discharge its obligations. By 1979, however, with its decision in *Ratti*,[27] later repeated in *Becker*,[28] the European Court had moved to an estoppel rationale: 'a Member State which has not adopted the implementing measures required by the directive . . . may not rely, as against individuals, on its own failure to perform the obligations which the directive entails'. The implication, of course, as was made clear to labour lawyers by the Court's decision in 1986 in *Marshall I*,[29] was that directives were directly effective only 'vertically' i.e. against State defendants, and not 'horizontally', i.e. as between non-State litigants.

The result was, and continues to be, pretty devastating for Community labour law. As explained above, most Community labour law is contained in directives and is therefore subject only to vertical direct effect. In particular, from the standpoint of a labour lawyer, the outcome looks arbitrary. Employees of the State may enforce against their employer the precise and unconditional obligations contained in all Community legislation, irrespective of the effectiveness of the national transposition process; non-State employees may not.[30] The European Court's decision in *Foster*,[31] by expanding the concept of the State for these purposes, may have increased the number of employees able to benefit from the doctrine of horizontal direct effect, but it has done nothing to lessen the underlying arbitrariness. If anything, it has increased it; for employers with no conceivable responsibility for the Member State's legislative failure may now find themselves caught by the doctrine of direct effect.[32]

[26] 'A directive shall be binding, as to the result to be achieved, upon each Member State to which it is addressed, but shall leave to the national authorities the choice of form and methods.'

[27] Case 148/78 [1979] ECR 1629.

[28] Case 8/81 [1982] ECR 53.

[29] Case 152/84 [1986] ECR 723.

[30] Of course, most systems of labour law do distinguish in some respects between the rights and obligations of State and non-State employees, but that occurs at the stage of framing the substantive obligations not when determining how rights, which the legislature has said are to be available in principle to all employees, are in practice to be assured.

[31] Case C–188/89, [1990] ECR I–3313.

[32] A particularly striking example is the willingness of an English judge to hold that a privatized and, therefore, wholly privately owned water company fell within the *Foster* criteria on the grounds that its activities were regulated by the State, in particular because

Again, the Court has sought to ameliorate the consequences of the distinction within the equality area by bringing as much as possible within Article 119, as against Directives 75/117[33] on equal pay, 76/207 on equal treatment, 79/7 on equal treatment in social security, or 86/378 on equal treatment in occupational social security schemes,[34] but even the Court cannot bring the whole of Community equality law within Article 119.[35] However the Court twisted and turned, the irrationality of the underlying distinction between directives and Treaty Articles, in terms of its labour law outcomes, could not be disguised.

C. The European Court and the National Courts

Deeply unsatisfactory though the distinction between directives, on the one hand, and Treaty Articles and regulations, on the other, may be in terms of the operation of the doctrine of direct effect, it is one which the European Court now seems conclusively to have adopted as part of Community law. In spite of spirited urgings to the contrary by several Advocates General,[36] the Court refused in 1994 in *Faccini Dori*[37] to take the opportunity to depart from its reasoning in *Marshall I*. Since the issue had been placed squarely before the Court by the Advocate General and the national litigation on this occasion involved two clearly non-State parties, one may regard the issue as finally settled.

Does the development and maintenance of the estoppel doctrine con-

the terms of its operating licence imposed upon it a 'public service' obligation: *Griffin* v. *South West Water Services Ltd* [1995] IRLR 15.

[33] Case 96/80, *Jenkins* [1981] ECR 911, treating this Dir. as simply spelling out what was already implicitly stated by Art. 119, thus rendering recourse to the Dir. to achieve the desired result unnecessary.

[34] In the case of these last three dirs. by expanding the notion of 'pay', so as to bring within Art. 119 a wide range of pension schemes and the conditions for access to them. See especially Cases 170/84 *Bilka-Kaufhaus* [1986] ECR 1607; C–262/88 *Barber* [1990] ECR 1889; C–7/93 *Beune* [1994] ECR I–4471; C–57/93 *Vroege* [1994] ECR I–4541; and C–200/91 *Coloroll* [1994] ECR I–4389.

[35] In any event, it is rather odd that Art. 119 is seen to pose no difficulties for horizontal direct effect, since Art. 119, like dirs., is addressed to the Member States and was expected to be implemented at domestic level by national legislation. See further n ?? below.

[36] See the Opinions of Van Gerven A.G. in Case C–271/91 *Marshall II* [1993] ECR I–4381, Jacobs A.G. in Case C–316/93 *Vaneetveld* [1994] ECR I–736 and of Lenz A.G. in Case C–91/92 *Faccini Dori* [1994] ECR I–3328. See especially Jacobs A.G. in *Vaneetveld*, who bluntly argued for a further move away from the international law model and the restoration of the *effet utile* rationale. 'It is unacceptable that the weakness of international law should be reproduced in the Community legal order. . . . [T]he role of dirs. in the EC Treaty has developed, as a result of the legislative practice of the Council, in a way which makes the language of Art. 189 of the treaty no longer appropriate. . . . There are sound reasons of principle for assigning direct effect to dirs. without any distinction based on the status of the defendant. It would be consistent with the need to ensure the effectiveness of Community law and its uniform application in all the Member States.' (At points 28 and 29.)

[37] For citation see n. 36 above.

stitute a failure of nerve on the part of the European Court? In the light of the temptation, which afflicts all Member States, not to implement fully some of the directives to which they agree at Brussels and the systematic failure of some Member States in this respect,[38] a case can clearly be mounted for regarding the Court's decision in *Dori* as a crucial missed opportunity. It is here, however, that the reactions of the national judiciaries have to be considered.

Although, as noted above, there are major advantages attaching to the system of enforcing Community rights through national legal systems, there is, nevertheless, a price to pay for piggybacking Community law on the national judicial infrastructure, and that price is the necessity to maintain the confidence of the national judiciaries in the European Court's project. In relation to the doctrine of the direct effect of directives that confidence was strained, at least in some quarters. After all, a natural reading of Article 189 of the Treaty of Rome suggested that its drafters had intended actions by the Commission or other Member States to be the only method of redress against a State which failed to discharge its duty of transposition. Direct effect of directives involved taking away from the Member States a role which, in contrast to regulations, Article 189 had clearly given them. Despite the political and resource arguments against relying wholly on the Commission or, even more fancifully, on other Member States to enforce the duty of transposition by way of complaints under Articles 169 and 170 and the (then) absence of legal sanctions attached to these Articles, it is perhaps not surprising that the doctrine of direct effect of directives was regarded as a step too far by some national courts. In particular, the French *Conseil d'Etat* and the German *Bundesfinanzhof* declared (or at least were widely perceived to have declared) in 1978 and 1981 respectively that the national authorities were exclusively competent to decide on the method of implementing directives, so that litigants could not invoke the provisions of a directive before the national courts.[39]

---

[38] For data on the transposition rates of the Member States in the employment and health and safety areas see European Commission, *European Social Policy—A Way Forward for the Union: A White Paper*, COM(94)333, 48 and 49. The rate of transposition of the employment and social policy dirs. varied from a high of 92% (UK and Portugal) to a low of 57% (Italy); and in the health and safety field from a high of all 11 dirs. transposed (France) to a low of none (!) (Spain, Greece, Italy, Luxembourg—figures as at 30 June 1994).

[39] *Ministère de l'Intérieur* v. *Cohn-Bendit*, Conseil d'Etat, 22 Dec. 1978 (1979) 15 *RTDE* 157 (note L. Dubois)(also reported in [1980] CMLR 543) and Bundesfinanzhof, VB 51/80, 16 July [1981] *Europarecht* 442 (note E. Millarg). The German court expressly followed the earlier decision of the Conseil d'Etat: '*In diesem Standpunkt stimmt der Senat mit der Entscheidung des franzosischen Conseil d'Etat vom 22 Dezember 1978 Nr, 11640 . . . in vollem Umfang uberein.*' In fact, the Conseil d'Etat, while rejecting direct effect, did not by any means rule out in its 1978 decision all legal challenges aimed at annulling domestic legislation on the ground that it was incompatible with the governing Community dir. Indeed, its subsequent decisions 'have brought its position into line with that advocated by the ECJ even though the conceptual basis remains quite distinctive' (Tatham, (1991) 40

These national reactions caused the European Court, as noted above, to shift rapidly from a broad *effet utile* rationale for the direct effect of directives to a narrower one derived from the idea of estoppel, on the basis of which compromise, as confirmed in *Marshall I*, the national courts fell into line.[40] The Court may have decided, apparently finally, against re-opening this settlement in the recent case of *Dori*, on the ground that this would be a breach of faith with the national courts. In the end, this is a matter of judgment about judicial politics which it is difficult to second-guess. An unstated but compelling limit on the Court's inventiveness is set by the need for its decisions to be acceptable to the national judiciaries. So far the Court has observed that limit, while boldly expanding the effective-ness of Community law. Whether, by the time of *Dori*, the national courts would have been prepared uniformly to accept the even bolder proposition which had been so controversial fifteen years earlier and whether such a step, even if accepted, would have enhanced the reputation of the European Court in the national legal communities is impossibly difficult to say.[41]

D. From Direct Effect to State Liability

That the European Court's decision not to press forward on the issue of the horizontal effect of directives was more of a tactical than a strategic decision is suggested by its subsequent boldness and inventiveness in creating alter-natives to direct effect, especially the principle of State liability. Already in *Von Colson*[42] in 1984 the Court had reacted to the stymieing of the full application of the doctrine of direct effect to directives by developing a doctrine of what might be termed 'indirect' effect.[43] This doctrine may be seen as imposing a duty of transposition on the national courts, as opposed to the national government, in line with the Court's view that Article 5 of the Treaty, requiring Member States to 'take all appropriate measures . . . to ensure fulfilment of the obligations arising out of the Treaty or resulting from action taken by the institutions of the Community', applied to all organs of the State including its courts. Concretely, the national courts 'are required to interpret their national law in the light of the wording and the purpose of the directive in order to achieve the result referred to in the third

ICLQ 907, 919. But it is crucial to note that this bringing into line would have been very much more difficult had the ECJ insisted upon the horizontal direct effect of dirs.

[40] This story is told, somewhat defensively, by P. Pescatore, a former judge at the ECJ, in 'The Doctrine of "Direct Effect": An Infant Disease of Community Law' in (1983) 8 *ELRev.* 155. See also T. C. Hartley, *The Foundations of European Community Law* (3rd edn, Clarendon Press, Oxford, 1994) 243–5 and 249–52.

[41] It should be noted that the Commission argued against horizontal direct effect of dirs. in *Vaneetveld*, n. 36 above.

[42] Case 14/83 [1984] ECR 1509.

[43] Fitzpatrick, 'The Significance of EEC Directives in UK Sex Discrimination Law' (1989) 9 *OJLS* 336.

paragraph of Article 189'.[44] After *Marleasing*[45] it is clear that this obligation applies as much to pre-existing national law as to laws enacted at national level for the express purpose of implementing the directive in question.

The *Von Colson* principle has the merit that it applies equally to litigation brought in the national courts against State and non-State defendants and, indeed, that it applies to the whole of the directive and not just those parts of it which are precise enough to meet the requirements of direct effect.[46] However, its weakness is that it is ultimately only a principle of interpretation and no genuine principle of interpretation can help a national court to overcome a flat contradiction between domestic law and an untransposed directive. Nor does it seem that the European Court expects national courts to use interpretation in this way.[47] This limitation on the doctrine of indirect effect is not surprising; if it were otherwise, the European Court would be imposing the horizontal direct effect of directives under another guise. If the European Court thought it unwise to impose the doctrine under one name, it is to be expected that it would find it no more attractive under another.

Instead, the energy of the Court over the matter of making Community law effective within the national legal systems has been channelled recently in the direction of the notion of State liability for failure to transpose a directive, a liability first clearly imposed in the *Francovich*[48] case. The notion of State liability involves a re-focusing by the Court on the specific provisions of Article 189, notably the obligation cast upon the Member State to transpose directives which are addressed to it. The novelty of the doctrine, however, is that it places in the hands of the litigant in the national court an equivalent to (perhaps even a more effective remedy than) the right of complaint to the European Court which the Commission and other Member States have under Articles 169 and 170 in the case of failure to transpose. If the doctrine of vertical direct effect of directives proceeds on the basis of a

---

[44] *Von Colson*, n. 42 above, at 26. [45] Case C–106/89 [1990] ECR I–4135.

[46] In *Von Colson* itself, n. 42 above, the Art. in question, Art. 6 of the Equal Treatment Dir., was not thought by the ECJ to be directly effective in the circumstances of that case: see para. 27 of the judgment.

[47] 'That obligation of the national court, "in so far as it is given discretion to do so under national law" . . . to interpret national provisions . . . in so far as possible in conformity even with a Directive without direct effect . . . is not completely watertight. It does not oblige the national court to interpret national law . . . *contra legem*. . . . The national court should, however, interpret ambiguous provisions . . . in accordance with Community law" *per* Van Gerven A.G. in his opinion in Case C–271/91 *Marshall II* [1993] ECR I–4367 at para. 10. However, this may be too narrow a formulation. The national court should first identify the applicable Community law and then, if possible, interpret the national law so as to conform with it, even if the national legislation is not on its face ambiguous: C. Docksey and B. Fitzpatrick, 'The Duty of National Courts to Interpret Provisions of National Law in accordance with Community Law' (1991) 20 *ILJ* 113 at 119. For striking examples of this process at work in the British courts see *Litster* v. *Forth Dry Dock & Engineering Co Ltd* [1989] ICR 341 (HL) and *Webb* v. *Emo Air Cargo (UK) Ltd (No. 2)* [1995]ICR 1021 (HL).

[48] Joined Cases C–6/90 and C–9/90, n. 14 above.

legal fiction that the State has done what ought to have been done by way of transposition, the doctrine of State liability fastens on the actual fact of non- or inadequate transposition and, in appropriate circumstances, makes the State liable for its default.

The boldness of this step should be fully recognized. What the Court has created is a new Community cause of action,[49] exercisable within national legal systems, which the Treaty had not provided for. It is capable of imposing upon traditionally sovereign legislatures liability for a failure to legislate or for defective legislation, a liability which only half the Member States recognize within their domestic laws and then subject to the most restrictive conditions. The boldness of the step and the determination of the European Court to continue down this path were demonstrated in the trilogy of decisions in which, five years later, the Court returned to the matter and fleshed out its cryptic remarks in the *Francovich* decision.[50] In *Brasserie du Pêcheur* the German government explicitly argued that Community legislation was needed to create a right to damages for those affected by Member State breaches of Community law and that for the Court to create such a right would be incompatible with the institutional balance established by the Treaty. This argument was robustly rejected by the Court. The existence and extent of state liability in damages 'are questions of Treaty interpretation' even though the Treaty contained no provision expressly dealing with the matter. Consequently, the Court had to mould such a right in discharge of its duty under Article 164 to ensure that 'in the interpretation and application of the Treaty the law is observed'.[51]

Having established the principle, however, the Court was rather restrained in its elucidation of the substantive principles of liability. The Court recognized two models it could follow: on the one hand, the Member States as mere implementers of policies decided at Community level with no significant choices to make themselves; on the other, a sharing of policy-making between the Community and the Member States. The former model would suggest state liability on a wide scale, the latter on a narrower one. The Court chose the latter model, even in relation to the transposition of directives, for which the Community's own, notoriously difficult to establish, liability under Article 215 for non-contractual harm was thought to provide the appropriate standard. The upshot was that to the conditions of liability established in the *Francovich* case—that the directive in question be

---

[49] The 'right . . . to obtain reparation' is 'founded directly on Community law' (ibid., judgment at para. 41).

[50] Joined Cases C–46/93 *Brasserie du Pêcheur* v. *Federal Republic of Germany* and C–48/93 *R* v. *Secretary of State for Transport ex p. Factortame Ltd.* [1996] IRLR 267; Case C–392/93 *R* v. *H.M. Treasury ex p. British Telecommunications plc* [1996] IRLR 300; and Case C–5/94 *R* v. *Ministry of Agriculture, Fisheries and Food ex p. Hedley Lomas (Ireland) Ltd.* [1996] All ER (EC) 493.

[51] At paras. 24 to 27.

intended to confer rights on persons, natural or legal, and that the non- or defective transposition be the cause of the plaintiff's harm—was added the requirement that the Member State should have 'manifestly and gravely disregarded the limits of its discretion'.[52]

However, it would be wrong to suppose that plaintiffs' lack of success in suing Community institutions under Article 215 will be fully replicated in actions before the national courts asserting the liability of the Member State. When transposing a directive, the State's discretion is clearly curtailed. It is no longer engaged in the business of making primary legislative choices but, rather, must integrate policies already chosen at Community level (or one of a number of defined policies) into the national legal system. The State clearly does not have the choice, as in *Francovich*, to decide that the policy should not be implemented in any way. Even when the State does act but transposes incorrectly, the *BT* case suggests that the discretion which the Court has in mind as justifying the Article 215 conditions for liability is not really a discretion operating at the policy level. Rather it is the discretion afforded to a subordinate who is given unclear instructions by a superior. Thus, in the *BT* case the United Kingdom escaped liability because the wording of the directive was imprecise, the United Kingdom's interpretation of its wording was plausible and held in good faith and the European Court had not removed through interpretation the ambiguities in the Directive.[53]

Where does this leave the overall ranking of the mechanisms which the Court has devised for securing the implementation of directives in the national legal systems of the Member States? There is no doubt that the Court places primary reliance on the quiet resolution of conflicts by the national courts through the use of the method of interpretation or of 'indirect effect'. Where that is not a powerful enough tool to deal with the problem, the relative ranking of direct effect and state liability is still to be settled. Although pressed by a number of Member States to do so, the European Court refused to give the state liability a supplementary role by confining its operation to those aspects of directives which are not directly effective.[54] Whether the Court will take the further step of giving state liability primacy by restricting the operation of the doctrine of direct effect, perhaps by confining it to those parts of directives intended to cast burdens on the State, remains to be seen. Such an approach would do something to remove the sting of the criticism made above that the doctrine of vertical direct effect, as it currently stands, produces an arbitrary distinction between public- and private-sector employees and employers.

It may be thought odd that the European Court should imagine that the

[52] *Brasserie du Pêcheur* at para. 55. It was the transposition of a dir. which was at issue in the *BT* case.

[53] *BT* case at paras. 41 to 45. In fact, this approach really undermines the initial classification of the case as one where the Art. 215 criteria are the appropriate ones.

[54] *Brasserie du Pêcheur*, at paras. 18 to 22.

national courts would accept the principle of State liability, while it feared that the horizontal direct effect of directives would prove too big a pill for them to swallow. However, national courts are not necessarily opposed to the expansion of Community law which it then falls to the national courts to apply. Such a process may well enhance the prestige of the national courts, especially *vis-à-vis* national governments. However, just as the European Court needs to keep a wary eye on the reactions of the Member States collectively to its decisions, so also national judiciaries need to be able either to disguise any expansion of their powers *vis-à-vis* national governments or to present it as a natural consequence—enforced upon rather than encouraged by the national judges—of the State's decision to join the Community. In this context, they have an obvious concern with the quality of the formal arguments for and against particular legal consequences of the State's failure to transpose a directive, either at all or in full. In this respect, both State liability and the estoppel basis of direct effect have the advantage of being more clearly linked to the traditional understanding of the structure created by Article 189 for directives than is the horizontal direct effect principle, which seeks to vault over the need for Member State transposition.[55]

E. Conclusion

Finally, how should labour lawyers view the affirmation of the rule which confines the direct effect of directives to vertical direct effect and the development of a principle of State liability as an alternative way of providing redress to those intended to be benefited by the Community instrument? Is it a matter of indifference? So long as the employee (say) is provided with an effective remedy, does it matter that it is a remedy against the State rather than that employee's (private-sector) employer? The first point to make is that the choice of State liability for non-implementation will indeed normally represent a decision about remedies. At best, opting for State liability involves a decision that the plaintiff shall be compensated in damages, rather than through any remedy of specific performance which might be available if the substantive liability could have been enforced against the person who would have owed the duty in question had transposition taken place properly.[56]

More problematic, at least in some Member States, will be the question of

[55] The blunt arguments of those who take the same views as Jacobs A.G. (see n. 36 above) are likely to be particularly problematic from this perspective.

[56] The force of this point, of course, depends heavily upon the availability of specific performance remedies in national labour law systems. As we shall see below in sect. III, Community law does not at present insist upon the adoption of any particular remedies in national systems to support Community obligations, so that, subject to the principle of effectiveness, remedies are a matter of subsidiarity.

the forum in which State liability claims will be brought, and in particular whether they can be brought in the specialist and perhaps more user-friendly labour courts or, on the other hand, must be assigned to generalist courts or specialist administrative courts which have no particular labour law expertise. While Community law provides the cause of action and so defines its scope, the 'detailed procedural rules' governing the enforcement of State liability are a matter for the legal systems of each Member State.[57] One can envisage a 'power struggle' between different sets of courts in at least some Member States, whose outcome will not necessarily be the provision of the most effective court for use by employees seeking to enforce rights derived from Community law.[58] This will not only detract from the practical enforcement of such rights, but will also prolong the division between employees in the private and the State sectors. The latter consequence will follow, at least unless, which is at present very uncertain, the Court also engages in a substantial retreat from the proposition that precise provisions in directives are covered by the doctrine of vertical direct effect.[59]

We have now examined the main stages in the drive by the European Court to make Community law fully a part of the rules which will be enforced by national courts and legal systems. Although decisions such as *Defrenne II, Marshall I, Von Colson* and *Francovich* would play a prominent part in any writer's account of this remarkably rapid and inventive doctrinal development on the part of the Court, it is surely clear that the labour law origins of these cases were a secondary consideration for the Court. What mattered was the opportunities they offered to consider (and usually push forward) the general principles of direct effect, indirect effect, and State liability, which would then apply to all relevant Community legislation, whether concerned with labour law or other topics.[60] In a sense Community labour law has simply slip-streamed along behind the more general concern

[57] *Francovich*, n. 14 above, at para. 42. Subject, of course, to the standard requirements that the procedural rules governing the Community cause of action must not be less favourable than those applying to comparable causes of action in domestic law and that, in any event, the procedural rules should not render the bringing of the Community claim 'impossible'.

[58] Cf. *Secretary of State for Employment* v. *Mann* [1996] IRLR 2, where the English Employment Appeal Tribunal held that *Francovich* claims should be heard in the general High Court rather than in the specialist industrial tribunals, partly, it would seem, because of a perception that such sensitive claims (*vis-à-vis* the government) should be handled by the more senior court which traditionally deals with claims against 'the Crown'.

[59] See the discussion above in text attached to n. 54.

[60] In my experience very few people can give an accurate and coherent account of the labour law problem underlying *Francovich*, and most writers do not attempt to do so. Perhaps this matters little, since it appears from subsequent litigation in the case that Mr Francovich is unlikely to recover anything from the State, since he worked for an enterprise of a type which the Italian State could legitimately exclude from the coverage of the national legislation implementing the Insolvency Directive! See Case C–479/93, *Francovich II*, 9 Nov. 1995, not yet reported.

of the Court to create what Snyder has termed a 'judicial liability system'[61] for the enforcement of Community norms within national legal systems.

III. Community Law and National Law: Remedies and Procedure

In the previous section we analysed the European Court's concern to ensure that Community rules were capable of giving rise to causes of action for litigants in national courts. In that section, however, we said very little about the way in which those causes of action were implemented within national legal systems. We shall examine that issue here. The Court's continuing concern with the effectiveness of Community law shows itself, but, once again, the Court's intervention into the potentially sensitive area of Member States' procedural law seems to have been accepted by the national courts, partly because, no doubt, such intervention has often led to a strengthening of their roles within their legal systems. The Court also seems to have avoided touching the raw nerves of the national governments, partly by limiting their financial exposure to decisions adverse to the Member States' interests and partly too, as noted above, because each Member States has an interest in other States providing remedies for breaches of Community law which are at least as effective as those provided by that Member State's own legal system.

In this process the European Court has begun to create a Community law of civil procedure, and to do so with very little guidance from the Treaty or the secondary Community legislation. It is perhaps this aspect of the Court's creativity in the procedural area which marks it off from the decisions discussed in the previous section and makes a bridge to those discussed in the next section. For all the Court's inventiveness with notions of direct effect, indirect effect, and State liability, it could be said that all the Court was doing was seeking to ensure that those causes of action, which the Treaty or the Community legislative process had defined, were made available, as anticipated, in the national courts. However, in relation to procedural matters the Treaty and the secondary legislation say very little, no doubt precisely because the drafters of those instruments intended to rely on the national mechanisms. Thus, Article 119, while firmly setting out the principle of equal pay, says nothing about the national procedural law which should govern its transposition at national level. Directives 75/117 and 76/207 are scarcely more helpful, containing

[61] F. Snyder, 'The Effectiveness of European Community Law' (1993) 56 *MLR* 19. In the light of the account given above, especially of the interplay between the ECJ and national courts, it may be thought that the word 'system' slightly overplays the matter. The grand design, if such existed, has clearly been qualified by pragmatic considerations of what would or would not be acceptable.

merely some generalizations on this topic, upon which, however, the Court was to build a considerable superstructure.[62]

However, there is an inherent contradiction in the reliance on national legal systems to enforce Community law, a contradiction that exists not only in relation to Community rules which are predicated on national transposing legislation but equally to those rules, such as many Treaty Articles and most regulations, which are directly applicable without such national legislation and, indeed, where national transposing legislation is usually forbidden.[63] The contradiction consists in the fact that the substantive obligations contained in general Community rules are, so far as the translation services of the Community can make them, identical in all the Community countries, and yet reliance on national legal systems for the enforcement of Community law necessarily involves the acceptance of variations in the practical impact of the norms in different Member States. The question for the European Court was whether this was a tolerable, even a rational, situation or whether, on the contrary, the court should develop doctrines which would tend towards less divergence among Member States' procedural laws.

A. Remedies

At a very early stage the European Court decided that the adequacy of the remedies provided by national legal systems to back up Community obligations was not a matter purely for the national governments and courts, even if, in the absence of precise Community procedural norms, the Member States necessarily enjoyed a wide discretion concerning the remedies they would provide. Two criteria were developed, namely, that the national remedies must be 'non-discriminatory' i.e. no less effective than those provided by the national system in support of comparable national rules, and effective. This formula, however, by itself did no more than state the dilemma. Comparability meant focusing on how well the remedies for breaches of the Community norms were assimilated to those of the national system; effectiveness, or at least any rigorous notion of it, meant the application of a non-national standard which might mean wrenching the Community norm out of its national setting and giving it, in domestic terms, extraordinary remedial support, thus emphasizing its distinctiveness

---

[62] Art. 6 of Dir. 75/117 on equal pay states: 'Member States shall, in accordance with their national circumstances and legal systems, take the measures necessary to ensure that the principle of equal pay is applied. They shall see that effective means are available to take care that this principle is observed.' Art. 6 of Dir. 76/207 on equal treatment takes a slightly different tack: 'Member States shall introduce into their national legal systems such measures as are necessary to enable all persons who consider themselves wronged by failure to apply to them the principle of equal treatment . . . to pursue their claims by judicial process after possible recourse to other competent authorities.'

[63] Case 39/72 *Commission v. Italy* [1973] ECR 101.

from purely national rules. Not surprisingly, perhaps, we can see that the Court over time has tended to the second position.

The crucial case here is *Marshall II*,[64] though for labour lawyers the story begins with *Von Colson*. There the European Court deduced from Article 189 of the Treaty and Article 6 of the Equal Treatment Directive[65] that the sanction chosen by the Member State for the transposing national legislation must 'be such as to guarantee real and effective judicial protection. Moreover, it must have a real deterrent effect on the employer.'[66] However, while indicating that the derisory sanction (reimbursement of out-of-pocket expenses) then available under German law for a discriminatory refusal to hire was inadequate, the Court refused to commit itself to a precise view of the sanction to be provided. That was a matter for the Member State (provided it acted within the effectiveness guideline) and, because of the breadth of this discretion, the Court declined to give Article 6 of the Directive direct effect. The German courts were accordingly left with the problem of trying to devise an appropriate remedy on the basis of an interpretation of the German law as it then stood.[67]

In *Marshall II*, encouraged by an industrial tribunal, the lowest level UK labour court, the European Court took a bolder approach. Relying on Article 6, the industrial tribunal ignored two domestic, statutory limitations on its remedial powers when it came to award compensation to Miss Marshall for her discriminatory retirement, namely, the limit on the total amount of compensation it could award a complainant and the absence of any power in its governing statute to award interest.[68] Both these limitations were part of the general remedial set-up within which the industrial tribunals operated and applied, for example, to race relations and unfair dismissal claims as well as to sex discrimination cases. The European Court agreed that both restrictions amounted to a breach of Article 6, which required the award of 'full' compensation. The Court thus rejected the more moderate approach of the Advocate General, based on 'adequate' compensation, which would have permitted Member States to impose a limitation on overall compensation, though not one as low as that then current in the UK.

This result illustrates the Court's preference for effectiveness over comparability in relation to remedies. As a consequence of this decision sex discrimination rights in Britain became much better protected than either

---

[64] Case C-271/91 [1993] ECR I-4367. To similar effect is the discussion of remedies in *Brasserie du Pêcheur*, above n. 50.

[65] Set out at n. 62 above.

[66] Para 23 of *Von Colson*, n. 42 above..

[67] For an account of the sequel see J. Shaw, 'European Community Judicial Method: Its Application to Sex Discrimination Law' (1990) 19 *ILJ* 228.

[68] [1989] 3 CMLR 389. The reference to the ECJ was made by the HL, so that the case went completely through the English court system before being referred.

other discrimination claims or most unfair dismissal claims, at least as far as compensation was concerned. So bizarre was the result in the domestic context that the UK Government felt obliged to extend the amending legislation to race discrimination as well as sex discrimination cases, even though the former do not fall within the purview of Community law.[69]

The boldness of the industrial tribunal's judgment was not confined to the substantive content of Article 6. How could the tribunal's interpretation of that Article benefit Miss Marshall in her action against the Health Authority unless it was directly effective, a conclusion which the European Court had rejected in *Von Colson*? The European Court obliged the industrial tribunal by now taking a different view on that issue: since the UK Government had chosen compensation as the appropriate remedy, it had exercised the discretion which Article 6 conferred upon it and, in relation to a claim for adequate compensation, the Article was in consequence directly effective.[70] Crucially, the outcome was to require the national courts to ignore, in *Simmenthal* and *Factortame* fashion, national limits on their remedies, and even to create remedies, in this case the award of interest, which, although known elsewhere in the national system, had not been made available to the industrial tribunals. The supremacy of Community law and the empowerment of national courts, even at the lowest levels, thus made themselves fully felt in the remedial arena.

B. Time Limits

Although the question of effective remedies is perhaps the most obvious and even the most important of the procedural matters with which the Court has had to deal, it is clearly not the only aspect of national civil procedure which is capable of producing variations in the impact of Community law in the Member States.[71] Of these additional procedural matters it is the

---

[69] Sex Discrimination and Equal Pay (Remedial) Regs. 1993 (SI 2798); Race Relations (Remedies) Act 1994. This is a good example of the 'spill over' effect of Community law. As a consequence of the lifting of the limit, some very large awards were made in favour of officers dismissed from the armed forces on becoming pregnant: *Ministry of Defence* v. *Cannock* [1994] ICR 918 (EAT). See also, subsequently, the Sex Discrimination and Equal Pay (Miscellaneous Amendments) Regs. 1996 (SI 438), permitting tribunals to award compensation in cases of indirect sex discrimination.

[70] The ECJ had given a broad hint in a similar direction in Case 177/88 *Dekker* [1990] ECR I–3841 at paras. 24–6. Thus, the direct effectiveness of Community obligations would seem to depend not only on whether the Community law is precise and unconditional, but also on how the Member State has responded to the obligation. An obligation might thus be directly effective in one Member State at a particular time, because that State had chosen compensation, but not in another, because that State had not enacted any transposing legislation?

[71] See also the cases on the burden of proof, with which there is not space to deal here: Cases 170/84 *Bilka-Kaufhaus* [1986] ECR 1607; 109/88 *Danfoss* [1989] ECR 3199; and

decisions on time limits which are the most illuminating. On the one hand, the Court has fashioned rules about time limits which increase the pressures on Member States to transpose directives in a timely and accurate fashion, but on the other hand the Court has shown an awareness of the destabilizing potential of judgments which seek to undo events which had previously been regarded as settled, especially if those previous events go back over many years. The exact balance which the Court has struck between those competing considerations has turned out to be more responsive to the arguments for not upsetting past dispositions, especially where the financial interests of Member State governments are at risk, than to the arguments for putting the maximum pressures on Member States to transpose directives.

The central time limits cases revolve, significantly, around article 4 of Directive 79/7 on the equal treatment of men and women in social security matters, i.e. the area of implementation of the equality principle which has the greatest potential impact on the public finances of the Member States. In the Irish case, *Emmott*,[72] the Court seemed willing to apply its estoppel theory with equal force to time limits on the substantive provisions of directives. There the applicant challenged a time limit in national law for the bringing of proceedings, which meant that, at the point when the Member State at last adequately transposed the Directive, the limit was long past for the commencement of the litigation about the applicant's treatment by the State. The Court held that 'until such time as the Directive has been properly transposed, a defaulting member State may not rely on an individual's delay in initiating proceedings against it in order to protect rights conferred on him by the provisions of the Directive'. The decision was put on the ground that, without transposition, individuals in the Member State are unable to ascertain the full extent of their rights. However, the result was applied to directly effective elements of the Directive as well as to those parts which were not,[73] even though the former, *ex hypothesi*, could have

---

C-400/93 *Royal Copenhagen* [1995] ECR I-1275. There are also many matters which the ECJ has not considered in the area of civil procedure which must have a major influence on the effectiveness of Community law, e.g. the costs of litigation. Although the UK is an expensive country in which to bring civil claims, it has a high level of litigation in the sex discrimination area partly because of the existence of statutory bodies with the duty (and the funds) to promote equality through, *inter alia*, litigation. Of the total Art. 177 equal pay and treatment references to the ECJ from all countries fully one third have been funded by the British Equal Opportunities Commission or its Northern Ireland equivalent. See C. Barnard 'A European Litigation Strategy: The Case of the Equal Opportunities Commission in J. Shaw and S. More (eds.), *New Legal Dynamics of European Union* (Clarendon Press, Oxford, 1995), 254.

[72] Case C-208/90 [1991] ECR I-4269. Although the case was decided on the basis set out in the text, it could as well have been put on the narrower basis that the Irish authorities had misled the Mrs Emmott into thinking that the delay would not prejudice her claim for benefit.

[73] See para. 21 of the judgment.

formed the basis of a suit in the national court before transposition and even though such directly effective parts were necessarily precise and unconditional and so could presumably have been used by the individual to deduce his or her rights without the aid of implementing legislation. One may conclude that the Court did not want the doctrine of direct effect to operate so as to reduce the pressure on Member States to transpose directives.

This was a most remarkable decision, which went against the principle common in national laws that time limits on the bringing of litigation should not be set aside simply because the law subsequently turns out to be (or becomes) different from what it was though to be at the time the failure to litigate occurred. On the other hand, it could be seen as a natural consequence of the principle underlying the notions of direct effect and State liability, namely, that the non-transposition of a directive is a wrong on the part of the State.[74]

There was then a sharp reverse of position in *Steenhorst-Neerings*[75] (concerning contributory benefits) and *Johnson II*[76] (concerning non-contributory benefits), where the time limit at issue related, not to the initiation of proceedings, but to the length of time an award of compensation could be backdated. In both cases, the national provisions stated that an award of benefit could not be backdated more than twelve months before the claim was made, even though in both cases it was clear that the withholding of the benefit in the earlier period had been in breach of the equality principle enshrined in Directive 79/7. In a significantly different choice of test, the Court said that the Member States had discretion to set such limits, subject to the twin controls of national treatment and the requirement that the time limit must not be such 'as to render virtually impossible the exercise of rights conferred by Community law'. In contrast to *Emmot*, the time limits in the two later cases did not deprive 'the applicant of any opportunity whatever' to assert her rights.

Although the 'virtually impossible' criterion is a test of some pedigree in Community law, its use by the Court was a considerable contrast to the references to the need for fully effective remedies in *Marshall II*. In fact, this constituted a backtracking from *Emmott*, for a Member State would now benefit from the non- or defective implementation of a directive, provided that the period of delay exceeded the limit on backdating and provided potential litigants in the national courts were sufficiently ill-informed not to avail themselves of the possibility of actions based directly on the directive

[74] The *Emmott* principle applies only to the invocation of limitation periods by the State. As with *Francovich* liability the force of the argument that the State should not be able to invoke time limits is heavily dependent upon whether the State had made good-faith efforts to transpose the dir. in question accurately. It is not clear, however, that the *Emmott* principle makes any allowance for such factors.

[75] Case C–338/91 [1993] ECR I–5475.

[76] Case C–410/92 [1994] ECR I–5483.

immediately after the date for implementation had passed. On the other hand, given the pressures on public expenditure in general and social security budgets in particular and the national sensitivities on both these issues, one can see the attraction to the Court of imposing some limit on the governments' financial exposure. Nevertheless, it is difficult to reconcile, except on a pragmatic basis, the Court's views on the strictness of the Member State's duty under *Francovich* to transpose directives and the condoning in these recent cases of Member States' benefiting from breach of this duty.[77]

Furthermore, it is also far from clear whether the *Emmott* doctrine applies to Treaty Articles which presuppose implementing legislation on the part of the Member State, notably the failure of Member States to pass legislation transposing the obligations in relation to equal pay contained in Article 119. In *Fisscher*[78] one of the pension cases discussed below, the Court laid down only the national treatment and 'not impossible' tests for national rules relating to time limits for the bringing of claims under Article 119 asserting the right to join occupational pension schemes. It is unclear whether this was because the defendant in the case was a non-State body or because the claim was based on Article 119. Even the former basis emphasizes once again the arbitrariness of the State/non-State distinction in labour law terms,[79] while the latter produces the odd result that the fundamental Treaty right to equality[80] is less well protected at a procedural level than rights contained in secondary Community legislation.

C. Collective Agreements

The Court's concern with effectiveness has had a particular impact on one matter which is close to any labour lawyer's heart, namely, the role of

[77] More recently, the European Court's decision in Case C–62/93 *BP Supergas* v. *Greece* [1995] ECR I–1883 suggests that *Emmott* is no longer the general rule even in relation to time limits on the initiation of litigation, so that *Emmott* is in future to be explained on the basis of the misleading actions of the Irish authorities rather than on her inability to establish her rights before transposition. See J. Coppel (1996) 25 ILJ 153. We wait to see what rules as to retrospection will be applied to claims against the State under the *Francovich* principle (as opposed to the cases discussed in the text, where it was the limits on the State's substantive liability which were in issue).

[78] Case C–128/93 [1994] ECR I–4583. The Eng. CA has taken the view that *Emmott* does not apply to Art. 119 claims, even where the defendant is an emanation of the State: *Biggs* v. *Somerset County Council* [1996] ICR 364.

[79] In effect, equality in relation to pension rights contained in State pension schemes will be better protected than in relation to such rights contained in occupational pension schemes, though it is to some extent a matter of historical accident whether in particular Member States protection against loss of income in old age is provided through state or occupational schemes.

[80] See below sect. IV.A.1 The Commission's proposal for a dir. amending Dir. 86/378/ EEC would apply the *Fisscher* ruling to all claims for equal treatment in relation to occupational pension schemes, even where these schemes are operated by state bodies.

collective bargaining and collective agreements in the regulation of working life. The Court's basic stance has been to prioritize a perhaps rather formal notion of effectiveness over the promotion of collectively bargained solutions. The issue first arose in relation to the use of collective agreements to implement directives and the result of the early cases, notably *Commission* v. *Denmark*[81] and *Commission* v. *Italy*,[82] was that implementation of labour law directives could be left in the first instance to collective agreements, but provided that such agreements gave rise to 'effective protection' and provided that the State itself established effective forms of enforcement for those workers who, for example on grounds of non-unionism, who were unable to rely on the collective agreement, where the sector in question was not covered by an agreement or where the collective agreement implemented the directive only partially. The Court seems to have been more concerned with removing temptation from the Member States to avoid the full impact of directives by utilizing methods of transposition which are non-transparent and easily changeable[83] than with promoting collective bargaining. Although labour lawyers may advance this criticism, it was probably more important from the European Court's point of view that its stance has been ratified by the Member States in Article 2(4) of the Agreement on Social Policy, which adopts a similar policy to that laid down in the Court's case law.[84] Further development towards giving collective agreements an enhanced regulatory role will require the working out of the still problematic procedure for involving the social partners, not in the implementation of legislation, but in the creation of Community-wide rules under Articles 3 and 4 of the Agreement.

The thrust of the Court's decisions in *Commission* v. *Belgium* and *Commission* v. *Italy* was that collective agreements may be used to implement directives, but not in such a way as to undermine the intent of these instruments to confer rights upon all workers, whether covered by collective agreements or not. In the cases in question it was indeed clear that the Community legislature had intended to confer rights upon all employees.

---

[81] Case 143/83 [1985] ECR 427.

[82] Case 235/84 [1986] ECR 2291.

[83] See Case C–102/79, *Commission* v. *Belgium* [1980] ECR 1473.

[84] It should also be noticed that the ECJ's position is not as far away from that of the International Labour Organization as is sometimes thought. That doyen of international labour lawyers, Wilfred Jenks, took the view that in the application of ILO Conventions 'the only proper starting point' must be 'the assumption that for all practical purposes legislation is normally indispensable unless the Convention otherwise provides': C. Wilfred Jenks, 'The Application of International Labour Conventions by means of Collective Agreements' (1958) 19 *Zeitschrift für ausländisches öffentliches Recht und Völkerrecht* 197, 199. A greater contrast is with the Social Charter of the Council of Europe which, in Art. 33, expressly permits implementation through agreements between employers and workers' organizations and then provides that the States parties to the Charter will be regarded as having fulfilled their obligations if the Arts. of the Charter which are implemented in this way 'are applied . . . to the great majority of the workers concerned'.

The interest of the recent decisions in *Commission* v. *UK*[85] is that they display a reluctance on the part of the Court to interpret directives, which were ambiguous on the point, in a way which did not give them universal effect. However, in insisting upon universality but failing clearly to prioritize the existing institutions of collective representation, the Court ran the risk of undermining rather than supplementing collective bargaining.

It will be recalled that both Directives 75/129 on collective redundancies and 77/187 on transfers of businesses require consultation in certain circumstances with the representatives of the workers concerned. Such representatives are defined as those 'provided for by the laws or practice of the Member States'. In the UK representation of workers has traditionally been via the institutions of collective bargaining, so that both the Labour Government, transposing the first Directive, and the Conservative Government, transposing the second, chose to require consultation with the representatives of the trade unions recognized by the employer for the purposes of collective bargaining. It followed from this decision that, if no union were so recognized, then no consultation would be required. At the time the first Directive was transposed, there was legislation in force under which employers could in appropriate circumstances be required to recognize a trade union. By the date of the transposition of the second directive that legislation had been repealed, but it is difficult to believe that that rather ineffective legislation, which had been introduced only in 1971, had had much impact in practice upon the scope of collective bargaining arrangements in the UK. These were, and always had been, essentially voluntary, so that the attachment of consultation rights to representatives of recognized trade unions meant, inevitably and unlike in countries with statutory works councils systems, some potentially large gaps in the coverage of the Directive. This was a tendency much exacerbated by the legislative onslaught on the power of trade unions in the 1980s, which employers have followed up in the 1990s by increasingly resorting to the derecognition of trade unions. The question for the Court was whether the definition of 'worker representatives' in the Directives meant that the Community legislature had wished to accept this situation. Was Member State autonomy in relation to the institutions of collective bargaining more important than the uniform impact of Community norms?

Not surprisingly in the light of its case law, the Court gave a negative answer to the question. The real criticism to be made of its judgments, however, is its failure to insist clearly on the Member State's obligation to provide an *effective* method of employee representation *vis-à-vis* the employer on transfers and redundancies. Naturally, the Court did not make the reintroduction of a legal obligation to recognize trade unions for the

[85] Cases C–382/92 and C–383/92 [1994] ECR I–2435, noted by P. Davies (1994) 23 *ILJ* 272, and Wedderburn (1994) *Int. JComp LLIR* 339.

purposes of collective bargaining either a necessary or a sufficient response on the part of the UK Government to its condemnation. It was not necessary, because all the Community law required was consultation, and it was not sufficient, because even compulsory recognition would not have covered, for example, workplaces where trade union membership was low or non-existent.

The real shortcoming of the judgments was that it was possible to read them and, especially, the Opinion of the Advocate General as requiring no more than the election by the whole workforce of employee representatives *ad hoc* for the purposes of consultation over the proposed redundancy or transfer; and, moreover, that such *ad hoc* representatives carried in Community law no greater weight than the representatives of the recognized trade union. Of course, the UK Government took full advantage of such implications. Under the Collective Redundancies and Transfer of Undertakings (Protection of Employment) (Amendment) Regulations 1995[86] employers will have to consult representatives of the employees in all cases covered by the Directive, but, even where a union is recognized for the purposes of collective bargaining, the employer will have the choice of consulting instead a non-union based body or even representatives elected *ad hoc*.

The result may be said to be a triumph for the form of consultation over its substance. It remains to be seen whether the Commission or the Court will have the stomach for a further encounter with the UK over this issue. As thing stand at the moment, the Court's boldness in seeking to re-order a Member State's system of collective representation has backfired. The degree of legal support in the UK for an independent and effective system of representation of the employees' interests has actually been reduced by the 1995 Regulations. As will be suggested below in relation to pensions, the Court should either have been bolder or have left well alone. It should either develop a comprehensive set of criteria for judging the effectiveness of Member States' systems of representation, rather along the lines of its criteria for judging the effectiveness of the remedies provided by the Member States' legal systems, or it should eschew *ad hoc* intervention. The latter leaves too much scope for national governments to subvert the aims of the Court's decisions.[87]

---

[86] SI 1995 No 2527. For a comment see M. Hall, 'Beyond Recognition? Employee Representation and EU Law' (1996) 25 *ILJ* 15. A challenge in the domestic courts on the ground that the Regulations did not comply with community law failed: *R v. Secretary of State for Trade and Industry ex parte Unison* [1996] IRLR 438, but there still may be an infringement action launched by the Commission.

[87] This is not to deny that, as a result of falling membership and employer policies, the British system of collective bargaining is in considerable trouble or that, in the hands of a more sympathetic government, the principle of worker- rather than union-based representation could play a role in the reinvigoration of the British system of representation. See Trades Union Congress, *Your Voice at Work* (London, 1995). What is disputed is the

IV. The European Court and Substantive Labour Law

It might be thought that the decisions of the Court, examined above, do not constitute good tests for the attitude of the Court towards labour law matters, because the issues which they raised were of general significance for relations between Community and national law and those general matters necessarily appeared more important to the Court than the substantive content of the rights which were at issue. In this section, therefore, we will examine a number of cases, including some already looked at above, where the Court was squarely faced with an issue of substantive Community labour law. Considerations of space forbid an examination of cases outside the area of gender equality, which is, of course, the area where the Court has made its greatest contribution. However, it will be suggested that the pressures towards an expansive view of Community law and the constraints upon such developments, which we have identified above, have also had a crucial impact in this substantive area.

A Equality as between Men and Women

1. *Equality as a Fundamental Right*

Non-discrimination has been held by the Court to be a general principle of Community law.[88] Article 119 and the equality directives have thus been placed in a context in which they are not simply examples of Community labour law but manifestations of a much broader principle which permeates all aspects of Community law. Moreover, the development by the European Court of a fundamental rights jurisprudence, which was not obviously required by the Treaty, was a central part of its battle to secure acceptance by the national courts of its doctrines of supremacy and direct effect.

It is a well-known story, which need not be repeated here,[89] that the German constitutional courts in particular were reluctant to accept the supremacy of Community law over even the Basic Law of Germany in the absence in Community law of any guarantees of constitutional rights which the Basic Law provided. The European Court responded by insisting upon supremacy but coupling it with the development of a Community doctrine of fundamental rights. The pressure on the European Court was, of course, not simply to announce the existence of such rights in principle but also to turn them into a legal reality. In other words, the need to keep

ability of the ECJ to bring about such a change in the absence of a receptive domestic climate and, even, its desire to do so.

[88] See in particular C. Docksey, 'The Principle of Equality between Men and Women as a Fundamental Right under Community Law' (1991) 20 *ILJ* 258.

[89] See T. C. Hartley, *The Foundations of European Community Law*, n. 40 above, 139–44.

national constitutional courts in line has been a continuing pressure on the Court to be active in this area.[90] This is not to say, of course, that, once the Court had perceived the need for a jurisprudence of fundamental rights, it found the task of developing it in any way distasteful.

The European Court was quick to see the fundamental rights potential of Article 119. In *Defrenne II*[91] the Court rescued the Article from its 'level playing field' origins and declared, famously, that it had a 'double aim' of which the social one was at least as important as the economic aim and, it has to be said, the former has in fact dominated the Court's subsequent thinking.[92] In *Defrenne III*[93] the point was put in explicitly fundamental rights language: 'The Court has repeatedly stated that respect for fundamental personal human rights is one of the general principles of Community law, the observance of which it has a duty to ensure. There can be no doubt that the elimination of discrimination based on sex forms part of those fundamental rights.'

The timing of this declaration was no doubt significant, for the Court was in the process of completing the first stage of the development of a Community doctrine of fundamental rights, having recently handed down its decision in *Nold II*[94] and being about to decide the case of *Hauer*.[95] However, this view of Article 119 was not just a way of giving the Court an even more effective retort to national constitutional courts; it also put the ECJ in touch with one of the most significant social movements in Western Europe of the post-war period, namely the struggle for the improvement of the position of women. So a broad view of Article 119 enabled the Court to appear in the vanguard of European social trends, to do something to mitigate the Community's overwhelming 'businessman's' image, and, in legal terms, to make advances on the social front from what appeared at first sight to be an impossibly narrow bridgehead in the shape of the Social Policy provisions of the Treaty of Rome.

Moreover, equality of treatment via its connection with Article 119 had a

---

[90] '[T]he most dangerous challenges to the primacy of Community law come from none other than the national constitutional courts and are rooted in fear lest Brussels produce rules which might damage their respective bills of rights': Mancini, n. 3 above, 14. That this is not a fear of the past is demonstrated by the German Federal Constitutional Court's decision on the Maastricht Treaty. See M. Weiss (1993) 9 *Int. J. Comp. LLIR* 351.

[91] Case 43/75 [1976] ECR 455,

[92] Of course, in pursuing social aims under Art. 119 the ECJ has often taken into account the economic costs of particular social policies (see, e.g., the discussion of the pension cases, below) but that amounts to using economic arguments as a limit on the social objectives of the Art., not using it to pursue economic objectives as such. For an examination of arguments of the former type see C. McCrudden and J. Black, 'Achieving Equality between Men and Women in Social Security: Some Issues of Costs and Problems of Implementation' in C. McCrudden (ed.), *Equality of Treatment between Women and Men in Social Security* (Butterworths, London 1994).

[93] Case 149/77 [1978] ECR 1365, at paras. 26 and 27.

[94] Case 4/73 [1974] ECR 491.   [95] Case 44/79 [1979] ECR 3727.

potential which other fundamental rights, such as legitimate expectations or proportionality, derived from general principles of the Member States' laws, did not have. The latter could be used to control the exercise of State power, whether by the Community institutions or by Member States acting within the scope of Community law, but could not be used to impose principles of conduct upon actors across the board, including in the private sphere. Article 119 and the equality directives could do this, especially with the development of the doctrines of direct and indirect effect, noted above. As with non-discrimination on grounds of nationality, and by contrast with the principle on non-discrimination on the ground of race or ethnic origin,[96] the legislative basis for the sex equality principle proved invaluable. To put the matter another way, gender equality as a fundamental principle could operate only within the Community sphere, so that, as was said in *Defrenne III*, the applicant could not sue in a national court basing herself on that fundamental principle when her complaint fell outside the (then) scope of Community equality legislation. Nevertheless, by using the fundamental rights argument to give a broad interpretation to Article 119 and the equality directives, the Court was *ipso facto* expanding the scope of the Community sphere and thus the impact of the principle of equality in national legal systems.

Armed with the tools of Article 119 and, as the 1970s progressed, the equality directives, and responding to the incentives described above, the Court took an increasingly bold view of what that legislation required of employers. One needs but list some of the highlights. After an initial hesitation,[97] the Court accepted a quite rigorous concept of indirect discrimination and then turned it to the benefit of (predominantly female) part-time workers.[98] It has done something to require transparency and justification of pay systems which produce apparently discriminatory results.[99] After apparently endless skirmishing, the Court has insisted upon equality in relation to retirement ages[100] and retirement benefits, including, most famously, pension benefits.[101] It has brought discrimination on

---

[96] See Hepple elsewhere in this volume.

[97] See Case 96/80 *Jenkins* [1981] ECR 911, where the ECJ's formulation of the indirect discrimination test was so inadequate that the referring national court developed its own more rigorous definition when the matter was remitted to it: *Jenkins* v. *Kingsgate (Clothing Productions) Ltd.* [1981] ICR 715.

[98] See Cases 170/84 *Bilka-Kaufhaus* [1986] ECR 1607; C–33/89, *Kowalska* [1990] ECR I–2519; C–184/89 *Nimz* [1991] ECR I–322. These decisions have led the UK courts in a similar direction without the need for references to the ECJ. See, e.g., *R.* v. *Secretary of State for Employment, ex parte Equal Opportunities Commission* [1994] ICR 317 (HL).

[99] See Cases 109/88, *Danfoss* [1989] ECR 3199 and C–127/92 *Enderby* [1993] ECR I–5535.

[100] Case 152/84 *Marshall I* [1986] ECR 723.

[101] Case C–262/88 *Barber* [1990] ECR I–1889 and its progeny.

grounds of pregnancy within the legislation.[102] Finally, as we saw above, it has insisted upon effective remedies for the redress of discriminatory conduct.

This is a considerable catalogue of achievements, but the Court's approach is not beyond criticism. The criticisms which have been advanced can be grouped under three headings: first, that the Court has sometimes taken on the solution of problems which could be satisfactorily resolved only by legislation; secondly, that its concept of equality has tended to be too formal and to become divorced from the social reality of women's disadvantage, the need to remedy which was the driving force behind the legislation; and, thirdly, that it has been too ready to allow the Member States to set the agenda for implementing the principle of equality, thus compromising on the rigor with which the principle is implemented. It will readily be seen that it is hardly possible to advance with any degree of consistency both the first and the third of these criticisms.

2. Over-extending the Judicial Role?

The argument here is based, not on a democratic premise (i.e. that such lawmaking ought to be carried out by a democratically responsible legislature rather than a non-accountable court), but rather on a technical argument, namely, that a case-by-case approach to the resolution of major social problems did not yield a coherent set of rules. This argument will be examined in the context of the Court's decisions on the application of the Equal Treatment Directive to pregnancy.

The Court's decisions on pregnancy raise the question whether it was wise to attempt to remedy disadvantage stemming from a uniquely female condition by employing the mechanism of anti-discrimination law, which is centred on the notion of a *comparison* between the positions of men and of women. Within a framework of equal treatment and, therefore, of comparison two coherent intellectual solutions seem to be available, though they both have disadvantages. The first position is to accept that no comparison with a male in an equivalent position is possible and then to draw the conclusion that the case falls outside the scope of equality law. The Court was unwilling to do this in the absence at the time of Community legislation dealing specifically with the position of pregnant workers, who would thus be left unprotected at Community level.

The second is to argue that a sensible comparison with a male can be made because, from an employer's point of view, the relevant fact is not the precise nature of the physical condition giving rise to the unavailabilty for work, but the unavailability for work itself and its likely duration. This approach tends to lead to the question: was the woman treated less favourably than a sick man would have been? If the emphasis is on the equality

[102] Case 177/88 *Dekker* [1990] ECR 3841.

of treatment by an employer of the men and women in its employ, this approach has a lot to be said for it. However, if the underlying policy is guaranteeing pregnant workers a minimum level of protection, then such a comparative approach may fall short of its objective. For example, if an employer treats sick workers in general ungenerously, this approach will permit it to treat pregnant women workers equally ungenerously.[103]

The Court developed a third approach, which was to accept, again, that no comparison with a male is possible but then to draw the opposite conclusion to that indicated above, i.e. that disadvantage inflicted on grounds of pregnancy or a pregnancy-related reason is direct discrimination because all pregnant workers are female. As the Court put it bluntly in *Dekker* (a case of refusal to hire for a pregnancy-related reason): 'Only women can be refused employment on the ground of pregnancy and such a refusal *therefore* constitutes direct discrimination on the ground of sex. A refusal of employment on account of the financial consequences of absence due to pregnancy must be regarded as based, essentially, on the fact of pregnancy.'[104] This approach in fact involves substituting for the comparison with the employer's treatment of an equivalent man a comparison with the employer's treatment of workers (male or female) who are not pregnant, usually in fact a comparison with the way the applicant herself was treated before she became pregnant. Any disadvantageous treatment of the woman for a pregnancy-related reason becomes discrimination and, indeed, in the eyes of the Court in *Dekker*, direct discrimination. Since direct discrimination can rarely, if ever, be justified, one arrives quickly at the position that any disadavantage inflicted upon a pregnant worker by an employer because of her pregnancy is unlawful.[105]

This is not an indefensible policy, but it is difficult to think of legal systems which adopt it; and it soon became clear that the Court was not prepared to adopt it either. What the Court was trying to do was to create a legal regime for the protection of pregnant workers, which gave them significant, free-standing legal rights but stopped short of requiring employers to disregard the fact of the pregnancy in all situations. On the basis

---

[103] The European Court rejected the 'sick-man' comparison in Case C–32/93, *Webb* [1994] ECR I–3567, at para. 25. However, it has received legislative endorsement in the United States in the Pregnancy Discrimination Act 1978 (s. 701(k) of Title VII of the Civil Rights Act 1964): a pregnant woman 'shall be treated the same . . . as other persons not so affected but similar in their ability or inability to work'.

[104] At para 12 of *Decker*, n. 102 above, emphasis added..

[105] Hare has suggested, in my view rightly, that the ECJ might have done better in *Dekker* to find the employer's act to have been *indirectly* discriminatory, thus putting it in the position of 'reconciling the protection of pregnant women with the expression of the employer's legitimate economic concerns over the availability of his work-force' (1991) 20 *ILJ* 124, 129. Perhaps, however, that was precisely the task the ECJ wished to give to the Member States.

of the interpretation of the equality laws which it had adopted, however, it became very difficult to explain why the more far-reaching consequence did not follow.

Thus, on the same day as it decided *Dekker* the European Court also held in *Hertz*[106] that a women dismissed on grounds of a pregnancy-induced illness but after the end of the period of maternity leave could not benefit from the principle that only women could be dismissed for a pregnancy-related reason and so such dismissals amounted to direct discrimination. Because the period of maternity leave was over, the woman could benefit only from the less far-reaching principle of comparison with a sick man. The decision revealed clearly enough the Court's underlying strategy of creating a special pregnancy and maternity-leave regime, but it hardly explained the apparent contradiction with the announced logic of *Dekker*.

An even clearer example of the difficulty is provided by the Court's rejection in *Gillespie*[107] of the argument that Article 119 applies to payments made by an employer during the period of maternity leave, this decision thus relieving the employer of the obligation to maintain full pay during this period. This result could be achieved only by expressly reintroducing the test of comparison with a man (the test which had been rejected in *Dekker*) and, having reintroduced it, by drawing the conclusion that the absence of an appropriate male comparator meant that there was no discrimination. 'Women taking maternity leave', said the Court, 'are in a special position which requires them to be afforded special protection, but which is not comparable either with that of a man or with that of a woman actually at work.'

The girations of the Court in *Hertz* and *Gillespie* demonstrate perhaps the unwisdom of the Court's embarking upon the attempt to hew out of the rock of discrimination law a specialized pregnancy and maternity regime. As Fredman has said, 'a satisfactory solution can only be achieved by abandoning the attempt to rely on a traditional equality-difference test. Instead, it is necessary to make a conscious and explicit decision on the social value of parenthood and to formulate legal rules to reflect this.'[108] On the other hand, in terms of *realpolitik* the Court's efforts could be thought to have been rather successful. If one focuses, not on the coherence of the Court's doctrine, but upon its impact upon the Community legislative process and, thus, its interaction with the Member States, the result becomes more creditable. The initial decision in *Dekker* helped to spur the Member States into giving serious consideration to the Commission's proposals on

---

[106] Case C–179/88 [1990] ECR I–3979.

[107] Case C–342/93 [1996] IRLR 214. The quotation is from para. 17.

[108] S. Fredman, 'A Difference with Distinction: Pregnancy and Parenthood Reassessed' (1994) 110 *LQR* 106. Of course, such a decision might, and in most actual legal regimes does, fall short of protecting the woman against all the adverse employment consequences of the pregnancy.

maternity rights and, ultimately, into legislative activity in the form of Directive 92/85, adopted under Article 118A of the Treaty. On the other hand, the subsequent decision in *Gillespie*, preserves the careful compromise on maternity pay, laid down in article 11 of the Pregnancy Directive,[109] from being undermined by a finding that workers are already entitled to a much greater right by virtue of the Treaty.

3. *Equality and Social Disadvantage*

If the Court's decisions in the area of pregnancy and maternity can be presented as the Court giving the legislative process a shove and then taking a back-seat once the Member States had spoken, its decisions in relation to pensions, and especially in relation to equality of pension ages, reveal the Court in an apparently bolder mode. In relation to equality of pension ages the Member States had already spoken in Directive 86/378 on equal treatment in occupational social security schemes. Article 9 of that Directive, coupled with Article 7 of Directive 79/7 on equal treatment in matters of social security, seemed to have left the Member States free not to equalize pension ages in occupational pension schemes until equalization was achieved in state retirement pension ages, in relation to which the 1979 Directive imposed on the Member States only an obligation to keep the existing inequality under review. The effect of the decision in *Barber*, requiring pension ages to be equalized on the basis of Article 119 of the Treaty, thus upset the Member States' legislative dispositions contained in secondary Community legislation. Was this a wise step for the Court to have taken?

The *Barber* decision was certainly technically defective in one very important sense. In the light of the existence of Directive 86/378, which the Court was in part overruling by applying Article 119 of the Treaty to the question of pension ages, but upon which employers had obviously relied, the Court decided to give its decision only prospective effect. However, the Court famously failed to make clear whether it was aiming to control pensions benefits *paid* after the date of its judgment or only benefits *earned* after that date. That ambiguity, besides causing consternation in the pensions industries of some Member States, gave the Member States the opportunity to decide the matter for themselves, at least for the period after the adoption of the Treaty on European Union, by adding the 'Barber' protocol[110] to that Treaty. This opted for the second and more restrictive view of the prospective effect of the judgment. Not surprisingly, perhaps, the Court itself in *Ten Oever*[111] then fell into line in relation to the period between its decision in *Barber* and the date of coming into force of the Protocol.

[109] This Art. falls far short of conferring upon workers on maternity leave a right to full pay and in fact in many ways reintroduces at a legislative level the 'sick man' comparison.

[110] Prot. Concerning Art. 119 of the Treaty Establishing the European Community.

[111] Case C–109/91 *Ten Oever* [1993] ECR I–4879.

Also left in doubt by the *Barber* decision were the types of scheme covered by the ruling, its impact on the Court's earlier decision in *Bilka-Kaufhaus*, the conditions under which retrospective access claims could be admitted in the national courts,[112] the position of survivors' benefits and of additional voluntary contributions, the legality of the use of actuarial factors in calculating pension contributions or benefits, the question of levelling up or levelling down, and the legal position of scheme trustees. It was a formidable list of unresolved issues which *Barber* generated. Although Cases C–109/91, *Ten Oever*;[113] C–110/91, *Moroni*;[114] C–152/91, *Neath*;[115] C–200/91, *Coloroll*;[116] C–128/93, *Fisscher*;[117] C–408/92, *Smith*;[118] C–28/93, *Van den Akker*;[119] C–7/93 *Beune*;[120] and C–57/93, *Vroege*[121] eventually provided answers to most, though by no means all, of these question, litigants paid a high price for the information. One may wonder whether this was not a classic situation for the rounded legislative approach rather than case-by-case determination.

On the other hand, supporters of the Court could say that in *Barber* the Court, far from upsetting a legislative solution which the Member States had arrived at, was rather dealing with their refusal to address legislatively a clearly established legal problem. As early as the Court's decision in *Defrenne I*[122] it had indicated, at least by way of negative implication, that occupational pension benefits were within the scope of Article 119[123] and its decision in May 1986 in *Bilka-Kaufhaus*[124] reinforced, positively, that negative conclusion. Yet Directive 86/387 of July 1986 persisted in treating the matter of equality in pension ages as if it was within national discretion. Moreover, the Commission's proposals of October 1987 for a directive

---

[112] See n. 78 above.

[113] [1993] ECR I–4879.

[114] [1993] ECR I–6591.

[115] [1993] ECR I–6935.

[116] [1994] ECR I–4389.

[117] [1994] ECR I–4583. In this case the ECJ held, *inter alia*, that part-timers wrongly excluded from access to pension schemes in the past should be entitled to retrospective admission only on payment of the contributions which they would have paid had they always been members. The need to find a large lump-sum has an obvious chilling effect upon the practical chances of past discrimination being effectively redressed. An attractive solution would have been to give the wrongly excluded part-timers the option to take a reduced pension (based upon what the employer should have contributed) without making up the past contributions. Surprisingly, this is what the UK Government proposed (see the Opinion of Van Gerven A.G. at para. 29) but the ECJ seems to have taken a stricter line: judgment at para. 37.

[118] [1994] ECR I–4435.

[119] [1994] ECR I–4527.

[120] [1994] ECR I–4471.

[121] [1994] ECR I–4541.

[122] Case 80/70 [1971] ECR 445.

[123] The ECJ said: 'Although consideration in the nature of social security benefits is not therefore in principle alien to the concept of pay, there cannot be brought within this concept . . . social security schemes or benefits, in particular retirement pensions, directly governed by legislation without any element of agreement within the undertaking or the occupational branch concerned, which are obligatorily applicable to general categories of workers.

[124] Case 170/84 [1986] ECR 1607.

'completing the implementation of the principle of equal treatment for men and women in statutory and occupational social security schemes', which would have required equal pension ages, remained unadopted.[125] Without the Court's intervention, clumsy though it was, inequality in pension ages would doubtless have persisted.[126]

This riposte, however, brings us to ask the question: how important was the elimination of the discrimination in pension ages? What was being attacked by Mr Barber was one of the few aspects of employment conditions which tend systematically to the advantage of women.[127] Securing access by men to that advantage was no doubt perfectly justifiable on the basis of a formal notion of equality,[128] but it did nothing to reduce the social disadvantage of women, which related to different aspects of pension provision altogether.[129] However, worse was to follow in the subsequent litigation. The end result is not that men have achieved the earlier retirement age of women but that, at least for the future, women will often find themselves governed by the higher retirement age of men. This is because in *Smith*[130] and *Akker*[131] the Court interpreted its previous jurisprudence on levelling-up, notably what it had said in *Defrenne II*, so as to confine it to situations where the employer or pension fund trustees had not taken explicit measures to eliminate the discriminatory measure, in this case, to equalize pension ages. Where such steps were taken, by contrast, that could be done, if the employer wished, on a levelling-down basis. Moreover, in that context any transitional measures to lessen the impact of this process on women would be unlawful.[132]

Of course, the decision of the employer to introduce uniform pension

---

[125] COM(87)494 final [1987] OJ C309–10, Art. 9.

[126] For a strong argument to this effect see D. Curtin, 'Scalping the Community Legislator: Occupational Pensions and "Barber" ' (1990) 27 *CMLRev.* 475.

[127] It is no more than a tendency. As with all pension issues, matters are not straightforward. In the UK until 1940 State pension ages were in fact equal and the introduction of a lower age for women tended to benefit retired men and non-working women but to act to the detriment of working women who were now often forced to retire at the new lower age when they would have preferred to continue in work: see Fredman, 'The Poverty of Equality: Pensions and the ECJ' (1996) 25 *ILJ*.

[128] Though one may wonder why the British Equal Opportunities Commission devoted such a large proportion of its scarce resources to supporting the litigation.

[129] Notably, of course, the greater chance of having spells out of paid employment or working only part-time.

[130] Case C–408/92 [1994] ECR I–4435.

[131] Case C–28/93 [1994] ECR I–4527.

[132] That levelling down was permitted by the ECJ should perhaps cause no surprise. It is what Art. 9 of the Commission's unadopted proposals would have allowed, and the ECJ has been much more receptive to levelling down in the application of the equality principle to the social security area. See Cases 126/86, *Zaera* [1988] ECR 8697 and 30/85 *Teuling* [1987] ECR 2487. Art. 9, however, would have permitted transitional arrangements to soften the blow to the disadvantaged group.

ages could not deprive men of their entitlement to equal treatment in the period before uniformity was introduced (nor, indeed, women of their pre-Barber advantages). However, the extent of that benefit to men was much reduced by the subsequent elucidation of the meaning of the prospective effect limitation. *Ten Oever, Smith,* and *Akker* together created a situation in which employers had the greatest possible incentive to move to formal uniform pension ages on a levelling-down basis i.e. by increasing the retirement age of women. So, when all the argument and excitement have subsided, the situation on pension ages can be seen to have changed very little for the benefit of men and a good deal to the detriment of women. Most men will benefit from lower retirement ages only in respect of pension benefits earned during the period from 17 May 1990 (the date of the *Barber* decision) until such time as the employer implements an equalization plan, which it is free to do on a levelling-down basis. At that point, if the employer chooses a levelling-down solution, the men will lose the advantage which the *Barber* case had brought them and the women will become worse off than they were before. So the likely end result of the litigation is that, for the future, the previously advantaged group (women) will have lost that advantage and the previously disadvantaged group (men) will continue to suffer the disadvantage. Paradoxically, the beneficiaries of the litigation may well turn out to be the employers, who have been presented with an opportunity to reduce their pension costs.

4. *Judicial Deference to the Member States*

Why should the Court have allowed the pensions litigation to produce such a sorry result? In part, the answer would seem to be that the Court is committed to a rather formal concept of equality and has lost sight of the social purpose behind the legislation. From a perspective of formal equality, provided men and women are treated equally, the fact that a decision may do nothing to redress the disadvantages suffered by women or, indeed, may reinforce them is not to be regarded as a criticism of the decision. Even when the Court was in the hey-day of its development of the Community equality legislation, such a tendency could already be indentified[133] and its recent decision in *Kalanke*[134] suggests that it is an inhibition which it has not subsequently overcome. In this case the Court held contrary to Community

---

[133] See S. Fredman, 'European Community Discrimination Law: A Critique' (1992) 21 *ILJ* 119. See also *Bilka-Kaufhaus,* n. 98 above, at paras. 38 ff., refusing to accept the argument, put forward in this case under the more difficult heading of Art. 119, that the employer was obliged to organize the pension scheme so as 'to take into account the fact that family responsibilities prevent women workers from fulfilling the requirements for such a pension'.

[134] Case C–450/93 [1995] ECR I–3051. The form of positive discrimination employed in the national legislation at issue was the 'tie-break': if all other factors were equal as between a female and a male candidate, the former was to be preferred. It has to be said, however, that the principle was implemented in a rather unsophisticated way in the case in question.

law a German national provision containing a mild form of positive discrimination in favour of women.

With this tendency towards formal equality already embedded in its
psyche there was clearly a risk that the Court would adopt a levelling-down
solution in the pensions cases. It is suggested, however, that there was more
to it than the attachment of the Court to a limited view of the nature of
equality. It is also suggested that there was more involved than the Court
suddenly taking fright at the large sums of money which would have been
required to be provided by employers in order to remedy the wrongs which
would have been produced by the more far-reaching interpretations of
Barber. Behind the headlines about the amounts of money involved was the
fact that, as became clear in the welter of post-*Barber* litigation, the Court
had put itself in a position where litigants were asking it to assume the
burden of determining the structure of an important area of social policy.
Not only might the Court have had doubts about its competence to do this
in the light of the mess which it had made of the prospective effect ruling in
Barber, but the litigation raised the question whether the Court was prepared to engage in wholesale overruling of the solutions which the Member
States had arrived at in Directive 86/378.

In *Barber* the Court may have thought it was doing no more than pushing
the Member States down the road towards equal pension ages along which,
in principle, they had already agreed to travel. If so, the flood of subsequent
litigation would quickly have disabused it and revealed that more was at
stake. The Court, it soon became clear, was in danger of becoming the
designer of the details of the national solutions. The inappropriateness of
that result was suggested not only by the turmoil into which the pension
industry was thrown in many Member States, not only by the reaffirmation
by the Member States of their interest in this area in the 'Barber' protocol of
the Maastricht Treaty, but also, and perhaps most important, by the introduction of the notion of 'subsidiarity' into that Treaty. Although formulated
in Article 3b of the Rome Treaty in terms of the Community's legislative
process, there is no doubt that the discontentments which found expression
in this new Article were in significant part engendered by the previous
decisions of the European Court of Justice.

The Court may well have thought that pensions were a bad topic to have
got into just before the emergence of this new principle for governing
relations between the Community and the Member States. It was highly
complex and so difficult to resolve speedily on a case-by-case basis and it
was politically sensitive within the Member States. So the backtracking
began: not just endorsement of the *Barber* protocol and the adoption of
levelling-down (though those were the most important decisions) but also
the preservation of national time limits to govern the domestic litigation,
the silence on the use of actuarial factors in defined-contribution schemes

and the express permission to use them in the calculation of employers' contributions to defined-benefit schemes, and the decisions to accept discriminatory treatment in relation to bridging pensions and additional voluntary contributions.[135]

The limited nature of the reforms arising out of this extensive litigation is perhaps best illustrated by looking at the Commission's revised proposals for amending Directive 86/387,[136] which are avowedly based on the Court's recent case law and which replace the earlier proposals of 1987. A comparison of the second set of proposals with Directive 86/387 shows how little of the 1986 Directive needs to be changed as a result of the recent cases, apart from the removal (from the date of the *Barber* judgment) of the derogation in respect of equal pension ages. Indeed, most of the changes which are proposed will operate to the detriment of workers, for example, the express acceptance of national time limits for the bringing of litigation and the clear statement that sex-based actuarial factors are acceptable outside the area of employee contributions to and benefits from defined-benefit pension schemes. In particular, the Commission's acceptance and, by implication its view that the Court has accepted, that benefits from defined-contribution schemes can vary as between men and women (to the detriment of the latter) on the basis of actuarial calculations that, in general, women live longer than men, is a major missed opportunity, given the incentives operating in at least some Member States for employers to move away from defined benefit to defined contribution schemes. It has never been satisfactorily explained why this actuarial fact is permitted to be used in the calculation of differential annuities when other, equally well-established, actuarial risks, such as occupation or smoking, are often simply pooled within the pension scheme or among the annuitants. It is a great pity that the Court did not grasp this issue since it was one of the few new issues litigated from which women stood to gain from the application of the equality principle.

One may conclude that a combination of deference to the Member States and a limited view of the reach of the equality principle led the Court into an unsatisfactory overall result in the pension cases. The position of women would have been better served if either the Court had decided in *Barber* to leave the question of pension ages entirely to the Member States or, if, having entered the fray, it had been prepared to play a bolder and more extensive role in advancing equality in pensions.

---

[135] For an excellent short review of the state of play see M. Tether, 'Sex Equality and Occupational Pension Schemes' (1995) 24 *ILJ* 194.

[136] Set out in (1995) *European Industrial Relations Review* No. 258 at 26.

V. Conclusion

At the beginning of this Chapter we noted that the view that the activism of British judges in the labour law area seemed often to have been animated by the individualistic property-based values of the common law. Hence the reservations of many British labour lawyers towards activism on the part of domestic judges. The activism of the judges of the European Court of Justice has clearly been driven by a very different set of concerns, which relate to the need to ensure the effectiveness of Community law, both substantively and procedurally, and to develop a Community doctrine of fundamental rights. Should labour lawyers be more positively disposed towards activism of the latter kind? Is effective Community law and a developed doctrine of fundamental rights at Community level necessarily conducive to the achievement of the goals of a progressive labour law?

Provided the policies embodied in the Community norms are acceptable, labour lawyers should welcome the effective implementation and enforcement of Community law within national legal systems. Indeed, British labour lawyers have tended to be unsympathetic about the Court's scruples *vis-à-vis* national judiciaries and, for example, have urged it on, though unsuccessfully, to abandon the division between the horizontal and vertical direct effect of directives.[137] Certainly, both the substantive and the procedural equality law of the Member States has been immeasurably strengthened by the ability of litigants to sue directly on the Community rules within national courts.

Yet, *Commission* v. *UK* suggests that a certain caution on the part of labour lawyers in giving a positive assessment to the activism of the Court may be appropriate where Community law occupies only a small part of the relevant area of law. There, insistence upon the 'full' implementation of Community law by a Member State may lead to a situation where partial but effective consultation via trade union representatives is replaced by comprehensive but rather ineffective consultation with *ad hoc* elected representatives. Of course, the Court may have viewed itself as simply supplementing the system of representation via collective bargaining with one based on elected employee representatives and it may be said that the potential for replacement of the former by the latter was the consequence of the Member State's particular reaction to the judgments. Was that not, however, a reaction which the Court should have foreseen? Would it not have displayed greater wisdom on the part of the Court in terms of the effectiveness of the consultation process if it had rather insisted upon the trade union as the only appropriate channel of communication in the British

---

[137] B. Fitzpatrick and E. Szyszczak, 'Remedies and Effective Judicial Protection in Community Law' (1994) 57 *MLR* 434.

system and perhaps even coupled this with a Community obligation to consult well-supported but unrecognized trade unions? These different policies might be said to represent a choice between a commitment to freedom of association, not yet a fully recognized principle of Community law, and simply ensuring that the Member States abide by the letter of a rather limited view of Community law.

A rather similar problem for the Court, that is, of its not controlling all the appropriate levers of power in a particular context, arises, too, where the Court's seeming aim, and certainly the impact of its judgments, is to stimulate the Community legislative process. As we saw above, the Court played this game with some skill in the maternity area—or, at any rate, one can say that things have not turned out too badly, despite the doctrinal confusion which has been generated. But in relation to uniform pension ages it is difficult to believe that the members of the Court can derive any real satisfaction from the outcomes of the cases. No fundamental right of women has been vindicated, simply the formal equality of the sexes, and that at a lower level of protection. Despite the formidable range of legal tools at its disposal in the equality area, the Court has not felt able to mount an effective challenge to the view, shared by most of the Member States, that the overriding policy issue in this area is the control of the costs to employers and, indirectly, the State[138] of providing pensions.

Is it even the case that the Court wanted to do better by the notion of equality but felt it politic, with an Intergovernmental Conference approaching, not to antagonize the Member States and the powerful pension lobby? We have seen that there is some evidence that, in fact, the Court's conception of equality is partly flawed. In other words, the welcome to be given by labour lawyers to the doctrines of direct effect, indirect effect, and State liability is very much conditional on the qualification made above: 'provided the policies embodied in the Community norms are acceptable'. One may imagine that labour lawyers will have a very different reaction to the effective enforcement of Community norms which cut across the goals of labour law. The supremacy of Community law may become less acceptable if Community equality law is seen to be less progressive than the national law which it supplants.[139] The Court's record in handling affirmative or positive action has not been impressive. In *Hofmann*[140] it permitted women-specific legislation which stereotyped the role of mothers *vis-à-vis* children, while in *Kalanke*[141] it refused to allow a mild job preference scheme, aimed

---

[138] A similar solicitude, this time for state pension costs, is to be found in the decisions of the ECJ permitting the exclusion of part-time employees, working fewer than 15 hours per week, from old-age pension schemes: Cases C–317/93, *Nolte* [1995] ECR I–4624 and C–444/93, *Megner and Scheffel* [1995] ECR I–4741.

[139] Of course, this was an aspect, too, of the Sunday Trading cases. See n. 7 above.

[140] Case 184/83 [1984] ECR 3047.

[141] N. 134 above.

at remedying past discrimination. In the latter case the question was not even whether Community law required affirmative action but whether that was permitted to the Member States. The Court abandoned a minimum-standards approach and may have cut off experimentation with affirmative action at Member State level.[142]

Given the limited purchase of Community law in the general area of labour law, at least in the pre-Maastricht period, it is of course unrealistic to chide the Court with not having developed an overall vision of Community social policy. Rather, the Court's focus on the development of an effective Community law has served the limited areas of labour law which have fallen within the purview of the Court well enough—with one or two notable exceptions mentioned in the previous paragraphs. However, if the Social Agreement manages to make the transition from being a mechanism for legislation over a broad front of labour law to the actual production of such law, then the Court may find itself under increasing pressure to develop a vision of Community labour law which is distinct from and additional to its vision of how the national legal systems incorporate and give effect to Community rules. It cannot be said that we yet have a clear view of how the Court will go about that task.

[142] Of course, something may yet be salvaged from the *Kalanke* debacle: it cannot be said that the ECJ is incapable of learning from its mistakes.

6

The European Court of Justice and the External Competences of the Community

FEDERICO MANCINI

In the autumn of 1994, when the European Court of Justice was called upon to give its Opinion on the Agreement establishing the World Trade Organization,[1] the procedure taking place in Luxembourg attracted much attention from the international public. The long-awaited outcome of the Uruguay Round negotiations was finally at hand and the opinion of the Court was one of the last hurdles before the entry into force of the Agreement.

Now, nearly two years on, the perspective is quite different: the Opinion of the Court enabled the Member States to ratify the WTO Agreement along with the European Community itself,[2] according to the formula of so-called mixed agreements. Against all odds the Agreement came into force on schedule, on 1 January 1995, and the World Trade Organization is now operating.

The main value of scrutinizing the Opinion at this later stage lies in gaining an understanding of the latest developments of the case law concerning the treaty-making power of the European Community and in analysing its consequences for the conduct of the external economic relations of the European Union. Therefore, I shall first try to summarize the Opinion and

---

[1] Opinion 1/94 of 15 November 1994 [1994] ECR I–5267. Among the comments published to date now see: Josiane Auvret-Finck, (1995) 31 *Revue trimestrielle de droit européen* 322; Rainer M. Bierwagen, 'Introductory Note' (1955) 34 *ILM* 683; Jacques H. J. Bourgeois, 'The EC in the WTO and Advisory Opinion 1/94—an Echternach procession' (1995) 32 *CMLRev.* 763; Jacques H. J. Bourgeois, 'L'avis de la Cour de justice des Communautés européennes à propos de l'Uruguay Round: un avis mitigé' (1994) 4 *Revue du marché unique européen* 11; Vlad Constantinesco (1995) 122 *Journal du droit international* 412; Jacqueline Dutheil de la Rochère, 'L'ère des compétences partagées. A propos de l'étendue des compétences extérieures de la Communauté européenne' (1955) 38 *Revue du marché Commun* 461; Karl Stefan Eisermann, 'Die Luftfahrtaußenkompetenz der Gemeinschaft' (1995) 6 *Europäische Zeitschrift für Wirtschaftsrecht* 331; Meinhard Hilf, 'EG-Außenkompetenzen in Grenzen—Das Gutachten des EuGH zur Welthandelsorganisation' (1995) 6 *Europäische Zeitschrift für Wirtschaftsrecht* 7–8; Meinhard Hilf, 'The ECJ's Opinion 1/94 on the WTO—No Surprise, but Wise?' (1995) 6 *European Journal of International Law* 245; Denys Simon, 'La compétence des Communautés pour conclure l'accord OMC: l'avis 1/94 de la Cour de justice' (1994) 4 *Europe*, Dec., 1–3.

[2] The WTO Agreement was concluded by Council Dec. 94/800/EC of 22 Dec. 1994 ([1994] OJ L336/1).

make some comments on it, while respecting the duty of discretion incumbent upon a judge. I shall then endeavour to illustrate its implications—indeed, the complications it has brought about for the representation of the Community within the WTO and other international fora. Finally, I should like to examine the advisability of amending the EC Treaty and putting into effect interim arrangements in order to overcome those difficulties and to ensure consistency in the conduct of the Community's external economic policy.

First of all, let us recall why the Court was asked to rule on the WTO Agreement. The Opinion procedure is just one more peculiarity of the Community decision-making process. According to Article 228 of the EC Treaty, the Council, the Commission, or a Member State may apply to the Court for a prior opinion on whether the envisaged conclusion of an international agreement by the Community is compatible with the provisions of the Treaty. If the Court considers that the proposed agreement is incompatible with the Treaty, it may come into force only pursuant to an amendment of the Treaty. Moreover, the Court has consistently held that its opinion may be sought on questions concerning the division between Member States and the Community of competence to conclude an international agreement.[3]

This was indeed what happened in the WTO case: the Court was not asked to decide whether this instrument was compatible with the EC Treaty —which was not in dispute—but rather to establish whether the Community's competence to conclude the Agreement was exclusive or merely concurrent with the powers of the Member States. If the former were found to be the case, the Community would conclude the WTO Agreement alone; otherwise, this instrument would have to be ratified by both the Community and its Member States according to the formula of so-called mixed agreements. In this connection, it may be recalled that, throughout the negotiating process, a Community procedure had been applied whereby the Commission acted as the sole negotiator *vis-à-vis* third countries, with the assistance of a committee of representatives of Member States and on the basis of negotiation directives issued by the Council. Nevertheless, it had been agreed that both the Community and its Member States would become original members of the WTO. The Member States' participation in the new body was therefore not really at stake, but the Opinion of the Court would determine whether their membership would correspond to real powers or be no more than a formality.

Let us examine the legal situation before the WTO Opinion. According to well-established case law, the Community enjoys exclusive competence to enter into international agreements, in the first place, by virtue of the

---

[3] See also Art. 107(2) of the ECJ Rules of Procedure.

express provisions of Article 113 of the EC Treaty, which empowers the Council to act in the field of the common commercial policy.[4] Secondly, the Court has consistently held that the Community has implied powers to act in the international sphere whenever the Treaty has endowed it with power to act in the internal sphere (*in foro interno, in foro externo*). However, as a rule such a competence becomes exclusive only where the Community has first acted in the internal sphere, thus occupying the field (the so-called doctrine of pre-emption).

As regards the first aspect, the Court's approach in progressively defining the scope of the common commercial policy had been based on the assumption that this concept has an open nature and must cover the same content as in a national context.[5] Therefore, Article 113 had been construed in an evolutive manner, to encompass, beyond the traditional instruments of any regulation concerning trade in goods (tariffs and quantitative restrictions), any measures which become necessary by reason of changes in international trade and trade negotiations. Over the years the Court considered, for instance, that Article 113 could provide the basis for concluding international commodity agreements designed to stabilize trade by operating a buffer stock[6] or for adopting such measures as the system of generalized preferences,[7] which are at the borderline between trade and development aid.

The second aspect, namely the Community's implied powers to conclude international agreements, had been based on the so-called ERTA doctrine. In the eponymous judgment of 1971,[8] dealing with a draft agreement on a classic labour-law topic (the working time of lorry and bus drivers), the Court had said that

each time the Community . . . adopts provisions laying down common rules, whatever form these may take, the Member States no longer have the right, acting individually or even collectively, to undertake obligations with third countries which affect those rules. As and when such common rules come into being, the Community alone is in a position to assume and carry out contractual obligations towards third countries affecting the whole sphere of application of the Community legal system.

Six years later, in its Opinion 1/76[9] the Court held that, in some cases, an internal competence could provide the basis for an exclusive external competence even though it had not yet been exercised in the internal sphere.

---

[4] The exclusive nature of the competence deriving from Art. 113 has been consistently reaffirmed since the Court's judgment of 15 Dec. 1976 in Case 41/76 *Donckerwolcke* v. *Procureur de la République* [1976] ECR 1921.

[5] The landmark decisions in this respect are judgment of 12 July 1973 in Case 8/73 *Massey-Ferguson* [1973] ECR 897; Opinion 1/75 of 11 Nov. 1975 in the *Local Cost Standard Case* [1975] ECR 1355; Opinion 1/78 of 4 Oct. 1979 in the *Natural Rubber Case* [1979] ECR 2781.   [6] Opinion 1/78, quoted.

[7] Judgment of 26 Mar. 1987 in Case 45/86 *Commission* v. *Council* [1987] ECR 1493, otherwise known as the *ERTA* decision.

[8] Judgment of 31 Mar. 1971 in Case 22/70 *Commission* v. *Council* [1971] ECR 263.

[9] Opinion of 26 Apr. 1977 *in the Laying-up Fund of the Rhine Case* [1977] ECR 741.

Although these principles were laid down in cases concerning a common policy, namely transport policy, it would appear from later decisions[10] that they apply in any area of Community activity.

In particular, the Court has expressly recognized in Opinion 2/91 that the powers conferred upon the Community in the social policy area, which is of special interest for the scholar to whom this Chapter is dedicated, may provide a basis for its external competence. This competence, however, is not exclusive when the relevant internal rules are directives laying down the 'minimum requirements' mentioned in Article 118A(2), of the Treaty. In this case, the Member States remain empowered to enact measures designed to ensure a better protection of working conditions or to apply for this purpose the provisions of an international convention.[11] Conversely, if the international agreement deals with an area already covered to a large extent by Community rules based on other Treaty provisions such as Article 100 or 100A, which do not enable the Member States to maintain or introduce more stringent norms, the competence of the Community acquires an exclusive character.[12]

It should be noted that, according to the Court, the typical provisions of international labour conventions concerning the consultation of management and the trade unions may fall within the competence of either the Member States or the Community, depending on the objective pursued by such consultation.[13] Furthermore, in the specific case of the conventions drawn up under the auspices of the ILO—which the Community, not being a member of this organization, cannot itself conclude—the external competence of the Community may, if necessary, be exercised through the medium of the Member States acting jointly in its interest.[14] However, as early as 1986 the Council and the Commission devised a procedure applicable to the negotiation of ILO conventions in the areas falling within the exclusive competence of the Community, in full compliance with the tripartite consultation mechanisms provided for in Convention No. 144 concerning Tripartite Consultations to Promote the Implementation of International Labour Standards and with the autonomy of 'both sides of industry'.[15]

In spite of these significant factors, when the Court was asked to rule on the WTO Agreement, the extent to which the Community needs to have acted in order to acquire exclusive competence was not entirely clear; nor was it clear in what way the envisaged international agreement would have

---

[10] See judgment of 14 July 1976 in Joined Cases 3, 4, and 6/76, *Kramer* [1976] ECR 1279, and Opinion 2/91 of 19 Mar. 1993, *Re ILO Convention No. 170 on Safety in the Use of Chemicals at Work* [1993] ECR I–1061.

[11] Ibid., Para. 18. [12] Ibid., Paras. 22–6.

[13] Ibid., Para. 32. [14] Ibid., Para. 5 and Paras. 37–8.

[15] Council Dec. of 22 Dec. 1986, unpublished but mentioned in the introductory section of Opinion 2/91, I–1067. The convention was adopted on 21 June 1976 (1976) 59 *ILO Official Bull.* 83.

to affect common rules adopted by the Community in order for the Member States to be deprived of competence in the international sphere. There was also room for discussion about the exact scope of Opinion 1/76.

The Court had traditionally displayed remarkable ingenuity in both areas, by expanding the notion of common commercial policy and by defining the Community's implied powers on the basis of a substantially federal approach. However, in a changed institutional and political context, after the Maastricht conference had refused to amend Article 113 of the Treaty in order to establish a common policy on external economic relations, the Luxembourg judges—as I shall point out further—could no longer afford to strain the Community's external competences against the will of the constituent power.

The WTO Opinion is a complex and intricate judicial document. It builds on previous case law, construing it narrowly yet stopping short of contradicting or overruling it. Nevertheless, it fails to draw all the potential consequences from that case law for the WTO Agreement, especially in the new areas of international trade negotiations, i.e. trade in services falling under the GATS Agreement and the Agreement on so-called TRIPS, the Trade-related Aspects of Intellectual Property Rights.

One should certainly welcome the clear message coming from Luxembourg concerning trade in goods. Putting an end to a long-lasting debate, the Court ruled that the Community enjoys exclusive competence in this area under Article 113 of the EC Treaty, even though the agreement concerns *inter alia* ECSC, Euratom or agricultural products.[16] Moreover, the Community's powers cover the Agreement on Sanitary and Phytosanitary Measures as well as the Agreement on Technical Barriers to Trade.[17] Thus, the Court unambiguously rejected the contention that Article 113 could not confer on the Community powers to conclude an international agreement which requires internal measures to be adopted under a different legal base: this is an important point of principle, although the reasoning of the Court in the rest of the Opinion may appear somewhat contradictory in this respect.

The recognition that trade in services may, at least in principle, come within the common commercial policy is another positive aspect of the Opinion.[18] The Court realized that the tertiary sector has become a vital element of an advanced economy and that nowadays any major international trade negotiation inevitably deals with services. The interpretation of Article 113 must keep step with such a fundamental evolution, if the Community is to maintain substantial powers in the area of international trade.

The trouble with services, however, is that they come in many shapes and forms. The GATS Agreement identifies four modes of supply: (1) cross-frontier supply not involving any movement of persons (as when a

---

[16] Paras. 22–9. [17] Paras. 30–3. [18] Para. 41.

stockbroker advises a client in another country by electronic mail); (2) consumption abroad (as when a tourist travels to another country, sleeps in a hotel there, eats in restaurants, and so forth); (3) commercial presence (meaning that a branch or subsidiary is established in another country); and (4) the presence of natural persons, whether employees or self-employed workers, in a country other than their homeland (as when a plumber is sent across the frontier in order to unblock someone's U-bend or a lawyer goes in order to earn even larger fees than he would at home). These distinctions were to prove extremely appealing to a cautious Court, anxious to hammer out carefully balanced, if not (as some commentators have pointed out) entirely convincing, compromises.

The Luxembourg judges noted that cross-frontier supplies not involving the movement of persons are very much akin to trade in goods. Therefore, there was no particular reason why they should not fall within the concept of the common commercial policy.[19] The Court declined to reach the same conclusion for the other modes of supply, the reason being that they involve movements of nationals of third countries, which are covered —it said—by separate provisions of the EC Treaty.[20]

Now, the accuracy of this statement may be questioned. First of all, the Annex on Movement of Natural Persons supplying Services under the Agreement expressly states that the GATS Agreement 'shall not prevent a Member from applying measures to regulate the entry of natural persons into, or their temporary stay in, its territory, including those measures necessary to protect the integrity of, and to ensure the orderly movement of natural persons across, its borders'. Secondly, the only provision of the EC Treaty dealing with such topics is Article 100c, the scope of which is limited to certain aspects of the visa policy. Moreover, we have seen that an argument of the same kind had just been rejected in the section of the same Opinion concerning trade in goods: the Community competence under Article 113 to conclude an international agreement is independent—the Court had said—of the legal base to be chosen for its implementation in the internal sphere. Lastly, the Court disregarded the fact that the establishment of a company incorporated in a third country may take place without the movement of nationals of the third country.

The other remark made by the Court in this context—that the existence in the Treaty of specific chapters on the free movement of natural and legal persons shows that those matters do not fall within the common commercial policy—has been found even harder to swallow in certain quarters, since those chapters concern only the situation of Community nationals in another Member State and have nothing to do with trade relations with third countries.

As far as transport services are concerned, the Opinion made clear that

[19] Para. 44.   [20] Paras. 45–7.

they do not fall under Article 113 since they are covered by a specific title on the common transport policy.[21] Again, this reasoning may not seem entirely consistent with the Court's findings concerning trade in goods and it certainly relies on a narrow reading of the *ERTA* judgment. The Court also examined a number of embargoes based on Article 113 and involving the suspension of transport services, which had been invoked by the Commission, but considered that they were not relevant precedents since the suspension of transport services was a mere adjunct to a principal embargo on products. Strangely enough, the Court forgot to mention a 1992 embargo against Libya regarding air transport only.[22]

The Court went on to hold that the Community could not claim exclusive competence under Article 113 concerning TRIPS.[23] Notwithstanding a clear connection between intellectual property rights and trade in goods, the former do not relate specifically to international trade and affect just as much internal trade. Once again, it has been objected that the same could be said of technical barriers, which the Court itself recognizes as belonging to the field of the common commercial policy.[24] However, according to the Court, only the prohibition on importing counterfeit goods falls within the scope of the common commercial policy.

The Opinion then examined whether a Community exclusive competence concerning services and TRIPS flowed from its internal powers, according to the principles established in the *ERTA* judgment or in Opinion 1/76. Without going into detail, let us say simply that Opinion 1/76 is construed narrowly: the possibility for the Community to claim an exclusive external competence even when a corresponding internal power has not yet been exercised is restricted to those exceptional cases where internal measures will not be effective.[25] On the other hand, as far as the *ERTA* judgment is concerned, I do not share the view put forward by certain commentators that the WTO Opinion represents a step back.[26] Admittedly, the Court requires that the Community must have achieved harmonization internally in order to enjoy exclusive external competence to conclude an international agreement which might affect these internal rules;[27] but the extent of such harmonization and the degree to which the common rules need to be affected have not changed, as the Court made clear some months later, in its Opinion concerning the OECD decision on national treatment.[28] Moreover,

---

[21] Para. 48.   [22] Council Reg. (EEC) 945/92, of 14 Apr. 1992 [1992] OJ L101/53.
[23] Paras. 55-71.
[24] See Auvret-Finck, n. 1 above, 329.   [25] Paras. 84–6.
[26] See Auvret-Finck, n. 1 above, 333; Bourgeois, 'The EC in the WTO', n. 1 above, 781; Constantinesco, n. 1 above, 417; Dutheil de la Rochère, 'L'ère des compétences partagées', n. 1 above, 466-469; Simon, "La compétence des Communautés", n. 1 above, 2–3.
[27] Paras. 95–6.
[28] Opinion 1/92 of 24 Mar. 1995, *Re OECD Decision on National Treatment* [1995] ECR I–521, para. 33.

it is accepted that internal legislative acts containing provisions on the treatment of third country nationals or expressly conferring on the institutions powers to negotiate with third countries may also provide the basis for exclusive external competence.

In practice, the conclusion is that the Community's exclusive competence based on implied powers covers only certain areas of the GATS and TRIPS Agreements, which means that the WTO Agreement must be concluded as a mixed agreement by both the Community and the Member States. But the extensive Community legislation concerning services, and particularly such sectors as transport services, implies that large parts of GATS fall within Community competence. In relation to TRIPS, the obvious inference is that, since no harmonization measures have been adopted in areas such as patents, industrial models, and undisclosed technical information, they therefore remain outside the Community's exclusive external competence. I would nevertheless like to point out that the Court vigorously rejected the contention that certain aspects of the enforcement of intellectual property rights are within a domain reserved to the Member States.[29]

Lastly, the Court decided to broach a subject on which its opinion had not been expressly sought, namely the duty of co-operation between Member States and the Community institutions to ensure unity of action *vis-à-vis* the rest of the world in the implementation of the WTO Agreement.[30] This circumstance alone shows that the judges were deeply concerned about the practical consequences of their ruling, both for the Community and for the functioning of the WTO Agreement: indeed, a paralysed European Community would be a fatal blow to the WTO itself. Moreover, co-ordination between the Community and the Member States in their respective fields of competence is of vital importance, all the more so by reason of the mechanism of cross-retaliation provided for in the Agreement. It must be conceded, however, that the Opinion does not go beyond a statement of principle, which may not prove very useful for the administration of the Agreement in Geneva.

This final section of the Opinion shows that the Court perceived the major difficulties inherent in the 'mixed agreement' formula: not only the WTO Agreement but any major trade arrangement—inevitably including trade in services—will require, from now on, sixteen ratifications (fifteen Member States and the Community) and endless discussions to determine who has jurisdiction on any particular point. Why, then, did the Court not accept that the Community's competence must be interpreted broadly from the start? The current political context doubtless played some part in the Court's restraint: judicial power cannot always make up for lack of vision on the part of the political actors, especially when such action would meet

---

[29] Para. 104.   [30] Paras. 106–9.

with strong opposition in some quarters. Experience shows that the Member States have always been more open and clear-sighted in designing general constitutional solutions at the highest political level than in the day-to-day administration of specific areas, which is generally left to the egoism of national bureaucracies, whose major concern is to maintain their own prerogatives. Now, the proposal to amend Article 113 to establish a common policy on external economic relations was not rejected by some obscure civil servant but by the Heads of State and Government meeting at Maastricht.[31]

The forthcoming Intergovernmental Conference (IGC) provides a fresh opportunity for reflection and action. With the motto 'less action, but better action' President Jacques Santer was certainly expressing a widely held view regarding the role of the Community: its institutions should focus on those matters where their intervention is most useful, or even indispensable. Rather than expand token Community competences in such marginal areas as culture or civil protection, where the institutions may produce little more than meetings of experts in Brussels and badly translated brochures, the crucial need is to deepen integration by strengthening the core of Community policies and by ensuring that the Community can cope with new challenges through an effective decision-making mechanism.

If this view is correct, there can be little doubt that, by any standard of subsidiarity, economic relations with third countries are better dealt with at Community than at national level. Two centuries ago, James Madison observed that what he called intercourse with foreign nations 'forms an obvious and essential branch of the federal administration. If we are to be one nation in any respect, it clearly ought to be in respect to other nations'.[32]

Madison's remark is just as relevant today—even to the opponents of a European federal supernation. It is understandable that the introduction of majority voting in the field of the common foreign and security policy—which will be one of the main items on the agenda of the IGC—may be seen as depriving the Member States of essential sovereign powers. But this kind of objection should not apply to external economic relations, since their traditional aspects have been conducted jointly for nearly three decades. Any reform extending the scope of the common commercial policy would merely reflect the changing nature of our economies.

From this point of view, it is clearly necessary that the European Union should speak with one voice in all international trade negotiations and in those fora where such negotiations are held—WTO, OECD, UNCTAD, FAO. Its action would gain in effectiveness, partly because our trading

[31] On the 'minimalist' philosophy which seems to guide the Court since the ratification of the Maastricht Treaty see G. F. Mancini and D. T. Keeling, 'Language, Culture and Politics in the Life of the European Court of Justice', to be published shortly in the *Columbia Journal of European Law*.

[32] *The Federalist Papers* (1788) No. 42.

partners need to know who is competent to negotiate without having to listen to lengthy lectures on European law. Moreover, I am inclined to believe that they would prefer to have one interlocutor rather than fifteen or, tomorrow, twenty-five, each of them endowed with a power of veto.

On the other hand, European public opinion is, I venture to say, more likely to accept a transfer of competences in particular areas where joint action is clearly desirable for everyone's sake—the establishment of a single market is the most recent example—than sporadic and confused interventions in matters of local interest. People may question why the Community should issue eco-labels for environmentally friendly dish-washers, but it seems unlikely that anybody will demonstrate to defend the power of a national transport ministry to negotiate an open skies agreement.

I am not naïve enough to believe that the coming IGC, based on a limited agenda, will set about overturning the general principles on the allocation of powers between the Community and its Member States. Nevertheless, the example of Maastricht should teach us some lessons. It would probably be wiser and more effective to apply the subsidiarity principle in earnest when defining Community competences, rather than pay lip service to it every time a new act is adopted. The institutions, endowed with clear-cut competences in essential areas, should then be in a position to carry out their tasks effectively.

The internal market is virtually complete, several Member States will be using a common currency in a few years' time—I still think—which means that the key elements of internal economic integration will soon be in place. Who would deny that its indispensable corollary is a true common policy on external economic relations, with simple procedures for taking all the essential decisions concerning international trade in goods and services in the Community context?[33]

In the meantime, pragmatic solutions must be found in order to limit and, if possible, overcome the disadvantages arising from mixed competences not only in the WTO framework, but also in other important fora such as FAO or the agreements with Central and Eastern European countries. I am afraid that Member States will not accept that the Community should exercise its virtual competences in order to fill the gaps in its exclusive competence, which would generally suffice to enable it to act alone: as regards the WTO, it appears from the Court's Opinion that not a single provision of the Agreement falls within a domain reserved to Member States. However, it could be possible to reach satisfactory solutions for

---

[33] In Pro. Constantinesco's words, *n*. 1 above, 'la vision des compétences respectives des Etats membres et de la Communauté que nous livre ici la Cour ne doit-elle pas aussi être comprise comme un message destiné précisément à ceux qui vont avoir la charge de réviser prochainement les traités? Sans un renforcement des structures et des compétences communautaires dans ces domaines, comment l'Union, première puissance commerciale du monde, pourrait-elle être à la hauteur de ses responsabilités?'

conducting negotiations as well as for representing the European Union's interests within the relevant international organizations.

Much depends, of course, on the goodwill of the Member States. In some instances they have been prepared to step back when this has led to a better defence of their common interests and more effective negotiation—just as in the process leading to the conclusion of the WTO Agreement. But these are mere concessions, revocable at any time and bound to disappear whenever essential interests of a Member State are at stake.

The Council and the Commission are now working hard to frame an arrangement on the Community's participation in the activities of the WTO, and I fervently hope that they will be successful. Without knowing the details of the envisaged arrangement, I foresee three main difficulties. First, unless the Community procedure is generalized, any *modus vivendi* can apply only to mixed or national competences, since Community powers may be subject only to the procedures provided for by the Treaty. Therefore, a preliminary classification of competences is necessary—and we all know that it is still extremely difficult to determine the exact scope of the Community's jurisdiction in any particular case, notwithstanding the Court's Opinion. Secondly, if Member States insist on being able to present an individual position when no agreement is reached, Community discipline will be fatally flawed. Our WTO partners would be entitled to react to an individual action of a Member State by retaliating against the Community as a whole. Even the dutifully behaved would then be tempted to follow their own course in matters falling within their jurisdiction. Thirdly, our partners may become tired of our internal bickering and require us to spell out in advance who has jurisdiction and who is entitled to vote on any particular point of the agenda—the so-called FAO procedure. That would lead to lengthy debates before any meeting and would inevitably impair the effective representation of European interests.

The Court has recently been called upon again to adjudicate on these issues in a case concerning the so-called FAO procedure.[34]

The Commission had challenged the Council's decision giving Member States the right to vote within the Food and Agriculture Organization for the adoption of the Agreement to Promote Compliance with International Conservation and Management Measures by Fishing Vessels on the High Seas. Although not contesting that competence to conclude such an agreement was shared between the Community and its Member States, the Commission contended that the main thrust of the Agreement did not fall within the competence of the Member States. Therefore, in accordance with the relevant section of an Arrangement between the Council and the Commission regarding preparation for FAO meetings, statement and voting, the right to vote should have been exercised by the Community.

[34] Case C–25/94 *Commission* v. *Council*, 19 Mar. 1996.

In its judgment the Court first rejected the objections to admissibility raised by the Council and by the United Kingdom, holding that the Council's vote, far from being a matter of procedure or protocol, had legal effects in several respects. On the one hand, it affected the Community's rights which attached to its membership of the FAO and its position *vis-à-vis* third countries. On the other hand, it had an influence on the content of the Agreement as well as on competence to implement it and eventually to conclude subsequent agreements on the same questions.

On the substance of the case, the Court's reasoning was that the main thrust of the provision of the Agreement falls within the exclusive competence of the Community to adopt conservation measures within the framework of the common fishery policy—indeed, it does not appear from the judgment that Member States have any competence at all. Therefore, the Court concluded, by deciding that Member States were entitled to vote, the Council had violated the duty of co-operation between the Community and its Member States, the content of which, in this case, had been specified in the relevant section of the Arrangement between the Council and the Commission.

The Court's reasoning flows from the need for unity in the international representation of the Community. We can therefore assume that, even apart from any specific institutional arrangement, the Treaty itself imposes on the Member States and the Community institutions an obligation to co-operate —both in the process of negotiating an international agreement and in the fulfilment of the commitments which stem from it.

If this is the case, any dispute between the Community and the Member States concerning their respective competences within WTO and other international fora can be brought before the Court. Of course, it is not practically possible to seek a Court's ruling every time such a dispute arises in international negotiations. I would emphasize, however, that the very existence of a judicial control should lead the political actors to comply with the duty of cooperation set forth by the Court. A mere skeleton in the WTO opinion, this duty has taken on flesh and blood in the FAO judgment. The Court has shown that, when the political actors fail to ensure Community discipline, it is ready to call them to order.

7

Instruments of EC Labour Law

WOLFGANG DÄUBLER

I. Does Labour Law Have Specific Instruments?

As part of the legal order, national labour law appears to share the nature of other fields of the law: the observer will find some constitutional provisions, a number of acts, regulations and decrees—and a good deal of judge-made law, which may either be formally binding, as in Britain, or have a nearly equivalent effect, as on the Continent.

On the basis of a very narrow conception of the legal order, there is no difference from, say, company law and civil law, which have structures that are roughly the same as this. If, however, we take a broader approach and ask what are the labour law rules that are applied in practice, the perspective changes. First and foremost, we find collective agreements at various levels— some of them applicable to the entire economy, others to a particular sector or industry, and yet others just to a single enterprise or even shop floor. In continental Europe, these agreements contain legally binding rules; in Britain, they are incorporated into the contract of employment, which under normal circumstances makes for a comparable result. In some legal systems, for instance the Danish one, the scope of collective bargaining is so far-reaching that traditional fields of labour law, such as protection against dismissal, are covered exclusively by collective agreements. In all EC countries the State-imposed law is complemented by autonomous law.

Collective agreements, however, are not the only specific labour law instrument. In everyday life on the shop floor as well as at enterprise level, rules exist which are respected but whose legal status is uncertain; their only 'source' and legitimation stem from the behaviour of employer and em- ployees. Such rules may concern fringe benefits, trade union rights, or work performance; they may be the result of negotiation or imposed unilaterally. These informal rules make up an important part of working life even though lawyers tend to minimize their significance or ignore it completely. Here again, therefore, State-imposed law is complemented by special rules outside the range of State legislation, in terms of both form and substance. There is no guarantee that these informal rules will comply either with laws or with collective agreements.

To argue that all this makes labour law defective would, however, be misleading. The different levels of rule-making tailor it to particular conditions with a high degree of flexibility. At the same time, they mean that formal changes in the law may have a very limited effect: the social partners may react in a way that re-establishes the status quo; shop floor rules may continue as if there had been no new legislation. This is, of course, by no means an automatic reaction, because it depends on the relative strength of management and of trade unions and other workers' representatives. The point to bear in mind, however, is that the law does not always present a binding guideline for the real-life behaviour of employers and employees.

II. Sources of EC Labour Law

Rules created by the EC concerning employees are legal rules in the formal sense. They are comparable to statute law and judge-made law within a national context. The complements described in Section I are, however, absent: there are normally no European collective agreements that apply directly to individual employment relationships and there are no Europe-wide informal rules, although they are conceivable in multinational corporations. That does not mean, however, that European labour law has more direct impact than national law. The fifteen national systems, comprising their laws, collective agreements, and informal rules, may delay or block the implementation of European legislation. This is obvious when Member States fail to fulfil the duties deriving from the Treaty or certain directives, but it may occur with even greater effect in less obvious cases where collective bargaining or informal rules do not comply with EC rules. The instruments of EC labour law are thus very fragmentary; they may be able to add some elements to national systems, but they cannot replace national labour law—not even in a very circumscribed field like sex discrimination or acquired rights in the event of the transfer of enterprises. This situation could well change with the advent of European collective agreements, especially at the level of multinational enterprises, but as we shall see, we are still some distance from that at present.

The monopoly of 'State'-imposed rules in EC labour law has many causes that cannot be analysed in detail. One of them may be the weakness of the trade union movement at European level compared with the national level: as yet, there has not even been any co-ordination of national collective bargaining across different Community countries, although it would have required relatively little effort. That there are any labour law rules at all is due not so much to pressure from a well-organized labour movement as to the fact that the Community needs support from the populations of the Member States. There are political reasons for closing the legitimation gap created by the underdeveloped democratic structure of the EC.[1] The traditional argument in favour of international labour standards, namely, equalizing the conditions for competitors in the world market, seems to be of very limited importance. Except in the field of health protection, EC labour law does not provide for substantive standards like a five-week holiday entitlement or protection against dismissal, in acknowledgement of the differing level of labour costs in individual Member States. Basically, it guarantees rights of equality for such groups as migrant workers and women that do not interfere with the high degree of difference between protective rules in separate Member States.

The fact that the only labour law is that created by the EC institutions implies that the 'instruments' used are not of a specific nature: we find almost every kind of legal technique, as also applied in other fields such as free movement of goods or competition law within the EC. The only reason we do not refer in a general fashion to well-known treatises of EC law is that EC labour legislation is concentrated in certain instruments and more or less abjures others (albeit not entirely).

We shall start with primary EC law, including international treaties and agreements made by the EC (Section III below), and then move on to secondary EC law as described in Article 189 of the EC Treaty (Section IV). Some atypical instruments are discussed next (Section V), followed by the legal status of agreements between the social partners in accordance with Article 118b of the EC Treaty (Section VI). We shall conclude with some remarks about the future (Section VII). All instruments will be described, as well as the decisions of the Court of Justice that implement them.

III. Primary Community Law

1. EC Treaty and EU Treaty

The EC Treaty contains some labour law-related rules with highly differentiated degrees of abstraction.

(a) Global Social Aims

According to the second and third statements of intent in the Preamble to the EC Treaty, the Community is resolved to ensure not only economic but also social progress, which is to be reflected in a constant improvement of living and working conditions. Reference to this objective is also made in Article 2 as amended by the EU Treaty, which includes among the declared tasks of the Community the promotion of 'a high level of employment and of social protection'. In the Single European Act, this is supplemented by the mention

---

[1] For more details, see W. Däubler, *Market and Social Justice in the EC—the Other Side of the Internal Market* (Gütersloh, Bertelsmann 1991), 73.

in its Preamble of 'social justice' as an objective, and one that is placed in the context of the Member States' constitutions and of human rights as guaranteed by international law.[2] The Treaty on European Union also mentions in its Article B the objective 'to promote economic and social progress'.

These broadly worded statements yield very few concrete conclusions. Essentially, their only effect is a general obligation on the EC institutions not to ignore the attendant social consequences inherent in policies implemented in various fields. People who are fond of formulae may see in these provisions a ban on Manchesterism, but it is difficult to imagine a decision of the Court of Justice declaring a regulation or directive invalid as conflicting with Article 2 of the EC Treaty. The way in which social objectives should be pursued, and their relative value in comparison with other goals, are left open.

(b) Concrete Policy Objectives

In Article 117—one degree of abstraction lower—the EC Treaty advocates an independent social policy that is basically entrusted to the Member States. Despite its cautious wording,[3] Article 117(1) is not just a political declaration of intent but a legally binding commitment. This is manifested more clearly in the French version of the text, where the use of the word *conviennent* carries the implication of 'convention'. In terms of substance, the general objectives of the Treaty are specified not only by the stipulation of an independent social policy, but also by the provision that there should not simply be harmonization or approximation of living and working conditions; rather, this harmonization is to be achieved 'while the improvement is being maintained'. This means, in addition, that the Community not only has to intervene to compensate for potential distortions of competition due to differences in social costs, but also has a mandate for promoting social evolution even where this precondition is not present.

According to the Court of Justice, however, this mandate does not create concrete obligations for the Community or for the Member States. Even if Member States lower their labour standards in a very substantive way (in the actual case concerned, allowing third-world working conditions on ships

---

[2] The precise wording of the third statement of intent in the Preamble reads as follows: '[d]etermined to work together to promote democracy on the basis of fundamental rights recognized in the constitutions and laws of the Member States, in the Convention for the Protection of Human Rights and Fundamental Freedoms and the European Social Charter, notably freedom, equality and social justice'.

[3] Art. 117 reads:
'Member States agree upon the need to promote improved working conditions and an improved standard of living for workers, so as to make possible their harmonization while the improvement is being maintained.

They believe that such a development will ensue not only from the functioning of the common market, which will favour the harmonization of social systems, but also from the procedures provided for in this Treaty and from the approximation of provisions laid down by law, regulation or administrative action.'

sailing under their national flag), nobody can invoke Article 117 as a barrier against social retrogression: Article 117 has a binding effect only as a guideline for the interpretation of other Treaty provisions.[4] Social aspects have to be taken into account not only in the framework of an independent social policy, but also in the context of economic policy action. With reference to Article 2 of the Treaty, the binding force of provisions like Article 102a and Article103(1) is no greater than that described above. The same is true of Article 75(1) dealing with common transport policy and Article39(2)(a) dealing with agricultural policy.

(c) Clear-Cut Powers: Freedom of Movement for Workers, Equal Pay, and the European Social Fund

The freedom of movement for workers laid down in Articles 48-51 is one of the 'fundamental freedoms' of the Common Market: a single economic area necessarily implies labour mobility. In 1970, Article 48 of the Treaty became directly applicable law in all Member States.[5] Equal treatment of migrant workers, i.e. a labour law rule, can thus be derived directly from the EC Treaty.

Article 119 of the Treaty contains the principle that men and women should receive equal pay for equal work. As the Court of Justice decided in the second *Defrenne* case, this Article is binding not only on the Member States but on private parties as well, especially employers and employees.[6]

A third relatively concrete provision refers to the European Social Fund, whose task under Article 123 of the Treaty is 'to improve employment opportunities for workers in the internal market and to contribute thereby to raising the standard of living'. According to the provisions of the Single European Act, this Fund is one of the so-called structural funds that grant subsidies to promote, in particular, government intervention in regions with high unemployment or in favour of problem groups.[7]

(d) Enabling Provisions, especially the Agreement on Social Policy

The Single European Act added Article 118a to the Treaty to enable the Council to enact directives by qualified majority voting in the field of the 'working environment'. The Commission and the Council have restricted their own powers to health and safety matters, leaving aside such important topics as 'humanizing the world of work'.[8] The absence of other specific

---

[4] ECJ, *Europäische Zeitschrift für Wirtschaftsrecht* (Beck, Munchen 1993), 288, Sloman Neptun; see X. Lewis, 'The Employment of Foreign Seamen on Board Vessels of a Member State' (1993) 22 *Industrial Law Journal* 235.

[5] [1974] ECR 359 and 1337.   [6] [1976] ECR 455.

[7] For more details see [1993] OJ L93/5 and 39.

[8] It must, however, be noted that EC health and safety legislation is very important and has added a great many protective measures to current law in countries like Germany or Italy. The most important text is the so-called Framework Dir. ([1989] OJ L183/1), but the dirs. concerning the handling of heavy loads ([1990] OJ L156/9) and visual display units ([1990] L156/14) also merit mention.

labour law provisions in the Treaty made it necessary to have recourse to the provision on the approximation of laws (Article 100) or to the general clause of Article 235. Both routes were accepted by the European Court of Justice, but they require a unanimous decision by the Council. The power of veto thus given to every Member State was upheld by the Single European Act, because Article 100a(2) excluded from the new qualified majority rule all 'provisions relating to the rights and interests of employed persons'.[9]

In its decision on Maastricht, the German Constitutional Court heavily criticized the broad interpretation given to Article 235[10] and has stated that such ECJ decisions would have no binding effect on the Federal Republic's courts, administration, and Parliament. The impact of this quite unusual reasoning is, however, relatively minor in the field of labour law: the Maastricht Agreement on Social Policy between eleven Member States (excluding the United Kingdom) contains, in its Article 2, a list of specified fields where directives may be enacted.[11] Even though it may not exhaust the whole of labour law, the subject fields are as broad as 'working conditions', 'information and consultation of workers', and 'protection of workers where their employment contract is terminated'. The Agreement is based on the assumption that the UK veto has to be overcome without imposing any obligation on the United Kingdom; its objective is not to extend the scope of Community legislation to new fields. This means that the matters covered by the Agreement may be equally well treated within the framework of the Treaty itself in instances where the UK Government is in agreement.

2. Treaties with Third States

On the basis of Articles 228, 238, and other provisions of the Treaty,[12] the Community has concluded a considerable number of treaties and agreements with non-member countries. Some of these agreements deal with labour law matters, and the following merit mention:

(a) The Agreement on the European Economic Area, which came into force on 1 January 1994. It extends all the Treaty provisions mentioned above

[9] On the respective scope of Art. 118a and Art. 100a(2), see the differing positions of R. Blanpain, *Labour Law and Industrial Relations in the European Community* (Kluwer, Deventer, 1991), 146 and E. Vogel-Polsky, *L'Europe Sociale 1993: Illusion, Alibi ou Réalité?* (Editions de l'Université de Bruxelles, Brussels 1991), 129 ff.

[10] See M. Weiss, 'The German Federal Constitutional Court's Approach to Maastricht,' (1993) 9 *The International Journal of Comparative Labour Law and Industrial Relations* 351.

[11] For a critical evaluation, see M. Weiss, 'The Significance of Maastricht for European Community Social Policy' (1992) 8 *The International Journal of Comparative Labour Law and Industrial Relations* 3; B. Bercusson, (1994) 10 *Industrial Law Journal* 23; the conformity with fundamental structures of the EC is stressed by T. Schuster, 'Rechtsfragen der Maastrichter Vereinbarungen zur Sozialpolitik', *Europische Zeitschrift für Wirtschaftsrecht* (1992), 178.

[12] An overview of all relevant provision is given by G. Bermann, R. Goebel *et al.*, *Cases and Materials on European Community Law* (West Publishing, St. Paul/Minn., 1993), 891.

to the signatory States, thereby establishing, for instance, free movement of workers across the whole area covered by the Agreement.[13]

(b) The Association Agreement between the Community and Turkey contains a vague programme to establish free movement of workers. There is a Second Protocol, with wording close to that of Article 48 of the EC Treaty; it was, however, held not to be self-executing by the European Court of Justice.[14] On the other hand, there is a decision made by the Association Council that considerably improves the legal situation of Turkish workers within the Community.[15]

(c) The Co-operation Agreement between the Community and Morocco contains provisions giving equal rights to Moroccan workers living legally in one of the Member States. According to the Court of Justice, at least some of these provisions have direct effect and can be invoked in national courts.[16]

(d) According to the Court of Justice,[17] the Community is entitled to conclude ILO Conventions in accordance with its powers as granted by the EC Treaty. In cases of joint competence, Member States and the Community have to act together; where the subject matter falls within the exclusive scope of (primary or secondary) EC law, it lies with the EC institutions to negotiate, sign, and ratify such Conventions. To date, there have been no concrete examples—a fact that should not surprise anyone, given the practical difficulties: the EC is not a member of the ILO and cannot easily provide for the tripartite representation required by the statutes of the ILO.[18] It has to be added that following the Court's decision it remains unclear whether a jointly concluded convention is part of primary Community law or has a legal status *sui generis*.

3. Fundamental Rights

Are there any fundamental workers' rights in EC law such as freedom to organize? Rights of this kind have been one of the most important instruments in developing the legal field that we nowadays call labour law.

Like the two other Community Treaties, the EC Treaty does not include a separate list of fundamental rights. The reason originally given was that, unlike political organizations, a purely economic community does not perform any acts for which fundamental rights would be relevant. This reasoning reflects a peculiarly narrow perception of fundamental rights, restricting them

---

[13] Cf. O. Jacot-Guillarmod, *Accord EEE* (Schulthess, Zürich 1992).

[14] Case 12/86 *Meryem Demirel* v. *Stadt Schwäbisch Gmünd* [1987] ECR 3719.

[15] Case C–192/89 *S. Z. Sevince* v. *Staatssecretaris van Justitie* [1990] ECR I–3461.

[16] See Case C–18/90 *Office national de l'empoi* v. *Bahia Kziber* [1991] ECR I–199.

[17] Opinion 2/91 [1993] OJ C109.

[18] Cf. L. Betten, (1993) 9 *The International Journal of Comparative Labour Law and Industrial Relations* 244.

to guarantees of participation in politics and protection against unjust imprisonment, seizure, and other forms of State action. The 'freedoms' covered by the Treaty are basically confined to national treatment; they are rights of equality that ignore all other possible needs for protection.

Subsequent legal developments have likewise had little positive impact on this situation. The fact that all Member States have ratified the European Convention on Human Rights does not mean that the Convention is now an integral part of Community law. This would presuppose that the Member States agreed to being 'succeeded' in their legal status by the Community; such an attitude seems fictitious. It would also presuppose a change in the Convention itself, which admits nobody but individual sovereign States to membership. The Preamble to the Single European Act, which mentions not only the European Convention on Human Rights but also the European Social Charter, is generally not interpreted as having integrated these two conventions into Community law.

In keeping with the EC Treaty's 'blindness to fundamental rights', the Court of Justice at first refused to monitor Community measures for their compatibility with fundamental rights.[19] It was not until 1969, in the context of the *Stauder* case, that the Court ruled that the provision at issue did not contain any elements capable of 'jeopardizing the fundamental human rights enshrined in the general principles of Community law and protected by the Court'.[20]

In its 1970 *Internationale Handelsgesellschaft* decision, the Court of Justice emphasized once again that it was its task to ensure the observation of fundamental rights as part of the general principles of law.[21] How these fundamental rights could be identified was paraphrased as follows: they would have to be inspired by 'the constitutional traditions common to the Member States', but they would also have to fit in with the structure and objectives of the Community.[22]

In the 1974 *Nold* case this was underlined once again, based on the following reasoning:[23]

'It [the Court of Justice] cannot therefore uphold measures which are incompatible with fundamental rights recognized and protected by the Constitutions of those States. Similarly, international treaties for the protection of human rights on which the Member States have collaborated, or of which they are signatories, can supply guidelines which should be followed within the framework of Community law.'

[19] Case 1/58 *Friedrich Stork & Co. v. High Authority of the European Coal and Steel Community* [1959] ECR 17, 26; Joined cases 36, 37, 38 and 40/59 *Präsident Ruhrkohlenverkaufsgesellschaft mbH, Geitling Ruhrkohlen - Verkaufsgesellschaft mbH, Mausegatt Ruhrkohlen - Verkaufsgesellschaft mbH and J. Nold KG v. High Authority of the European Coal and Steel Community* [1960] ECR 423; Case 40/64 *Marcello Sgarlata and Others v. Commission of the EEC* [1965] ECR 215.
[20] Case 29/69 *Erich Stauder v. City of Ulm, Sozialamt* [1969] ECR 419, 425.
[21] Case 11/70 *Internationale Handelsgesellschaft mbH v. Einfuhr- und Vorratsstelle für Getreide und Futtermittel* [1970] ECR 1125, 1134.   [22] [1970] ECR 1134.
[23] Case 4/73 *J. Nold Kohlen - und Baustoffgroßhandlung v. Commission of the European Communities* [1974] ECR 491, 507.

This reference to international conventions was specified in subsequent decisions, in particular with regard to the European Convention on Human Rights. In the *Rutili* case, [24] for instance, measures taken by alien-registration authorities were assessed on the basis of Articles 8 to 11 of the European Convention on Human Rights, and the Court decided for the first time that the right to organize is part of Community law.

By and large, the Court's decisions deserve commendation, but significant deficiencies of protection remain. Is the collective autonomy of the social partners a general principle which EC legislation has to respect? Can fundamental rights be invoked against social powers provided that their exercise is regulated by EC law? What is the precise meaning of freedom to organize? Does it also include the right not to unionize? None of these questions can be answered with certainty from the existing decisions of the Court of Justice.

In addition to these 'intrinsic' points of criticism, there is also an objection to the basic assumptions of the model. Problems relating to fundamental rights have so far mainly arisen in the context of atypical Community actions, for instance with respect to bans on agricultural crops, Member States decrees based on Community law regarding migrant workers and particular decisions taken by the Community *vis-à-vis* specific companies or their employees. However, this still leaves typical Community action—the opening up of markets. Even if construction or transport companies are exposed to cut-throat competition, for example, it is not possible according to the current interpretation of fundamental rights to define the opening-up of markets as such as an infringement of fundamental rights, even though the disruption of workplaces and workers' lives may be as devastating as direct (and possibly illegal) State action. It will not be.possible to deal with the real problems of the Common Market and Monetary Union on the basis of a traditional list of fundamental rights. Instead, certain social and economic minimum standards need to be set, both at Community and at Member State level, in order to prevent or reduce labour cost competition, social dumping, evasion of legal provisions, and hardship generated by processes of restructuring.

To date, the Community has not yet created such a text. The 'Community Charter of the Fundamental and Social Rights of Workers', adopted by the Member States with the exception of the United Kingdom at the Strasbourg summit in December 1989, is a declaration of good intent without any direct binding effect. [25] It may become a guideline for the interpretation of EC labour law, but its political impact is much more important than its legal content.

IV. Secondary Community Law

Article 189 of the EC Treaty gives the Council and the Commission a series of specific instruments as a way of enacting legislative and quasi-legislative

---

[24] Case 36/75 *Roland Rutili* v. *Minister for the Interior* [1975] ECR 1219, 1232.
[25] The text can be found in: *Social Europe* 1/1990 and in G. Bermann *et al.*, *European Community Law, Selected Documents* (West Publishing, St. Paul/Minn., 1993), 661.

measures. These enactments constitute secondary EC law, the validity of which depends on compliance with the EC Treaty and other primary EC law sources. They comprise binding regulations, directives, and decisions and non-binding recommendations and opinions. In labour law, these various instruments have been used in quite specific ways. Relatively detailed directives are the most commonly used form of legislative intervention.

1. Regulations

According to Article 189(2) of the EC Treaty, a regulation shall have 'general application' and be 'binding in its entirety and directly applicable in all Member States'. This means that regulations can create rights and obligations for individuals comparable to acts of national parliaments.

Regulations play a certain but not decisive role in labour law. They have been issued in the fields of freedom of movement for workers[26] and social legislation relating to trans-frontier road transport.[27] To date, there has been no regulation in the field of equal treatment for men and women, although Article 235 of the Treaty, normally taken as the legal basis in this field, would enable the Council to enact a regulation. The proposed European Company Statute[28] is to be in the form of a regulation, but employee participation has been excluded and placed once more in a separate directive.

2. Directives

According to Article 189(3) of the EC Treaty, a directive shall be binding 'as to the result to be achieved', but shall 'leave to the national authorities the choice of form and methods'. The Member States are therefore to keep some decision-making power over implementation, and not to be confined to mere execution of the directive. The Treaty is silent on the subject of sanctions in the event of a Member State failing to fulfil its obligations under a directive; the only way of enforcing a directive seems to be the procedure in Article 169.

The reality is far removed from this legal pattern. In the field of labour law in particular, directives have been used to impose relatively specific obligations on the Member States that leave them almost no decision-making power. The directives on the approximation of laws relating to the principle of equal pay for men and women[29] and on the implementation of the principle of equal treatment for men and women as regards access to employment, vocational training and promotion, and working conditions[30] serve as ex-

---

[26]   The most important one is Council Reg. 1612/68 on freedom of movement for workers within the Community [1968] OJ L257/1.

[27]   Reg. 3820/85 [1985] OJ L370/1.

[28]   Cf. Leupold, *Die Europäische Aktiengesellschaft unter besonderer Berücksichtigung des deutschen Rechts. Chancen und Probleme auf dem Weg zu einer supranationalen Gesellschaftsform* (Aachen, 1993).

[29]   Dir. 75/117 [1975] OJ L45/19.

[30]   Dir. 76/207, [1976] OJ L39/40.

amples. The Court of Justice accepts this way of using directives, following its general inclination to strengthen the powers of the European institutions (while staying within the bounds of what still seems to be acceptable to the Member States).

To allow detailed rules was only a first step for the Court. If a Member State omits to comply with a directive after the 'adaptation period' normally allowed has expired, individuals are entitled to invoke the provisions of that directive in their relations with a Member State or other public authority: the State concerned may not, according to the Court, rely on its own failure to fulfil the obligations that a directive requires.[31] The only condition is that the provision in the directive concerned must be unconditional and precise enough to be applied without further State intervention. There is, however, no 'horizontal' effect in such instances: an employee cannot invoke a provision of the directive against his private employer. This would mean imposing obligations on the employer, a consequence deemed inappropriate by the Court of Justice.[32] The national judge is, however, obliged to interpret national law in conformity with the requirements of the directive, which in many cases may make for a similar effect.[33]

In certain situations, where a directive that is not self-executing has the purpose of attributing concrete rights to individuals, a non-complying Member State has been held liable in damages to citizens who would be better off if the directive had been implemented in due time. The most prominent case deals with a labour law matter. When Italy had failed to implement Directive 80/987 on the approximation of laws relating to the protection of employees in the event of their employer's insolvency,[34] three employees sued the Italian Republic for not having fulfilled its duty to create a guarantee institution that would have paid the employees' outstanding claims for the three months immediately preceding the bankruptcy judgment. On referral under Article 177 of the Treaty, the Court stated that Community law provides for damages in such a case.[35]

Viewed as a whole, directives have become increasingly similar to regulations. To cross the borderline between the two and enact regulations instead of directives would, however, be pointlessly to provoke at least some Member States: the fact of having no horizontal effect and of offering the Member States at least a symbolic power of decision makes directives politically more acceptable than regulations. Recent legislation (for instance, on European

---

[31] Case 148/78 *Pubblia Ministero* v. *Tullio Ratti* [1979] ECR 1629.

[32] Case 152/84 *M. H. Marshall* v. *Southampton and South-West Hampshire Area Health Authority (Teaching)* [1986] ECR 723; Case 80/86 *Criminal proceedings against Kolpinghuis Nijmegen BV* [1987] ECR 3969.

[33] Case 14/83 *Sabine von Colson and Elisabeth Kamann* v. *Land Nordrhein/Westfalen* [1984] ECR 1891; Case C–106/89 *Marleasing SA* v. *La Comercial Internacional de Alimentación SA* [1990] ECR I–4135.   [34] [1980] OJ L283/23.

[35] Joined cases C–6/90 and C–9/90 *Andrea Francovich e.a.* v. *Italian Republic* [1991] ECR 5357.

works councils[36] and data protection[37]) continues to follow this trend. Under the Maastricht Treaty it may even correspond to a legal obligation, since the principle of subsidiarity enshrined in Article 3b of the EC Treaty obliges the Community to restrict 'centralized' European rules to fields where Member State activity is insufficient to achieve the proposed objective. The dominant position of directives in social policy matters is underlined by Article 2 of the Maastricht Agreement on Social Policy, which provides for the enactment of directives, but not regulations or decisions.

3. Decisions

According to Article 189(4) of the EC Treaty a decision shall be 'binding in its entirety upon those to whom it is addressed'. If a decision is addressed to a Member State, citizens may invoke its provisions against the non-compliant State under the same conditions as directives[38]. In labour law, decisions play a minor role; to the best of my knowledge, they are used only when the Commission is granting money from the European Social Fund. A rather important exception, however, was the Commission's attempt to set up a communication and consultation procedure on migration policies in relation to third-State citizens by a decision based on Article 118 of the Treaty. The Court pronounced part of the decision void because the Commission was not entitled under that article to prescribe the objectives of the procedure and to extend it to the cultural integration of foreign workers.[39]

4. Recommendations and opinions

According to Article 189(5) of the Treaty, recommendations and opinions 'shall have no binding force'. This wording, however, does not explicitly exclude the use of these instruments in certain circumstances as guidelines for the interpretation of EC law or national law. The Court of Justice has stated this principle in a case relating to occupational illness;[40] the German Federal Labour Court has followed it in a case concerning the age of retirement.[41] The fact that recommendations and opinions are thus a kind of soft 'law' may be an incentive to avoid directives in matters where Member States might be hostile to specific measures. The problem of sexual harassment in the work-place is an example: despite the undisputed importance of the problem, the

---

[36] [1994] OJ L254/64.

[37] See W. Däubler/Th. Klebe, P. Wedde, *Kommentar zum Bündesdatenschutzgesetz*, (Bund, Kuln, 1996).

[38] Case 9/70 *Franz Grad* v. *Finanzamt Traunstein* [1970] ECR 825.

[39] Joined cases 281, 283 to 285 and287/85, *Federal Republic of Germany and Others* v. *Commission of the European Communities* [1987] ECR 3203.

[40] Case C–322/88 *Salvatore Grimaldi* v. *Fonds des maladies professionnelles* [1989] ECR 4407, 4419.

[41] Federal Labour Court (=BAG) [1993] *Der Betrieb* 1993, 443, 444.

Commission and the Council have so far resorted only to non-legally binding acts.[42]

V. Atypical Acts

The list of instruments in Article 189 of the Treaty is not exhaustive. In practice, EC institutions often use non-specific forms of action whose binding force depends on the circumstances.[43] There are 'resolutions', 'programmes' and 'declarations'. There are 'decisions' in a broad, non-technical sense, encompassing what the Germans (and the German version of the texts) call *Beschlüsse* and merely expressing the will of the decision-making body without referring to Article 189(4). In the social policy field, the Council Decisions establishing Community action programmes for the disabled,[44] and the educational programme to promote the mobility of university students ('Erasmus'[45]) are notable examples.

The 'rules' established by this route have been dubbed *droit européen souterrain*;[46] they merit careful analysis in all cases where the Community grants subsidies without any other legal basis. It seems clear that the Council and the Commission are bound by their own declarations and have to respect fundamental rights, especially the right to equal treatment. But the temptation to implement or foster social policy measures through financial intervention alone, in order to avoid the complicated legislative process with all its stumbling-blocks, may be great. In the future, the Community will probably be obliged to create clearer structures that imply not only transparent rules but also independent institutions: as in a nation State, EC social policy needs institutional differentiation to achieve higher efficiency and better control. Nobody would seriously propose that all national social policy should be concentrated in a single Ministry and a few 'social funds'. The more the Community plans to act in the social arena the more it must follow the example of the nation State or develop comparable instruments.[47]

It seems appropriate to mention in the context of 'atypical' acts Conventions between the Member States, which may or may not be based on Article 220 of the Treaty but are all closely related to EC activities. Two of them have an important impact on labour law:

[42] Details and references in: W. Däubler, M. Kittner, K. Lörcher, Internationale Arbeits- und Sozialordnung (2nd edn., Bund-Verlag, Cologne, 1994), No. 420.
[43] Overview in Th. Oppermann, *Europarecht* (Beck, Munich, 1991), No. 487.
[44] See e.g. the Council Decision of 18 Apr. 1988 concerning 'Helios' [1988] OJ L104.
[45] Council Dec. of 14 Dec. 1989 [1989] OJ L395.
[46] G. Lyon-Caen, 'L'avenir de l'Europe Sociale', in *Actes du Colloque européen, Quel Avenir pour l'Europe Sociale: 1992 et après?* (Editions CIACO, Brussels, 1992), 56.
[47] Cf. D. Merten, R. Pitschas (ed.), *Der Europäische Sozialstaat und seine Institutionen*, (Duncker und Humblot, Berlin, 1993).

(1) The Brussels Convention of 27 September 1968 on Jurisdiction and the Enforcement of Judgments in Civil and Commercial Matters,[48] as amended by the Convention of San Sebastian of 26 May 1989,[49] regards lawsuits concerning the employment relationship as falling within its scope. It is completed by the Protocol on its interpretation by the Court of Justice,[50] which confers on the Court the same powers as under Article 177 of the EC Treaty. The very existence of the Protocol proves that the Convention, though relying explicitly on Article 220 of the Treaty, is not part of Community law.

(2) The Rome Convention of 19 June 1980 on the Law Applicable to Contractual Obligations[51] contains, in its Article 6, rules on the employment relationship. It is not based on Article 220 of the EC Treaty, and the Second Protocol relating to its interpretation by the Court of Justice has not yet been ratified; nevertheless, the close connection with the legal system of the EC is obvious.[52] The Convention does not harmonize labour law as such but merely co-ordinates the different legal orders. The idea is that at least the choice of applicable law should not depend on different national rules within a common market.

VI. 'Agreements' in the Framework of the Social Dialogue

According to Article 118b of the Treaty, the Commission is to endeavour to develop the dialogue between management and labour at European level 'which could, if the two sides consider it desirable, lead to relations based on agreement'. Article 4 of the Maastricht Agreement on Social Policy seems more precise: '[s]hould management and labour so desire, the dialogue between them at Community level may lead to contractual relations, including agreements'. Does the Community have, here, a new instrument for developing labour relations?

It may initially seem easy to answer in the affirmative on reading the text of the Maastricht Agreement. Not only is the social dialogue to be promoted by the Commission, but according to Article 3(4) of the Maastricht Agreement the social partners are entitled to 'interrupt' the drawing up of a proposal by the Commission for a period of nine months, while they attempt to reach their own solution. Furthermore, the effectiveness of their talks has been upgraded by the provision in Article 4(2) permitting them to request the implementation of their common position by Council decision.

However, without going into details here,[53] the reader's initial impression

---

[48] [1978] OJ L304/77.   [49] [1989] OJ L285/1.
[50] [1971] OJ L304/97.   [51] [1980] OJ L266/1.
[52] Cf. R. Plender, *The European Contracts Convention. The Rome Convention on the Choice of Law for Contracts* (Sweet and Maxwell, London, 1991), 105.
[53] See the contributions by Treu, Sciarra, and Weiss to this volume.

must quickly be corrected. The new 'instrument' lacks almost all the characteristics necessary for it to be used: apart from the fact that this agreement is a contract, we know nothing of its other features. Which legal system is to apply to it? Are the parties entitled to a choice of law? Can there be any binding effect on the member organizations of the social partners? Perhaps even on the individual employment relationship? Must a 'European collective agreement' respect national laws, or does it share the supremacy of Community law? Is the Council obliged to issue such an implementing decision at the joint request of European employers and unions? May it add or delete any provisions? What does 'decision' mean? Is it conceived in the broad sense as encompassing directives and other acts in accordance with Article 189 of the Treaty, or is it confined to 'decision' in the narrow sense of Article 189(4)? The list of questions can easily be continued.[54]

It would, of course, be possible to find an answer to all these questions without resorting to pure speculation or wishful thinking. But the effort seems premature. So far, the social partners have consistently preferred 'joint opinions',[55] which can hardly be called 'agreements'. To do more would require, at least on the employers' side, a new definition of the role of UNICE and CEEP. Surely, however, national employers' organizations and unions will, like others, rely on the subsidiarity principle. Are they likely to defer power to Brussels when everybody else tries to get it back to London, Madrid, Paris or Bonn? If in the future they reach agreement on certain issues, it will only be to combine their lobbying power. Whether this proves useful or not, a joint visit by employers and unions to the Commissioner's office will not need an elaborate legal framework. The EC will continue to use the traditional instruments.

VII. Prospects for the Future

The overview of sources of EC labour law given here reveals a wide variation in the legislative instruments concerned. This variation lies not only in the use of primary EC law as well as international agreements and various forms of secondary EC law, but also in their considerable differences as to the content: in some cases broadly worded statements, and in other precise and detailed provisions.

EC labour law has nothing of the nature of a European *code du travail*—there is no 'system', no clear and comprehensive concept behind it. This may be explained by the fact that EC social policy has always occupied a precarious

---

[54] For further questions see: W. Däubler, 'Europäische Tarifverträge nach Maastricht' [1992] *Europäische Zeitschrift für Wirtschaftsrecht* 329 ff.; A. Ojeda Avilés, 'European Collective Bargaining: A Triumph of the Will?' (1993) 9 *The International Journal of Comparative Labour Law and Industrial Relations* 279 ff.

[55] See the documentation in Commission of the European Communities, *Community Social Policy, Current Status 1 January 1993* (Luxembourg, 1993), 120 ff.

position within the activities of the Community. On an abstract level, the decision-makers have always recognized the necessity of certain steps in the social field, but their will to take concrete measures has not—to put it diplomatically—always been evident. In the absence of a well-organized European labour movement, the main political reason for taking action in the field of labour law is the need to win support from the populations of the Member States. Unfortunately, this need is defined in quite a different way according to whether the example followed is that of Bismarck or of Governments which react only to upheavals and riots.

In reality, there are good reasons for the Community to develop its social policy. And, as we have shown, the EC Treaty contains sufficient provisions to enable this to be done. To banish social policy to the bottom of the list of priorities would seriously undermine the legitimacy of the Community in the event of anything other than favourable circumstances. Its position is different from that of a nation State. As a 'fragment of a State', its activities are essentially restricted to the economic sphere; even the Maastricht Treaty has not changed it for the time being. If expectations in the critical area of the economy prove to be disappointed to any great extent and the Community is consequently perceived as the (actual or supposed) creator of unemployment and other social problems, it has no real power to take countermeasures. It lacks the capacity to gain the loyalty of the vast majority of its citizens through shared cultural values or the provision of public benefits such as internal and external security. There are three further areas of deficiency:

(1) Although the European Parliament is democratically elected, it has only a limited right of veto over Community moves to lay down standards. It possesses no right to initiate legislation and is able to block only quite specific projects; to that extent, even the German Reichstag was in a stronger position under the 1871 Constitution.
(2) Community decision-making lacks transparency. The Council of Ministers, the actual legislature, meets behind closed doors; interested citizens cannot discover, as they can in the various Parliaments of the Member States, who supported or who contested particular decisions.
(3) This lack of democracy and lack of transparency are both heightened by the absence of European-level media. Press, television, and radio, as well as most interest groups, are still organized along national lines. This means that their controlling function can be exercised effectively only at national level. Brussels, Luxembourg, or Strasbourg are treated as 'spheres' outside their own countries—a change in the composition of the Commission is little more important than a vote of confidence in the Belgian Parliament.

An institution built on such weak foundations must ensure that the interests and wishes of individual citizens are somehow fulfilled within the Community (not fully, of course, but to a certain extent at least). The first Danish referendum on the Maastricht Treaty made it clear that the Community needs to exercise regard for the individual and that it will be putting its own existence in jeopardy if it continues to rely solely on market mechanisms, confining itself in other respects to a kind of background function. This does not mean that an effective social policy would be enough in itself to remedy the lack of legitimacy and bring about stability: without such a policy, however, the Community's future prospects will look even less certain.[56]

The Community's problems have intensified with the Maastricht Treaty. The increase in its powers means that its lack of legitimacy will become more and more obvious.[57] Even before the advent of currency union, the restrictions on national government deficits laid down in the new Article 104c of the EC Treaty will considerably reduce the scope for action in the field of social policy at present enjoyed by many Member States. Once a single currency for some or all Member States has been introduced, the exchange rate mechanism will no longer exist as a means of compensating for different productivity levels. A declining level of productivity, whether relative (i.e. in comparison with other Member States) or absolute, will have to be offset by 'cost reductions', particularly cuts in labour costs. In addition, it will no longer be possible for individual Member States to adopt a counter-cyclical economic policy.[58] When they cease to be able to 'compensate' in the traditional way it will rest on the Community to take the appropriate measures.

This increased pressure for action will now, however, be matched by what has been only a modest improvement in the instruments available. Although the decision-making process is, in principle, made easier by the Maastricht Protocol on social policy, the Treaty itself does not provide for any improvements in this sphere. In particular, it creates no new institutions, apart from the so-called 'cohesion' fund. This means that the Community will very probably find itself in a predicament, since it has only modest methods at its disposal to counter the enormous socio-political risks. The Community's strategy on the path to currency union is reminiscent of that of a wayfarer journeying through a primaeval forest who convinces himself that his merry songs will turn snakes and other beasts into harmless creatures. More soberly, the Community will be putting its very existence in jeopardy if it pursues its monetary and economic policy as if it were a federal State but without possessing the opportunities for adjusting social policy that are properly available to such a State.

---

[56] On the importance of social policy as a means of establishing legitimacy, see R. Pitschas, *Die öffentliche Verwaltung* (1992), 277.

[57] Cf. P. VerLoren van Themaat, 'Les Défis de Maastricht. Une nouvelle Étape importante, mais vers quels Horizons?' [1992] *Revue du Marché Commun (RMC)* 205.

[58] Ibid.

8

European Collective Bargaining Levels and the Competences of the Social Partners

TIZIANO TREU

1. The Abstention of Community Law in Collective Bargaining Regulation

Collective labour relations, and collective bargaining in particular, have so far lain outside the range of European Community law. The reasons are rooted more in the practice and politics of the Member States than in the law of the Community. Even before the Single European Act and before Maastricht, it would not have been impossible to justify legal intervention by the Community in many aspects of collective labour relations. Differences in industrial relations practices bring about differences in employment conditions: consequently, it could have been argued that the harmonization of national practices is important in order to avoid distortion of competition and/or to promote free movement of labour. It is no more arbitrary to use such an argument to justify the harmonization of industrial relations than to justify, for example, a directive on the transfer of undertakings. The impact on competition of differences in national regulations is no less direct in the former area than in the latter. Indeed, a similar line of reasoning has been used by the European Commission, starting from the early 1970s, to justify its recurrent attempts to harmonize through directives the differing regulation of information, consultation, and participation in the various member countries.

The absence of Community law in collective labour relations can be explained by the argument of national divergences and peculiarities. The industrial relations systems within the Community do indeeed differ in many fundamental features. Comparative analysis shows that all major industrial relations models, judged according to various indicators, are represented. But difference alone may not be a sufficient explanation.

National differences in collective bargaining or industrial conflict practices, areas in which Community-level regulation has been eschewed by the Commission, are no greater than thoseexisting between different systems of information and consultation, in which the same Commission has tried for decades to intervene.

The reasons for this uneven approach would appear to lie deeper in the very nature and practice of industrial relations as perceived by national actors.

Degrees, levels, and types of legislation are influenced by many variables which are themselves historically changing in the Member States; and these variables are also relevant at the European Community level. The most important are related to the content of the various aspects of industrial relations, to their closeness to the social autonomy of the partners and the basic interests of each national community. Drawing from the comparative experience, one can mention certain issues which go to the very roots of the collective system, such as the right to organize and internal union affairs. In most European States, with the recent exception of the United Kingdom, these issues are wholly free from legal regulation as such. Other matters, such as industrial conflict, are equally fundamental to the partners' autonomy but are usually subject to legal regulation because they directly influence social power relations and public interest. The difficult balance between freedom and limitation of conflict is, however, considered so critical to the national interest that is kept within the authority of the individual Member States.

These two groups of issues, together with pay, are excluded from European-level regulation not only *de facto* but also *de jure*. This remains true even under the Maastricht Protocol, which has extended Community competence to regulate labour matters. The exception of pay well represents the key importance of the national interest, because pay is the 'bottom line' issue of both individual and collective labour relations.

The more interventionist attitude of the EC authorities, in the area of information, consultation, and participation rights, again both *de facto* and *de jure*, may be explained by at least two reasons: first, in the tradition of most European countries these issues have been regarded as belonging not strictly to the sphere of the partners' autonomy but to the functioning of the enterprise as an institution; and secondly, the harmonization of company law is considered a fundamental condition of the functioning of the single European market.[1]

2. Support without Regulation in the Maastricht Social Protocol

Collective bargaining as such appears to be in an intermediate position with respect to supranational regulation. It shares with the former group of issues its closeness to the social partners' autonomy and critical importance to the balance of social power. And in the European tradition it is the central institution of collective labour relations. In most national systems collective bargaining is not, like internal union affairs, wholly exempt from legal regulation; but legal intervention is mainly directed at regulating procedural aspects and reinforcing the legal effects of collective agreements, not dictating rules of substance or influencing the merit of negotiation.

[1] G. and A. Lyon-Caen, *Droit social international et européen* (8th ed., Dalloz, Paris, 1993), 343 ff.

In fact collective bargaining has not traditionally been included in the regulatory agenda of the European Community.[2] Even the Maastricht Treaty Social Protocol is ambiguous in this respect. The lack of any mention of (national) collective bargaining as one of the possible areas of EC regulatory powers is probably not sufficient to exclude such powers. They may be derived from the reference by the Protocol to the 'representation and collective defence of the interest of workers', an expression which can also include collective bargaining.[3]

But the lack of any explicit reference to collective bargaining as an object of Community law is surprising, to say the least, given the importance of this institution and the very tradition of the Community. Manifestations of the interest of the European authorities and the social partners in (supranational) collective bargaining date back almost to the origins of the Community.

This interest has been expressed with growing intensity: starting from the support for EC-level sectoral bipartite or tripartite committees, which have been operating in many sectors since the 1960s; moving on to the promotion of social dialogue at Val Duchesse, subsequently endorsed by the Single European Act as an instrument of European social policies likely to evolve into 'real' collective bargaining; and culminating in the recognition, by the Maastricht Social Protocol, of European-level collective bargaining as a possible primary source of Community law.

This European policy towards collective bargaining is in line with the promotional as opposed to regulatory attitude common to many national traditions. But it carries it to the extreme: i.e. to the point of ignoring national collective bargaining practices as an object of regulation and support and concentrating attention on separate supranational initiatives of social dialogue and bargaining. Differences in national practices, law, and (even) basic conceptions of collective bargaining are not seen as an insurmountable obstacle to Community intervention. On the contrary, they seem to be taken for granted if not accepted as a form of inevitable diversity.

Any phase of harmonization of national practices as such is omitted; common European objectives are to be pursued directly at the supranational level, creating the independent legal institution of the 'European collective agreement'.

The innovation introduced in this respect by the Maastricht Protocol needs some clarification. Under pre-existing Community law and practice, trilateral action at supranational level has had, roughly speaking, two possible outcomes. The most frequent has been the issuing of 'joint opinions' by the social partners, which are characterized by a content of variable precision and by

---

[2] See different opinions by F. Scarpelli, 'Diritto comunitario, diritto sindacale italiano e sistema di relazioni industriali, principi e compatibilità' [1993] *DRLI* 163; R. Del Punta, 'Rappresentanze dei lavoratori e diritto comunitario', ibid., 189.

[3] M. Weiss, 'The Significance of Maastricht for European Community Social Policy' [1992] *Int. J. CLLIR* 8.

rather uncertain or weak legal status.[4] They can promote harmonization through their persuasive power both on the Community and on the constituent national organizations.[5] Even the more precise of these opinions have been framed only as policy guidelines intended to promote future collective activity and relying on the internal cohesion of the organizations.[6]

The second possible outcome has been collective agreements in the strict sense. Their legal identity dates back to before Maastricht and even before 1986;[7] however, lacking specific Community regulation, they could operate only according to national principles and regulations. Their legal effectiveness *vis-à-vis* the EC authorities was not significantly different from that of the 'joint opinion'; again because the parties were inclined to agree only on broad guidelines rather than on specific regulations.

Even the influence on their constituents was not necessarily any greater. The only common technique available to transpose the agreed commitments from European to national level was and still is, the obligations internal to the social partners' organization. The difference from the 'joint opinion' is that here the commitment is not unilateral (each party *vis-à-vis* its own constituents) but bilateral. But the nature, effects and enforceability of these commitments still depend on the national rules concerning collective bargaining and internal union relations, which were and are different.

The strengthening of the representative powers of the EC-level sectoral committees and the European unions has not reached the point of giving supranational organizations a superior hierarchical standing over the national social partners.[8]

Effectiveness was more easily guaranteed in the case of transnational enterprise agreements and obligational clauses. In a few instances, like the CEEP agreement of 6 September 1990, the partners' bilateral commitment has been particularly strong, going beyond a mere invitation to their national

---

[4] Wedderburn, 'Community Law and Workers' Rights: Fact or Fiction in 1992?' (1991) 13 Dublin Univ, L J 1, 34.

[5] Lyon-Caen and Lyon-Caen, n. 1 above, 331 ff.; F. Guarriello, *L'ordinamento comunitario e autonomia collectiva. Il dialogo sociale* (Angeli, Milan, 1992), 113 ff.; M. Weiss, 'Social Dialogue and Collective Bargaining in the Framework of a Social Europe', in G. Spyropoulos and G. Fragnière (eds.), *Work and Social Policies in the New Europe* (European University Press, 1991), 65 ff.

[6] An appraisal of these results in J. Goetschy, 'Le dialogue sociale européen de Val Duchesse: un premier bilan' [1992] *Travail Emploi* 264.

[7] M. Despax, 'Les conventions collectives de travail européennes [1965] *DS* 616 ff.; G. Schnorr, 'La convention collective européenne, son opportunité, les possibilités de la réaliser et les problèmes juridiques qu'elle pose' [1971] *DS* 157 ff.; G. Lyon-Caen, 'Négociation et convention collective au niveau européen' [1973] *RTDE* 585 ff. and [1974] *RTDE* 1 ff. More recently, E. Triggiani, 'Il contratto collettivo di diritto comunitario [1979] *RDE* 231 ff.

[8] Cf. Guarriello, n. 5 above, 102 ff.; B. Veneziani, 'Il sindacato europeo e le relazioni industriali' [1990] *Lav. Inf.* n. 17, 9 ff.; M. Grandi, 'Parti sociali e contrattazione nell, 'Unione europea' [1993] *Lav. Dir.* 76 ff.

constituents and imposing on them a sort of duty to bargain in accordance with the guidelines set in Brussels. Even here, however, the effects of this duty and any consequences of its violation were to be judged according to national legislation.

The Maastricht Protocol has made explicit the recognition of the social partners' autonomy in shaping their collective relations. It has confirmed the legal identity of European-level collective agreements, but also the fact that their legal effectiveness in principle follows the national rules. These rules differ so greatly, particularly with respect to the so-called 'normative' part of agreements, that enforceability may be extremely uneven in the various countries, thereby reducing the potential harmonizing capacity of the agreement.[9] In addition, the Protocol has created another rather extraordinary possibility, namely, a type of European-level agreement which can be made directly and generally enforceable by a Council decision. This innovation and the power granted to the social partners to pre-empt EC initiatives recognize a (formal) priority of the consensual method over authoritative norms as a source of Community law.

The technique used in the Maastricht Protocol with regard to recognition of a European-level collective agreement is not totally new. A somewhat similar approach can be found in the case of the European company and workers' participation. Here, too, the proposed directive takes into account the diversity of national systems and aims at creating a new institution at the European level open to employee participation, which the interested parties (companies and employees) may or may not adopt in their national system. This choice, once adopted, would amount to bypassing the diversity of national systems of company law and workers' participation, allowing the same parties to choose between different models of workers' participation. But the similarity ends there.

Once a given type of workers' participation is selected within a corporation which adopts the European company statute, this type would operate directly at the national level and would exclude other forms of regulation both of the company as such and of workers representation. By contrast, the European-level collective bargaining envisaged by the Maastricht Protocol may coexist, and in fact is meant to coexist, with national collective bargaining, operating according to national laws and practice.

Not only that; European agreements, once concluded at the European level (sectoral or interprofessional, i.e. economy-wide), may operate on the national systems either directly via a Council decision, or indirectly via national collective agreements which implement the European agreement according to

---

[9] See different opinions in this respect: Lord Wedderburn, 'Inderogability, Collective Agreements and Community Law [1992] *Ind. Law Journal* 248 ff.; S. Sciarra, 'Il dialogo fra ordinamento comunitario e nazionale del lavoro: la contrattazione collettiva' [1992] *DLRI* 728 ff.; Guarriello, n. 5 above, 51 ff.

national rules (i.e. with the relevant differences concerning their legal effects, scope and extension).[10]

3. A Counter-productive or a 'Necessary' Choice?

This choice raises a number of difficult questions and doubts. In an area as critical as collective bargaining, abandoning any attempt to harmonize national instruments in favour of creating a new European-level institution may be politically counter-productive, if not paradoxical.

The question is particularly serious given that the practice of transnational collective agreements is as yet scarcely developed in the Community. A policy choice is not the same thing as some intellectual exercise which can be easily anticipated. I have in mind here the attempts made by some scholars to create a legal model of a European-level collective agreement in the mid-1960s, when the practice of collective bargaining was unknown at supranational level and also little developed in many national systems.[11] Even that intellectual exercise may not have been without its counter-productive consequences in so far as it has given priority to the shaping of a common legal model of the European-level collective agreement rather than fostering convergent national collective bargaining practices which might develop outside any legal impediments.

For the same reason, the Maastricht creation of a European-level collective agreement, particularly in the 'strong' version of an authoritative source of law,[12] might be judged alien to, if not contrasting with, the principle of subsidiarity which is now given universal tribute. This aspect of the choice was not in fact analysed in advance either in public debate or by experts.

The 'political' answer to any such objection is clear. The European authorities, spurred on by the social partners, have opted for a consensual source (the European-level collective agreement) in order to keep authoritative legal instruments (such as directives and regulations) at a 'lighter' level. In this respect the choice may be seen as in line with the subsidiarity principle, because it implies that consensual sources of regulation should be preferred, wherever feasible, to non-consensual or heteronomous sources.

---

[10] This latter alternative does not entail any obligation on the Member States or on the social partners and the European authorities: see R. Blanpain, *Labour law and industrial relations of the European Union* (Kluwer, Deventer, 1992), 28 ff.; B.Bercusson, 'Maastricht: A Fundamental Change in European Labor Law' [1992] *Ind. Rel. Journal* 177; B. Fitzpatrick, Community Social Law after Maastricht [1992] *Ind. Law. Journal* 3, 199.

[11] See n. 7 above.

[12] See some sceptical remarks about this choice by Weiss, n. 3 above, 12; Sciarra, n. 9 above, 746.

4. The Ambivalence of the Social Partners

Whatever opinion may be on this point, the choice made at Maastricht must take into account certain variables which are likely to operate more as obstacles than as factors favouring this choice. Most of them concern the social actors who promoted the protocol. The major weakness in this respect lies in their respective motivations in supporting it: although the preference for consensual, as opposed to legal, regulation shared by the social partners is convergent with the official motivation of the European authorities, it is in itself ambiguous.[13] To date, a negative concern to avoid legal interference from the Brussels Eurocrats seems prevalent over any positive wish to conclude agreements at supranational level. It is mainly the employers who ostensibly prefer some future but unlikely agreement to legal activism on the part of the Commission. But certain trade unions in fact share, beyond what is officially declared, this opposition to relinquishing national bargaining power to supranational organizations. No significant success has been achieved in the preparation of supranational negotiations; even in the mature area of the European Works Council (EWC), attempts to agree on common rules have failed.

The general agreement of 31 October 1991, which gave the green light to the Social Protocol, has so far remained an unrepeated precedent. The legal recognition of this European-level instrument is in danger of remaining an admirable example of legal creativity without practical consequences. Even worse, it might serve to reduce the legitimacy of legal instruments such as the directives without providing a concrete consensual alternative. Given these premises, it seems less urgent to explore the legal aspects of future European-level collective agreements than to clarify the prerequisites for their development (possibly in order to promote them).

5. European Social Actors: Management Initiatives and Multinational Enterprise Agreements

A first prerequisite, often mentioned in political and scholarly discussions, concerns the organization and powers of the social actors, i.e. the evolution of both trade unions and employers' associations from national organizations into European bodies endowed with sufficient capacity to negotiate.

The reasons for and process of internationalization are not symmetrical for the two sides, employers and unions.

[13] See W. Streeck, The Rise and Decline of Neocorporatism, in *Economic and Political Changes in Europe; Implications for Industrial Relations* (3rd IIRA European Regional Congress, Cecucci, Bari, 1993), 35 ff.; idem., *The Effect of European Integration on National Industrial Relations*, Paper, Washington, DC, 27–29 May 1993.

Only for the latter is internationalization a totally new process which must necessarily be shaped in order to implement transnational rules. Enterprises as economic entities are themselves already supranational; they can also use this dimension in their capacity as employers to the extent that they deem necessary. This dimension is at the same time easier and yet not necessary, since enterprises can directly implement common practices and rules of industrial relations in different countries without changing their organization.

In the case of multinational enterprises in particular, the options are open now that socio-political conditions in most Member States favour unilateral human resource management practices as a possible alternative to bilateral collective labour relations. For multinational enterprises, the former are an instrument of harmonization which can operate fully via the usual channels of corporate organization without having to resort to 'external' relations (with a minimum of interference by Community law and institutions). While these reasons indicate that the initiative for supranational organizations is likely to rest with the trade unions, it does not necessarily follow that this is the case.

The opposite might seem to be true, judging from the fact that the few examples of supranational collective agreements known to date (around thirty) have been concluded at the enterprise group level and following management initiative.[14] These trends confirm that the enterprise is at present the 'easiest' vehicle or environment for supranational experiments in bargaining.

But the significance of these experiments is again ambivalent. They do not necessarily represent an implementation of the Maastricht policy. For various reasons the enterprise group is not *per se* a European level of collective activity. The scope of the agreement coincides not with the Community Member States butwith the scope of the enterprise organization or part thereof.[15]

The same conclusion is confirmed by the content of such agreements. They are not specifically related to issues relevant for the Community, whether belonging to the *aquis communautaire* (e.g. an agreement specifying the

[14] Cf. G. Bergougnoux, 'Projets européens les politiques d'entreprise: B.S.N. [1990] *DS* 671 ff.; P. Langlois, 'La négociation collective d'entreprise. La politique communautaire' [1990] *DS* 673 ff.; A. Jobert, 'La négociation collective dans les entreprises multinationales en Europe', in G. Devin (ed.), *Syndicalisme, dimensions internationales* (Erasme, Paris, 1990), 313; M. Gold and M. Hall, *European level information and consultation in multinational companies: an evaluation of practice* (European Foundation for the Improvement of Living and Working Conditions, Dublin, 1992); F. Guarriello, 'Accordi di gruppo e strutture di rappresentanza europee' [1993] *Lav. Dir* 1; M. Hall, F. Marginson, K. Seisson, 'The European Works Council: Setting the Research Agenda', *Warwick Papers in Industrial Relations*, Nov. 1992, no. 41; W. Streeck and S. Vitals, *European Works Councils: Between Statutory Enactment and Voluntary Adoption* (Univ. of Wisconsin, mimeo, 1993); *I comitati d'impresa europei*, ed. by C. Stanzani (EL, Rome, 1993).

[15] See the remarks by A. Lyon-Caen, 'Après Maastricht: quel espace contractuel européen? [1992], *Les Cahiers de la fondation Europe et Société*, no. 25.

implementation of existing directives) or anticipating future programmes of action.

Instead, most analyses confirm that the issues and functions of these agreements are linked to policy priorities of the individual enterprises, even more than to their specific economic position.[16] External influences come more from national industrial relations practices and policies, including trade union interests, than from Community indications.

Even less surprising, the actors on the employees' side are heterogeneous and not structured on a European scale. Their basis is usually an aggregation of enterprise employee representatives, institutionalized to a varying degree according to the country (more in Germany than in France) and supported externally by sectoral union committees (the most vital form of union supranational organization).

Probably the closest link with the Community institutional framework may be found in the content of some agreements aimed at fostering common human-resource-management policies in intrafirm training and mobility; but the link with the European issue of free movement of labour is at best indirect.

The weak link between (supranational) enterprise agreements and the Community dimension should not be over-emphasized as evidence that these agreements have or will have an 'anti-European' evolution. It simply shows that experiments in industrial relations follow the easier line of development. In the present state of Community law and practice, this is precisely the group enterprise. Once the policy has been adopted by management, the enterprise's supranational identity guarantees the agreement its scope and effectiveness.

This is particularly true since the agreements known to date have a mainly procedural rather than 'normative' content. The diversity of the legal nature and effectiveness of collectiveclauses in the various Member States chiefly concerns so-called normative clauses, i.e. those which regulate individual terms and conditions of employment. Procedural clauses have a more uniform legal basis, at least in continental Europe, in the law of contracts.[17] Moreover, when they imply obligations mainly on the employers' side, such as the information and consultation clauses common in these European-level agreements, they do not even need a common legal support. Their effectiveness is directly guaranteed in the national industrial relations system by the identity of the actors committed to fulfil them, i.e. the multinational enterprises themselves.

This effectiveness might be less certain where these collective clauses concern union and employee conduct, such as no-strike clauses, whose status

[16] See with different approaches: P. Marginson, 'European Integration and Transnational Management Unions, Relations in the Enterprise' (1992) 30 *Brit. J. Ind. Rel.* 529-45; Streeck, Vitols, n. 14 above.

[17] P. Rodière, *La convention collective de travail en droit international* (Litec, Paris, 1987).

is somewhat diversified and controversial in the various national systems, notably Italy. These arguments are, however, hypothetical, since the existing enterprise agreements are shaped in terms more resembling those of a statement of policy than a legally binding obligational clause.

In absolute terms there is nothing to prevent all collective clauses, including normative ones, from operating in the various countries according to their different legal rules. But the influence of collective regulation on the individual employment relationship, which is the essence of normative clauses, requires, in the absence of legal backing, a form of joint determination by the actors, i.e. employers, unions, and employees (who are required to consent), much stronger than that for procedural clauses: and this determination is far from strong in the present situation.

6. The Legal Status of the Multinational Enterprise Agreement

In short, enterprise agreements may be an easy vehicle for supranational collective activity precisely because they do not require any supranational legal recognition but may be effectively promoted by the very organization of the enterprise.

Even so, their effectiveness could well profit from supranational support. But this can conceivably come in indirect rather thandirect forms. Adoption of the directive on European works councils (EWC) would give a common institutional status to the actors on the employees' side, albeit shaped in different forms, which would certainly stabilize and possibly promote supranational agreements of this type. In any event, multinational enterprise agreements are bound to operate in each national system according to the local rules, as indicated in the first of the two alternatives provided for by the new Article 118B. They will not acquire any legal status in Community law, even according to the second alternative which implies approval of agreements by a Council decision. Even though Article 118 B mentions collective agreements without further qualification, and so could be referred to collective agreements of any scope,[18] an enterprise agreement, no matter how widely multinational, is not appropriate for transformation into a Council decision.

The rationale of this specific rule lies in the possibility of using collective agreements as 'material content' of a rule valid for Community-wide industrial relations.

When proposing such a solution, the Maastricht constituents probably had in mind a type of economy-wide agreement like that concluded on 31 October 1991, or the general rules which have been recurrently discussed at Val Duchesse and then approved by the parties in the form of the *avis commun*

---

[18] R. Blanpain, *Labour Law and Industrial Relations of the European Union* (Kluwer, Deventer, 1993), 62; more restrictively, Weiss, n. 5 above, 11.

(joint opinion). Even though this assumption on the part of the constituents does not *per se* bind the interpreter of the text, enterprise agreements are particularly remote from the Maastricht perception of using collective agreements as a source of law, directly binding on the social partners in the various national systems. The particular parties, issues and solutions entailed in such agreements are traditionally so close to the life of the enterprise concerned as to defy legal generalization: and it is difficult to imagine any change in these characteristics in the future.

7. European-level Economy-wide Agreements

At the other extreme, the scope of economy-wide agreements gives them the greatest potential for becoming the instrument of the new source of Community labour law decided at Maastricht. All the common rules in the field of industrial relations have so far been conceived in general terms, because the harmonization pursued by the Community was related to fundamental rules of horizontal or cross-sectoral relevance. But the realization of this potential is dependent on a number of conditions, here too concerning the social actors: their policies and organization.

It is well known that the practice of economy-wide agreements and the underlying powers of the signatory confederations is far from homogenous in the Member States. In certain countries such as Italy, Spain, and France, such pacts have sometimes acquired the form of binding agreements regulating terms and condition of employment; but even here they have more often maintained the character of broad policy guidelines addressed to the social partners themselves, to Parliament and to government. Even in these countries, they are the most unstable and uneven level of bargaining. In other national systems, Germany providing a notable example, the first type does not exist at all because both the trade-union and the employers' confederations lack the capacity to represent their constituent organizations, and *a fortiori* individual employees and employers, in collective bargaining; and even the second type of policy agreement is barely known.

This has influenced the original structure of the ETUC. The confederation has the nature of an umbrella organization rather than a negotiating structure, thereby reflecting the weakness of most national confederation members.[19]

Such diversity of experience and the lack of representative peak organizations on the two sides have so far been bridged by Community practice in two ways: by excluding *a priori* that the results of Val Duchesse may acquire the status of collective bargaining; and by using the existing powers of the European confederations not in the preparation of formal Acts but in informal lobbying activity *vis-à-vis* the European authorities. Following Maastricht, the

[19] M. Weiss, n. 5 above, 65.

duty imposed on the Commission to consult the social partner organizations prior to any Community action formalizes this lobbying activity and consequently requires more rigorously defined credentials for the confederations.

The pressure for more precise representativeness will further intensify if and when the peak European trade union and employers' organizations leave the safe ground of the 'joint opinions' and engage in real bargaining.

One could minimize the need for a specific mandate to the confederations by arguing that in the 'strong' version of Article 118B it is the Council decision, not the collective agreement, which has binding effects on the social partners and within the national systems. But this solution might be a dubious and possibly counterproductive short cut. It would widen the gap between the two alternatives proposed in Article 118B by acknowledging the structural weakness of agreements as compared with Council decisions, something which both the social partners and the Commission might find difficult to accept. Moreover, it would invalidate the very assumption on which the Protocol choice rests, i.e. the preference for a consensual/representative form of Community as opposed to authoritative regulation.

Much will depend on the content of bargaining. Political bargaining on general social and economic issues of the type experienced in some European countries (in whatever form) remains close to non-binding documents of the past, in particular the joint opinions of Val Duchesse. Consequently, the necessary mandate to the confederations among themselves and the Commission might remain vague. But the price paid would be a weak influence of the document among the social partners, *vis-à-vis* their constituents and the EC authorities.

For general agreements of this type, even a Council decision might be insufficient to give them legal effectiveness. If we follow the notion that Council decisions approving European-level agreements have the nature of regulations, they would axiomatically exclude an excessively vague content. Policy documents are more suited to recommendations than to regulations. Here, the institutional choice provided by the protocol appears to be too rigid in the present state of European labor relations.[20] This type of agreement would not be much more than a joint opinion submitted by the employers' and trade-unions' confederations to the Commission in the obligatory consultation procedure set by the protocol, i.e. less useful as a regulatory technique than as a proposal for concerted action. Such an outcome would minimize the institutional evolution sought first by the Single European Act and then at Maastricht: their main institutional innovation was precisely to go beyond social dialogue as a mere lobbying activity preparatory to the normative process of the EC authorities and to recognize the direct relevance of collective agreements as a source of Community law.

At the other extreme, an agreement concerning terms and conditions of

[20] Sciarra, n. 9 above, 744.

employment would require a specific mandate to the European-level negotiators on both sides. This remains true even assuming that European agreements of this scope would in any case use regulatory techniques different from
those known to a national tradition of collective agreements, less detailed,
and shaped more in the form of framework agreements than of actual
normative documents. Here, too, however, for the implementation of agreements via the Council a limit to this vagueness would derive from the rigid
technique of the Council decision. Specific agreements of this kind seem
unlikely in the near future, even on issues which might be appropriate for
EC-level regulation like some of those already presented in directive proposals and repeatedly discussed at Val Duchesse with significantly convergent
opinions.

The most realistic content of 'general' agreements might consist of guidelines for subsequent negotiations as it has been in the examples known to
date. These general agreements would be founded more on procedural than
on substantive rules concerning the forms and issues of lower-level negotiation. Even so, the political sensitivity and controversial nature of most issues
now on the agenda must not be under-estimated. In this case also, the outcome
of bargaining on these matters might not be a European collective agreement
to be implemented via a Council decision (with the complication mentioned
above) but a joint document to be used by the Council in order to support a
(flexible) directive: something not greatly different from and not necessarily
any more influential than the joint opinions of Val Duchesse.

The use of the collective instrument indicated by the Protocol therefore
proves to be difficult even for the general agreements which were the proto-
type envisaged by its signatories.

8. Sectoral Collective Bargaining

Sectoral collective bargaining likewise presents specific problems in this
respect. It represents the backbone of the bargaining structure in most
continental European countries. Yet, paradoxically, almost no formal projection at supranational level has occurred so far. The paradox is in fact only
apparent: it shows how great a distance separates practices like bilateral
consultation, joint opinions, *de facto* convergence between different systems,
and genuine European-level collective bargaining.

In recent years these practices have developed, in particular, in the sectors
which are strategically most relevant for the Community and more open to
foreign competition. The joint opinions issued by bipartite or tripartite
committees have often been influential on Community policies in areas
extending beyond labour matters.[21] In some cases the social partners have
come close to actual bargaining. National collective bargaining has in certain

[21] See Goetschy, n. 6 above.

sectors been inclined to favour common policies, if not to adopt a specific content; this runs counter to the trend in other areas of Community activity where divergence has often prevailed. Sectoral organizations of employers and employees at European level have acquired growing authority, to the point that (more on the union side than the employers' side) their national constituents, as representing the site of bargaining power in most continental countries, have declared themselves willing to delegate actual bargaining functions to their European representatives on an *ad hoc* basis. For these reasons many experts believe that sectoral social dialogue is the most promising first step towards actual European collective bargaining.[22]

In spite of these developments, the very importance of the sectoral level of bargaining makes the conclusion of supranational agreements a difficult goal. In national practice, sectoral agreements have a comprehensive content relating to pay and other employment conditions. Even taking into account the recent trend towards decentralization, they constitute the basic 'labour law' for employees working in the sector concerned.

Any projection of such a comprehensive type of agreement at European level would represent the outcome of a mature process of harmonization. This seems to be the case regardless of the form of implementation, i.e. whether the enforcement of agreements remains entrusted to the national social partners in accordance with national rules or is supported by a Council decision.

A realistic step could conceivably be experimentation with *ad hoc* agreements confined to specific issues: i.e. something less ambitious than the sectoral agreements known to national traditions but more readily acceptable to the social partners and their national constituents. This selective approach might minimize the obstacles and bridge the differences which remain in the (roughly) common practice of sectoral agreements.

Judging from the various national experiences, only certain functions of the collective agreement have a reasonable possibility of being extended to the supranational scale: in particular, information and consultation on industrial restructuring and its social consequences, which more and more often cut across individual countries. Other more ambitious matters of content such as the creation of a common job classification, 'a common industrial grammar' (as A. Lyon-Caen calls it) capable of assisting supranational mobility, are less likely.

For this reason, it seems to me that the Europeanization of the collective bargaining system cannot proceed simply through an imitation or extension of

---

[22] Lyon-Caen, n. 15 above, and 'La régulation de branche dans l'Europe communautaire', in S. Negrelli and T. Treu, 'Stato, mercato, management e relazioni di lavoro nelle telecomunicazioni europee', in Fondazione Regionale Pietro Seveso/Sip, *Relazioni di lavoro e telecomunicazioni in Europa* (Angeli, Milan, 1991), 13 ff.

national institutions; it implies a mixture of innovation and adaptation in the form of flexible and limited experiments.

If this is a realistic process, the enforcement of these partial agreements could conceivably be left to the diversity of national rules. This appears the most likely solution even assuming that national unions agreed to give a full and uniform mandate to their Brussels representatives. The meaning and effectiveness of this mandate might be uniformly perceived within the individual organizations themselves. But its external relevance in each legal system would vary according to the rules concerning the effects of collective agreements on the individual members (employees, employers) of the signatories, particularly as regards systems of enforcement. To use an Italian expression, the *inderogability*[23] and direct effects of these agreements could not be uniformly achieved at European level, but would still depend on the national systems.

An extension of sectoral agreements by Council decision would not meet the objections which have been raised in relation to multinational enterprise agreements. In the traditions of most continental European countries, sectoral agreements are considered the most suitable for legislative extension. The extension procedure has the precise intention of harmonizing pay and other employment conditions at a minimum level for all firms operating within given sectors. An extension across different European countries would correspond to the same function. But the impact on the employment conditions of national firms would be multiplied, as would the pressure, consequently, to resist such a direct form of harmonization.

9. Different Alternatives for Convergence

The arguments discussed so far show that the problem of transforming collective bargaining into a European institution extends far beyond the aspects of the legal recognition and effectiveness of collective agreements and the internal organization of the collective actors.

If European-level agreements are to be used as instruments of harmonization or (to use a 'softer' word) convergence, they encounter all the obstacles and resistance which the process of harmonization has already experienced. Harmonization via collective agreements may possibly be more legitimate than statutory harmonization, but it may also be even more difficult if it aims at defining its object more stringently, i.e. at harmonizing not only basic legal principles and procedures but actual terms and conditions of employment for employees throughout the Community.

The post-Maastricht scenario is far from clear. The Maastricht protocol has given European-level collective agreements not only explicit recognition but

[23] See Lord Wedderburn, n. 9 above, 245.

also greater legal authority than was previously possible. The Maastricht institutional arrangements in fact anticipated the actual practice of bilateral labour relations. The general socio-political climate as it has developed since Maastricht, together with the internal resistance within (and controversies between) the social actors regarding the Europeanization of collective bargaining, are now making the process extremely difficult. Thus a comprehensive approach to harmonization aimed at equalizing all employment conditions, as it was dreamed of in the 1970s, is at present illusory.

The fact of having involved the social partners more deeply in the process of harmonization does not reduce its complexity.

Choosing between the different alternatives is critical: it can hardly be done according to a 'once and for all' top-down decision. Harmonization from above[24] has met with increasing resistance over the last twenty years. It is unlikely to be any more successful if pursued by the social partners in the turbulent environment of the 1990s.

Even social partners better organized and more stably entrenched than those prevailing in Europe would find it difficult to 'sell' their members a top-down decision. An inductive and experimental process is not only more realistic but inevitable, particularly since many indicators demonstrate the persistence of nationalism in industrial relations as in other areas.[25] Only precise analysis of national practices and policies can suggest to both the European authorities and the social partners the best methods of promoting transnational industrial relations and their most suitable objects.

The social partners, no less than the Community authorities, will have to reconsider a basic question: namely, to what extent they are willing and able to agree on the specific regulation of employment conditions intended to be binding on the individual or, instead, only on broad guidelines to be further discussed and loosely applied. The institutional identity and effectiveness of European-level collective bargaining may, like European directives, be inversely proportional to its scope. Broad understanding on general issues, which is typical of economy-wide practices, might remain for some time the intermediate option between joint opinions and true collective agreements; at this economy-wide level procedural guidelines might prevail.

Multinational enterprise agreements could prove the most vital and legally identifiable instrument in the short run, capable of influencing not only legal rules but actual employment conditions in different countries. But they will not necessarily be useful for harmonization or even convergence between different national practices beyond the boundaries of the firm. The expansive influence of best enterprise practices on national systems is highly unpredictable, and may not be any greater where enterprise agreements are operating

[24] See a survey in T. Treu, 'Social Policy in the Legal Order of the European Union', FIDE Congress, Rome, 12–15 October 1994.
[25] See Streeck, *The effect of European integration*, n. 13 above, whose analysis is wholly convincing on this point.

on a multinational scale. The harmonization of industrial relations within large multinational firms is at best ambivalent. It may contribute to general convergence via imitation effects, or it may simply create another form of dualism in an already diversified scenario.[26]

The sectoral level remains a relatively solid ground for national industrial relations, but may not be ripe for true European bargaining. Even partial experiments may require lengthy preparation, i.e. convergent efforts and cross-comparison of national practices, before reaching the Brussels level.

Given the uncertain prospects of bargaining at different levels, it is premature to assume any 'articulation' or hierarchy between these levels in the terms known to national collective bargaining.[27]

National systems are still the primary determinants of European common rules, of both legal and contractual origin. The Maastricht policy has simply strengthened the Community's authoritative powers and the social partners' scope for shapinga European collective labour law system.

The institutional identity of these national systems, again both legal and voluntary, is so solidly entrenched in tradition that it cannot easily be replaced by a supranational policy such as that proposed at Maastricht (nor, on the other hand, by sheer market forces). The influence of national systems on the shaping of social Europe will probably be greater than expected, at least in the short run, given the slowing-down of the Maastricht policies (not only in the social sphere).

It is uncertain which will be the more heavily affected by this slowing-down: the normative activity of the European authorities or the bargaining initiative of the social partners. Here again, the position of the two sources of Community law is asymmetric. Authoritative sources (directives and regulations) have the 'advantage' of being backed by the relatively solid institutions of the Community and by forty years of fairly intensive normative output. Significantly enough, confidence in the use of directives as more effective than purely consensual instruments is still widely shared, by the trade unions as well. Consensual sources, i.e. collective agreements of various levels and coverage, have less tradition and almost no institutional or organizational background, but might have more social authority and legitimacy.

10. A Selective Use of Legislative and Collective Initiatives

In the Maastricht philosophy these two sources are not meant to be alternative. They might be complementary:[28] the extension of the EC's normative powers

---

[26] See examples in S. Negrelli and T. Treu, 'L'integrazione europea comme fattore di stabilità delle relazioni industriali italiane' [1994] *RIDL* 50 ff.

[27] See the remarks of Lyon-Caen, n. 15 above. The very expression 'level of bargaining' is itself inappropriate, since it can strictly be used only with respect to a collective bargaining structure which is operating as a system.

[28] An interactive influence of the two sources has already been experienced in the

in labour matters is a potential incentive for collective bargaining, and the social partners might profit from a stronger Community. But post-Maastricht events have shown that this institutional solution rests on politically shaky grounds. Our analyses and the previous experience suggest certain conditions and a 'caveat'. They indicate the need for an inductive and selective approach to harmonization, an approach which applies to both legislative and contractual sources. But they have different implications for each, according to their nature.

Authoritative sources, as often suggested by scholars, should curb their ambition to harmonize specific legal rules and terms and conditions of employment. This specific harmonization would be an impossible task even for political institutions more solid than the present ones. Since Maastricht this task has lost priority. Moreover, such an approach would present a serious risk of mere formalism, given the diversity of national systems, particularly in collective labour relations. The European authorities still have a decisive role to play in the development of social Europe, at least in the view of those who do not believe in the harmonizing virtues of market forces and are also sceptical of the various proposals for neo-voluntarism.

But the role of the European Union would be more effective if concentrated in two directions: first, establishing and giving general currency to basic individual and collective rights, something which may pertain to the Court of Justice even more than to the Council;[29] and secondly, to support the institutional conditions necessary to foster some measure of economic and social convergence between the national systems.

Support for the social partners in collective activity is an obvious priority according to the Maastricht protocol. The European authorities would act in much the same way as most national States did in the past in order to promote the institutions of industrial relations. Another priority is to encourage convergence in the socio-economic conditions which are the structural basis of norms and institutions. As defined by Lyon-Caen, that implies specifically, harmonizing the social conditions of growth: education, quality of manpower, technological skills, basic infrastructures, and basic social security. This is a most challenging task which presupposes a deep knowledge of and respect for the national systems. It also requires direct collaboration by the social partners, however.

Community. The influence of the EC authorities on collective bargaining can be direct (via regs. and dirs.) or indirect (through support for negotiating parties). And recently, the negotiations between the social partners on European works councils came close to reaching an agreement; their impasse has relaunched the Commission's legislative initiative, with a text inspired by the social dialogue route. See B. Bercusson, 'European Labour Law and Sectoral Bargaining' [1993] *Ind. Rel. Journal* 257 and idem, *Report to the FIDE Congress*, Rome 12–15 Oct. 1994.

[29] S. Simitis, 'Europeizzazione o rinazionalizzazione del diritto del lavoro' [1994] *DLRI* 641; Sciarra, n. 9 above; eadem, 'Social values and the multiple sources of European social law' [1995] *European Law Journal* 60.

The social partners, who have been called upon prematurely to play a major role in social Europe, should be equally or even more selective. Their closeness to the reality of employment conditions should not prompt them to follow a regulatory approach. As indicated above the harmonization of specific contractual terms or provisions may be even more difficult than harmonization of the legal rules of industrial relations.

Experimental efforts to promote convergence between collective bargaining systems, with the latter remaining national, seem more effective, at least in the short run, than creating a false architecture of European bargaining. The only practicable method appears to be the generalization of selected similarities between national practices, supported by the actors and the European authorities, as a preparation for future supranational agreements. Even then, the function of these supranational agreements would probably be less regulatory than promotional, and better directed at establishing transnational consensual procedures than regulating specific conditions of employment.

The absolute priority is to create the institutions of a European collective system: namely, effective supranational trade-union and employers' organizations; common procedures concerning the presence of workers' representatives in supranational enterprises; mutual recognition of bilateral institutions and practices; information and consultation on labour market and industrial policies affecting labour conditions; procedures for the monitoring and possibly settlement of supranational labour disputes.

9

Collective Agreements in the Hierarchy of European Community Sources

SILVANA SCIARRA

The Social Chapter: Theories and Practice of Collective Bargaining

The Maastricht Compromise

The adoption of the Protocol on social policy, annexed to the Maastricht Treaty, represents an innovation in Community law. This is for several reasons, analysed in depth by commentators over the last few years, which have opened up a new road for legal thinking and for the intervention of European institutions.

Before starting to follow this road, the main arguments that will be presented here may be mentioned: changes in the social field, important in themselves as well as in the general context of European developments, have not proved vigorous enough to place social policies among the main objectives of the Union, nor to elevate them to visible political priorities. The most significant outcomes of the last few years are to be found outside the Social Chapter, among the measures to fight unemployment,[1] slowly emerging from the very general macro-economic choices which generated them. They, too, need to find a stronger coherency and to acquire the appropriate tools to bind Member States to a consistent common action.

The image which more accurately illustrates the order governing the European Community in the social field is that of a 'multitiered system',[2]

---

[1] Such as the White Paper on *Growth, Competitiveness and Employment,* COM(93)700 final, 5 Dec. 1993; the Green Paper on *European Social Policy: Options for the Future,* COM(93) 551, 17 Nov. 1993; the White Paper on *European Social Policy: A Way Forward for the Union,* COM 94(333), 27 July, 1994 and the recent *The European Employment Strategy: Recent Progress and Prospects for the Future,* COM(95)465, 11 Oct. 1995. On these initiatives, see E. Szyszczak, 'Future Directions in European Union Social Policy Law'(1995) 24 *ILJ* 19. See also the results of the European Council's meetings held at Essen (EC, Bull. 12–1994, I) and Cannes (EC, Bull 6–1995, I), in Dec. 1994 and June 1995 respectively, in which employment issues are related to measures to increase competitiveness. All issues related to employment are of course mentioned in the latest Commission's plan of action for 1996. See COM(95)512.

[2] S. Leibfried and P. Pierson (eds), *European Social Policy between Fragmentation and Integration* (Brookings, Washington, 1995), particularly in the editors' Introductory chapter 'Multitiered Institutions and the Making of the Social Policy (15 ff.) and in their concluding chapter, 'The Dynamics of Social Policy Integration' (432 ff.). See also in a

whereby Member States have inevitably lost part of their sovereignty, without ceasing completely to influence centralized decision-making.[3] Similarly, the abandonment of traditions and practices in national legal systems does not imply the construction of a supranational legal order; denationalization may bring about closer observation of other legal systems, through comparative methodologies, but does not automatically create a new harmonized system of rules.[4] From the broader point of view of a hierarchical system of norms, the lack of a set of constitutionally based social rights undermines the possibility of innovative reforms of general relevance. The existence of concurrent law-making systems, despite all this, puts in motion a very slow process, based on partnership rather than on separation of powers,[5] in a constant search for equilibrium between 'Communitarization' and renationalization.

From the perspective of legislative intervention, this implies recourse to a multiplicity of sources, including collective agreements, aimed at meeting the needs of market-building while maintaining an internal equilibrium in state-building. It also implies a multiplicity of regulatory techniques, including non-binding measures, which often create the preconditions for the enforcement of individual and collective rights.

The 'escape route'[6] found by governments while choosing to adopt the Social Chapter is an example of this state of affairs. The body of literature devoted to the many questions left open by the drafters of this document allows a number of conclusions to be drawn regarding the state of scholarly opinion, taking into account over-emphatic reactions[7] as well as more realistic —if not disenchanted—views.[8] The range of comments and interpretations is such as to represent in itself an interesting new patrimony of European labour law; in years to come, the results of confrontations between lawyers and

broader perspective F. Scharpf, *Community and Autonomy. Multilevel Policy-Making in the European Union*, EUI Working Paper RSC n. 94/1.

[3] The question of sovereignty in the EU is examined by N. McCormick, 'The Maastricht Urteil: Sovereignty Now' [1995] 1 *ELJ* 259.

[4] S. Simitis, 'Europeizzazione o rinazionalizzazione del diritto del lavoro?' [1994] *DLRI* 641.

[5] As observed by S. Cassesse, 'La costituzione europea' [1991] *Quaderni costituzionali*, 487 ff., particularly 503, with regard to the transformation occurred to the European Community.

[6] Leibfried and Pierson, n. 2 above, 37.

[7] Such as in B. Bercusson, 'Maastricht: A Fundamental Change in European Labour Law' [1992] *ILJ* 177, and 'The Collective Labour Law of the European Union' in [1995] *ELJ* 157, where the Agreement is qualified as 'the founding constitutional basis for the collective labour law of the EU'.

[8] Lord Wedderburn, 'Labour Standards, Global Markets and Labour Laws in Europe', in W. Sengenberger and D. Campbell (eds.), *International Labour Standards and Economic Interdependence* (International Institute for Labour Studies, Geneva, 1994). Paradigmatic of this cautious, if not sceptical stance, is the approach adopted by W. Streeck in his most recent writings; see 'Neo-Voluntarism: A New European Social Policy Regime?' [1995] *ELJ* 31, and 'European Social Policy after Maastricht: the "Social Dialogue" and "Subsidiarity"' (1994) 15 *Economic and Industrial Democracy* 151.

political scientists could well develop into sources of inspiration for new and more solid reforms. A summary of such analyses is necessary in order to guide the reader of this chapter along the legal and political lines that have highlighted the post-Maastricht literature.

The introduction of derogations from Article 148(2) of the Rome Treaty, by way of a Protocol signed by all of the then twelve Member States and authorizing just eleven to sign an Agreement, gave rise to doubts about the legal nature of such sources and their inclusion in Community law.

As to the Protocol, Article 239 of the EEC Treaty, not amended after Maastricht, leaves little doubt that all protocols are an integral part of the Treaty to which they are annexed and that they prevail as *lex specialis* over that Treaty, whenever incompatibility is at stake.[9] In the particular case of social policies, such an incompatibility arises from the unwillingness of the United Kingdom to adopt the same social standards as other Member States. This institutionalization in Community law of a political disagreement, provoked mainly by domestic reasons of coherence with internal economic choices,[10] raises the fundamental question of how different rules of the game can govern the same internal market. The principle of differentiation, adopted in international law to allow for autonomous and—when necessary—specialized regulations which are binding only for some states, acquires in this field a meaning all of its own, carrying consequences for the entire edifice of EC social rights and adding to their uncertainty and instability.[11]

[9] D. Curtin, 'The Constitutional Structure of the Union: A Europe of Bits and Pieces', (1993) 30 *CMLRev*, 17; C. Curti Gialdino, *Il Trattato di Maastricht sull'Unione Europea*, (Istituto Poligrafico e Zecca dello Stato, 1993), 144 ff.; G. F. Mancini, 'Regole giuridiche e relazioni sindacali nell'Unione Europea', in *Il Protocollo sociale di Maastricht: realtà e prospettive* (Suppl. Notiziario Giurisprudenza del lavoro, Roma 1995), 14 (also published in English translation). In a broader perspective see also C. Cattabriga, 'Limiti materiali alla revisione comunitaria: il caso dei protocolli allegati al Trattato di Maastricht' [1994] *Riv. Diritto Europeo* 256, who refers to the two Court Opinions on the EEA agreement, where the Court has developed a notion of material limits to the revision of the Treaties (Opinion 1/91 of 14 Dec. 1991 [1991], ECR I–6079 and Opinion 1/92 of 10 Apr. 1992 [1992] ECR I–2821). According to Cattabriga protocols must also respect such limits (at 248); though the Social Chapter is not expressly mentioned, its inclusion in the Maastricht Treaty as a Protocol downgrades it in the constitutional hierarchy of sources and prevents its inclusion in the hard core of Community constitutional values developed by the Court in parallel with the concept of material limits to the revision of the Treaties.

[10] P. Davies and M. Freedland, *Labour Legislation and Public Policy: A Contemporary History* (Clarendon Press, Oxford, 1993), 594 ff., analyse the 'vigorous rearguard action' conducted by the UK since the adoption of the Social Charter and, later on, when the Labour Party's inclination towards Community social policies became even clearer. On the EC social dimension as related to the developments of British labour law, see Lord Wedderburn 'Companies and Employees: Common Law or Social Dimension?' [1993] *LQR* 220.

[11] In the *Report prepared by the Commission for the Reflection Group* (EC Commission, Brussels, 1995), no mystery is made of the fact that the legal basis provided for in the Agreement may bring in itself distortions of competition. See the Ch. on internal policies, at 49. This is why the Commission has tried to favour, whenever possible, recourse to the legal basis in the EC Treaty, perpetuating the related contradictions and limitations.

As to the Agreement on Social Policy, those who have argued in favour of an intergovernmental agreement, thus denying its Community nature, were perhaps too anxious to emphasize the weakness of the solution adopted at Maastricht and the need to react against reluctant institutions and ambivalent Member States.[12] Such a position reflects a state of mind which operates against the step-by-step approach traditionally adopted for social policies and is unaware of the important implications that any Community source—albeit a very weak one—may have in building up further developments.

The majority of commentators have, instead, argued for the inclusion of both sources in Community law, mainly for 'topographic' reasons,[13] that is to say, the links established in the Protocol with the 'institutions, procedures and mechanisms of the Treaty'.[14] The Commission has made such a point in a Communication[15] and actual developments have gone in this direction: Directive 94/45 on the establishment of European Works Councils[16] was the first to be approved on the legal basis of the Agreement. The reality, therefore, is that

[12] See E. Vogel-Polsky, *Evaluation of the Social Provisions of the Treaty on European Union agreed by the European Summit at Maastricht on 9 and 10 December 1991*, Report prepared for the Committee on social affairs, employment and working environment of the European Parliament, 7 Feb. 1992 (DOC EN\CM\202155 PE 155.405/I). The same author levelled sceptical remarks at the adoption of the Community Charter of Fundamental Social Rights of Workers in 'What Future is there for a Social Europe following the Strasbourg Summit?' [1990] *ILJ* 65.

[13] As described by G. F. Mancini, n. 9 above, 35, who finds such arguments more convincing than those based on Art. 220 EC and oriented to prove that the Agreement is the result of negotiations by Member States.

[14] S. Sciarra, 'European Social Policy and Labour Law. Challenges and Perspectives', in *Collected Courses of the Academy of European Law 1993*, Vol. IV Bk 1 (Martinuss Nijhoff Publishers, The Hague, 1995); E. Whiteford, 'Social Policy after Maastricht', (1993) *ELRev* 18 202 ff., underlining, despite the Community nature of the sources in question, the dangers in abandoning fundamental principles of the Community legal order. Curtin, n. 7 above, raises some doubts about the community nature of the acts (the 'Directives') adopted on the basis of the Social Agreement, followed by E. Szyszczak, 'Social Policy: A Happy Ending or a Reworking of the Fairy Tale?', in D. O'Keeffe and P. Twomey (eds.), *Legal Issues of the Maastricht Treaty* (Wiley Chancery Law, London, 1994), who also investigates the possible ways in which the ECJ could play a related part as far as these acts are concerned. The legal status of the Social Chapter is also analysed by C. Barnard, 'A Social Policy for Europe: Politicians 1, Lawyers 0' (1992) *IJCLLIR* 8 15, whose particular perspective consists in finding out the possible effects which the Social Chapter would be able to produce in the UK, under both the 'international law' and the 'Community law' theses.

[15] COM(93)600 Final, 14th Dec. 1993, *Communication concerning the application of the Agreement on social policy*, now largely quoted in the 1995 Report on the Community Charter and on the Protocol (COM(95)184 Final, 24 May 1995), issued on the basis of Art. 7 of the Agreement on social policy, taking into account developments regarding both documents.

[16] [1994] OJ L254/64. See R. Blanpain and P. Windey, *European Works Councils. Information and Consultation of Employees in Multinational Enterprises in Europe* (Peeters, Leuven, 1994) and C. McGlynn, 'European Works Councils: Towards Industrial Democracy?' (1995) 24 *ILJ* 178. See also the proceedings of a conference held at the European University Institute, Workers' information and consultation in European banks, Supplement to *Notiziario di giurisprudenza del lavoro*, Rome, 1995

of a problematic translation of the Social Chapter into Community practice; reformism enacted through very slow moves seems to have been the principle followed by all the actors involved, leaving legal interpreters happy (or unhappy) with their predictions and yet veiling important problems in a mist of uncertainty.

One such problem has to do with the competence of the Court of Justice to adjudicate on the acts—including collective agreements and Council decisions —which may be the product of the Social Chapter.[17]

In particular, it is difficult to ascertain whether collective agreements—as regards Article 4 of the Agreement—can be included at all within the scope of Article 173 and whether preliminary ruling proceedings can be started under Article 177(b). We shall come back to this point later while anticipating that an implicit competence of the Court may be assumed in judgments on a Council decision, if this is neither a recommendation nor an opinion. However, the ambiguous treatment reserved for social policy issues is strikingly different from that provided for other matters, as shown in the new version of Article 173, which explicitly mentions the Court's competence in regard to acts of the European Central Bank (ECB).[18]

The origin of such ambiguities lies in the British dislike for the Social Chapter, as already mentioned; this was the eventual outcome of a long and often hard battle fought by two protagonists of the 1980s: Jacques Delors on one side and Margaret Thatcher on the other, both of them simultaneously symbols and protagonists of political commitment and strong, albeit opposing beliefs on social policy.[19] It is difficult—and perhaps not all that productive— to try to imagine whether the outcome at Maastricht would have been different had there not been such a strong confrontation. The very fact of having ceded such an important role to a single government giving precedence to considerations of state sovereignty over those of uniform Community law, is an indication of the very weak power exercised by organized interests and by the associations representing them at a European level.

This must be said despite the fact that the final text of the Agreement approved at Maastricht by the Member States reproduces almost entirely

[17] Yet another problem is challenging the Agreement via an Art. 177 reference for its incompatibility with the *acquis communautaire*. See Whiteford, n. 14 above, 20.

[18] Cattabriga, n. 9 above, 258 recalls Art. 164 of the Treaty as the leading norm in interpreting any new competence of the Court, even those attributed by international agreements. The Community's constitution is at stake, together with its fundamental scope, when the Court is given new powers to intervene. An implied competence might therefore represent an assault on the constitutional principles of the Community, even when—as in the Social Protocol—the norms from which such a competence may be inferred are primary Community law.

[19] G. Ross, *J. Delors and European Integration* (OUP, Oxford 1995); M. Rhodes, 'A Regulatory Conundrum: Industrial Relations and the Social Dimension', in *European Social Policies*, n. 2 above, 78 ff.

what the social partners had agreed upon on 31 October 1991, signing a document which will certainly be remembered in the history of European social developments.[20]

From a legal point of view the core of disagreement between the Member States is to be found earlier on, in an obstinate quarrel on the Treaty legal basis, when legislation had to be proposed. Article 118A, as amended by the Single European Act, was the battleground: it appeared too narrow for those who wanted to apply the qualified majority vote provided for measures relating to health and safety of workers, and too wide for those who claimed unanimity to be the golden rule for labour matters.[21]

Maastricht and the intriguing solution found in the last few hours before the end of the negotiations, when the United Kingdom refused to sign the Agreement but adhered to the Protocol,[22] enlarged the legal basis for matters to be decided both unanimously and by a qualified majority vote. Moreover, the field was potentially opened up for the social partners to perform more powerfully, as we shall see below. The solutions envisaged in the Social Chapter are, nevertheless, far from satisfactory. This value judgement, based on a systematic interpretation of both the Protocol and the Agreement, running parallel as they do to the relevant norms of the EEC Treaty,[23] coincides with the empirical observation of the very limited use that has been made of the new tools available.

One could argue that the price paid for the last-minute compromise reached at Maastricht was too high and that not enough thought was given to the underevaluation of constitutional principles governing social policies. It could also be argued that the delay in the Treaty's ratification damaged the Protocol's potential, to the point of discouraging the social partners from making use of it.[24] Indeed, even if this is a feasible explanation the Agreement brings in itself a 'contradiction'[25] as painful as a thorn in the flesh of the new social

---

[20] G. Ross, 'Assessing the Delors Era and Social Policy', in *European social policies*, n. 2 above, 380.

[21] For a review of the problems related to the legal bases of EC labour law, see Lord Wedderburn, 'European Community Law and Workers' Rights after 1992: Fact or Fake?' and 'Freedom and Frontiers of Labour Law', in *Labour Law and Freedom. Further Essays in Labour Law* (Lawrence & Wishart. London, 1995; P. Davies, 'The Emergence of European Labour Law', in W. McCarthy (ed.), *Legal Intervention in Industrial Relations: Gains and Losses* (Blackwell, Oxford, 1992; M. Weiss, 'The Significance of Maastricht for European Community Social Policy' [1992] *IJCLLIR* 3 ff.; S. Sciarra, 'Social Values and the Multiple Sources of European Social Law' [1995] 1 *ELJ* 60. See also K. Banks, 'L'article 118A element dynamique de la politique sociale communautaire' (1993) *Cahiers de droit européen* 537; A. Lo Faro 'EC Social Policy and 1993. The dark side of European Integration?' [1992] *Comp. Lab. Law Journal* 1 ff.

[22] C. Curti Gialdino, n. 9 above. 143, underlining how the opting-in of 11 Member States was a solution opposite to the one adopted for the Monetary Union.

[23] See the phrase in the Protocol 'this Protocol and the said Agreement are without prejudice to the provisions of this Treaty, particularly those which relate to social policy which constitute an integral part of the *acquis communautaire*'.

[24] G. Ross, 'Assessing the Delors Era and Social Policy', n. 20 above, 384.

[25] LordWedderburn, 'Labour Standards, Global Markets and Labour Laws in Europe',

dimension, namely, the express exclusion (Article 2.6) of the right of association from Community competence.

The European Union's objectives as set in Article B, Title I, include economic and social cohesion and link it to the establishment of economic and monetary union; Article F.2 expresses the European Union's obligation to observe the 1950 European Convention on Human Rights (ECHR) and the constitutional traditions of Member States as general principles of Community law. This might imply that a 'collective dimension', built on the right to associate that is common to the most important and best-established European legal systems, accompanies the freedom of movement granted as fundamental to all European workers.[26] It could also be argued that the new *status civitatis* enshrined in the Treaty, aimed at the creation of a supranational level of citizenship, cannot conflict with Article 11 of the ECHR; the result is a 'Communitarization' of that particular fundamental right, leading to the inclusion of a collective dimension in the Treaty itself.[27]

It cannot, however, be denied that, unlike the definition of an internal market provided for in Article 7A, social policy lacks an 'identity' and 'cannot lay claim to an obvious constituency'; this is due to the difficulty in bringing together all the various provisions, which are scattered throughout the Treaties, but also to the fact that the notion of a European labour market is still very vague, as is also that of a European labour movement.[28]

For all these reasons, no broad interpretation[29] and no generous and far-sighted initiative of the social partners could compensate for the lack of a solid constitutional basis on which to found the development of collective rights at Community level. This lacuna is even more yawning and more worrying if one thinks in terms of expansion of the Community; the notion of

in W. Sengenberger and D. Campbell (eds.), n. 8 above, 'Freedom and Frontiers of Labour Law', n. 21 above. On the meaning of the freedom of association principle, see Lord Wedderburn, 'Freedom of Association and Philosophies of Labour Law' (1989) 18 *ILJ* 1.

[26] J. Aparicio Tovar, 'Contrattazione collettiva e fonti comunitarie', in A. Baylos, B. Caruso, M. D'Antona, S. Sciarra (eds.), *Dizionario di diritto del lavoro comunitario* (Monduzzi Editore, Bologna, 1996).

[27] M. Rodriguez-Piñero, 'La negociacion colectiva europea hasta Maastricht' [1992] II *Relaciones Laborales* 40; M. A. Moreau, 'Tendances du droit social communautaire: des droits sociaux en quête de reconnaisance' [1994] *Droit Social* 614, inferring that European citizenship is not to be interpreted separately from the *acquis communitaire* but requires, nevertheless, the constitutionalization of social rights.

[28] J. Shaw, 'Twin-track Social Europe—the Inside Track', in D. O'Keeffe and P. M. Twomey (eds.), n. 14 above, 296-297.

[29] An example of which can be found in Bercusson, 'The Collective Labour Law, n. 7 above, especially 158-9, where it is indicated that collective labour law has its European roots outside the specific subject matter and is therefore the result of spill-over; in such a notion 'reflections' from national experiences are included, as well as ECJ case law. It remains difficult to prove that such reflections do exist and are indeed being 'spilled over', since the legal bases so far provided in Community law are very distant from constitutional traditions of Member States in collective labour law. It is even more difficult to label as 'spill-over effect' the legal implications of ECJ case law, which, on the contrary, bring about effective changes in national legal systems and may give rise to specific rights of individuals in the national courts.

the *acquis communautaire*, running like a red thread through the leading principles of the European Union, does not in itself suffice to overcome the absence of fundamental rights in the Treaties, nor to export binding principles across borders, in the context of wider external relations.[30] The Court has not adopted a high profile on this matter, preferring not to act as a constitutional court or to indicate in an orderly way the European legal system's priorities.[31]

The consolidation of stronger principles in the Treaty could make room for a more relevant role for the Court and the commencement of a heroic period of social rights. The most important confrontation is currently taking place between institutions; this is in itself an example of how 'functional spillover can generate political spillover'.[32] From the perspective of the Social Chapter this implies that soft law and other non-legally binding measures such as collective agreements are a means to an end, useful for the diffusion of principles which should then consolidate into rights.[33]

Collective Agreements: Neo-voluntarism *v.* Neo-corporatism

The image of a multi-tiered system mentioned at the beginning may be evoked again when describing the typology of collective agreements presented in the Social Agreement. Before analysing in detail the legal nature of and effects produced by such collective sources, it should be noted that none of the theories traditionally applied to collective bargaining for the purposes of analysing this legal and social phenomenon within an institutional frame of reference seems to apply satisfactorily to the European scene. The reason for this lies in the absence of supranational actors—management and labour— comparable to national actors.

Voluntarism,[34] traditionally used in labour law theory to signify the primacy of collective agreements over the law, does not apply to the European system of collective labour relations. Nor can a comparison be drawn between the European single market and a snapshot view of a national economic system within which industrial relations theories have placed the activity of collective

[30] See the Agreement on EEA, signed at Oporto on 2 May 1992 and in particular section V (where arts. 118A, 118B and 119 are recalled) and Art. 78, including social policies among the matters for which co-operation must be pursued among the signatories. In the annexed declarations reference is also made to principles and rights of the 1989 Social Charter.

[31] C. Curti Gialdino, 'Some reflections on the *acquis communautaire*' (1995) 32 *CMLRev*, 1089.

[32] S. Leibfried and P. Pierson, 'The Dynamics', n. 2 above, 442.

[33] S. Sciarra, 'Social Values and the Multiple Sources of European Social Law' [1995] 1 *ELJ* 60. More generally see B. Hepple, 'Social Values and European Law' [1995], *Current Legal Problems* 39 ff.

[34] The term is used differently in this context from the sense adopted by Streeck, n. 8 above at 31 ff. For a critique of legal abstention, leading to voluntarism both in labour law theory and policies, see H. Collins, 'Against Abstentionism in Labour Law' in J. Eekelaar and J. Bell (eds.) *Oxford Essays in Jurisprudence* (OUP, Oxford, 1987), 79 ff.

organizations, thus theorizing the strict correlation between the economic and legal elements of the bargaining process. This is mainly due to the fact that, by the express choice made in Article 2.6 of the Social Agreement, European collective bargaining does not deal with pay, making it something inherently different from traditional negotiating machinery at a national level. The lack of a clear normative function coincides—in the specific case of supranational collective agreements—with the lack of a standardization function, that is to say with the proper setting of labour costs and the indication of the impact of wages on the economic system as a whole.

Nor can we compare European institutions to individual States when interacting as regulators and/or as negotiators with national social partners. In an enlarged scheme of reference such as that of a supranational single market, the dynamics of interest representation reproduce themselves almost indefinitely, as in a hall of mirrors, because of the continual need to solve different problems at different levels of decision-making. The overlapping of national and supranational powers in initiating trilateral negotiations, together with the impossibility of identifying the nature of the exchanges and the expected outcomes, are clear indications of an imperfect balance between imperfect actors.

The only way of demonstrating that these intuitions are correct is to look at the various types of collective agreements enshrined in the definitions of the Social Agreement and verify whether they belong to the same legal species.

The first type, referred to in Article 2.4 of the Agreement, constitutes a novelty in European social law: both the procedure, as an offer emanating jointly from the social partners to transpose directives by means of collective agreements, and the option that is left open to States whether or not to accept their offer, represent an innovation. Although the initiative comes from the social partners, Member States are held responsible for non-implementation of Community law, should the 'necessary measures' introduced by agreement represent an insufficient or incorrect transposition and therefore not fulfil the final obligation, as under Article 189.

One may argue, as a consequence of Article 2.4, that it is the State's responsibility to verify whether collective agreements are generally applicable and meet the standards indicated by the ECJ,[35] both for the generality of employees involved and for the areas of activity concerned. If the obligations of the Member States in this respect, are to be interpreted widely, it may prove difficult to isolate the autonomy of the social partners in a vacuum,

---

[35] Case 91/81 *Commission* v. *Italy* [1982] ECR 723; Case 131/84 *Commission* v. *Italy* [1985] ECR 3531; Case 143/83 *Commission* v. *Denmark* [1985] ECR 427. J. Aparicio Tovar, n. 26 above, 180, underlines that collective agreements are by definition a weaker tool than directives, if nothing else for the fact that they do not have an unlimited duration. If they were lacking an expiry term, however, they would be the result of a more self-restrained collective identity, less dynamic when dealing with European norms than it is when dealing with domestic issues.

whereby they act independently of the standards required at a supranational level. This is particularly relevant with regard to the legal enforceability of collective agreements and to the breadth of their scope.

Even interpretations developed in national case law,[36] through rulings on the legally binding function of collective agreements and their enforceability on a case-by-case basis, may prove to be a controversial tool if used beyond national frontiers. Although it might appear contradictory to the process of internationalization, which is also affecting interest organizations and involving management and labour alike, the social partners continue to be better defended as to their prerogatives when they remain within national boundaries. This is so for several reasons. The assimilation of contractual sources to other legal sources reflects harmonized choices made within each legal system taken as a whole. Different techniques, such as devolution from the law to collective agreements or extension of agreements through law,[37] must imply coherent mechanisms in national labour law, whereby the real power of collective organizations to act as negotiating agents is somehow recognized in legislation so that legal consequences from collective bargaining may be inferred. Furthermore, the meaning of the expression 'social partners' varies considerably from country to country, linked as it is to concrete functions and activities which unions and employers' associations are asked to perform at various levels.[38] The role of the State, as in Article 2.4, would inevitably imply a preliminary evaluation of the social partners' ability to perform as powerful and capable negotiators within the scope of the Agreement and, indeed, within the framework of Community law. Far from reflecting the scheme of collective *laissez faire*, the model put forward here is that of an interventionist state, acting as legislator behind the scenes of voluntary negotiations. The Court of Justice's competence to intervene on such acts would in any case be related to the role played by the State: whether as duly observing Community law or as in breach of it, the State features as the direct interlocutor of the Court, responsible in the end for the proper functioning of its internal bargaining machinery.

Collective agreements, as presented in Article 4 and referred to in Article 3.4 of the Agreement are of a different type from that described above.

There can be the case of agreements used as alternative measures to

[36] The example of Italy can be quoted, where the lack of legal enforceability for collective agreements has been counterbalanced by a powerful interpretation in case law, allowing for a *de facto* extension of the scope of bargaining even beyond the parties signatories to them. See G. Giugni, *Diritto Sindacale* (Cacucci, Bari, 1995); Lord Wedderburn, 'Inderogability, Collective Agreements and Community Law' (1992) 21 *ILJ* 245.

[37] Lord Wedderburn and S. Sciarra, 'Collective Bargaining as Agreement and as Law: Neo-Contractualist and Neo-Corporatist Tendencies of our Age', in A. Pizzorusso (ed.), *Law in the Making* (Springer-Verlag, Berlin-Heidelberg, 1988).

[38] A. Lo Faro, 'Maastricht ed oltre' [1993] *Diritto delle Relazioni Industriali* 125 ff., especially at 141. See also M. Roccella and T. Treu, *Dritto del lavoro della Comunità Europea* (Cedam, Padova, 1995), 34.

directives, following the elaborate procedure set out in Article 3. Here the Commission is required to act as promoter of consultation and of the dialogue between management and labour. The latter may be active to a varying degree in such a procedure, depending on matters of internal coherence and overall strategy; what is out of the question is that the social partners have a new 'right'[39] to act as the official interlocutors of the Commission and to be part of the law-making process.[40] Drawing a parallel with concertation or neo-corporatist arrangements, useful as it may appear in order to describe the new roles assigned to all three actors involved, is not so simple. Not only do we find that the Commission is left with no relevant discretionary powers,[41] bound as it is by the objectives of the Agreement (Article 1), in which social policies are inextricably linked with 'the need to maintain the competitiveness of the Community economy'; it also has to be borne in mind that Community action as envisaged in Article 3 is confined within the bound of the competence assigned by Article 2 for decisions to be taken by qualified majority or unanimously.

The other possible notion of a European collective agreement is that resulting from a fruitful dialogue, whenever both parties express the 'desire' to engage in contractual relations (Article 4.1). We have to assume that this specific type of agreement, envisaged in Article 4.2, can be negotiated only by supra-national European associations; it remains to be seen whether a

---

[39] This is emphasized by the Commission Communication concerning the application of the Agreement on social policy, COM(93)600 Final, 14 Dec. 1993.

[40] The first application of the Art. 3 procedure was related to the adoption of the European Works Council Directive. The fact that an agreement was almost reached by the social partners may optimistically be seen as a sign of proper functioning of the Social Agreement. It can also be argued that the adoption of a directive was a victory of the Commission over reluctant social partners, especially over the employers' opposition to it.

During the course of 1995 another Commission proposal went through the two-stage consultation provided for by Art. 3: the parental leave directive proposal, whose first step dates from 1983. In this second case, the result of the social partners' negotiations was different, a draft framework agreement having been reached in Nov. 1995 between ETUC, UNICE, and CEEP. The conclusion of the framework agreement, which took place in Dec. 1995 (see Agence Europe No 6627, 15 Dec. 1995, 9), does not hide the substantial poverty of its content. Throughout the bargaining round, the British CBI was present—as was expressly stated—in the capacity of observer and non-voting participant. The Commission proposed the adoption of the Agreement; the Dir. is the final outcome of the whole procedure: Dir. 96/34 EC, of 3 June 1996 [1996] OJ L145.

Finally, a third Art. 3 consultation was undertaken by the Commission in Sept. 1995, with regard to atypical work issues.

[41] A. Ojeda Aviles, 'European Collective Bargaining: A Triumph of the Will?' (1993) 9 *IJCLLIR* 290. An overview of the institutional framework which never did allow for corporatist arrangements to succeed is in P. Teague, *The European Community: The Social Dimension* (Kogan Page, London, 1989), 87 ff. See also W. Streeck and P. Schmitter, 'From National Corporatism to Transnational Pluralism: Organized Interests in the Single European Market' (1991) 19 *Politics & Society* 133. The potentialities of the Social Chapter are analysed in the perspective of the setting-up of a European corporatist decision-making model by D. Obradovic, 'Prospects for Corporatist Decision-making in the European Union: The Social Policy Agreement' (1995) 2 *Journal of European Public Policy* 1350.

precondition for being defined as such is to be an association covering all forms and expressions of organized interests in all Member States, and so representative of European employees. Although soft law helps the interpreter to find a reasonable solution,[42] it is far from clear how the criteria adopted at a national level in order to measure representativeness may be transplanted to a European level. The difficulty is due to the fact that, even when referred to in domestic legislation, the notion of a representative union is subject to constant changes, either because of varying value judgements expressed in case law, or because of varying political orientations of national parliaments,[43] or because of varying membership and affiliation numbers and, consequently, varying bargaining power. This is why European representativeness should not be thought of as a reproduction of existing criteria but as a unique concept, mainly linked to the capacity of both European management and labour to be active and present across industry and across Member States, despite the lack of constitutional guidance in the Treaty. The current situation, whereby the most urgent reform is also the most difficult to achieve, leaves the whole matter of collective bargaining and its social and political relevance in a limbo, towards which varying degrees of optimism may be adopted.

In both of these latter cases (Article 3 and Article 4) one can argue that, unlike the procedures indicated in Article 2.4 (where discretion is left to the States and where—as under Article 169—the Commission could bring an action before the Court), the rules of the game are set at a European level and the Commission and the Council are asked to play an institutional role. The difference between the two types of agreement relates only to their scope, the former functioning as an alternative to other Community actions and the latter dealing with matters outside the scope of Article 2.[44]

This is why both types of agreement are to be qualified as 'European' in a more stringent and appropriate way, although their inclusion among the acts of the institutions—as under Article 177(b)—remains debatable. Despite the recognition they receive in the Maastricht Agreement, which goes far beyond the weak formulation of the social dialogue in the SEA, management and labour are in no way treated as European institutions. Their public role, either as holders of the right to be consulted by the Commission or as

[42] See again the Communication quoted at n. 39 above.

[43] Recent Italian developments are a living example of a changing—if not disappearing—notion of a representative union. Following the result of a referendum which repealed part of the relevant legislation (Article 19 of the 1970 Workers' Statute), no agreement has been reached so far in Parliament on a new formulation of the law. The result is a purely factual importance of those unions which are able to impose themselves as bargaining agents at national and local level. See G. Giugni, 'La rappresentanza sindacale dopo il referendum' [1995] *DLRI* 357 ff., particularly 366.

[44] Agreements outside the competence of the Social Agreement would not generate any direct legal effect within national legal systems. See G. Lyon-Caen, 'Le droit social de la Communauté européenne après le Traité de Maastricht' [1993] *Recueil Dalloz* 152.

initiators of the bargaining procedure regulated by Article 4, does not result in the ability to produce a new category of Community acts. European collective bargaining remains in the realm of procedures; it attempts to solve complexity through the inclusion of organized interests in the decision-making process, but it is not capable of assigning new rights to individuals and creating a new competence of the Court under Article 173.

This can be quoted as another example of 'partnership'[45] between nation-states—and in particular between national organizations—without the creation of a new separated power. Consequently, mere agreements reached under Article 4 are gentlemen's agreements from which no rights and obligations arise and which are therefore not interpretable by the Court;[46] nor is there an obligation on the Member States to apply them directly or to amend legislation with a view to transposing them, as explicitly stated in Declaration No. 2 at the end of the Social Chapter.[47]

By contrast, a Council decision jointly requested by the signatory parties on a proposal from the Commission seems closer to acts of the Council, other than recommendations and opinions, as referred to in Article 173, even if its origin lies in a voluntary and autonomous bargaining activity of the social partners. This may be one of the reasons why the European Parliament has indicated that agreements should be implemented by a Council decision, pending a more structural reform to be adopted at the 1996 Intergovernmental Conference, namely, the implementation of the Social Protocol as a whole through legislation.[48]

No theoretical framework appears suitable to include and describe European collective bargaining as it emerges from the Social Chapter. The argument that collective agreements reached under Article 4 do not possess legal enforceability does not prove the victory of neo-voluntarism, nor of a Community collective *laissez faire*; even the terminology adopted to describe the hierarchy of sources in national systems of labour law seems inappropriate for the consolidation of European norms. What is missing is the legitimacy of representative associations within Community law; this causes the lack of any

[45] See earlier text and n. 5.
[46] G. F. Mancini, 'Regole giuridiche', n. 7 above, 38. See also A. Ojeda-Aviles, n. 41 above, 286, who talks of agreements 'not generally applicable' and J. Aparicio Tovar, n. 26 above, 187, who specifies that neither Community agreements nor national agreements implementing them share the effects of Community law, that is to say 'prevail on internal law' and ensure uniformity.
[47] Of which it is said that it 'has limited legal significance and is not justiciable'. See E. Szyszczak, n. 14 above, 321.
[48] The Parliament's position, expressed in the plenary session on 23–24 Feb. 1994 (DOC A3–0091/94 in [1994] OJ C77/30) following the Commission's Communication, is now given full account in the *Report on the Community Charter of the Fundamental Social Rights of Workers* which has been presented by the Commission jointly with the *Report on the Social Protocol*, in compliance with Art. 7 of the Agreement. See COM(95)184 Final, 24 May 1995, 39–40.

normative significance for European collective agreements and leaves to them the weaker—although not unnecessary—role of framework agreements.

As for the procedural importance of information and consultation, it must be stressed that the Social Chapter has greatly innovated the social dialogue, transforming it from a non-regulatory institution into a pre-regulatory technique which binds the Commission to new rules. Failure to comply with this new obligation may result in infringement of Community law, in line with what the Court has stated in regard to the duty to consult the European Parliament in the law-making process.[49] As yet, procedural labour law seems to be the only answer to unresolved institutional problems. In the current interlocutory phase, this is no minor achievement for social policies: included as they are in a more democratic decision-making machinery, they also appear, through the lens of the Social Chapter, more visible and transparent than before.[50]

Subsidiarity and the Social Agreement

The Relationship between Legal and Voluntary Sources

Article 2 of the Agreement ('With a view to achieving the objectives of Article 1, the Community shall support and complement the activities of the Member States') is an indication of how a partial loss of sovereignty did occur for Member States in the social field.[51] This is so despite the statement in Article 2.5 that directives based on the Agreement and implemented by management and labour do not prevent Member States 'from maintaining or introducing more stringent protective measures compatible with the Treaty'. This norm must be read in conjunction with Article 3b, which constitutes the guiding principle for the attribution of competence and the conferral of powers by the Treaty.

Declaration No. 16 on the hierarchy of Community Acts, attached to the Maastricht Treaty, calls upon the 1996 Intergovernmental Conference to review the classification of Community acts. The initial indications given by the Commission,[52] together with the results of academic research carried out

[49] G. Tesauro, 'Le procedure di consultazione delle parti sociali nel Protocollo sociale', in *Il Protocollo sociale di Maastricht: realtà e prospettive* n. 9 above, 140; S. Sciarra, 'Il dialogo tra ordinamento comunitario e nazionale del lavoro: la contrattazione collettiva' [1992] *DLRI* 715.

[50] The critical evaluation given in the ECOSOC's Opinion culminated in the suggestion —albeit not unanimous—to introduce an 'independent secratariat', with the task of monitoring the consultation procedures. See B. Bercusson and J.J. van Dijk, 'The Implementation of the Protocol and Agreement on Social Policy of the Treaty on European Union' (1995) 11 *IJCLLR* 3.

[51] P. Langlois, 'Europe sociale et principe de subsidiarité' [1993] *Droit Social* 203.

[52] *The Principle of Subsidiarity, Communication of the Commission to the Council and the European Parliament*, SEC (92)1990 Final, 27 Oct. 1992.

meanwhile,[53] will shortly be the subject of evaluation at a political level and will prove extremely relevant for social policy too.

In accordance with the philosophy of the Commission's document, most binding instruments must be viewed as the last resort; therefore it would seem an implicit consequence that the law should give way to voluntary sources. However, this still obscure aspect of subsidiarity must be co-ordinated with other relevant aspects, including the choice of legal basis in the Treaty. That is why such a principle must be viewed as 'part of decision-making, not a precondition for it'.[54] When recourse to a binding instrument is unavoidable, the Commission favours the choice of framework directives, laying down basic rules, and goes on to state that this choice must imply a hierarchy of norms to be recognized as an official constitutional principle.[55] This is even more necessary for social policy, the legal foundations of which are scattered throughout the Treaties and uncertain in their orientation, thus increasing the weakness of the supra-national law-making process.

Because of the new importance attributed to collective agreements in the framework of Community measures, subsidiarity has also been given a further function, relating to the nature of the measure—contractual or legal—to be adopted and not the legal subject—the Community or the Member State—adopting it. Horizontal subsidiarity—as it is referred to—does not seem to add anything further to what Article 2 already states; nor does it alter the existing balance between States and social partners.[56] Whereas in national labour law traditions the relationship between law and collective agreements is a symptom of mutual recognition between different systems of norms and the product of harmonized developments on both sides, in the European context such a model does not automatically apply. Delegation to voluntary sources, as we might attempt to describe collective agreements *ex* Article 2.4, does not imply the recognition of a specialized function for them. On the contrary, traditional ways of measuring the social partners' autonomy—such as a balance between countervailing powers and the ability to negotiate either through conflict or through dispute resolution machinery—do not appear central to attainment of the final outcome, that is to say, compliance with Community standards via the evaluation of the State, which remains an essential part of the above mentioned procedure set in Article 2.4.

Horizontal subsidiarity, as referred to in the choice between law and collective agreements, may be used only as an indirect way of interpreting the

---

[53] G. Winter (ed.), *Sources and Categories of European Union Law. A Comparative and Reform Perspective* (Nomos, Baden, 1996), forthcoming.

[54] Communication n. 52 above.   [55] Ibid. 16.

[56] In the Commission's Communication on the Social Agreement mention is made of a 'dual form of subsidiarity in the social field', the second one being the choice 'at Community level' of a legal or contractual approach. A different interpretation is given by B. Bercusson and J.J.van Dijk, n. 50 above, 10 ff., who argue in favour of transposing the notion of dual subsidiarity also at national level, and claim to base their argument on 'a careful reading' of the Protocol.

competence of European institutions and evaluating the adequacy of the measures to be adopted. The social partners, although integrated into the law-making process, are in no way comparable to institutions of the Community; their still uncertain legitimacy to act as representative of management and labour means that they act as quasi-supranational structures, split between the requirements of the single market and of loyalty to individual States. Consequently, European collective agreements are not explicitly included among Community acts, nor do they find a clear legitimacy in Community law. Since they have not yet proved, in practice, to fulfil specific aims, recourse to such tools remains merely programmatic, both in legal writings and in practical terms. With a view to future and even more general reforms it is correct to argue, with reference to collective agreements also, that 'the Community act should legally be defined by its origin, i.e. its being made by the legislature process, but not by its content or function'.[57] This would imply a formal inclusion of collective agreements in the hierarchy of Community sources only when they become incorporated in a Council decision. Furthermore, a clear definition should be given of the term 'decision', which has so far been left to the imagination of interpreters and never tested in practice.

In the existing legal framework, the dangers hidden behind horizontal subsidiarity are subtle: to rationalize the role of Community legal instruments by linking them to voluntary sources which, as they stand, neither run parallel to the law nor can be ranked at an equal level, may prove of little effectiveness. This is so both for semantic reasons (what we mean by European collective agreements) and for reasons relating to bargaining agents and their tasks (who bargains for whom?).[58] The lack of legitimacy within Community law—as already mentioned—is aggravated by the difficulty of communication between labour law systems, each inclined to maintain intact their own national peculiarities. It is also for this reason that new rules should be written into the constitutions of supranational organizations, for both management and labour.[59] Although the results would still remain unpredictable in the social

---

[57] G. Winter (ed), n. 53 above, 21.

[58] M. Le Friant and A. Höland, 'La reconnaissance des contrats collectifs par le droit communautaire', in G. Winter (ed), n. 53 above, who also underline the uncertain definition of the social partners to be consulted by the Commission and suggest that the interpretation of European collective agreements should depend on the organizational nature of the bargaining agents, namely, they should be multi-industry organizations, not merely industrial ones. The Commission argued similarly: Communication, n. 39 above, 22. See also the social partners' joint proposal, of 29 Oct. 1993 (in: Joint Opinions, v/1986/94), in which the envisaged criteria are: to be organized horizontally or sectorally at European level, to be formed of 'representative' organizations in Member States, to be present in EEA countries also, to be voluntary organizations, able to conduct collective bargaining, and to be 'instructed by their members to represent them in the framework of the Community social dialogue' (point 4). This last point is of particular relevance when discussing European collective agreements and trying to position them in a hierarchy of sources.

[59] See the ETUC Statute—as amended at the 8th Congress held in Brussels in May 1995—at Art. 13, stating that the Executive Committee, 'the supreme authority' of the confederation, has the power to determine the composition and the mandate of the

field, a hierarchical structure of norms would certainly serve the initial purpose of imposing common and uniform rules as a starting point for all Member States and for the social partners as well. It is therefore disappointing that the report prepared for this purpose[60] should have devoted such little attention to collective agreements and the unsolved interpretative problems raised by the Social Chapter.

Furthermore, the group of independent experts set up by the Commission in 1994, and asked to give indications on how to simplify and reduce Community legislation, produced a report[61] carrying somewhat ambiguous consequences for employment and social matters. While indicating that 'fundamental rights and principles directly applicable in the Member States' should be agreed upon, the experts did not openly address the issue of collective agreements and their legal nature in the overall system of Community measures; they simply declared that the social partners should 'agree as soon as possible on arrangements which would render legislative initiative on the part of the Community superfluous'. Much criticized by the employers' association UNICE for its lack of clarity, the *Molitor Report* has nevertheless reawakened the imagination of the business community. The expressed preference for autonomous choices of the social partners at national level whenever confronting employment issues[62] is yet another sign of a multi-tiered system of social policies which becomes inclined towards state-building as soon as the market requires stronger guiding principles. Law, even when merely announced as a possibility, acts as a powerful deterrent, inducing the social partners to opt for collective bargaining as the least dangerous of the available choices.

The Relationship between Different Levels of Regulation

The principle of subsidiarity, as it has just been argued, does not serve the additional purpose of indicating choices—to be made at national level—between voluntary and legal means. Nevertheless, a relationship does exist between law and collective agreements, even in the current situation where the hierarchy of Community sources has not yet been redefined.

We must start by saying that the supremacy and direct effect of Community law are doctrines which are also applicable to national collective agreements,

delegation for negotiations on a case-by-case basis. It also specifies that decisions on the outcome of negotiations shall be taken by the same body, following precise voting procedures which are also aimed at involving the organisations directly concerned in negotiations, holding, when necessary, internal consultations.

[60] Winter (ed.), n. 53 above.

[61] *Report of the group of independent experts on legislative and administrative simplification*, COM(95)288 Final, 21 June 1995 (*Molitor Report*).

[62] *Agence Europe*, No. 6510, 28 June 1995, 15.

irrespective of their scope, their legal nature and their being or not being legally binding.[63] This reflects the impact of Community law on national systems seen as a whole, including all sources and means of regulation. Similarly, domestic labour law is left free to maintain, or supplement with more protective measures, those laid down at Community level. There is a dual link between national and supranational systems of norms, aimed at guaranteeing mutual respect between sources and providing enforcement for rights, regardless of their origins.

This model of reciprocal inclusion has not lost its original value and has been proposed again in recent directives. Only some are worth mentioning, because of the particular relevance of the subject matter and also the special systems of derogation they introduce.

In the Directive on the organization of working time,[64] collective agreements are seen either as a parallel source to which detailed and more minute regulations could be reserved (rest breaks, weekly working time[65]) or as a channel for the introduction of more favourable provisions (Article 15). Both these functions are traditionally fulfilled by the social partners in most European legal systems and may be interpreted as a way of specifying legal regulations more precisely or even refining their content. A different function is the one assigned to collective agreements—even at a level lower than the national or the regional one—for the introduction of derogations (Article 17). In all the various cases envisaged by the Directive, collective sources must continue to comply with the protection of workers' health and safety; they are seen therefore as a measure to compensate individual rights and re-establish an equilibrium which might otherwise be contrary to the basic principles set in the Directive.

Because of the general importance which protective measures have in this sensitive area of labour law, it is explicitly stated that Member States in which collective agreements are not legally enforceable or in which laws on working time are in force must allow derogations by way of collective agreements (Article 17.3). Regulatory powers remain in the hands of national legislatures whenever questions of public policy are at stake; this takes place either through national statutes 'ensuring the conclusion of collective agreements' or through a formal authorization made by the state to undergo derogations.

[63] The ECJ has had several opportunities to affirm this. Some meaningful examples are: Case 165/82, *Commission* v. *UK* [1983] ECR, 3431; Case 170/84, *Bilka Kaufhaus GmbH* v. *Weber von Hartz* [1986] ECR 1607; Case 184/89, *Nimz* v. *Freie und Hansestadt Hamburg* [1991] ECR 297.

[64] Council Dir. 93/104/EC, of 23 Nov. 1993 [1993] OJ L307/18.

[65] Bercusson, 'The Collective Labour Law' , n. 7 above, 164, interprets Art. 4 on breaks as assistance of the primacy of collective agreements over legislation 'in determining the EU standard', whereas this appears to be one of the many cases in which it is the State's choice whether to enforce Community law through collective agreements or law or, as frequently happens, through a combination of these two (Art. 4 specifies that national legislation is required if collective agreements fail to regulate the matter).

The *Molitor Report*[66] has commented on the Working Time Directive, putting forward a strong plea for flexibility for both employers and employees and stating that a clear rule should be established for the calculation of a reference period in determining weekly working time. The suggestion is that it should be longer than four months—as at present indicated in Article 16.2—and reach twelve months for the compensation of overtime, to allow the Member States and social partners to introduce different provisions. This detailed proposal, unusual when compared with the *Report*'s otherwise abrupt style, indicates that account must be taken of national traditions, often stemming from collective bargaining, when dealing with flexibility issues; it also shows that the maximum requirement set at Community level serves the purpose of protecting individual employees' health and safety and is therefore not subject to derogations *in pejus*. A traditional hierarchy of norms seems to be still in its place and to fulfil its traditional aim, even in the perspective of a reform which is intended to make the entire European legal system more efficient and oriented towards greater competitiveness.

The Directive on European Works Councils[67] is unique as regards establishing a relationship between law and voluntary sources. Reference is made to collective agreements reached prior to the deadline indicated in the Directive for implementation by Member States and in any case before the transposition of the Directive itself (Article 13); such agreements are thought of as a measure preferable to the law, as far as the parties signatory to them are concerned. The obligation on Member States to comply with Community norms by inserting them into national legal systems is, unusually, shifted to collective sources, which do not technically represent an alternative means of implementation but a way of exempting Community-scale undertakings or Community-scale groups of undertakings from observing the Directive while nevertheless complying with its principles. The role left to Member States is still significant, since it is their obligation to ensure that management and labour meet the deadline; in any case they have to 'take all necessary steps enabling them at all times to guarantee the results' imposed by the Directive (Article 14).[68]

Both these examples have been chosen in order to show that collective bargaining at national level is not referred to as a variable independent of the

---

[66] N. 61 above. sec. 4, point 9.

[67] Quoted at n. 16 above.

[68] It remains to be ascertained whether the subsidiary requirements indicated in the annex represent a minimum floor for collective agreements also. If the latter could go below the standards set in the annex, Art. 13 might become a way of evading the Directive's main function and introducing a less strict regulation through voluntary sources. Not only would this go against the spirit of the Dir.; it would also create a situation in which the State's responsibility would be to ascertain that collective agreements signed pursuant to Art. 13 are not a derogation *in pejus* from Community law and that management and labour have not used their bargaining power against the regulatory power of the State.

rest of the legal system. Directives do not impose choices between the measures to be adopted in fulfilling Community obligations; subsidiarity, as a leading principle governing the distribution of competence, does not affect national legal systems, nor does it touch the internal balance between legal and voluntary sources.

Market-building: Collective Bargaining and Title VI of the Maastricht Treaty

European social policy has been described as a multi-level system of regulation, in which various bodies and institutions are active and in search of a more coherent legislative strategy; reasons have also been advanced why collective agreements do not have clear legal standing, even after their appearance on the scene. The underlying implication of such deliberations is that, after Maastricht, labour law is different from what it was before and so labour lawyers are commenting on it. This is the unexpected result of an unusual combination of events: a Treaty lacking fundamental social rights, social partners lacking strong powers, and institutions lacking a clear legislative initiative. And added to all these uncertain institutional choices there are further constraints.

Title VI on economic and monetary policy, in particular Article 103 of the Treaty on European Union (TEU), is an important source, together with Title XIV on economic and social cohesion. Whereas the former puts the Council in a position to co-ordinate Member States' initiatives and ensure that they comply with broad economic policy guidelines, the latter grants financial assistance to projects in the field of environment and trans-European transport infrastructure networks, through the Cohesion Fund.[69]

Following the Delors White Paper[70] and the issuing of the guidelines by the Council, the social partners have repeatedly produced their own point of view,[71] which is relevant to the content of this Chapter. The co-ordination of economic and monetary policies at Community level is seen as a precondition

---

[69] Council Reg. 1164/94, 16 May 1994 [1994] OJ L130/1.

[70] *Growth, Competitiveness*, n. 1 above.

[71] See *The Framework for the Broad Economic Policy Guidelines*, 5 Dec. 1993. This document must be read in conjunction with the first Council Recommendation of 22 Dec. 1993, issued on the basis of Art. 103.2 The guidelines are issued approximately every six months. The Joint Opinion elaborated by the Macroeconomic Group of the Social Dialogue (May 1995) was explicitly aimed at the preparation of the following EU guidelines and addressed not only to the Commission but also to the EcoFin and Social Affairs Councils, deploring the fact that previous Opinions had not been given sufficient attention by Member States. This is no minor detail when describing the institutionalization of what can hardly be described as an informal consultation mechanism. The Madrid Summit (December 1995) witnessed the first joint report from the EcoFin and Labour and Social Affairs Councils, addressing the Intergovernmental Conference with the pressing issue of unemployment. See *Agence Europe* No 6629, 17 Dec. 1995, 5 ff.

for an increase in growth and in competitiveness. The implications of the guidelines for employment and collective bargaining are perceived as incumbent at all levels of negotiation. First of all, control and moderation in wage negotiations should be aimed at reducing inflation and indirectly at reducing short-term interest rates. This in itself is a strategy, which includes the social partners for the simple reason that consensus is indispensable to reach the aims stated: 'social consensus, reflected in collective agreements, would help central banks to accelerate their interest rate reductions. . . . Such reduced interest rates will alleviate the charges on business and budgets . . . helping exports and investments and so recovery in the Community'. Therefore, Article 103.2 of the Treaty 'is designed to create a coherent framework for a co-ordinated strategy', having inevitable effects on collective bargainers.[72]

Furthermore, the social partners have openly stated that no contradiction is to be envisaged between productivity growth and employment creation, especially when certain conditions are met to allow for redistribution of productivity.[73] Among such conditions, social dialogue is considered essential for the acceptability of sectoral changes and for the reform of labour markets, as well as for the adoption of measures which would facilitate the re-absorption of unemployed workers through labour mobility, special training schemes, and active labour market policies. In the subsequent Council guidelines[74] the link between job creation and competitiveness appears to be more clearly specified; in reading these documents, the impression is that a common language is being adopted by European institutions and social partners and that the inclusion of the latter in the policy-making process does not produce feelings of divided loyalty, but rather a sense of shared aims and objectives.

Neither the Council guidelines nor the social partners' Opinions on them are legally binding documents; they create purely political obligations on Member States, which may or may not be reflected in the relationship governments establish with the social partners at a national level. The reason such matters need to be mentioned when discussing collective agreements in the hierarchy of European sources is not to pay uncritical homage to well-established macro-economic choices; it is rather the discovery of some coherence within the institutional machinery which must be brought forward and discussed.

The lack of legal enforceability of collective sources as regulated in the Social Chapter—meaning, as has been argued above, that no normative effects on national labour law systems are produced by European collective agreements—is counterbalanced by the political and economic constraints within which national negotiations must take place, in order to comply with Maastricht standards and help solve problems of structural unemployment. Targets

[72] Pts 5 and 9 of the 1993 social partners' joint document, n. 58 above
[73] See Joint Opinion of May 1995, n. 71 above.
[74] Council Recommendation adopted on 10 July 1995 [1995] OJ L191/24; EC Bull. 718–1995, points 1, 3, 6, and 2).

set in the Maastricht Protocol are vague and improbable, whereas the aims of Title VI, much as they may appear largely unfulfilled, do fall within the most distinct character of Community policies. Market-building proceeds through the issuing of economic guidelines which are relevant and involving for European social partners; state-building is a counterpart to this process and has effects on collective negotiators, inasmuch as they obey the rules of the market and pay heed to economic constraints. Governments choose to enact concertation with the social partners[75] because of national priorities, which may become more stringent as a consequence of supranational targets. The main point to stress is that economic and monetary policies do not generate collective bargaining of a traditional kind and might even have an indirect effect in modifying styles of bargaining at national level, imposing a less conflictual attitude as a consequence of wage restraint under the threat of rising unemployment.[76] The criticism levelled at the weak foundations of social policies, including collective bargaining, much as it might appear repetitive, is in fact central to the current debate and must not be abandoned.

Market-building represents a visible trend in more recent documents such as those analysed above, which may be described as additional and even more sophisticated products of political spill-over, carrying nothing but indirect effects on the construction of a European system of collective labour relations.

In this line of expansion it is important to mention other developing strategies which appear increasingly relevant for the role to be fulfilled by collective actors. Following the Delors White Paper and pursuant to a Recommendation by the Essen European Council, a group was set up to advise on economic policy, with a view to achieving European competitiveness. The first *Ciampi Report*,[77] issued in June 1995, is mainly centred on proposals for a better functioning of the internal market. 'Competitiveness' it is said in the Report, is at times perceived as something of an obsession, undermining national cultures, displacing jobs, dividing peoples, encouraging social dumping by low-wage countries or more advanced nations. . . . Competitiveness implies elements of productivity, efficiency, profitability. But it is not an end in itself or a target. It is . . . a tool for achieving targets'.[78] The philosophy underlying the *Report*, as also the Delors White Paper, is to take action against unemployment attacking 'structural disadvantages'—such as

---

[75] One of the most relevant examples is the 1993 Protocol signed in Italy during the Ciampi government, widely recognised as a significant step forward for the Italian economy. See also recent developments along similar lines in Germany and Portugal in early 1996.

[76] In the Presidency Conclusions issued at the Madrid summit it is specified that measures on wage restraint fall within the social partners' sphere of action. See *Agence Europe*, n. 71 above, 9.

[77] So called after the name of its chair. See Competitiveness Advisory Group, *Enhancing European Competitiveness*, First Report to the President of the Commission, the prime ministers and Heads of State, Brussels 1995.   [78] Ibid. 2.

institutional and market fragmentation, limited labour mobility, different labour market regulations—which provoke a loss in relative European performance compared with Japan and the United States. One of the envisaged answers is the adoption of the European Company Statute, aimed among other things at cutting the costs incurred by incorporated subsidiaries regulated by different laws in different Member States, together with further steps in fiscal and social legislation.

The victory of *lex mercatoria* over social rights is too easy an answer, although the implications for measures to be taken in the social field are—at least in this first *Report*—rather weak and indeed confined to a short paragraph on human resources as 'major factors in productivity, quality and innovative capacity'.[79] Factors, not a strategy in itself, since more innovative interventions are to be found elsewhere in the creation of 'knowledge resource centres', presented as the tentative structures in which information supply and demand will be facilitated. Information and knowledge are becoming the key words of new social policies aimed at combating unemployment; macro-economic policies are the framework within which Labour Ministers must confront national and European economic institutions, as well as the social partners.

European collective bargaining is not, at first sight, part of this scheme of intervention, although partnership and social consensus are ingredients of the economic policy recipe concerned and appear to be taken for granted. This implication is echoed in the second *Ciampi Report*,[80] in which some examples of joint action involving management and the social partners are given. They have to do with combining professional training and technology transfer, means to improve employees' learning capacity in the long run, the combination of work and study, especially for young employees, and the establishment of training schemes involving government and the social partners which are aimed at extending the promised improvements to 'outsiders' and particularly to the long-term unemployed and low-skilled. Collective bargaining could be part of the equipment necessary to the adoption of a new view of social policies; in this regard labour lawyers might correctly and vigorously argue that it should indeed be the main tool to be used in developing a new profile of collective identity.

While all new ideas remain in an indistinct area of policy-making, reflecting once again the tension between the centre and periphery of the Community, something must be said regarding the establishment of stronger legal principles from which such new policies should be generated and reinforced.

In the *Westendorp Report*[81] important statements are made in the section

---

[79] Ibid. 20. This subject is likely to be the core of the third *Report*, expected in June 1996.

[80] Issued with the same title as in n. 77 in Dec. 1995. See especially 21 ff.

[81] Progress Report from the Chairman of the Reflection Group on the 1996 Inter-governmental Conference, *Agence Europe*, No 1951/1952, 27 Sept. 1995. 15.

devoted to policies. The Union should 'strengthen the social content of the Treaty'; in order to do that, it should propose to reword Article 103 so as 'to incorporate the idea of giving priority to employment', making it an objective within a global policy. The Swedish delegate, bringing a breath of fresh air into the debate, had indeed proposed that a new Chapter, entitled Employment Policy, should be inserted in the Treaty, to follow the one on Economic Policy. Not only should employment be highlighted as a matter of common concern; it should also be required, through specific procedures, that co-ordinated strategies be adopted and that social dialogue be directed at strengthening the links between decentralized labour markets and broader economic policies.[82]

Furthermore, the *Molitor Report*'s vague references to social rights when addressing the issue of enhanced competitiveness through the simplification of legal and administrative measures, as mentioned earlier,[83] reinforce the need to open up the debate on the hierarchy of European norms and to do so starting from fundamental constitutional values. This is the rationale behind proposals[84] to include in an amended new version of Article 117 of the EC Treaty social rights as they stem from the constitutional tradition of Member States and to enlarge the scope of Article F.2 of the TEU, including the 1961 Social Charter and the 1989 Community Charter among the sources to refer to for the enforcement of fundamental rights. It could also be significant to refer to social rights in Article 3 TEU, so that economic growth could be balanced by a more compelling reference to common actions to be pursued at a supranational level.

Even when discussing issues of constitutional reform, the image of a multi-tiered system that was mentioned at the beginning of this Chapter still appears appropriate. A constant interchange between different actors is required for achieving institutional changes. One of the principles to bear in mind is to include collective agreements in the changes and to treat them both as an outcome and as a source of social policies.

[82] The Swedish proposal was presented at the Reflection group in Sept. 1995 and discussed widely, although not unanimously accepted. See *Agence Europe* No 6558, 8 Sept. 1995, 12.

[83] See note 61 above.

[84] Such as those by R. Blanpain, B. Hepple, S. Sciarra and M. Weiss, *Fundamental Social Rights: Proposals for the European Union* (Peeters Leuven, 1996)

10

Workers' Participation in the European Union

MANFRED WEISS

1. The Task

Workers' participation in a broad sense—be it via institutionalized models or collective bargaining, via trade unions or elected bodies—is a common feature throughout the Community. The question arises, however, to what extent it affords workers or workers' representatives influence in management's decision-making. When the problem is put this way, the differences become evident.[1] Some countries provide statutory arrangements to make sure that workers' representatives are informed, consulted, or even asked for their agreement before management takes specific measures. In other countries, everything depends on the strength of trade unions to put pressure on management. But the distinction is not only between formalized structures which provide rights of information, consultation, or even codetermination and informal systems which leave everything to the trade unions' activities. It also reflects a differing tradition of industrial relations models. In Germany, for example, workers' integration in management's decision-making is the result of a long history of thinking in terms of reforming the capitalist system by restricting management's unilateral powers.[2] In Britain, on the contrary, as an example of the other end of the spectrum, the labour movement has traditionally taken the view that decisions of a strategic, planning and economic nature properly belong to the sphere of management: the trade unions' role is not to become integrated in decision-making but to endeavour to fight for the modification of such decisions for the workers' benefit.[3] These differences are commonly referred to as co-operative versus conflictual approaches. Whatever the explanation for all these differences may be, their end result is that in some member countries the scope for unilateral decision-making is

[1] For a survey see M. Biagi, 'Forms of Employee Representation at the Workplace', in R. Blanpain (ed.), *Comparative Labour Law and Industrial Relations in Industrialised Market Economies* (4th ed., 1990), i, 109.
[2] Cf. T. Ramm 'Workers' Participation, the Representation of of Labour and Special La Seur Courts', in B. Hepple (ed.), *The Making of Labour Law in Europe* (Mansell, London/New York, 1986), 243.
[3] Cf. A. Neal, 'Co-Determination in the Federal Republic of Germany: An External Perspective from the United Kingdom', in A. Gladstone, R. Lansbury, R. Steber, T. Treu and M. Weiss (eds.), *Current Issues in Labour Relations* (De Gruyter: Berlin/New York, 1989), 129–145 (139).

significantly greater than in others, and that management's obligations regarding information, consultation, or even engaging in a co-determination procedure are by no means on an equal level throughout the Community.

The approximation of these differing degrees of workers' participation in management's decision-making would appear to be appropriate for at least two reasons. First, a continuation of the differences would mean distortion of competition. The existing discrepancy between varying levels of participation may not only lead to disadvantages for companies in countries with highly developed systems of workers' participation, but may also be a temptation for companies to relocate to countries where unilateral decision-making is still the rule.[4] In the case of transnationally operating companies, there is a danger that measures leading to disadvantages may be taken in the country where less resistance from workers' representatives is to be expected. The notorious strategy adopted by AKZO in the early 1970s serves as an illustrative example.[5] Secondly, and perhaps even more importantly, it should be stressed that, in a Community which has now commenced its progress from a purely economic alliance to a political union, more than the strictly economic dimension must be taken into account. In a perspective of promoting industrial democracy as a stabilizing element of political democracy, workers throughout the Community should have an equally fair opportunity to influence decisions of which they constitute the subjects.

However, the task of harmonizing models of workers' participation is not so easy as it may seem at first glance. It would not be very helpful simply to provide identical models for every country. If, for example, the French *comité d'entreprise* were simply to be turned into a German *Betriebsrat*, including all the rights connected with the latter body, the respective functions of the two would by no means be the same. Such an approach would ignore the fact that these actors and institutions would still have to operate within very different general frameworks. Neither the structure of trade unions nor the system of collective bargaining would be comparable. The mechanisms of conflict resolution would remain very different: this would apply not only to the classic instrument of industrial action, i.e. the strike, but also to the system of adjudication by the courts. In short, the functional impact of any particular institution depends on its interrelationship with all the other elements of a given industrial relations system.

Whether and to what extent management decisions are influenced or even shaped by workers' participation can be evaluated only if an overall view is taken of a given system as a comprehensive and complex entity. In one system, statutory arrangements may play an important role in promoting workers'

---

[4] This is one of the most frequently used arguments in Germany. See M. Weiss, 'Labour Law and Industrial Relations in Europe 1992: A German Perspective' [1990] *Comparative Labor Law Journal*, 411 (422)

[5] See R.Blanpain, *Labour Law and Industrial Relations of the European Community*, 1991, Kluwer: Deventer, 153.

influence on management's decision-making. In another system, the strength and autonomy of the trade unions as principal actors may be the decisive factor. In yet a third system, a combination of statutory and contractual elements may lead to such influence.[6] Consequently, it is not helpful to focus solely on specific isolated institutions in order to gain an impression of workers' influence on management decision-making, nor is it helpful simply to compare identically or similarly labelled institutions in different systems.[7]

This basic insight has far-reaching consequences: it demonstrates the limits of any attempt at harmonization. Full harmonization would be attainable only if in all fifteen countries the totality of the industrial relations systems (actors, instruments, and institutions) were the same. Given that each industrial relations system to a great extent reflects the specific cultural and political history of the individual country concerned and that the results of this historical development are immensely heterogeneous, such a perfectionist strategy of harmonization would obviously be neither realistic nor desirable. Therefore, it should be eliminated from the discussion at the very outset. In particular, it should not be used as a justification for doing nothing.

But even bearing in mind that particular institutional models necessarily have a different meaning in each country, depending on the other elements of the individual country concerned, there is still no alternative to the pragmatic approach of attempting to promote some approximation of the national institutional arrangements. Harmonization in this sense can mean no more than a narrrowing of the gap between the different Member States. It certainly will not produce structures which are identical in functional terms.

The task, however, consists in more than harmonization. No matter how highly developed a given system of workers' participation may be, hitherto it has ended at the relevant country's border. If decisions are made elsewhere by the headquarters of a transnational company or by the parent company of a transnational group, workers' participation, at least as yet, has no access. This shortcoming has to be seen as a challenge in view of the fact that the transnationalization of undertakings and of groups of undertakings is rapidly increasing within the Community. For some time now there has been a steady growth in mergers, takeovers, and joint ventures. During the 1980s acquisitions by the 1,000 largest undertakings in the Community, whether via mergers or by purchase of majority shareholdings, have doubled every three years. To quote just two figures: whereas in the period 1984–85 only 208 such acquisitions took place, in the period 1988–9 the number rose to 492. If all the mergers are analysed it can be stated that the number of cases where undertakings located in different Member States were involved has increased

---

[6] For these different types of regulation see M. Biagi, n. 1 above, 199.
[7] Cf. J. Schregle, 'Workers' Participation in the Federal Republic of Germany in an International Perspective', in A. Gladstone, *et al.*, n. 3 above 105 (106).

significantly since 1987.[8] There is no doubt that the single market as established since 1993 will accelerate this process of transnationalization.[9] Therefore, the need to extend workers' influence beyond national borders is becoming increasingly urgent.

2. The Community's Response

The Community's activities in this area are based mainly on three considerations. First, there is the idea of harmonizing the models of workers' participation in the different Member States in order to approximate the conditions of competition, increase transparency and thereby reduce transaction costs and also to facilitate transnational mobility. Secondly, Community models of company law are to be created, distinct from and independent of the existing structures in the individual Member States, to be available as an option alternative to domestic law and thereby facilitating transnational employment within the Community. Thirdly, the workers' rights which to date have stopped short at the borders of a particular member country are to be extended to the headquarters of transnational undertakings or to the controlling company of a transnational group.

So far, the Community has developed three strategies to fulfil this complex task. The first, and as yet most successful, strategy consists in the introduction and harmonization of information and consultation procedures in relation to certain specific issues: collective dismissals, transfer of undertakings, and, most recently, health and safety. The second strategy refers to workers' participation in corporate boards. This includes the proposal for a fifth company law Directive on the structure of public limited companies and the powers and obligations of their organs, as well as the proposal for a European company statute and, now, three other models of Community-type company law. The third strategy aims to improve channels of information and consultation in transnationally operating undertakings and groups of undertakings. This encompasses the proposal for a Directive on procedures for informing and consulting employees (the so-called Vredeling proposal) and the recent Directive on the establishment of a European Works Council in Community-scale undertakings or groups of undertakings for the purposes of informing and consulting employees.

---

[8] See Introduction to the proposal for amending the Council directive on the approximation of the laws of the Member States relating to collective redundancies [1991] OJ C310.

[9] Cf. A. Calcon, L. Frey, R. Lindley, A. Lyon-Caen, H. Markmann, and S. Simitis, *Labour Market, Fundamental Rights and Social Policy in the Community*, 1992, Brussels, 28.

2.1 The Legal Basis for the Community's Activities

Even before Maastricht it was generally accepted that Article 100 of the Treaty of Rome provides a sound basis for measures taken by the Community in this area. The problem was, however, that Article 100 requires a unanimous decision in the Council, thereby presenting a serious obstacle to getting a proposal passed. This explains why, in reference to the proposal for intro-ducing workers' participation in the European company, the problem arose whether it could be based on an Article referring to harmonization of company law (Article 54(3)(g)) allowing the Council to decide by a qualified majority.[10] This debate is now of purely historical interest and will therefore not be discussed further here.

The Social Protocol to the Maastricht Treaty allows qualified majority voting for 'information and consultation of workers' but insists on unanimous voting for measures relating to 'representation and collective defence of the interests of the workers, including co-determination'.[11] This not only implies that the Community's competence in this area should be uncontested from now on. Since the Protocol is not intended to worsen the Community's position, it is difficult to conceive that 'representation and collective defence of the interests of workers, including co-determination' should now require unanimous voting for the fourteen (originally eleven) Member States if it had previously been possible for the fifteen (originally twelve) Member States on the basis of qualified majority voting. There is no indication whatever that this amendment was intended to increase the Community's difficulties as far as its basic competence is concerned. Hence, the sophisticated controversy about Article 54(3)(g) versus Article 100 of the Treaty of Rome may be dispensed with here: whether it is matter of workers' participation in corporate boards for fifteen Member States or for fourteen, the requirement for unanimous voting in the Council can no longer be questioned.

However, it is difficult to draw the dividing line between 'information and consultation of workers' on the one hand and 'representation and collective defence of the interests of workers, including co-determination' on the other. In the context of the fourteen Member States covered by the Social Protocol this is, nevertheless, the line of demarcation between qualified majority voting and unanimous voting. The recent Directive on European Works Councils is a very good example of how arbitrary it may be to draw this demarcation line. In view of the wording of the Protocol it may well be doubted whether this Directive could be passed by qualified majority.[12] However, given the political

---

[10] See R. Blanpain, n. 5 above, 186.
[11] On this distinction see M. Weiss, 'The Significance of Maastricht for European Community Social Policy' [1992] *International Journal of Comparative Labour Law and Industrial Relations*, 1992, 3 (7).
[12] See M. Weiss, n. 11 above, 7.

intention of the authors of the Protocol there is no doubt that they wanted this to become possible.[13]

Even though it is self-evident that the subsidiarity principle plays an important role in this area as well as in all other branches of Community politics, the issue will not be further examined in this very brief survey.

2.2 Workers' Participation in Respect of Certain Specific Issues

The initial steps in this direction were taken by the Community's first Social Action Programme of 1974, which was the outcome of the spectacular Paris summit of 1972.[14] In 1975 the Directive on the approximation of the laws of the Member States relating to collective redundancies was passed[15] and two years later the Directive on the safeguarding of employees' rights in the event of transfers of undertakings, businesses or parts of businesses[16] followed. Without going into detail it may simply be said that both Directives establish an information and consultation procedure in the context of collective redundancies and transfers of undertakings. The actors on the workers' side are the workers' representatives according 'to the law and practice' of the respective Member State. In some countries these Directives were implemented only after Community intervention and with extraordinary delay. Even where implementation took place quickly, problems remained. There was and is no guarantee that a body acting as workers' representative will be available everywhere. To take just the most interesting example: in Britain, according to the Employment Protection Act 1975 'workers' representative' in this context meant an independent trade union recognized by the employer. Until 1979 recognition of a trade union was obligatory under certain conditions. As a result of the changes made by the Thatcher Government it is now left to the employer's discretion whether a trade union is to be recognized and, if so, which one. The employer is legally entitled not only to refuse recognition but also to withdraw it without giving any reasons. Owing to the factual decline in trade union power in Britain derecognition has increased significantly in the past few years.[17] In short, and to make the point: under such a régime it is purely a matter of chance whether a representative exists to be informed and consulted. In such circumstances, formal transposition of the Directive is obviously far from being real implementation.[18]

Both Directives related only to cases where the decision on collective

---

[13] See R. Blanpain and P. Windey, *European Works Councils* (Peters, Leuven 1994), 58.
[14] Cf. A. Jacons and H. Zeijen, *European Labour Law and Social Policy* (Tilburg University Press, Tilburg, 1993), 3.
[15] [1975] OJ L48.   [16] [1977] OJ L61.
[17] For details of this legal structure see G. Morris and T. Archer, *Trade Unions, Employers and the Law* (Blackwell, Oxford), 139–43.
[18] This is also the opinion of the European Court of Justice in Cases C–382/92 and C–383/92, *Commission v. United Kingdom* [1994] ICR 664 (ECJ).

redundancies or on transfer of undertakings was made within the particular company concerned. However, they did not cover cases where workers, employed in a subsidiary, are affected by decisions taken by the holding company of a group, which may be located within the same country or abroad. Consequently, the Directive on collective redundancies was amended in 1992.[19] According to the amended version, the Directive now applies irrespective of whether the decision on collective redundancies is made by the employer or by the parent undertaking controlling the employing company. At the same time the minimum requirements for the content of information and consultation were specified and enlarged. Originally, it was intended to incorporate an effective sanction in the Directive, making the dismissals null and void if the Directive's requirements were not observed, but this attempt failed.[20] Recently the Commission has presented a proposal to amend the Directive on the transfer of undertakings in the same way as the Directive on collective redundancies. This is proving, however, to be more complicated since it is combined with the controversy over whether the European Court of Justice's judgments should be codified and/or corrected at the same time.[21]

The biggest step so far in establishing a Community-wide model of workers' participation was taken by the Directive of 1989 on the introduction of measures to encourage improvements in the safety and health of workers at work, the so-called Framework Directive.[22] There it says in Article 11(1): 'Employers shall consult workers and/or their representatives and allow them to take part in discussions on all questions relating to safety and health at work. This presupposes the consultation of workers, the right of workers and/ or their representatives to make proposals, and balanced participation in accordance with national laws and/or practice.' What 'balanced participation' means in this context remains relatively obscure. But given that it is to be understood as something other than the consultation mentioned in the same paragraph it can only be interpreted as providing a stronger degree of influence.[23] It will be the European Court of Justice's task to clarify the meaning of this concept if it is asked to examine the means of implementation in the various countries. There is, however, no doubt that the astonishingly generous wording of the Framework Directive reflects the general consensus within the Community on making health and safety standards effective.

---

[19] [1992] OJ L245/3.

[20] Cf. C. Bourn, 'Amending the Collective Dismissal Directive: A Case of Re-arranging the Deckchairs?' [1993] *The International Journal of Comparative Labour Law and Industrial Relations*, 227 (240); see also M. Weiss, 'Die europarechtliche Regelung der Massenentlassung' [1992] *Recht der Arbeit*, 367 (370).

[21] Proposal of 8 Sept. 1994 [1994] OJ C274/10.

[22] [1989] OJ L183/1.

[23] Cf. M. Weiss, 'The Industrial Relations of Occupational Health: The Impact of the Framework Directive on the Federal Republic of Germany' [1990] *International Journal of Comparative Labour Law and Industrial Relations*, 119 (127).

2.3 Workers' Representation on Corporate Boards

The proposals for establishing workers' representation on and participation in corporate boards have their roots in the late 1960s.[24] The preparatory work of this period yielded two results: the first proposal for a European company Statute of 1970[25] and the first proposal for a Fifth Directive on the structure of public limited companies of 1972.[26] Whereas the European company proposal seeks to add a new Community dimension of company law to the already existing array of national company laws, the proposed Fifth Directive has to be seen as an attempt to harmonize existing company law. Thus, it must be perfectly clear from the very start that the Fifth Directive would have a significantly more far-reaching impact on undertakings in the Community than the proposed European company Statute. The latter would always remain an optional alternative to the otherwise still available national models. Or, to put it another way, whereas a system of workers' participation which has been incorporated into national company law cannot be circumvented, such circumvention would always remain possible if workers' participation were confined to the additional and therefore merely optional pattern of a European company. This difference may explain why workers' participation in the context of the European company has a significantly better chance of being realized—as will be shown—than the same proposal in the context of a Fifth Directive.

The first drafts of both proposals[27] started with the same significant mistake: they ignored the one-tier system of company law as it exists in quite a few member countries and instead exclusively favoured a structure which made sense only in a two-tier system based on a division of labour between an executive board with management functions and a supervisory board with essentially monitoring functions. The proposals contained a mixture of the models of workers' representation on the supervisory board as then existed in the Netherlands and in Germany: a naïve and utterly hopeless attempt to impose the institutional arrangements of two Member States upon all the others. Hence it is not surprising that these first drafts met with nothing but strong resistance.

It is, however, somewhat surprising that even in the amended draft of the European company Statute of 1975[28] the original pattern was maintained. Compared with the first draft, which provided only a representation of one third from the workers' side as against two thirds for shareholders' representatives, the new draft merely changed the board composition: one third

---

[24] Cf. W. Kolvenbach, 'EEC Company Law Harmonization and Worker Participation', *University of Pennsylvania Journal of International Business Law*, 1990, 709–788 (764–765).

[25] [1970] OJ C241/1.   [26] [1972] OJ C131/49.

[27] For details see W. Kolvenbach, n. 24 above, 720–2 and 765

[28] [1975] *Bull. EC*, Suppl. 4.

workers' representatives, one third shareholders' representatives, and another third reserved for persons agreed on by the other two groups.

Despite their obvious failings, these first drafts had an important impact. They sparked off a highly controversial debate which in fact marked the beginning of a real awareness of the differences in the basic structures of company law, differences in trade union structures and trade union policies, and differences in the role played by law in industrial relations in the various Member States. The Commissions's *Green Paper* of 1975 on Employee Participation and Company Structure in the European Community[29] served as a very informative and stimulating input to this debate, in the course of which the heterogeneous nature of the industrial landscape throughout the Community was discovered to its full extent. Against this background it became more and more apparent that future drafts and amendments would have to abandon the approach of imposing one identical model on all the other Member States. Otherwise the chances of realization in the political process would tend towards zero. It is therefore no surprise that the drafts which were finally amended and presented in the 1980s looked quite different.

The amended and so far latest draft of the Fifth Directive dates from 1983.[30] This new draft no longer offers only one fixed menu for all the Members States seated around the Community table, but replaces it by a sort of cafeteria system in which each Member State is able to choose whatever best suits its taste. First of all, it contains models for the one-tier structure of company law as well as for the two-tier structure. It must, however, be stressed that the one-tier system is somewhat modified to look like a two-tier system. The board of directors is now divided into a smaller number of managing members and a larger number of monitoring members, thereby arriving at a division of labour similar to that between a management board and a supervisory board in a two-tier structure.

As far as the two-tier system is concerned, there is a choice of four models. First, the representation of workers German-style, leaving each Member State free to fix the proportion of worker representatives at between one third and a half, in the latter case providing a casting vote for the shareholders' representatives. This option also includes the alternative of three groups as previously contained in the amended draft of the European company Statute of 1975. Secondly, a model as used in the Netherlands could be chosen: the supervisory board co-opts members who are neither workers' nor shareholders' representatives. According to the third model a separate body representing the company's employees has to be established. This body has the right to regular information and consultation on the company's economic situation. The rights of this separate body are in essence the same as the information rights of the supervisory organ appointed by the general meeting. Furthermore, this body must be consulted in the same way as the supervisory

[29] [1975] *Bull EC*, Suppl. 8.   [30] [1983] OJ C240/2.

organ. The separate body is supposed to meet prior to each supervisory board meeting and must be provided with all the documentation and information relating to the agenda for the supervisory board meeting. Lastly, the fourth model introduces workers' participation by way of collective agreements. Where, however, such an agreement cannot be reached within a certain period, Member States must regulate workers' participation in accordance with one of the other options. If the one-tier system is chosen the same rules apply, at least in principle.

The proposal not only offers a significant degree of flexibility, but also allows workers' participation to be circumvented altogether: if the majority of workers vote against it, a participation model does not have to be introduced.

It was mainly this latter possibility which led to the fact that the European Trade Union Confederation (ETUC) described the new draft as 'reactionary'[31] and that the German Trade Union Congress (DGB) simply interpreted it as an 'insult' to workers.[32] On the other side, the British Trade Union Congress (TUC) as well as the Union of Industrial and Employers' Confederations of Europe (UNICE), in spite of the increased flexibility, objected to the attempt to spread the system of workers' participation to countries where such a tradition was so far unknown.[33] In view of the opposition from both sides— which of course related to many other points not mentioned here—it is no surprise at all that, by a kind of general consensus, this latest draft was very soon considered to all intents and purposes moribund.

The more it proved that the integration of workers' participation into the national company law structure of each member country remains illusory, at least for the time being, the more efforts were renewed to introduce workers' participation on a Community scale by way of redefinition of the European company Statute. Consequently, in the Commission's *White Paper* of 1985 on completing the internal market the European company Statute was mentioned as one of the goals to be achieved by the end of 1992.[34] In 1987 the European Council requested the relevant bodies 'to make swift progress with regard to the company law adjustments required for the creation of a European company'.[35] Urged on by these initiatives, in 1988 the Commission drew up a memorandum in which the key problems of a Statute for a European company were listed.[36] In this memorandum the European Parliament, the Council, and the two sides of industry were invited to express their views. On the basis

[31] European Trade Union Confederation, *ETUC Position on the Amended Proposal for a Fifth Directive*, 1984 (adopted by the ETUC Executive Committee at its session in Brussels on 9–10 Feb. 1984).

[32] Press release by Deutscher Gewerkschaftsbund (DGB) of 28 Nov. 1983.

[33] See W. Kolvenbach, n. 24 above, 729–30

[34] Commission of the European Communities, *Completing the Internal Market*. White Paper from the Commission to the European Council, Com.No. 310, 1985

[35] [1987] *EC Bull*, 6.

[36] Commission of the European Communities, Memorandum, COM No. 320, 188 [1988] *Bull EC*, Suppl. 3.

of the feedback obtained from these actors, the Commission prepared a new draft Statute, which was presented in August 1989.[37] In order to achieve the necessary flexibility, the element of workers' participation was now separated from the Statute proper, which is contained in a draft regulation: workers' participation is to be covered by a Directive. There are, however, safeguards that the regulation cannot be passed without the Directive: the two are closely interrelated.

The range of options is very similar to the alternatives provided in the latest draft for the Fifth Directive: first, the German model in which the workers' representatives may have a minimum of one third and a maximum of one half of the seats, without a casting vote for the shareholders' side in the latter version; secondly, the Dutch model of co-option; thirdly, the separate body for workers' representation with specific rights of information and consultation; and last systems agreed by collective agreements. Where such an agreement cannot be reached, the most advanced national model in the respective Member State would have to be applied. If no such model exists, the Directive stipulates a set of minimum standards for information and consultation. Most importantly, the possibility of opting out of workers' participation altogether is abolished.

In an apparent effort to cover the entire area of company law, the Commission has presented in the meantime three more proposals for further Community company law models: European associations, co-operative societies and mutual societies. Again, workers' participation is not contained in the Statute itself but in a related Directive.[38] According to the Commission the aim of the drafts is to provide the benefits of the internal market also to these types of association, in the same way as to the European company.

The three proposals contain an identical concept of participation. Board representation is to be established in companies with at least fifty workers. However, the concept of participation in these proposals is only of a subsidiary nature: the national law on workers' board representation is normally to be applied; only if no national system of workers' participation exists for these types of association, or if it does not cover all companies down to fifty workers, does a workers' participation structure have to be established, taking account of the very ambiguous and complicated provisions of the proposed Directives.[39]

The Commission's perfectionism in extending workers' participation to these additional types of association seems less than helpful at a time when the debate on the European company is at its height. The energies that need to be devoted to the latter one are thereby distracted.

---

[37] [1989] OJ C263/41.
[38] [1992] OJ C99; see also the amended proposal in [1992] OJ C236/1.
[39] See also A. Jacobs and H. Zeijen, n. 14 above, 119.

2.4 Information and Consultation in the Transnational Context

As indicated earlier, the possibility for workers to obtain information and be consulted before important management decisions are taken is by no means identical or even similar throughout the Community. Some countries have institutional mechanisms—based on statute or on collective agreements—to make sure that information and consultation take place, while others do not. And as already mentioned, even where information and consultation arrangements exist, they become irrelevant once a company develops a structure which transfers the centre of decision-making beyond the borders of the country concerned. National institutional arrangements on information and consultation can operate only within the national framework. If the real decisions are taken by the headquarters outside the country concerned, information and consultation rights become useless. It is therefore no surprise that the main initiative to establish a framework for information and consultation on a European scale came from the labour movements in countries where such arrangements already existed and where the degree of frustration had steadily increased because, on the one hand, the transnational perspective was becoming more and more important but, on the other hand, it was not accessible to the traditional instruments available within the national framework.

2.4.1 The Vredeling Proposal

The first draft of a Directive on procedures for informing and consulting employees, the so-called Vredeling proposal of 1980,[40] named after the then Commissioner of Social Affairs, was originally focused solely on transnational undertakings with subsidiaries in different Member States. Only later, in the amended draft of 1983,[41] were national undertakings with a complex structure included in order to eliminate unequal treatment of workers of national and transnational companies in countries where no institutional information and consultation arrangements existed. Those who had resisted the first draft most strongly, ie the Union of Industrial and Employers' Confederations of Europe (UNICE), insisted on equal treatment of national and transnational undertakings.[42] Instead of simply giving up the initiative, the Commission tried to reconcile UNICE's position with its own by eliminating the discrimination in the second draft.

According to this amended draft, the envisaged information and consultation procedure applied if 'a total of at least 1000 workers is employed in the Community by the parent undertaking and its subsidiaries taken as a whole', no matter whether the undertaking lay wholly within the scope of one member

---

[40] [1980] OJ C297/3.   [41] 1[983] OJ C217/3.
[42] Cf. UNICE position (19 Feb. 1981), in R. Blanpain, F. Blanquet, F. Herman, and A. Mouty, *The Vredeling Proposal* (Kluwer, Deventer 1983), 75 (80).

country or whether it had a transnational structure. If the decision-making centre of the undertaking was outside the Community the procedure was to be applied if at least 1,000 workers were employed as a whole in subsidiaries within the Community.

The proposal did not in any way affect the given structure of workers' representation. As in the Directives relating to specific issues, the actors in the case of information or consultation were 'the employees' representatives provided for by the laws or practices of the Member States'.

If the parent undertaking was within the Community, a body representing all the employees of the parent undertaking and its subsidiaries within the Community could be created by means of an agreement to be concluded between the management of the undertaking and the employees' representatives. This remained the only indication of an institutional innovation, and of course merely an optional one.

At least once a year the management of the parent undertaking was to forward to the management of each subsidiary within the Community information on the activities of the parent undertaking and its subsidiaries as a whole, mainly relating to structure, economic and financial position, the probable development of the business and of production and sales, the employment situation and probable trends, and investment prospects. Each subsidiary's management then was required to communicate this information without delay to the employees' representatives. If the subsidiary failed to fulfil this duty, the employees' representatives were entitled to approach the parent undertaking's management direct.

Much more important than the communication of this general information was the special procedure to be followed if certain specific decisions were to be taken: closure or transfer of an establishment or major parts thereof; restriction of or substantial modifications to the activities of the undertaking; major modifications with regard to organization, working practices or production methods, including modifications resulting from the introduction of new technologies; introduction of long-term co-operation with other undertakings or the cessation of such co-operation; and, lastly, measures relating to workers' health and industrial safety. In these cases the management of the parent undertaking, via the management of the subsidiary affected, was required to provide precise information, including details of the grounds for the proposed decision, the legal as well as the economic and social consequences of such decisions for the employees concerned, and the measures planned in respect of such employees.

Once the employees' representatives received this information in writing they were allowed thirty days within which to give their opinion. Implementation of the planned decision was not permitted before either this opinion was received by the management or the thirty-day period had expired. In other words, the workers' representatives not only were informed and consulted, but also had an instrument for at least delaying implementation of the decision. This delay would even have to be observed in cases where information could not be communicated in view of the secrecy rule contained in the proposal, according to which secret information was not to be disclosed if such disclosure could substantially damage the undertaking's interests or lead to the failure of its plan.

Member States were to provide for appropriate penalties for failure to comply with the obligations laid down in the Directive. In cases where the parent undertaking had its headquarters outside the Community, either a specific agent authorized to fulfil the requirements laid down in the proposal or, in the absence of such an agent, the management of each subsidiary concerned within the Community was to be held responsible and therefore possibly liable to sanctions.

In the debate on the Vredeling proposal this so-called 'hostage solution', as well as the extraterritorial effect of the proposal as such, played a dominant part. Whereas—at least in principle—the European Trade Union Confederation (ETUC) supported the proposal,[43] business organizations within and outside the Community strongly opposed it. In addition to the extraterritorial argument, mainly used by the U.S.[44] and the Japanese[45] business communities, the proposal was criticized because it would lead to delays, difficulties in the planning and implementation of envisaged measures, and consequently reduced competitiveness. Somewhat in contradiction to these arguments, it was stressed that Community legislation in this area is neither necessary nor feasible since the existing OECD Guidelines on Multinationals as well as the relevant ILO tripartite Declaration would in any case be observed voluntarily.[46]

Several attempts were made to reconcile the conflicting views. In a strategy of ongoing consultation with the Member States, the so-called 'new approach', the EC authorities tried to achieve a consensus. This proved to be a futile hope, however. Hence, in 1986 the Council decided to freeze the issue until 1989, when the debate was supposed to be reopened.[47]

2.4.2 *The Directive on Establishing a European Works Council*

The new Directive[48] is the result of fresh efforts to revitalize social policy. The notion of the social dimension became a key issue in the discussions on the realization of the internal market. In addition, the institutional

---

[43] See W. Kolvenbach, n. 24 above, 753

[44] Memorandum of the Council of American Chambers of Commerce—Europe and Mediterranean of 18 May 1981, in R. Blanpain *et al.*, n. 42 above. 86.

[45] Keidanren Position of 22 June 1982, ibid., 97–9.

[46] Cf. W. Kolvenbach, n. 24 above, 748.

[47] Cf. A.Jacobs and H. Zeijen, n. 14 above, 155.

[48] Council Dir. 94/45/EC of 22 Sept. 1994 on the establishment of a European Works Council or a procedure in Community-scale undertakings and Community-scale groups of undertakings for the purposes of informing and consulting employees, [1994] OJ L254/64.

strengthening of the social dialogue at EC level by the Single European Act's amendment of the Treaty led to an increased involvement of the social partners throughout the Community. This explains why the initiative to adopt a Community Charter of Fundamental Social Rights of Workers enjoyed widespread public attention and became the subject of very heated and controversial debates. When in December 1989 in Strasbourg the Charter was adopted by eleven Member States (with abstention of the United Kingdom[49]) the content was reduced to a minimum on which practically everybody could agree. Hence, the topics contained in the Charter were also agreed upon by at least the majority of business organizations and their spokesmen. It is important in this context to mention that section 17 of the Charter reads as follows: 'Information, consultation and participation for workers must be developed along appropriate lines, taking account of the practices in force in the various Member States. This shall apply especially in companies or groups of companies having establishments or companies in two or more Member States of the European Community'. In section 18 the main situations requiring such information, consultation, and participation were specified. And in the Commission's Social Action Programme to implement the Charter the introduction of a Community instrument on employee information, consultation, and participation procedures in transnational undertakings was proposed. In short, and to make the point: both the legitimacy of such an instrument and the pressure to introduce it had increased tremendously compared with the period when Vredeling was being debated.

Furthermore, the Commission had succeeded in involving the social partners to an astonishing degree in the initial preparation of the draft of the new proposal. Bad experience in the past has changed the legislative process significantly. Nevertheless, the proposal, first presented in 1991[50] and then modified several times, in the end was not accepted unanimously in the Council. Therefore, there was no other way left but to follow the path opened up by the Social Protocol of Maastricht. On 22 September 1994 the Council adopted the Directive.

The Directive on the establishment of a European Works Council seeks to achieve the same goal as Vredeling, but uses a very different strategy.

First of all, it covers only transnational undertakings and groups of undertakings with at least 1,000 employees within the fourteen Member States and with at least 150 employees of the undertaking or of different undertakings of the group in each of at least two different Member States. The restriction to transnational undertakings and groups of undertakings may be explained by the wording of the Charter, which in this case evidently serves as a basis of legitimacy.

---

[49] For details see Lord Wedderburn, *The Social Charter, European Company and Employment rights. An Outline Agenda* (Institute of Employment Rights, London, 1990).
[50] [1991] OJ C39/10.

The focus of the Directive is on the establishment of a body representing the interests of all the workers of the undertaking or group of undertakings within the Community: the European Works Council (EWC). In order to establish such a European Works Council a relatively complicated procedure is provided for. First, the employees' representatives in each establishment or group undertaking must form a so-called special negotiating body composed of representatives from each Member State in which the Community-scale undertaking or group of undertakings employs at least 100 employees. Then the EWC is to be set up by written agreement between the central management of the Community-scale undertaking or of the controlling undertaking of the group on the one hand and the special negotiating body on the other. Where a Community-scale undertaking or group of undertakings has its central management or its controlling undertaking outside the fourteen Member States, the EWC must be set up by written agreement between its representative agent within these Member States or, in the absence of such an agent, the management of the establishment or group undertaking with the largest number of employees on the one hand and the special negotiating body on the other.

This agreement must determine specific matters: the nature and composition of the EWC; its functions and powers; the procedure for informing and consulting the EWC; the place, frequency, and duration of its meetings; and, lastly, the financial and material resources to be allocated to the EWC. Whether such an agreement is to be concluded, and in what manner, depends entirely on the parties on both sides. If the special negotiating body decides by a two thirds majority not to request such an agreement, that is already the end of the matter. Only if the central management refuses to commece negotiations within six months of receiving such a request or if after three years the two parties are unable to reach an agreement do the subsidiary requirements set out in the Annex to the Directive apply.

These subsidiary requirements are the only form of pressure available to the special negotiating body. They expressly limit the European Works Council's competence to information and consultation on matters which affect either the transnationally operating undertaking or group of undertakings as a whole or at least two subsidiaries of the undertaking or two undertakings of the group situated in different Member States (1(a)). The organizational structure of the European Works Council is prescribed to a certain extent (1(b) to (e)). In addition to the European Works Council a specific committee consisting of at most three members is provided for (1(c)). The European Works Council must be informed and consulted once a year on general aspects of the undertaking's or the group's policy (2). If measures with significant disadvantages for employees are at stake, additional information and consultation of the committee is required before these measures are executed. Those members of the European Works Council representing the constituency affected by the measures in question are entitled to participate in this meeting

(3). It is important to stress that the right of the European Works Council or the committee to meet alone before the meetings with central management is guaranteed (4) and that support by experts is provided if necessary (6). All costs are to be borne by the central management (7). However, the Member States are entitled to specify these guarantees, especially to limit the volume of funding.

In accordance with the principle of subsidiarity the Directive contains a clause which is intended to confirm already existing voluntary agreements and to stimulate the conclusion of new ones up till the 22 September 1996 or the date of national implementation of the Directive. Under Article 13 the Directive does not apply to undertakings or groups of undertakings which already have an agreement on a system of transnational information and consultation covering 'the entire workforce' or which conclude one by the earlier of the dates mentioned above. The content of such an agreement is left to the parties, as it is in the case of the Directive. Priority is given to the actors. However, it is by no means clear how representative the parties to such an agreement have to be or how strictly the notion 'covering the entire workforce' is to be taken.[51]

2.4.3 Problems of Implementation

The Directive establishes a transnational structure for which from the very beginning the national legislator has no competence. At least as far as the core of the relevant rules is concerned, the logical consequence would have been to use the instrument of a regulation, thereby creating directly applicable European law and to a large extent eliminating the problem of implementation. However, the Social Protocol provides a basis only for Directives in this context. Recourse to a regulation was therefore legally prohibited. Nevertheless, it would have been possible to specify the terms and concepts used in the Directive more closely, in order to achieve a relatively homogenous European framework. And it also would have been possible to clarify that it is exclusively the task of the European Court of Justice to interpret the various concepts: the legal nature and effect of the agreement under Article 6, the 'objective criteria' (see Article 8(2)) allowing dispensation from the duty to inform and the timing of information under section 3 of the Annex (not only before or also after a decision is made), to give just a few examples. But this is not the path followed by the Directive. It provides only a very vague and non-specific framework, leaving a considerable leeway for national implementation. The danger is obvious: implementation in each Member State may be significantly different. This could lead not only to decreased transparency of the regulatory framework but also to unintended competitive advantages and disadvantages among the Member States. In order to reduce this danger and to

[51] See R. Blanpain and P. Windey, n. 13 above, 98.

achieve as much harmonization as possible a co-ordinating committee for implementing the Directive has been established by the Commission.[52] Even though this committee, consisting of representatives of each Member State covered by the Directive, has purely advisory functions, it may well be doubted whether and to what extent it is compatible with the sovereignty of national Parliaments. Clearly, however, this is an attempt to achieve in another way the effect, at least in part, which would have been achieved by a regulation or by a more specific Directive.

Even if the co-ordinating committee is successful in laying the ground for relatively homogeneous patterns of national implementation, it cannot be ignored that the rules and institutions of national law are first of all subject to the national courts' interpretation. The danger therefore remains that, despite the committee's efforts, similar concepts will drift apart.

The Directive uses concepts which are well established and relatively clearly defined in some Member States. In other Member States the same concepts have no meaning whatever and can be made meaningful only by defining them in the course of implementing the Directive. To take an example: according to Article 9 the central management and the European Works Council must work 'in a spirit of co-operation'. In Germany, where this principle has a long tradition, this is understood (among other implications) to exclude any recourse to industrial action as a means of resolving disputes between central management and European Works Council. Whether it will have the same meaning in an Italian or French context is open to doubt. In spite of the coordinating committee's efforts, it may be predicted that national implementation will exhibit significant divergences. It would definitely have been better if the Directive had clarified what such a concept is supposed to mean in a Community context.

It is highly questionable whether the Directive's occasional reference to national law makes sense. To take just one example: according to Article 10 members of special negotiating bodies and European Works Councils 'shall, in the exercise of their functions, enjoy the same protection and guarantees provided for employees' representatives by the national legislation and/or practice in force in their country of employment'. This inevitably results in individual members of the same representative body enjoying very different levels of protection. It seems doubtful that this helps to strengthen the cohesion within such a body. Rather, the unequal degrees of protection are likely to preclude cohesion and so undermine efficiency.

One of the basic problems of implementation refers to the question whether the national legislator is entitled to improve on the Directive's requirements in favour of the employees.[53] Article 7(2) does not solve the problem: it may

[52] For details see C. Savoini, 'The Prospects of the Enactment of Directive 94/45/EC in the Member States of the European Union', in [1995] *Transfer* 245–51 (250).
[53] See R. Blanpain and R. Windey, n. 13 above, 87.

simply be read as a prohibition on any worsening of the provisions set out in the Annex. Article 12, which would have been the place to clarify the question, is also silent. Recourse, therefore, has to be had to Article 2(2) of the Social Protocol, whereby the Community legislator is entitled to set only minimum standards. It thus seems very unlikely that the Community legislator is empowered to extend its own competence to such a degree. At any rate, it did not happen here: the Directive is silent on the matter.

Nevertheless, it should be clear that deviation from the Directive is allowed only to a certain extent. It may be helpful in this context to make a distinction between organizational rules and rules referring to the actual powers of the bodies set up. Evaluating whether one organizational structure is more or less favourable for the employees in comparison with another can be very difficult. Owing to the complexity of such organizational structures, all that can be said is that they are different. Hence it seems to be advisable to consider purely organizational rules (composition of the special negotiating body or the European Works Council, etc.) to be neutral on the scale 'worse or better'. Consequently they are not to be modified by the national legislator.

It is a different matter when it comes to powers of a body representing the employees' interests: the more powers it has, the better for the employees. Consequently, at least in principle, the national legislator could improve the powers of the European Works Council. There is, however, a clear-cut borderline: the national legislator cannot go beyond information and consultation because it would then be stepping into an area for which a different legal basis in the Social Protocol would be relevant. But the national legislator remains entitled to improve on the instruments of information and consultation (by extending the procdure to more issues etc.) to make them more effective. Whether it would be politically wise for a national legislator to do so is, of course, a different matter altogether and beyond our scope here.

3. Conclusion

The least controversial and so far most successful strategy is, obviously, the establishment of information and consultation procedures in respect of certain specific issues. Despite many shortcomings in implementation, these attempts have so far had a very important effect. They have helped greatly to increase awareness of the strengths and weaknesses of the structure of workers' representation in the various countries, putting pressure on countries where existing arrangements made it difficult to implement the Directives. In the case of the United Kingdom, for instance, the European Court of Justice has considered the possibility, referred to earlier, of refusing trade union recognition at will, thereby eliminating the actor necessary for the envisaged procedure, to be a violation of the respective Directives.[54] Consequently, the United Kingdom has no choice but to adapt the existing pattern to the requirements set out in the Directives. In short, the strategy of establishing workers' participation in respect of certain specific issues is an appropriate tool for strengthening the structure of workers' representation throughout the Community. Hence, the Community should develop this channel further. There are many more issues to be covered by information and consultation procedures.

As far as workers' participation in corporate boards is concerned, this may still be too much of a reformulation of traditional perceptions of company law and industrial relations, at least in some Member States. And it may well be that in functional terms workers' participation in corporate boards makes sense only when there is some experience of how to co-operate with each other. Therefore it may be wise not to give the Fifth Directive first priority on the agenda. The smoother route via the optional model of a European company seems to be much more appropriate. Also, the shift of paradigm from imposing one and the same structure for all Member States to a simple offer of optional alternatives cannot be overestimated as a precondition for turning an illusory concept into a realistic approach. It will afford each Member State an opportunity to find out which of the optional models best suits its overall structure, and thereby gain experience.

The ideal instrument for paving the way for experience with workers' participation, and thereby creating the basis for further institutional arrangements, seems to be the strategy which targets information and consultation in the context of transnational undertakings and groups of undertakings. Of course the recent Directive—as shown above—contains many deficiencies and leads to difficulties of implementation. Leaving aside these more technical aspects it must, however, be stressed that the shift of paradigm from an essentially substantive regulation of rights and duties ('Vredeling') to a purely procedural arrangement, leaving all the decisions to the actors involved, is a step in the right direction.[55] It is predominantly an invitation to both companies and trade unions to develop a structure best suited to the needs of the particular undertaking or group of undertakings. The difference consists merely in the fact that the Directive will increase the pressure to conclude such agreements and to shape them indirectly by threatening minimum conditions in the event of failure to reach such an agreement.

The effect of the Directive will depend very much on the involvement and backing of the trade unions. In all countries covered by the Directive it will of necessity lead to a debate within the labour movement on what kind of structures might be desirable. The partners in the social dialogue could play an important role here. While the European legislator provides the basic

[54] See note 18 above.
[55] See M. Weiss, 'Europäische Betriebsräte' (1992) *Zeitschrift für Rechtspolitik*, 422-26 (426).

institutional framework, the actors in the social dialogue could support activities directed at reaching agreements within the undertakings and groups of undertakings covered by the Directive. For example, model agreements could be developed to facilitate implementation of the Directive's goal.[56] This strategy offers the utmost flexibility, calls for imaginative thinking, and invites experimentation. Instead of a homogeneous model, a multitude of different models may compete with each other.

If this perspective is correct, the question arises whether such a strategy does not miss the basic goal: to establish an equilibrium, a more or less equal standard of information and consultation within the Community. But, as already indicated at the start, any expectation of harmonization in this sense would be a futile and unrealistic hope. Neither the Directive on European Works Councils nor the Directive on workers' participation in the European company will achieve such uniformity. They will merely succeed in narrowing the gap and opening the door to the idea of workers' participation throughout the Community. Of course, as has been shown above, the Directive on European Works Councils should have been formulated differently in order at least to equalize the basic rules for the actors involved. But it is more important that it embodies a basic decision to overcome the co-existence of conflictual and co-operative systems in the long run, giving preference to the latter. It merely initiates a learning process. What will ultimately be necessary in order to achieve an equal level of workers' participation in functional terms will have to be discovered by experimenting with the range offered by such a type of Community legislation, focusing on procedure. The Community legislation itself is to be understood as only a first step in an organic development.

The second shift of paradigm is similarly important: from decentralized ('Vredeling') to centralized information and consultation. Transnational measures envisaged by the controlling undertaking may lead to different effects, advantageous or disadvantageous, for employees in different Member States. Therefore, it is important to banish the fear that employees in one country could have earlier and better information on these issues. This fear can be overcome only by a mechanism which institutionalizes simultaneous information and consultation in a forum where all employees of the different Member States are represented.

It may, however, be asked whether such a stimulus is necessary at all, or whether everything would be better left to the undertakings themselves, for voluntary arrangements.[57] But the fact cannot be ignored that little use has been made in the past of the possibility of establishing such voluntary

---

[56] On the role the social dialogue could play in reference to such model agreements see M. Weiss, 'Social Dialogue and Collective Bargaining in the Framework of a Social Europe', in G. Spyropoulos and G. Fragniere (eds.), *Work and Social Policies in a New Europe*, 1991 European Interuniversity Press: Brussels, 59-75 (69).

[57] See UNICE, Position Paper of 7 Oct. 1991.

structures. It was only the real threat of the recent Directive which initiated a good number of such agreements. And the option provided by Article 13 of the Directive has proved ultimately effective in significantly encouraging the conclusion of further voluntary agreements.[58] This shows that legislative pressure is essential in order to overcome the marginal nature of such agreements.

To avoid running into any problems with the principle of subsidiarity the Directive is confined to transnational undertakings and groups of undertakings. In addition, the Social Charter, as shown above, provides special legitimacy for the Community to fill the transnational gap. This, however, implies a special problem. If workers' representatives have a right to information and consultation in transnational undertakings where national law does not provide similar rights within domestic companies, there will obviously be segmentation of the internal labour market of the Member State concerned, leaving the workers in domestic companies in a worse position.[59] This, however, is to be considered a significant deficiency only if workers' participation is perceived as something static. From a dynamic perspective it looks quite different. It is very likely that an established pattern for transnational companies will put pressure on the national legislator to raise the rights of workers in domestic companies to the same level. Hence it turns out that in this respect also the Directive functions as a stimulus.

Representatives at the level of the controlling company of a group or the headquarters of a transnational undertaking may encounter conflicts of loyalty if measures are to be taken which are disadvantageous for their local constituency but reasonable for the workforce of the group or undertaking as a whole. This conflict probably cannot be eliminated altogether. But it could be reduced if another dimension could be improved: horizontal communication between workers and workers' representatives within a transnational undertaking or group of undertakings. The Directive does not prohibit such communication, but nor does it promote it. The Directive should be amended in this respect. But the call for an amendment may be wishful thinking, because such a strategy would entail significant costs. Therefore, in the absence of such legislation trade unions throughout the Member States should endeavour to make such horizontal communication one of their main tasks.[60]

---

[58] See H. Krieger and P. Bonneton, 'Analysis of existing voluntary agreements on information and consultation in European multinationals', in [1995] *Transfer* 188, and P. Bonneton (ed.) *Voluntary Agreements on Information and Consultation in European Multinationals*, Working Paper No. WP/94/50/EN of the European Foundation for the Improvement of Living and Working Conditions, Dublin.

[59] See the critical approach by M. Rood, 'Workers' Participation: The New Initiatives at European Level' [1993] *The International Journal of Comparative Labour Law and Industrial Relations*, 319 (323).

[60] See M. Weiss, 'Der soziale Dialog als Katalysator koordinierter Tarifpolitik in der EG', in M. Heinze and A. Söllner (eds.) *Arbeitsrecht in der Bewährung*, 1994, 1253 (1266).

Lastly, the Directive on European Works Councils is a good example of the unacceptability of a Europe à la carte. This model, as used in the Maastricht Social Protocol and Agreement, allows Member States to pick and choose which Community policies to accept. The Directive shows clearly that Member States cannot thereby escape the factual consequences of Community legislation. Owing to its opting-out the United Kingdom, legally speaking, is treated like any other non-member country, such as the United States or Japan. *De facto*, however, the United Kingdom is of necessity confronted with negative effects. Unlike other Member States, it cannot develop its own regulatory framework for U.K. transnationals by implementing the Directive. According to Article 4(2) of the Directive another Member State's legislation will be relevant, an effect which makes it more difficult for the headquarters of United Kingdom transnationals to cope with the Directive's requirements. As far as transnationals with headquarters outside the United Kingdom are concerned, British employees are clearly not covered by the Directive. This does not of course preclude the possibility that decisions affecting them disadvantageously will be taken by the central management abroad. But the fact that they are not represented on the European Works Council means that they are left out of information and consultation as institutionalized by the Directive. In this context it is enlightening to see that transnationals concluding voluntary agreements on works councils at the level of central management have included their U.K. employees.[61] And an increasing number of U.K. transnationals are signing agreements, although not legally required to do so. This shows that, at least in this context, the self-imposed abstention is proving de facto to be a sort of national masochism. The difficulties involved in deviating from the legal structure and acting in accordance with the interests of U.K. transnationals and U.K. employees may hopefully lead to the decision on 'opting out' being replaced by a decision to join in once again.

[61] See the examples in P. Bonneton, n. 58 above, 151 and 184, also compare R. Blanpain, B. Hepple, S. Sciarra, M. Weiss, *Fundamental Social Rights: Proposals for the European Union* (Peters, Leuven, 1996), 7.

11

Equality and Discrimination

BOB HEPPLE

1. Introduction

All Member States of the EC have enacted legislation against sex discrimination, including the right to equal pay for women and men. This has largely been due to the impact of Article 119 of the EC Treaty which provides that 'Each Member State shall . . . ensure . . . the application of the principle that men and women should receive equal pay for equal work.' This directly applicable provision has been supplemented by five Council directives on pay, employment and vocational training, aspects of statutory and occupational social security, and self-employment.[1]

However, legal intervention against other forms of social discrimination remains patchy at national level, and non-existent at Community level. As Bill Wedderburn has said, 'pressures for fair and equal treatment cause the law to intervene (though with what effect needs careful investigation) but not always with the same intensity'.[2]

---

[1] Council Dir. of 10 Feb. 1975 on the approximation of the laws of the Member States relating to the application of the principle of equal pay for men and women (75/117/EEC) ('Equal Pay Dir.'); Council Dir. of 9 Feb. 1976 on the implementation of the principle of equal treatment for men and women as regards to access to employment, vocational training and promotion and working conditions (76/207/EEC) ('Equal Treatment Dir.'); Council Dir. of 19 Dec. 1978 on the progressive implementation of the principle of equal treatment for men and women in matters of social security (79/7/EEC) ('Social Security Dir.'); Council Dir. of 24 July 1986 on the implementation of the principle of equal treatment for men and women in occupational social security schemes (86/378/EEC) ('Occupational Social Security Dir.') which the Commission proposes to amend in the light of ECJ decisions; Council Dir. of 11 Dec. 1986 on the application of the principle of equal treatment between men and women engaged in an activity including agriculture, in a self-employed capacity, and on the protection of self-employed women during pregnancy and motherhood (86/613/EEC) ('Self-Employed Dir.'). Draft dirs. on parental leave and on the reversal of the burden of proof in discrimination cases were at one time proposed by the Commission, but in the face of oposition have been withdrawn and, at the time of writing, have been submitted for consultation under the Maastricht Social Dialogue procedures.

[2] Lord Wedderburn, *The Worker and the Law* (3rd edn., Harmondsworth, 1986) 447. The Comparative Labour Law Group's study, *Discrimination in Employment* (ed. F. Schmidt) (Stockholm, 1978), dealt with race, nationality, national origin, and sex, but added discrimination in private and personal life, and 'from a rather different direction', Wedderburn's masterly ch. 6 on 'Discrimination in the Right to Organise and the Right to be a Non-Unionist'. These latter topics fall outside the scope of the present Ch.

Despite the European Court of Justice's much-vaunted respect for human rights as 'one of the fundamental principles of Community law',[3] including the rights to privacy[4] and religion,[5] the EC has done little to extend human rights outside the area of sex discrimination and equal pay. Discrimination on grounds of nationality is prohibited as against citizens of the Member States, and the Maastricht Treaty develops the concept of citizenship of the European Union (EU), but so-called 'third country' (non-EU) nationals who make up 2.5 per cent of the resident population of the EU (as high as 5.2 per cent in Germany and 3.8 per cent in France) are unprotected.[6] Doubts have even been expressed about the competence of the EC to legislate on matters of racial discrimination,[7] so revealing a mighty gap between legal reality and the political will expressed by the EC Heads of State and Government, together with those of other members of the Council of Europe, in the Vienna Declaration of 9 October 1993. In this they promised to take action against the resurgence of racism and xenophobia which 'threaten democratic societies and their fundamental values and undermine the foundations of European construction'. Four EC States (Denmark, Greece, Ireland, Luxembourg) have no specific legislation against racial discrimination in employment,[8] and in other Member States the legislation tends to be limited in coverage, for example to recruitment or dismissal.[9]

In other areas of discrimination, the EC has not gone beyond resolutions and other 'soft' measures. Over the past three decades the number of people aged over 60 in the Member States has risen from 46.5 million to 68.6 million, a trend set to continue.[10] Discrimination against older workers (40+), tends to be more subtle and covert than racism and sexism, but no EC country has followed the lead of the United States by enacting an Age Discrimination in Employment Act[11] Women, who face the 'double jeopardy' of sexism and

---

[3] Case 149/77, *Defrenne* v. *Sabena* [1978] ECR 1365 at paras. 26–27, and see further below, 247.

[4] Case 29/69, *Stauder* v. *Ulm* [1969] ECR 419 at para. 7; Case 136/79, *National Panasonic* [1980] ECR 2033.

[5] Case 30/75, *Prais* v. *Council* [1976] ECR 1589.

[6] John Salt, 'Current and Future Migration Trends Affecting Europe', in *People on the Move: New Migration Flows in Europe* (Council of Europe, Strasbourg, 1992), 48 and Table 4.

[7] See below, 243–5.

[8] In Northern Ireland, there is legislation against discrimination on grounds of religion or political opinion, but not racial discrimination, a matter currently under review.

[9] Ian Forbes and Geoffrey Mead, *Measure for Measure: A Comparative Analysis of Measures to Control Racial Discrimination in the Member Countries of the European Community* (Employment Department, Research Series No. 1, 1992), esp. 72.; see, too, Commission of the European Communities, *Legal Instruments to Combat Racism, and Xenophobia* (Directorate General Employment, Industrial Relations and Social Affairs, Brussels, 1992).

[10] *Social Europe*, 1/93, 21.

[11] The Age Discrimination in Employment Act 1967, which has been amended on several occasions, now protects everyone aged 40 and over: see generally, Mack A. Player, *Employment Discrimination Law* (St.Paul, Minn., 1988), ch. 6.

age barriers which have a disparate impact on those with family responsibilities, have found only limited protection through the concept of indirect sex discrimination.[12] But measures, based on the Community Charter of the Fundamental Social Rights of Workers, have been limited to a few recommendations, communications, decisions, and voluntary initiatives.[13]

A not dissimilar story can be told about persons with disabilities, who make up one in ten (30 million) of the population of the Member States.[14] Although a majority of the Member States[15] have constitutional or other legal provisions which refer to the right of persons with disabilities to equal treatment or recognition in employment, the dominant philosophy is still one of assistance rather than of rights against discrimination. The primary legal tool is the use of quotas,[16] which appear to be under-achieved and unenforced except in Germany. Measures under the Community Charter have focussed around action programmes (HELIOS I and II),[17] and a directive which aims to promote an improvement in the travel conditions of workers with motor disabilities.[18] The Medium-Term Social Action Programme (1995–7) proposes a number of other 'soft' measures, including a code of good practice in employment.

Wedderburn's enormous contribution to comparative labour law scholarship rests upon his recognition of 'the need to judge the meaning of law primarily by reference, not to its formal drafting but to the entire social and

---

[12] Trevor Buck, 'Ageism and Legal Control', in B. Hepple and E. Szyszczak (eds.) *Discrimination: the Limits of Law* (London, 1992), 250–2.

[13] Communication from the Commission of 24 Apr. 1990 (COM(90)80 Final); Council decision of 26 Nov. 1990 (91/49/EEC); Commission Dec. of 17 Oct. 1991 (91/544/EEC); Council decision of 24 June 1992 (92/440/EEC). The Observatory on Ageing and Older People was established in 1991 to analyse the impact of social and economic policies on older people. The three-year action programme (1991–3) for the elderly aimed to raise consciousness on these issues, but did not propose legislation. The Commission submitted proposals for further action in Mar. 1995 (COM(95)53).

[14] European Communities, *Disabled Persons*, Statistical Data (Luxembourg, 1993), ii.

[15] Those which have not done so are Denmark, France, Ireland, and Luxembourg: see generally, B. Doyle, *Disability, Discrimination, and Equal Opportunities: A Comparative Study of the Employment Rights of Disabled Persons* (London, 1995), ch. 3.

[16] E.g. France: 6% for undertakings with with 20 or more workers; Germany: 6% for employers with 16 or more workers; Italy: 15% from pool of 'sheltered' workers including 12% disabled persons for employers with over 35 workers; Netherlands: 5% under reintegration measures agreed by both sides of industry, failing which 3–7%; Spain: 2% for employers with 50 or more workers; Britain: 3% for employers with 20 or more workers.

[17] Council Dec. 88/327/EEC of 18 Apr. 1988 establishing a second action programme for Handicapped People in the EC Living Independently in Open Society (HELIOS), [1988] OJ L104/38, and Council Dec. 93/136/EEC of 25 Feb. 1993 establishing a third action programme (HELIOS II—1993–6) [1993] OJ L56/30. The Recommendation of 24 July 1986, on the employment of disabled people (86/379/EEC), was described by the European Parliament as 'weak in form and content' ([1986] OJ C148/84).

[18] This was introduced under Art. 118A EC; for the amended proposal see [1992] OJ C15/18

cultural context that determines its meaning and effect in application.'[19] In this spirit, the starting point of this Chapter must be to explain the haphazard and limited nature of Community action against social disadvantage in the single market. Secondly, the Chapter aims to provide a critique of the principle of 'equality' and the concept of 'discrimination', as these have emerged in the EC law on questions of gender and nationality. Finally, conscious of Wedderburn's insistence that the effect of legal intervention in this field needs 'careful investigation', the Chapter considers the effectiveness of laws which treat equality as an individual right.

Equality and the Market

Anti-discrimination laws are concerned with some aspects of the inequalities in income and job opportunities amongst those who work or seek work. The globalization of the market system, of which the expanding European Union is part, has been accompanied by a growth in inequality of this kind. To the traditional explanations for structural inequality,[20] such as class and family background, sex, ethnic origin, and geographical variations, we need to add the new international division of labour.[21] Western Europeans, like Americans, are becoming part of an international labour market encompassing Africa, Asia, Latin America, as well as Eastern Europe and the territories of the former Soviet Union. Barriers are crumbling, and the walls of the European Union may offer no more than temporary respite from the inequalities produced by global competition.

As already noted, anti-discrimination laws in the Community have focussed primarily on one form of inequality, that between men and women. The very limited impact which these laws appear to have had on reducing inequality is not surprising when one appreciates the segregation of women in poorly-paid jobs and their concentration in the services sector.[22] The rates of participation of women in the labour market in the Community have increased significantly over the past two decades, although with important regional variations. Most of the new jobs created have gone to women.[23] But a recent study[24] has shown

[19] Lord Wedderburn, 'The New Politics of Labour Law: Immunities or Positive Rights'. in *Employment Rights in Britain and Europe* (London, 1991), 98.

[20] See e.g. V. George and R. Lawson, *Poverty and Inequality in Common Market Countries* (London,1980), 16–21.

[21] Robert B. Reich,*The Work of Nations* (London, 1993), 172.

[22] The proportion of the workforce in the Community employed in services is just over 60% (having increased by 12 million in the 1980s); in the North of the Community the figure is closer to that in the USA (70%); on average 18% of those in services are part-time (38% in the Netherlands, 28% in the U.K. and Denmark), the vast majority of these being women: *Employment in Europe 1992*, EC Brussels, 1993, 71 ff.

[23] Ibid.125.

[24] Jill Rubery and Collette Fagan, *Occupational Segregation of Women and Men in the European Community*, Social Europe, Supplement 3/93.

that gender segregation is, if anything, greater in countries with high levels of participation, particularly if this is associated with high levels of part-time and temporary work. Changes are occurring, but pulling in two directions, with women increasing their representation in both high-level professional jobs and low-level jobs. Women have high shares of jobs in service and clerical occupations, with public sector work being a particular gender trap associated with declining relative pay. At the same time, women do better in moving up the jobs hierarchy in predominantly female occupations. Women now make up about half of all higher education students in most EC countries. These well-educated women are likely to have career aspirations similar to those of men. Although they fare less well than men because of family responsibilities, they do better than less well-educated women for whom it is harder to find suitable jobs which enable them to reconcile work and family.

Another recent study,[25] emphasizes the high degree of occupational segregation in the rapidly expanding part-time female workforce, which largely cancels out any trend to integration in the declining full-time workforce. The increasing inequality *within* the female workforce is due to factors such as class background, family responsibilities, the length and quality of education and training, and working time patterns.

In view of these deep, structural characteristics of inequality between men and women, why did the founders of the EC, who believed firmly in the virtues of economic neo-liberalism, decide to intervene in the labour market through the provisions of Article 119? The debate between the protagonists and opponents of Article 119 during the negotiations is reminiscent of the controversy between U.K. Governments and other Member States in the 1980s and 1990s over the social dimension.

At the time of the Treaty negotiations, although nearly all the Six States had constitutional provisions declaring equality between men and women, and four of them had ratified the ILO.Equal Remuneration Convention of 1951 (No. 100), only France (by legislation of 1957)[26] had specific legislation requiring equal pay. The French argued that they would be at a competitive disadvantage if they alone had to bear the costs of equal pay. The Germans and the Benelux countries, on the other hand, maintained that the harmonization of indirect or social costs would be the inevitable outcome of the establishment of the Common Market. This was similar to the position taken by a Committee of Experts established by the European Coal and Steel Community in conjunction with the International Labour Office.[27] The

[25] C. Hakim, 'Segregated and Integrated Occupations: A New Approach to Analysing Social Change' (1993) 9 *European Sociological Review* 289; and more generally, *Key Issues in Women's Employment* London (Hakim, London 1996), esp. ch. 6.

[26] A. Arseguel and B. Reynes in *Equality Law Between Men and Women in the European Community* (Louvain-La-Neuve, 1986) ii, 117.

[27] ILO Studies and Reports (New Series) No. 46, *Social Aspects of European Collaboration* (Geneva, 1956). At the time, according to the ILO, in France the average

Committee distinguished between the *general level* of labour costs, which were said to reflect different levels of productivity, and *inter-industrial* patterns of costs, where it was said that intervention was justified in particular industries with exceptionally low wages or social costs, thus giving them a competitive advantage.

The Title on Social Policy (Title III) of the 1957 Treaty was a compromise between the German and French positions. On the one hand, the exhortatory Article 117, circumscribed by Article 118, declared that improved working conditions and an improved standard of living 'will ensue ... from the functioning of the Common Market, which will favour the harmonisation of social systems', and also referred to 'the approximation of provisions' (in effect under Article 100). On the other hand, Article 119 (and Article 120 on the equivalence of paid holiday schemes) sought to pay lip service to French demands for protection from 'social dumping'. The commitment to achieve 'equal pay for equal work' was weaker than the ILO standard of equal pay for work of equal value, which was rejected as too vague to be implemented at Community level. The objective of achieving equal pay by the end of the first stage (1962), and when this failed by the extended date of 1964,[28] was, in Warner's words, 'either made without conviction or was remarkably naïve'.[29]

Steps to implement Article 119 were taken only after a series of actions[30] brought under Article 119 by Gabrielle Defrenne, a Belgian air hostess, advised by Professor Eliane Vogel-Polsky, and a report to the Commission in 1972 by Evelyne Sullerot, a French sociologist, which concluded that there was still widespread sex discrimination in the Member States. The Equal Pay Directive widened the concept of equal pay by including a reference to equal value, and the Equal Treatment Directive, based on Article 235 of the EC Treaty, introduced the principle of equal treatment as regards access to employment, vocational training, promotion and working conditions. The reason for these extensions of the apparently limited provisions of Article 119, and its later elevation into a fundamental principle of equality,[31] has to be found in the political rather than the economic or legal sphere. Action

earnings of women were 91% of those of men, compared to 78% in Germany, and 66% in Britain.

[28] EC Bull. 1962/1, 7–9 (pay differentials to be reduced by 15% by 30 June 1962; 10% by 30 June 1963; and all discrimination to be abolished by the end of 1964).

[29] J. Warner, 'EC Social Policy in Practice: Community Action on Behalf of Women and its Impact in the Member States' (1984) 23 *Journal of Common Market Studies* 141, 143.

[30] Case 80/70, *Defrenne* v. *Belgian State (No.1)* [1971] ECR 445; Case 43/75 *Defrenne* v. *Sabena (No.2)* [1976] ECR 455; Case 149/77 *Defrenne* v. *Sabena (No.3)* [1978] ECR 1365.

[31] C. Docksey in C. McCrudden (ed.), *Women, Employment and European Equality Law* (London, 1987), 3 comments that 'had it been formulated more recently, it might well have been expressed more positively in terms of a fundamental principle of equality which is to be progressively implemented'. See further, below, 246–53.

against sex discrimination provided a vehicle for politicians to appease women voters. As Ellis points out, sex equality 'provides a relatively innocuous, even high-sounding platform by means of which the Communities can demonstrate their commitment to social progress'. Moreover, 'to accede to demands made by the [European] Parliament in the sphere of equal rights between the sexes has provided the Community's executive with a useful way out of heeding its advice in other fields'.[32] The result has been what Neilsen calls 'state feminism', that is ,equality laws 'which are neither mobilised for, nor implemented by, women, and which create rights only on an individual basis'.[33]

The lack of a similar political impetus against racial discrimination helps to account for the absence of EC legislation on this subject. Whether they are described as 'ethnic minorities' (United Kingdom and the Netherlands), 'guest workers' (Germany), or 'migrants' (most other countries), the Member States have within them significant diverse populations, particularly in large cities. Many were recruited when rapidly expanding economies in Western Europe were short of labour, and they often did jobs which the host population did not want to do. They still tend to be segregated in unskilled and semi-skilled jobs and concentrated in production and service sectors. They are more likely to under-achieve at school and to have poorer access to training and promotion than host country workers. They face higher levels of unemployment than the host population, and they suffer widespread discrimination even if, as is increasingly the case, they were born and bred in the country.[34] Without exception, it is members of the visible minority populations (currently amounting to about 9 million people or 2.6 per cent of the EC population) who suffer most from both direct and indirect discrimination.[35] Yet, it remains true to say that in most European countries the 'problem' is still looked at in the way it was in Britain a quarter of a century ago. 'Rarely, if ever, is the interaction between immigration,colour and social inequality seen as part of a dynamic social process'.[36]

There is every justification for the EC to act against racial discrimination. If freedom of movement, one of the fundamental premises of the Internal Market, is restricted for women because of their lack of mobility, then *a*

---

[32] Evelyn Ellis, *European Community Sex Equality Law* (Oxford, 1991), 40; see too K. O'Donovan and E. Szyszczak, *Equality and Sex Discrimination Law* (Oxford, 1988), 195.

[33] O'Donovan and Szyszczsak, n. 32 above, 195, referring to Ruth Neilsen, *Equality Legislation in a Comparative Pespective—Towards State Feminism* (Copenhagen,1983).

[34] Roger Zegers de Beijl, *Discrimination of Migrant Workers in Western Europe* (I.L.O. World Employment Programme Working Paper, Geneva, 1990), 44; Mary Coussey, *Tackling Racism and Xenophobia* (European Committee on Migration, Discussion Paper, Council of Europe, Strasbourg, 30 July 1993), 3.

[35] Ian Forbes and Geoffrey Mead, n. 9 above, 73.

[36] Bob Hepple, *Race, Jobs and the Law in Britain* (2nd edn., Penguin, Harmondsworth, 1970), 19.

fortiori racial discrimination must impede the free movement of nationals of the Member States who suffer colour discrimination when they attempt to exercise this freedom.[37] The process of creating a single 'European' identity can foster exclusionary and disparaging treatment of populations of immigrant origin whose race, ethnic origin, or nationality are different from those who regard themselves as 'Europeans'; the accompanying racism and xenophobia are dangerous sources of political instability. Moreover, the very operation of EC measures establishing the Internal Market is likely to result in indirect discrimination. For example, Council Directive 89/48/EEC on a general system for recognition of higher education diplomas awarded on completion of professional education and training of at least three years' duration may unjustifiably exclude members of groups of migrant origin whose qualifications have not been recognized by competent national authorities.[38] The absence of any individual or public legal remedy under EC law in this respect also illustrates that national law such as the British Race Relations Act 1976, may offer greater protection than is available in other Member States.[39] This is just as much a 'distortion of competition' as that which the French feared in the case of equal pay laws. Yet EC law remains narrowly confined to discrimination on grounds of 'nationality'.

Article 6 of the EC Treaty (formerly Article 7) prohibits any discrimination on grounds of nationality, but this applies only 'within the scope of application of this Treaty, and without prejudice to any special provisions contained therein'. One such 'special provision' is Article 48(2) which provides that 'freedom of movement shall entail the abolition of any discrimination based on nationality between workers of Member States as regards employment, remuneration, and other conditions of work and employment'. This Article is amplified by the directly applicable Regulation 1612/68 which spells out in detail the rights of nationals of Member States to take up work in other Member States under the same conditions as nationals of that Member State. Article 7 of Regulation 1612/68 protects workers who are nationals of a Member State from discrimination by reason of nationality 'in respect of any conditions of employment and work, in particular as regards remuneration, dismissal and should he become unemployed, reinstatement or re-employment'. Thus the Treaty, and the Regulation see non-discrimination as an essential step towards free movement. Yet the ECJ has interpreted Article 48 as limiting the general principle in (what is now) Article 6, so as to treat Article 48 as applying only to those workers who possess the nationality of one of the Member States.[40] The 8.5 million non-EC nationals legally resident

---

[37] E. M. Szyszczak, 'Race Discrimination: The Limits of Market Equality?' in Hepple and Szyszczak (eds.), n. 12 above, 125, 126.

[38] Szyszczak, n. 37 above, 127.

[39] Cf. *Hampson* v. *Department of Education and Science* [1990] IRLR 302 (HL).

[40] See generally, C. Greenwood, 'Nationality and the Limits of Free Movement of Persons in Community Law' (1987) 7 Yearbook of European Law 185, for a review of the

or working in the EC have no rights under Article 48 and the Regulation. The concept of 'European citizenship' in Articles 8 to 8e of the EC Treaty as amended by the Treaty of European Union does nothing to protect these third country nationals.

The argument that the EC has no competence to take measures against racial discrimination lacks conviction. Use could be made of Articles 7 (measures to establish market including free movement), 100 (approximation of provisions directly affecting the functioning of the market), and 235 (measures where Treaty does not provide appropriate powers), in order to adopt a directive on this subject. Alternatively, it has been argued that use could be made of Articles 117 and 118 of the EC Treaty by the European Commission to build a system of fundamental human rights for non-EC migrants within the Community, provided that the Commission can show that such measures are necessary for the functioning of the Community labour market as a whole.[41] However, despite a series of Community reports on the growth of racism and xenophobia,[42] a Joint Declaration of the Parliament and Council of 11 June 1986,[43] a reference in the Preamble to the Community Social Charter of December 1989 to the need to combat every form of discrimination including that on grounds of race or colour, and a Resolution of the Council of 29 May 1990,[44] there is still no legislative measure on racial discrimination. The growing demand for such legislation has recently been sidestepped by a Joint Declaration adopted at a Social Dialogue Summit on 20 October 1995. This gives advice on preventing racial discrimination and promoting equal treatment at the workplace, but is no substitute for directly applicable legislation. One of the questions addressed by this Chapter is whether the sex discrimination model, with its concept of formal equality of treatment and its relative neglect of substantive equality, its emphasis on individual rights, and its reliance on national implementation and enforcement, is adequate to the task of eliminating racial discrimination.

It is sometimes argued that, since markets are sets of unplanned spontaneous exchanges which reward individual efforts and abilities and so generate grossly unequal outcomes, they cannot be successfully manipulated through legislation. According to this static individualist economic model, anti-discrimination laws have not increased, and may even have diminished the

cases, and generally B. Sundberg-Weitman, *Discrimination on Grounds of Nationality* (Amsterdam, 1977). For earlier debate, see W. Bohning 'The Scope of the EEC System of Free Movement of Workers' (1972) 9 *Common Market Law Review* 81, and compare D. Eden and S. Patijn's rejoinder (1973) 10 *Common Market Law Review* 81.

[41] Szyszczak, n. 37 above, 140, reviewing the decision of the ECJ in Cases 281/85, 283–5/85, *Germany and others* v. *Commission* [1988] 1 CMLR 11.

[42] Evrigenis Report, submitted to European Parliament in 1985, PE 97.547; Ford Report submitted to European Parliament in 1990 (see Recommendation 31 proposing a dir. on racial discrimination).

[43] 86/C 158/01.

[44] 90/C 157/01.

aggregate welfare of women.[45] Against this dismal view of the Chicago school, there is the real world in which successful business organizations make use of equal opportunities practices in order to recruit and develop the most efficient staff and to build up diverse workforces which reflect their local markets so enabling them to make their organizations better informed, more adaptable, and closer to their customers.[46] In this dynamic approach to the market, the role of anti-discrimination legislation is to create a framework—in Wedderburn's famous phrase, a 'floor of rights'—within which enterprises can improve their efficiency by improving access, training, and promotion on the basis of job abilities rather than on arbitrary and irrational criteria such as sex or race. However, the absence of a comprehensive and positive approach to equality, and the haphazard attitude of Community law to the many forms of arbitrary discrimination, has limited both the symbolic and instrumental impact of the law.

3. Equality as a Fundamental Principle of EC Law

Can the seeds of such a comprehensive and positive approach to equality and discrimination be found in the Treaty and the case law of the European Court of Justice? Several Articles of the Treaty expressly prohibit forms of discrimination, such as Articles 6 and 48(2) (nationality), Article 37 (state monopolies), Article 40(3) (common agricultural policy), Articles 52 and 60 (right of establishment), Articles 92 and 95 (state aids), as well as Article119 (equal pay). Each of these has been said by the Court to be 'merely a specific enunciation of the general principle of equality which is one of the fundamental principles of Community law. This principle requires that similar situations shall not be treated differently unless differentiation is objectively justified.'[47]

The source of the principle is the concept of *Gleichheitssatz* in the constitutional law of the Germanic countries, where it is implied from the definition of the *Rechtstaat* as a means for protecting the subject from misuse of power. It may be compared with the last clause of the 14th Amendment to the United States Constitution which provides that no State shall 'deny any person within its jurisdiction the equal protection of the laws'. Although mainly intended for the benefit of the freed slaves, the equal protection clause has been developed into a general test of validity of state and local governmental actions which classify individuals for different benefits and burdens under the law. As such it is 'the most important concept in the U.S.

---

[45] Richard A. Posner, 'An Economic Analysis of Sex Discrimination Laws' 56 *U Chi. LR* 1311 (1989).

[46] See Mary Coussey and Hilary Jackson, *Making Equal Opportunities Work* (London, 1991), 2.

[47] Joined Cases 117/76 and 16/77, *Ruckdeschel* [1977] ECR 1753, para. 7.

Constitution for the protection of individual rights' in respect of state action.[48]

In the field of EC labour law, the principle suffers from two major limitations. The first is its restricted sphere of application. It has been confined to situations of judicial review of administrative or legislative action by the Community (under Articles 173 and 184), and to the interpretation of Article 119 and secondary legislation on equality between men and women. So Community officials were able to invoke it in order to challenge staff regulations which discriminated directly or indirectly on grounds of sex in relation to expatriation allowances.[49] And the ECJ has been able to justify liberal interpretations of Article 119 on the basis that the principle of equal pay is part of a general fundamental right to equality.[50] This right is said to be derived from the constitutional traditions of the Member States,[51] and from international standards such as those enshrined in the European Convention on Human Rights, the European Social Charter, and ILO Conventions, such as Conventions No.100 (Equal Remuneration) and No.111 (Discrimination in Employment).

However, the ECJ has not been prepared to treat breach of this fundamental right as a free-standing basis for legal action by individuals. There must be some other EC law 'for the principle to bite on'.[52] This is illustrated by the third *Defrenne* case,[53] decided before the coming into force of the Equal Treatment Directive, when the ECJ rejected the allegation that a general principle of EC law had been breached on the ground that at the time the Community had not assumed responsibility for supervising and guaranteeing the observance of the principle of equality between men and women in working conditions other than remuneration. The Community judges, like those in civil law systems generally, see their role as interpreters and enforcers of enacted law, and not as lawmakers.

This means that in practice the ECJ has done little more than to apply the principles of equal pay for equal work and equal treatment for men and women as enacted by the Community. It has not developed a generally enforceable right to equality for men and women. *A fortiori*, it has not developed such a right in other areas of social discrimination.

A second and even more significant weakness is the restrictive interpretation

[48] J. E. Novak and R. D. Rotunda, *Constitutional Law* (4th edn., St Paul, 1985); and see generally, P. G. Polyviou, *The Equal Protection of the Laws* (London, 1980).

[49] Case 20/71, *Sabbatini* [1972] ECR 345 (indirect discrimination); Cases 75 and 117/82, *Razzouk and Beydoun* [1984] ECR 1509 (direct discrimination). Cf Case 246/83, *De Angelis* [1985] ECR 1253.

[50] Case 43/76 *Defrenne* v. *Sabena* [1976] ECR 455 at 472, para. 12; Case 149/77, *Defrenne* v. *Sabena* [1978] ECR 1365 at 1368, paras. 26–27. See generally Ellis, n. 32 above, 117–34; C. Docksey, 'The Principle of Equality Between Women and Men as a Fundamental Right under Community Law' (1991) 20 *ILJ* 258.

[51] See e.g. German Basic Law, Art. 3.2; Italian Constitution, Art. 3; Preamble to French the Constitution of 1946, Art. 1 reaffirmed by the Constitution of 1958.

[52] Ellis, n. 32 above, 132.

[53] Case 149/77 [1978] ECR 1365.

which has been given to the concept of equality in both legislation and case law. This is a point which has been strongly argued from a feminist perspective both in the United States,[54] and in Europe.[55] The main criticism is that the concept is dependent on a norm of comparison, which is generally the existing (white) male norm. The principle is that like must be compared with like. The situation of the man and the woman being compared must be the same. The absurdity of pure reliance on a male norm in cases of discrimination on grounds of pregnancy was recognized by the ECJ in the *Dekker*[56] case. The protection of the Equal Treatment Directive was extended to a woman refused employment on grounds of pregnancy although there were no male applicants. The discrimination was 'on grounds of sex' because only a woman can be refused employment by reason of pregnancy. However, in the more difficult *Webb*[57] case, where a woman had been appointed to replace another woman on maternity leave and was dismissed when she announced that she, too, was pregnant, the Court suggested by implication that the dismissal of a woman on a fixed-term contract may be justified if she is, by reason of pregnancy, unable to fulfil the purpose of the contract. In the *Hertz*[58] case, the ECJ reintroduced the need for a male comparator where pregnancy-related illness extends beyond the period of obligatory maternity leave, the justification being that illness at this time was no different from that of men. The male norm is usually the reference point in legislation, as well. For example the Directive on Pregnant Workers 92/85/EEC uses the norm of sick pay as the basis for calculating minimum maternity pay. Pregnancy and confinement are treated as comparable to a male 'illness', rather than as a condition unique to women.

The more general weakness of the comparative approach is that it tends to ignore the occupational segregation and labour market disadvantages of women discussed earlier. Existing employment and pension benefits are structured according to the expectations of the male full-time worker in continuous employment from the age of 16 to that of (male) retirement. This assumes that the domestic and family needs of the man will be taken care of by his (unpaid) wife. The comparative approach fails to achieve equality for the many women who do not conform to this male norm. The legal rationalization is either that the circumstances of the man and woman are not similar, or that the discrimination is 'objectively justified', a defence which gives priority to the employer's business needs.

[54] See, for example, C. Smart, *Feminism and the Power of Law* (1989). 138–46; C. A. Mackinnon, *Feminism Unmodified* (1987), ch. 2.

[55] See, e.g. Sandra Fredman, 'European Community Discrimination Law: A Critique' (1992) 21 *ILJ* 119, and 'A Difference with Distinction: Pregnancy and Parenthood Reassesed' (1994) 110 *Law Quartely Review* 106; N. Lacey, 'Legislation against Sex Discrimination: Questions from a Feminist Perspective' (1987) 14 *Journal of Law and Society* 114.

[56] Case C–177/88, [1990] ECR 3841.

[57] Case C–32/93 [1994] ECR I—3567, applied by the HL in [1995] IRLR 645.

[58] Case 179/88 [1990] ECR 3979.

An example is to be found in the case of *Birds Eye Walls Ltd.* v. *Roberts.*[59] There was alleged to be direct discrimination in the case of men and women between the ages of 60, which is the state pensionable age for women in Britain, and 65, the state pensionable age for men, because a woman who retired early on ill-health grounds received a smaller bridging pension from her employer in those years than her male counterpart. From the age of 60 the woman's bridging pension was reduced by the amount of state pension she received or was deemed to receive, but no such reduction was made in the case of a man until the age of 65. The ECJ held that there was no discrimination because the situations of the woman and man were different. The bridging pension was a supplement to their financial resources and took account of changes with the passage of time, including receipt of state pension at different ages. The European Commission and the Advocate-General had argued for a similar result on the basis that, although there was direct discrimination, it was objectively justified.[60]

Against these criticisms, it may be argued that the concept of indirect discrimination provides a potentially powerful challenge to apparently neutral criteria and practices (male norms) which have a disproportionate adverse impact upon women. The introduction of this concept into Community law is a remarkable example of judicial creativity, which cannot be fully recounted here. Suffice it to say that Article 119 and the various equality directives make no explicit reference to indirect discrimination. It has been developed by the ECJ, at first on the basis of American and British provisions but now going well beyond those models.

Most recently, in the case of *Enderby* v. *Frenchay Health Authority*[61] the Court held that, where statistics disclose an appreciable difference in pay between two jobs, one carried out almost exclusively by women and the other predominantly by men, Article 119 requires the employer to show that the difference is based on objectively justified factors unrelated to sex discrimination. The importance of this decision is that it extends the situations in which the evidential burden of proof shifts to the employer. Previous decisions had established that the employer must justify disadvantage to women arising from particular arrangements, such as part-time work.[62] It had also been held that where a pay system is lacking in transparency, it is for the employer to prove that his practice in the matter of wages is not discriminatory.[63] In *Enderby*,

[59] Case C–132/92 [1994] IRLR 29.
[60] Case C–152/91 [1994] IRLR 91. Cf *Neath* v. *Hugh Steeper Ltd.* [1994] IRLR 91 where the ECJ avoided deciding whether the use of actuarial factors differing according to sex in funded defined-benefit occupational pension schemes were justifiable, by ruling that transfer benefits and lump-sum options are not 'pay' for purposes of Art. 119.
[61] Case C–127/92 [1993] IRLR 591.
[62] Case 170/84, *Bilka-Kaufhaus* [1986] IRLR 317, para. 31; Case C–33/89, *Kowalska* [1990] IRLR 447, para.16; Case C–184/89, *Nimz* [1991] IRLR 222, para. 15.
[63] Case 109/88, *Danfoss* [1989] IRLR 532, para.16.

the Court went further and was willing to infer indirect discrimination from the mere fact that the woman belonged to an almost entirely female occupation or profession. The Court appears to have agreed with the Advocate-General that less attention should be directed to the existence of a requirement or hurdle by means of which women suffer disadvantage, and more to the discriminatory result.

However, even this result-oriented approach suffers from two potentially major limitations. The first is that it still depends upon a comparison between representative groups of men and women. Indeed, in the field of equal pay, the ECJ has rejected the argument that the woman should be allowed to make a comparison with the 'hypothetical' male comparator, i.e. to ask how a man would have been treated, on the ground that this is too imprecise and would require comparative studies of entire branches of industry.[64] Thus, although a woman may compare herself with a man actually employed either contemporaneously or previously on work of equal value, she cannot improve her pay if she works in a segregated workforce with no relevant male comparator. Moreover, the Court appears to have rejected the possibility of comparisons with men in different establishments or employed by different employers in the same industry or service.[65]

A second potential limit is that proof of significant disadvantage does no more than raise a *prima facie* case of indirect discrimination. The employer may still provide evidence of objective justification. This involves a value judgement, and the impact which the law on indirect discrimination has on the labour market will depend upon how sympathetic the court is to the employer's business needs. The ECJ has been nudging national courts towards what, in the United States, would be called a 'strict scrutiny' test. This is 'that the means chosen [by the employer] correspond to a real need on the part of the undertaking, are appropriate with a view to achieving the objectives pursued and are necessary to that end'.[66] It is for national courts and tribunals to assess whether or not there is a 'real need', and the means chosen are 'appropriate' and 'necessary'. For example, following the ECJ's lead,[67] the British House of Lords (the highest appellate court) declared that thresholds prescribed by legislation which indirectly discriminated against part-time women workers were incompatible with Community law. The House of Lords rejected generalizations by the Government, such as that the thresholds were needed to keep a 'fair balance' between employers and employees. Since there was no means of ascertaining whether, as the Government claimed but others disputed, the thresholds were an incentive to

[64] Case 129/70, *Macarthys* [1979] ECR 1275.
[65] Case 43/75, *Defrenne (No.2)* [1976] ECR 455, paras. 19 and 22; cf. the argument by A. G. Verloren van Themaat in Case 143/83, *Commission v. Denmark* [1985] ECR 427.
[66] *Bilka-Kaufhaus*, n. 62 above, at para. 36.
[67] Case 171/88, *Rinner-Kuhn* [1989] ECR 2743.

employers to create part-time jobs, it was held that it had not been shown that the objective of creating more jobs would actually be achieved by the thresholds.[68]

The ECJ has also recently taken a robust approach to attempts to use 'market forces' to justify indirect discrimination. In the *Enderby* case the Court held that, although it is for national courts to determine whether and to what extent the shortage of candidates for a job and the need to attract them by higher pay constitutes an objectively justified ground for the difference in pay between the jobs in question, the relationship between that justification and the pay differential must be precise. If only part of the difference is explained by a factor not related to sex, then the principle of proportionality must be applied and only that part of the differential will be upheld.[69] In the same case the ECJ held that the mere fact that rates of pay for the jobs compared were arrived at by distinct non-discriminatory collective bargaining processes carried on by the same parties is not sufficient objective justification for the difference in pay between the two jobs. The ECJ is clearly anxious to stop any circumvention of the principle of equal pay by using separate bargaining processes, and also to emphasize that the principle applies to the effects, and not simply to the processes by which pay is determined. As Advocate General Lenz said: 'since justification of the discriminatory result is called for, it cannot be sufficient to explain the causes leading to the discrimination . . . If an explanatory approach were accepted as sufficient justification that would lead to the perpetuation of sexual roles in working life.'[70]

There are, therefore, signs that the ECJ is conscious of the need to keep the defence of objective justification within strict bounds. However, the value judgement inherent in the concept of equality means that arguments can be made, and sometimes accepted, which reduce its scope. An example of this is the argument advanced by the European Commission and the Advocate-General in recent cases, that direct discrimination can be justified.[71] The distinction between direct and indirect discrimination is fundamental to

---

[68] *Equal Opportunities Commission* v. *Secretary of State for Employment* [1994] 1 All ER 910; see, too, *R.* v. *Secretary of State for Employment, ex parte Seymour-Smith* [1995] IRLR 478, in which the English Court of Appeal held that the two-year qualifying period to claim certain employment rights in the U.K. amounted to unjustifiable indirect discrimination against part-time workers, the vast majority of whom are women. (This decision is currently the subject of an appeal to the HL.)

[69] The language used by the Court in this regard (at 595) is, unfortunately, not free from doubt (cf. the clearer Opinion of A. G. Lenz at 99). It seems that if it is not possible to determine precisely what proportion is attributable to a sex-free factor, then the differential in pay may be permitted 'in whole or in part' provided that factor was 'sufficiently significant' to provide objective justification. It is suggested that this is to be read in the light of A. G. Lenz's opinion in the way formulated in the text.

[70] [1993] IRLR 599. Cf. Case 400/93 *Royal Copenhagen A/S* [1995] IRLR 648, where the ECJ suggested that the fact that pay was determined by collective bargaining was a relevant factor.

[71] In *Birds Eye Walls Ltd* v. *Roberts* [1994] IRLR 29, at 35; and *Neath* v. *Hugh Steeper Ltd.* [1994] 1 All ER 929, 967–70.

British anti-discrimination law, which is modelled on that of the United States.[72] Direct discrimination occurs when one person is less favourably treated on grounds of sex (or race) than another person is treated or would be treated in similar circumstances. No justification is possible because the less favourable treatment is on one of the prohibited grounds.[73] However, in Continental countries, a much more generalized conception of 'disadvantageous treatment' is familiar. This requires comparability of situations and also lack of justification. So German writers connect the condition of equal situations with the condition of *Rechtfertigung aus der Natur der Sache*: the justifying fact excludes the equality of situations which is inherent in the notion of discrimination.[74]

The ECJ has indicated that, in cases of direct discrimination on grounds of sex (including pregnancy) without more, no justification is possible.[75] The problem arises in cases where sex-related criteria, such as different state pensionable ages or actuarial calculations which differentiate between the life expectancy of men and women, are the reasons for the discrimination. It has been argued[76] that these situations could equally be classified as ones of indirect discrimination, so making it arbitrary to limit the justification defence. The British lawyer would contend that this argument is based on a fallacy. If the criterion is sex-neutral then no question of direct discrimination arises. This could only be a case of indirect discrimination. On the other hand, if the criterion is sex-related then the discrimination is on the prohibited ground of sex, and hence not justifiable. This distinction is essential to a conceptual framework which seeks to prevent gender-stereotyping of women and men. Vague notions of justification are likely to perpetuate the sexual division of labour.

The overriding constraint on the principle of equality in a market system, which the defence of justification illustrates, is that of cost. Although the ideology and prejudices which were once used to justify arbitrary discrimination may now be generally rejected, the cost of remedying past discrimination is regularly used as an excuse for preserving the status quo. One example of this is the issue of retrospection of the decision of the ECJ in the *Barber* case.[77] The ruling of the ECJ was that occupational pensions are pay for the purposes of Article 119. Consequently discrimination between men and women in regard to benefits is prohibited. The ECJ recognized that this judgment could have serious financial consequences for employers and pension schemes, and

[72] Sex Discrimination Act 1975, s. 1(1); Race Relations Act 1976, s. 1(1).
[73] *James* v. *Eastleigh Borough Council* [1990] IRLR 228 (HL).
[74] B. Sundberg-Weitman, n. 40 above. 46.
[75] Case 177/88, *Dekker* [1991] IRLR 27.
[76] A. G. van Gerven in *Birds Eye Walls Ltd* v. *Roberts*, 35. Note, too, the confusion between 'covert' and 'indirect' in discrimination in early cases on nationality such as Case 152/73, *Sotgiu* v. *Deutsche Bundespost* [1974] ECR 153, and equal pay such as *Defrenne (No.2)*, above.
[77] Case C–262/88 [1990] ECR I–1889.

has subsequently made it clear that equal treatment in occupational pensions applies only to benefits payable in respect of periods of service subsequent to 17 May 1990 (the date of the *Barber* judgment), except for those who instituted legal proceedings before that date.[78] Thus the Court anticipated the coming into force of a Protocol which the signatories to the Maastricht Treaty of European Union had been persuaded to accept by the powerful pensions fund lobby who argued that the cost of not discriminating on grounds of sex would be too much for them to bear. The result is that equality in occupational pension schemes will not be achieved until well into the 21st Century. Behind the stated reason of 'legal certainty', lay the Court's acute awareness of 'the way in which occupational pension funds are financed'.[79]

The answer to the question raised at the beginning of this section must therefore be that the so-called 'fundamental right' to equality in Community law is illusory. It does not provide a free-standing basis for enforcing equal treatment between women and men, let alone a universal right in other situations of arbitrary discrimination. The very concept of 'equality' developed by the ECJ on the basis of Article 119 and the five sex equality directives is based on a male norm of comparison and tends to neglect occupational segregation and the labour market disadvantages of women. The concept of indirect discrimination does have the potential to overcome many aspects of institutionalized inequality between women and men, but it has been limited by the need for comparison between women and men in similar situations and by the defence of objective justification. Despite the recent trend towards strict scrutiny of this defence, there are powerful vested interests influencing the Member States and the courts. The immediate financial consequences of equality for these interest groups have tended to outweigh the social and economic costs to individuals who suffer from discrimination and disadvantage.

4. Equality as an Individual Right

Article 119 and the directives are based firmly on the premise that equality is an individual right, and that individuals must have access to a court or

[78] Case C–109/91, *Ten Oever* [1993] IRLR 601; Case C–152/91, *Neath* [1994] 1 All ER 929.

[79] *Ten Oever*, para.18; *Neath*, para. 15. The ECJ has excluded from the scope of Art. 119 statutory social security schemes determined by considerations of social policy rather than the employment relationship (Case C–7/93 *Beune* [1994] ECR I-4471); single-sex schemes (Case C–200/91 *Coloroll* [1994] ECR I-4389; and additional benefits stemming from additional voluntary contributions by employers (*Coloroll*). Moreover, once equality between men and women in pension schemes has been achieved there may be a levelling-down of benefits so long as this is done equally for men and women (Case C–28/93, *van den Akker* [1994] ECR I-4527). See Generally, C. McCrudden and J. Black, chap. 7 in *Equality of Treatment between Women and Men in Social Security* (London, 1994), 169–74.

tribunal to enforce this right.[80] In the Member States, too, the law has usually developed within the traditional forms of civil adjudication for the resolution of individual disputes, although sometimes unlawful discrimination is both a civil wrong and criminal offence.

The weakness inherent in this approach is obvious if one accepts that social disadvantage is suffered *collectively* by groups. In the case of direct discrimination this requires proof of the treatment of groups so that inferences of less favourable treatment on grounds of sex or race can be drawn. In the case of indirect discrimination, it is the effect of criteria and practices upon groups that must be examined. The individual straitjacket inhibits the development of collective or group procedures and remedies.

First, the European legal systems have not developed the class action, which was so important to the growth of anti-discrimination suits in the federal courts in the United States. The class action allows a common question of fact or law between each member of the class and the defendant to be tried in one action. The class might include not only those members of the group who actually applied for jobs and were rejected but also those who would have applied but for the discriminatory practice. Proof of the pattern or practice of discrimination is eased by admitting evidence of discrimination against any member of the class and there is wide scope for the production of documentary and other evidence. Once the pattern or practice is proved in a class action, the burden of proof shifts to the defendant to show that he did not discriminate against the individual. Any member of the class can intervene. It is not necessary for each member of the class to prove his or her loss. There is a wide range of remedies including calculation of substantial deterrent damages on a class-wide basis. The class action was a general procedure particularly well-suited to developing the substantive law of indirect discrimination. In recent years, its use has been rather seriously restricted by conservative courts, but the early cases remain as an interesting model of civil litigation which recognizes the group interest.

There are a few avenues by which some of the disadvantages of individual actions can be avoided. One is the possibility of infringement proceedings brought under Article 169 of the EC Treaty by the European Commission against a Member State which is alleged to have failed to fulfil its Treaty obligations. This was used, for example, to compel the United Kingdom to include in its law the concept of equal pay for work of equal value,[81] and to provide a remedy in respect of discriminatory collective agreements.[82] Recently, in Britain the right was established for the Equal Opportunities Commission to bring proceedings for the judicial review of legislation which

[80] Equal Pay Dir. Art. 2; Equal Treatment Dir. Art. 6; Case 222/84, *Johnston* v. *Chief Constable RUC* [1986] IRLR 263, paras. 13, 18.

[81] Case 61/81, *Commission* v. *United Kingdom* [1982] ECR 2601.

[82] Case 165/82, *Commission* v. *United Kingdom* [1983] ECR 3431.

is incompatible with EC law.[83] The EOC is a statutory body which has a duty to work towards the elimination of discrimination and to promote equality of opportunity between men and women. Among its powers are those of assisting individuals with legal advice or representation. A similar power is possessed by the Commission for Racial Equality in the field of racial discrimination. Research has shown that without this kind of assistance, individuals have much reduced chances of success.[84] Individuals, particularly if unrepresented, are not in a position to gather and to present the statistical material and other evidence of social facts which are crucial to discrimination litigation.

Secondly, the tailoring of individual remedies through litigation may do relatively little to change the underlying structures and practices which produce disadvantage. Recently, the ECJ has opened the possibility of substantial awards of compensation by national courts or tribunals. It has said that 'where financial compensation is the measure adopted to achieve the objective [of real equality of opportunity], it must be adequate, in that it must enable the loss and damage actually sustained as a result of the discriminatory [action] to be made good in full, according to the applicable national rule.'[85] This principle of effective enforcement appears to apply not only to discriminatory dismissals but also to other actions such as recruitment and harasssment. The award must take into account factors such as the effluxion of time, and so include interest, and also 'moral damage', equated in the British context with 'injury to feelings'. This decision has already had a significant impact in the United Kingdom, forcing the Government to lift the previous upper limit on compensation awards and resulting in more substantial awards.

However, the ECJ's criteria for compensation are carefully hedged by the acknowledgment that it is for the Member State to decide on the nature of the remedy and that this is to be determined 'according to the applicable national rule'. The effectiveness of the remedy will be heavily dependent upon the usual sanctions provided by the particular legal system. So in most countries there is no possibility of an order to engage a worker denied employment on unlawful grounds. Moreover, the remedies remain essentially individual. What is missing is the kind of remedy developed in class actions in the United

---

[83] *Equal Opportunities Commission* v. *Secretary of State for Employment* [1994] 1 All ER 910 (HL).

[84] See generally, B. Hepple, 'The Judicial Process in Claims for Equal Pay and Equal Treatment in the U.K.', in C. McCrudden (ed.), n. 31 above, ch. 7, and literature there cited; J. Gregory, *Dispensing Informal Justice* (EOC Research Discussion Series No. 5, 1993).

[85] Case C–271/91, *Marshall* v. *Southampton and Southwest Hampshire Area Health Authority (No.2)* [1993] IRLR 445. In the UK it has been held that the aim of 'deterrence' required under EC law does not mean that exemplary (punitive) damages can be awarded: *Ministry of Defence* v. *Meredith* [1995] IRLR 539. National systems may limit the period for which remedies are to be awarded: Case C–410/92, *Johnson* v. *Chief Adjudication Officer (No.2)* [1995] IRLR 157.

States, such as a court-supervised mandatory injunction requiring affirmative action.

Even if such legal remedies were introduced at national level—and the chances of this happening seem small—it is doubtful if they would succeed in the long run without collective support at the workplace. This raises the question of the 'boundary between collective autonomy and statutory intervention',[86] an issue which Wedderburn has always emphasized is central to labour law in a democratic society. While legislation at European and national level can provide a 'floor of rights', it will have little impact unless it stimulates voluntary action by employers and trade unions to bring equality issues into the mainstream of industrial relations. For unions this presents a major problem. Traditional approaches to wage bargaining have tended to have an adverse impact upon women. Unions have fought hard to maintain differentials based on skills and grades, and have argued for the 'family wage' which is based on the notion that the breadwinner should be paid enough to support himself and his wife and children. As Dickens observes in the British context, this 'has helped underpin male wages, yet it also serves to legitimate low wages for women, and help justify the widely held belief that women should not take jobs when men are unemployed. Historically, faced with a choice of strategies based on wage-earner solidarity with women and their protection via collective bargaining, or exclusion of women and legal protection, the union movement opted for the latter.'[87] Equality law is as much about removing direct and indirect discrimination from collective agreements as it is about doing so in the case of employer's pay structures. Indeed, some of the ECJ's most notable decisions have been directed at collective agreements.[88]

It is, of course, true that employers have far more opportunities than unions to change pay structures and other practices which impact adversely on women and racial minorities, because they can do so without collective agreement. The point being made here is that equality is, by its very nature, a collective issue because it affects not only individuals but groups of workers. A key part of any equality strategy must therefore be to raise 'equality awareness' among negotiators when dealing with matters like working time and pay.[89] This in

[86] Jon Clark and Lord Wedderburn, *Labour Law and Industrial Relations* (Oxford, 1983), 220.

[87] Linda Dickens, 'Anti-discrimination Legislation: Exploring and Explaining the Impact on Women's Employment' in *Legal Intervention in Industrial Relations: Gains and Losses* W. McCarthy (ed.) (Oxford, 1993), 103, 111–12.

[88] E.g. Case C–184/89, *Nimz* v. *Freie und Hansestadt Hamburg* [1991] IRLR 222 (seniority payments for part-time workers in German public service collective agreement); Case 33/89, *Kowalska* v. *Freie und Hansestadt Hamburg* [1990] IRLR 447 (severance payment in same agreement); cf. *Enderby* v. *Frenchay Health Authority*, above, which establishes that a non-discriminatory collective bargaining structure is not in itself 'objective justification' for indirect discrimination.

[89] Trevor Colling and Linda Dickens, *Equality Bargaining—Why Not?* (HMSO, London, 1989), 48; see too, L. Dickens, B. Townley and D. Winchester, *Tackling Sex Discrimination Through Collective Bargaining* (HMSO, London, 1986).

turn requires pressure on collective bargaining both within unions and also from external agencies such as the European Commission and national equal opportunity bodies. The Maastricht Social Policy Agreement presents a unique opportunity for social dialogue on equality issues. It is, however, questionable whether the structures and current priorities of European-level collective bargaining can adequately represent the interests of women and other disadvantaged groups.

5. Conclusion

The argument of this Chapter is based on the premise that the single market is as much a legal and political construction as an economic one. In particular there are political choices between, on the one hand, allowing market forces to produce grossly unequal outcomes and, on the other hand, mobilizing business organizations to make use of positive equal opportunities practices, on the foundation of a Community-wide floor of rights, in order to build up efficient, decently treated, and diverse workforces. The latter choice requires a broad and comprehensive principle of equality enforced by an effective legal strategy which embraces not only equal pay and equal treatment for men and women, but also the discrimination and disadvantage suffered by other groups, such as racial minorities, persons with disabilities, and older workers.

We have seen how Community law in this area has responded, and then only slowly, to political and legal pressures. Any doubts about the competence of the Community institutions to legislate outside the field of sex discrimination obviously needs to be removed in the next round of negotiations for the revision of the Treaties. However, the fundamental question will remain whether the symmetrical male/female discrimination model, with its narrow conception of equality as an individual right, is a suitable basis for the extension of Community action. The liberal philosophy which sees the occupational segregation and disadvantage of women as the outcome of competitive individual choices and seeks to remedy this by awarding compensation only to those women who are able to make comparisons with an existing male norm, leaves the structures of inequality relatively unscathed. The same criticism applies in cases where individual members of racial minorities are judged according to the stereotypes of the white majority, or persons with disabilities are matched to the norm of the fully abled.

What is required is a legal framework which recognizes the collective or group character of social disadvantage and discrimination. The concept of 'group rights' is problematical from a legal perspective,[90] but it has the benefit of focussing on the need to empower disadvantaged groups. Forceful

---

[90] Cf. Nicola Lacey, 'From Individual to Group?', in Hepple and Szyszcak (eds.), n. 12 above, 112–19.

arguments can be made that special treatment for disadvantaged groups is neither unjust nor immoral, nor is it incompatible with the principle of employing people on 'merit' (itself a suspect concept).[91] From this perspective, the outlines of a Community-based action programme are already becoming clear. This would include a wide range of measures at both Community and national level, including contract compliance, affirmative action policies, and more precise targeting of cohesion measures. The national legal systems will have to develop appropriate forms of class or group action and remedies which compensate members of a group and not only individuals. Where these do not exist, effective publicly-funded human rights agencies need to be established. Employers and trade unions need to be motivated to make equality an all-pervasive feature of collective agreements and pay structures.

Too much attention has been paid by lawyers to the formal right of individuals to equal opportunity, and not enough to substantive equality of outcome for disadvantaged groups. Article 6(3) of the Maastricht Agreement on Social Policy appeared to point in a new direction. Building on Article 2(4) of the Equal Treatment Directive, it provides that 'this Article shall not prevent any Member State from maintaining or adopting measures providing for special advantages in order to make it easier for women to pursue a vocational activity or to prevent or compensate for disadvantages in their professional careers'. However, in the recent *Kalanke*[92] case, the Court has reaffirmed the symmetrical model of equality embodied in Article 119. The Bremen Law on Equal Treatment for Men and Women in the Public Service provided that, where there was under-representation of women in any relevant personnel group within a department, women with the same qualifications as a man must be given priority. The Bundesarbeitsgericht held that this was compatible with German constitutional and statutory provisions because it did not involve a system of strict quotas, but rather a system of priority where both sexes were equally qualified, thus helping women overcome current disadvantages which are the result of past discrimination. However, the ECJ held that tie-break legislation, which gives women priority in recruitment, is contrary to Community law. The Court appears to support the distinction drawn by Advocate-General Tesauro in his Opinion in this case between equality of 'starting points' and equality as to 'points of arrival'. While measures which allow women to improve their ability to compete in the labour market are lawful, those which give them priority in recruitment or promotion are not.

It is unlikely that the *Kalanke* judgment will be the last word on the subject. In particular, the decision does not rule out targeting and numerical goals as a

---

[91] See generally, Bhikhu Parekh, 'A Case for Positive Discrimination' in Hepple and Szyszczak (eds.), n. 12 above, 261–80; and Gwynneth Pitt, 'Can Reverse Discrimination be Justified?' ibid. 281–99.

[92] Case C–450/93 [1995] IRLR 660.

means of monitoring equal opportunities policies. If the case leads advocates of equality to recognize the limits of individual rights against discrimination based on Article 119, it may have the positive result of shifting the focus of future Community law and policy towards a broader range of affirmative action—such as child care, parental leave, and educational and social measures—which will promote substantive equality for disadvantaged groups.

12

Economic and Social Cohesion and the European Social Fund

FERNANDO VALDÉS DAL-RÉ

1. Introduction

Of all the structural funds which the institution now known as the European Union (EU) has organized to carry out policies aimed at modernizing, improving, and rationalizing productive structures, infrastructures, and services in the Community countries, the European Social Fund (ESF) is the only one whose creation has a constitutional basis; that is, it is covered by the primary legislation of the Community.

Taking into consideration the legal principles contained in the Treaty of Paris of 1951, which gave the High Authority the right to grant aid for the resettlement and re-training for new employment of workers who might lose their jobs as a result of the progressive establishment of the European Coal and Steel Community,[1] Article 123 of the Treaty of Rome (TR) provided for the creation of a Social Fund with a dual promotional function: on the one hand, to promote job opportunities within the Community and, on the other hand, to increase the geographical and occupational mobility of workers, in order 'to improve employment opportunities for workers in the common market and to contribute thereby to raising the standard of living'.

The first of these tasks corresponds to what we now call 'job creation', perceived as a set of measures aimed at mobilizing unused human resources. The second task, which is more difficult to define from a single perspective, is implemented through a variety of actions, ranging from vocational training to the retraining of workers, and covering matters such as assistance in migration processes or the resettlement of workers made redundant by processes of industrial restructuring.[2] The ESF, together with freedom of movement for workers and social security benefits for migrant workers, is one of the most traditional and decisive institutions among the Community social policies. Furthermore, it has been, at least up to 1988, an autonomous instrument in

---

[1] Cf. Arts. 46, 56, and 68 of the ECSC Treaty. See M. Paolini, in *Commentario al Trattato istitutivo della Comunità Economica Europea*, R. Quadri, R. Monaco and A. Trabucchi (eds.) (Giuffré, Milan, 1965), 981.

[2] Cf. A. Martín Valverde, *El Fondo Social Europeo y la política de empleo en la Comunidad Europea* (Madrid (Ed. La Ley), Madrid, 1986), 16.

the service of Community employment policy. It is in fact the autonomous instrument *par excellence* of this policy.

The purpose of this paper is, specifically, to analyse the legal system in force in the ESF. In order to do this, we shall pitch our reflections at an intermediate level of abstraction: we do not intend to examine the ESF in the context of the broad principles that shape Community policies ('European social area', 'Community social policy', 'Community employment policy'). Nor do we intend to delve into a detailed analysis of day-to-day administrative practice or to recount the regulatory vicissitudes that the ESF has undergone throughout its history, since its commencement on 20 September 1960.[3] Lastly, it is not our intention to judge the contribution of the Fund to the matters for which it was established. Our purpose, a far less ambitious one, is confined to offering a general view of the operation of the ESF as a financial instrument, placing it from the outset in its appropriate perspective within the construction of the European Union: the attainment of economic and social cohesion.

2. Economic and Social Cohesion and the European Social Fund

Although a long-established term in Community jargon, 'cohesion' is far from being a well-defined concept with an unambiguous meaning. On the contrary, it is a notion capable of encompassing up to three different aspects (political, economic, and social), which nevertheless share 'solidarity' between all the geographical areas in Community territory as a common link. This solidarity aims to promote integrated and overall development within the framework of the Europe of the Fifteen. In its political dimension, 'cohesion' implies, among other aspects, an awareness of European citizenship and participation at all levels of public administration—Community, national, regional and local—in the process of European union.[4] As regards its economic aspect, cohesion implies a reduction in the disparities between different areas and, therefore, a co-ordinated development of all nations and regions in order to facilitate, in real terms, competition within the single market. It is more difficult to express the social side of cohesion, which advocates in a general, vague way a reduction in the inequalities in regard to rights and social services between European citizens in more prosperous areas and those in areas lagging behind in development.[5]

[3] The first ESF norm was EEC Reg. 6/1960, of 25 Aug. Since the Reg. did not contain any indication of when it should come into force, this took place 20 days after its publication in the OJ as prescribed by Art. 191 of the TR.

[4] See G. Cordero Mestaza, 'La cohesión en la Europa del Mercado Único y de la UEM' (1992) 51 *Papeles de Economía Española* 35.

[5] See E. González-Posada, 'La CEE y su cohesión social: proyectos y realidades' (1993) 4, *Revista de Estudios Europeos* 17–32.

To sum up, and attempting to combine the last two aspects, economic and social cohesion reflects a situation, formulates a principle, and defines an objective. The situation reflected is the existence of a true and real divide which separates the regions of the European Community into two, to a far greater extent than in any other major economic and political area in the industrialized world.[6] The principle that it formulates is solidarity between all the geographical areas included in the Community. The objective that it tries to attain is reduction of the disparities of all kinds that exist within the limits of the Community; or, to view it from a different perspective, the progress and 'upward' levelling of all the nations and regions in the Community.

The achievement of economic and social cohesion has featured, at least *avant la lettre*, throughout the entire historical process of the creation of the EU. A faint trace of this objective was represented in legal terms in Article 2 of the TR, where the Community takes on, among other functions, responsibility for promoting 'throughout the Community a harmonious development of economic activities, a continuous and balanced expansion'. However, during the first thirty years of the Community´s existence, social and economic cohesion was little more than an issue for reflection and debate within exclusive Community circles;[7] it was a programming objective, lacking any visible concrete effect or expression within the political framework of the Community.

A first, though modest, attempt to give more regulatory content to economic and social cohesion was made by the European Single Act (ESA), when it introduced into the Treaty establishing the EEC a new Title, number V, devoted to precisely this issue. Within this set of provisions, and after confirming as Community objectives the development and pursuit of actions aimed at 'strengthening' cohesion by reducing 'disparities between the various regions and the backwardness of the least-favoured regions' (Article 130a), it requires the Member States to direct and co-ordinate their economic policies in such a way that these objectives are taken into account in the implementation of the common policies and of the internal market (Article 130b). At the same time, Article 130d provided for the alteration of the existing structural funds by placing all of them, therefore including the ESF, in the service of economic and social cohesion.

In spite of the fact that, as a result of what was precribed in the Article mentioned above, the funds were reformed in 1988 by doubling their budgets, the measures that were taken were obviously insufficient to give substantial

---

[6] Cf. Economic and Social Committee, *Opinion on economic and social cohesion* (92/C 98/18) [1992] OJ C98/50, para. 1.1.1.

[7] See, e.g. the reports by Werner ('Rapport Interimaire concernant la réalisation par étapes de l'Union Economique et Monétaire' (EC Bull. Suppl. 7, 1970) or MacDougall 'The Report of the Study Group on the Role of the Public Finance in Europe Integration' (Série Economía y Finanza, CEE no. A13, (1977). A complete study of these issues is in National Institute of Economic and Social Research, *A new strategy for economic and social cohesion after 1992* (European Parliament Research and Documentation Papers, Luxembourg, 1991).

content to a cohesion policy. This was so, first of all, because the Single European Act (SEA) was not accompanied by any adjustment of budget allocations to its governing principles,[8] and secondly, because Article 130b was never enforced as regards the development of common policies by the Member States in order to achieve the publicly declared objective of cohesion. In practice, the Community decided to consider that this objective was adequately covered with the sole use of structural funds.[9]

The problem of cohesion was to be received with a renewed impetus by the Treaty of Maastricht (TM). First, the establishing Treaty was the subject of important amendments. Economic and social cohesion was directly and explicitly included among the principles that inform Community action (Articles 2 and 3). There were also the various provisions of the Title devoted to cohesion (the former Title V and present Title XIV), in which the Commission is required to submit a report on 'the progress made towards achieving economic and social cohesion' (Article 130b(2)) to all Community institutions every three years. The Council was also empowered to take measures, besides those given to the Funds (Article 130b(3)), aimed at achieving cohesion. A new fund was created, with the purpose of providing a financial contribution to 'projects in the fields of environment and trans-European networks in the area of transport infrastructure' (130d(2)). Lastly, a Protocol on economic and social cohesion was adopted, which was to be incorporated as an annex to the establishing Treaty.

The TM has meant a reinforcement of the legal bases established to achieve the objective of economic and social cohesion. The structural funds, both the old ones and the newly created one, continue to have a leading role in the EU, although it is not exclusive to them. Their aim is to achieve cohesion, and their effective operation will depend, logically, on the decisions that are adopted in the immediate future concerning Community budgets and other policies.[10] But for the moment, the winds that blow over cohesion are still weak and cold, which is not surprising since the very concept of cohesion has 'too weak a content'[11] to lead us to expect a rapid process of real convergence within the Community.

---

[8] The Padoa-Schioppa report ('Efficiency, Stability and Equity'. A Strategy for the Evolution of the System of the European Community', EEC, Apr. 1987) formulated an accurate diagnostic of these inadequacies. See Cordero, n. 4 above, 42.

[9] See German Institute of Economic Research, *Regional effects of Community policies* (European Parliament Research and Documentation Papers, Luxembourg, 1991).

[10] For a first evaluation of cohesion policy, see A. Hanneouart, *Economic and Social Cohesion and the Structural Funds: An Introduction*, in A. Hanneouart (ed.), *Economic and Social Cohesion in Europe: A New Objective for Integration* (Routledge, London, 1992) 1 ff.

[11] Cf. C. Lyon-Caen and A. Lyon-Caen, *Droit social international et européen* (8th edn., Dalloz, Paris, 1993), 264.

3. The Legal Framework of the European Social Fund

Although it has undergone many reforms and changes in its legal status throughout its history, the ESF has always retained the same structure in its regulatory design or framework, which consists of three types of provisions.[12] The first type is that of rules of general configuration, stated in the primary legislation. The second type is that of rules of operation, which usually take the legal form of Decisions and, more frequently, EEC Regulations. Finally, there are rules for the selection of programmes, which make use of ad hoc instruments of great versatility and go by various names: 'management guidelines' or 'Community support frameworks'.

The formulation of these three regulatory groups follows a relatively simple scheme. The rules of configuration make up the general structure or framework of the ESF at a double level: functional (by stating its main objectives) and organizational (by granting basic competences). The rules of operation define explicitly 'mid-term' objectives and, at the same time, determine the forms of assistance, the criteria for their distribution and the rules for the granting process. The rules on selection have the status of 'operational' complement of the above rules, and their aim is to 'achieve further specification or definition of preferences in short-term actions'.[13]

Initially, the rules of configuration were contained in Articles 123 to 125 of the TR. Following the amendment of the establishing Treaty, first by the SEA and later by the TM, the rules are: (a) Article 123, which states the general objectives of the Fund and to which we shall refer later; (b) Article 124, which assigns to the Commission responsibility for administering the Fund; (c) Article 125, which assigns to the Council responsibility for adopting, in accordance with the unanimity rule, implementing decisions concerning the Fund; (d) Article 130b, which places the actions of the structural funds, thus including the ESF, and all other Community financial instruments in the service of the objective of economic and social cohesion, and also requires the Commission to submit a report every three years to all the Community institutions on progress in the field of cohesion and on the manner in which the Funds have contributed to the achievement of that objective; and (e) Article 130d, which empowers the Council to adopt, by unanimity, provisions on the co-ordination of the Funds both with one another and with the other existing financial instruments.

The rules of operation of the ESF have also undergone, to a greater extent than the rules of configuration, an important regulatory evolution, especially as a consequence of the co-ordinated performance of all the Funds with a structural aim that was introduced in the amendment of the Treaty estab-

---

[12] See A. Martín Valverde, 'El Fondo Social Europeo', in Centro de Documentación Europea, Universidad de Valladolid, *El Espacio Social Europeo* (Lex Nova, Valladolid, 1991), 35.
[13] Ibid.

lishing the EEC by the SEA. At present, there are three rules of operation for the ESF: (a) Council Regulation (EEC) n° 2081/93 of 20 July 1993[14] on the tasks, effectiveness, and co-ordination of the structural funds; (b) Council Regulation (EEC) n° 2082/93 of the same date,[15] laying down provisions as regards co-ordination of the activities of the different structural funds; and (c) Council Regulation (EEC) n° 2084/93, also of the same date,[16] which contains provisions exclusive to the ESF. While the first of these Regulations acts as a framework for all the structural funds, the other two are complementary detailed rules, one of which is 'horizontal' in nature (2082/93) while the other is definitely 'vertical' (2084/93). Apart from this, the legal effect of this new set of Regulations is subject to a 'review clause', since the Council will have to re-examine them, at the request of the Commission, before 31 December 1999.[17] In this way, the traditional policy of mid-term review of the rules of operation of the Funds is continued. This policy was already provided for in the Regulation of 1988 and has been specifically applied to the ESF since it was first created.

Lastly, the rules for the selection of ESF programmes and concrete actions, which constitute the Fund's 'operating instructions',[18] are essentially contained within the so-called 'Community support frameworks' (CSF), which the Commission establishes for each Member State and for the different plans that they submit.[19] The reform of 1993 seems to have eliminated in this way the previous 'management guidelines'.[20] This was very probably caused by the principles that inform the management of funds, especially the principle of partnership, to which we shall refer later.

4. Characteristics

In the introduction to this Chapter, we have already mentioned that the creation of the ESF by the Treaty of Rome was aimed at the development of an employment policy. It is not our purpose to decide whether, during the course of its history, the ESF has indeed developed within the definition of its objectives and means of action, an employment policy which belongs

---

[14] [1993] OJ L193/5. This Council Reg. amends the previous Council Reg. (EEC) 2052/88 ([1988] OJ L185/9).

[15] [1993] OJ L193/20. This Council Reg. amends the previous Council Reg. (EEC) 4253/88 ([1988] OJ L374/1).

[16] [1993] OJ L193/39. This Council Reg. amends the previous Council Reg. (EEC) 4255/88 ([1988] OJ L374/21).

[17] Cf. Reg. 2081/93, Art. 19.

[18] Cf. Martín Valverde, n. 2 above, 36.

[19] On the CSF, see Arts. 8 ff of Reg. 2081/93 and Arts. 8 to 13 of Reg. 2082/93. On the 'Plans', see Arts. 5 to 7 of Reg. 2082/93.

[20] The 'management guidelines' of the ESF-1988 can be found in [1989] OJ C45/6. On their scope, see G. Gallizioli, *I Fondi strutturali delle Comunità Europee* (Cedam, Padua, 1992), 205.

exclusively to the Community as being independent of those of the Member States. In order to answer this question we should first have to analyse whether, in the light of the present distribution of responsibilities for employment at Community or national level, we can properly speak of a Community employment policy as such.[21] Whatever one's views on this issue, the purpose of the this Chapter is to determine the traits or elements which can be taken as the defining characteristics of the ESF.

The ESF is, first of all, one of the several structural funds organized by the European Community. The 'structural' designation of these Community funds has at least a double meaning: the first, a temporal one, shows a wish to endow their actions and means with continuity and permanence; the second, a functional one, links their actions with an aim to modernize the structures of Community systems of production of goods and services. Because it is a structural fund, the ESF is also a financial instrument which grants monetary aids. Unlike other Community financial instruments wich do not possess this quality (the European Investment Bank, for example), the financial contributions granted by the ESF take the form of 'subsidies' rather than credits or loans. Finally, the aid granted by the ESF is basically oriented towards employment and, more particularly within this field, towards vocational training. The range of action of the ESF is, therefore, within the limits of what we may call active manpower policies.

Until the reform of 1988, the ESF—as well as the other existing funds—had functional and budget autonomy. This reform, in compliance with the new provisions of Article 130d of the establishing Treaty as amended by the SEA, established instruments for the co-ordination of the structural funds, both with one another and with the other financial instruments. Although it has retained its organizational autonomy, the ESF has lost its previous double autonomy. Functionally, although it continues to act in the field of employment policy, the ESF co-ordinates its actions with those of the other instruments, within the framework of the objectives and criteria instituted by the rules of operation[22] and aiming at the attainment of economic and social cohesion. Financially, the Framework Regulation (2081/93) states that there should be a common budget allocation for all the Funds for the 1994–9 period.[23]

5. Aims

As noted earlier, Article 123 of the TR assigned the ESF to the field of employment policy, entrusting it with the dual function of encouraging the

---

[21] An answer in the negative can be found in, among others, Lyon-Caen and Lyon-Caen, n. 11 above, 255; M. Rocella and T. Treu, *Diritto del Lavoro della Comunità Europea* (Cedam, Padua, 1992), 158.   [22] See Rocella and Treu, n. 21 above, 172.
[23] The total budget for this period amounts to 141,471 million ECU, 70% of which is destined for Objective (1). See Art. 12 and Annex II of Reg. 2081/93.

growth of job opportunities and the geographical and occupational mobility of workers within the Community. The amendment of Article 123 by the TM has enlarged the ESF´s scope of influence by adding a new aim, which is to facilitate the adaptation of workers to industrial change and to changes in production systems, in particular through vocational training and retraining. In a nutshell, it is possible to say that the financial assistance granted by the ESF now covers the important aspects of employment policy, including most of 'what concerns the development of human resources and the improvement of the labour market'.[24]

Both before and after it was amended, the above mentioned Article 123 of the TR limits itself to defining broad areas or guidelines for the actions of the ESF; moreover, these areas are defined by concepts which allow for an important degree of flexibility, which is the actual function of the rules of configuration. Starting from this general statement of the ESF's range of action, it has been its rules of operation that have made the objectives more precise and concrete, in accordance with the economic and social circumstances which coincided at each moment in its history.[25]

In the historical period corresponding to the first fund (1960–71), in which, once the phase of reconstruction of the European industrial fabric was overcome, the principal problems came from the initiation of the common market (migratory processes within the Community). At this point, the fundamental objectives of job creation and geographical and occupational mobility were materialized in assistance for vocational rehabilitation, for the re-settlement of migrant workers and for guaranteeing the same level of pay for workers affected by processes of industrial restructuring. In its second period (1972–83), the fund had to cope with a new economic situation which was characterized by, among other factors, the employment crisis in certain sectors, new requirements in vocational training, and changes in the structure of the economically active population. Therefore, the objectives of the ESF were then aimed at the placement in new employment of workers coming from the agricultural sector or affected by the crisis in the textile industry. They were also aimed at the elimination of structural under-employment, the training of a skilled workforce and the absorption into the labour market of groups with special employment problems (women and minors). In its third period (1983–8), one of greater economic growth during which Europe emerged from the crisis of the 1970s and early 1980s, the rules of operation gave the ESF more active functions in employment policy which took

[24] Cf. H. C. Jones, 'El Fondo Social Europeo en el periodo 1994–1999' (1993) 19, *Europa Junta* 13.

[25] A good summary of the history of the ESF and of the relationship between its field of action and the economic context can be found in the special issue, devoted to the Fund, of *Europe Sociale* (1991, n° 2). Also see Gallizoli, n. 20 above, 72 ff. and Martín Valderde, n. 2 above, 31 ff.

shape in, on the one hand, in vocational training actions which would facilitate access to stable jobs and, on the other hand, in the promotion of employment opportunities, contributing in particular to the integration into working life of young people and less-favoured workers, as well as the adaptation of workers to technological change and the reduction of regional imbalances within the labour market.

The reform of 1988 introduced important changes in the definition of the ESF´s objectives. First, from the quantitative point of view, the list of objectives experienced a drastic reduction in comparison with the previous periods. However, as a consequence of the provisions contained in Article 130d of the TR, in the SEA version, the objectives of the ESF are stated in co-ordination with the other structural funds. Article 1 of Council Regulation (EEC) 2052/88 of 24 June 1988 defines the following five objectives: (1) to promote the development and structural adjustment of regions whose development is lagging behind: (2) to convert the regions seriously affected by industrial decline; (3) to combat long-term unemployment; (4) to facilitate the integration into working life of young people; and (5a) to adjust agricultural structures in order to reform the common agricultural policy and (5b) and to promote the development of rural areas. Among the objectives that shape the actions of the structural funds, the implementation of those stated at (3) and (4) was assigned specifically and exclusively to the ESF, which was also to participate in the implementation of the others, with the exception of Objective (5a), by financing employment and vocational training programmes, as well as programmes for the creation of self-employment activities.

Neither youth unemployment nor the situation of the long-term unem-ployed has been a target issue foreign to the operational history of the ESF. The former had already been provided for in the rules of operation of the ESF–1983, while the latter was mentioned in the rules for the selection of priority programmes of the same ESF–1983.[26] By 1988 the situation in the labour market had suffered a major setback, which affected young people in particular; at the same time, the length of periods of unemployment increased.[27] This resulted in the definition that the ESF–1988 gave of its specific objectives, on which the assistance granted by this Community instrument was to concentrate.

The rules of operation prescribed for the structural funds in 1993 have introduced some changes in the formulation of the ESF´s objectives. First,

---

[26] See E. Toffanin, 'La vocation principale du FSE. La lutte contre le chômage de longue durée et l'insertion professionelle des jeunes' (1991) 2 *Europe Sociale* 24 ff.; and V. Panagos, 'La politique "anti-chômage" et les jeunes chômeurs dans les Communautés Européennes' [1991] *RMC* 797 ff.

[27] 'From 1983 to 1988, the number of long-term unemployed people increased from 4.5 million to 5.5 million (22%) in the Europe of the Ten and to 7.3 million in that of the Twelve, that is from 45% to 52% of the total number of unemployed people'. Cf. Economic and Social Committee, n. 6 above, para. 1.1.12.

Objective (3) is newly defined, combining the former Objectives (3) and (4) and therefore covering all actions relating to the long-term unemployed and the integration of young people into working life. At the same time, as had already been stated in the former rules, actions taken under this objective are not confined to these two types of worker but are also to include the short-term unemployed and even those who are under threat of becoming long-term unemployed. Moreover, this objective covers actions aimed at facilitating the integration into the labour market of people who lose their jobs as a result, among other circumstances, of industrial restructuring or migrations within the Community.

Secondly, and as a development of the task entrusted to the fund by Article 123 of the TR as amended by the TM, a new Objective (4) is established, with a view to facilitating the adaptation of workers to industrial change and to changes in production systems. Its aim is to increase competitive performance in companies, by giving adequate training to workers in order to improve their job prospects.[28] Lastly, and concerning Objectives (1), (2) and (5b), the actions of the fund are mainly aimed at supporting employment growth and stability.

6. Forms of Assistance

In the previous section we examined the objectives that the ESF serves. However, the field of application of this structural fund would not be adequately delimited if we did not refer, however briefly and schematically, to the forms of assistance that the fund itself grants. For this purpose, we must distinguish between (a) actions and (b) what in the 'ineffable'[29] language of the Community is called 'eligible expenditure'.

a. Types of Action

The objectives that have been specifically assigned to the ESF are realized and implemented in three types of action or programme: one for vocational training, one for employment aids, and one for the creation of appropriate training and employment structures. Each of these programmes, besides having a general content in common with all the objectives, also has its own specific purpose. Thus, the commmon content for vocational training, for example, consists in the acquisition of the knowledge necessary to occupy a post, including the updating of any previous knowledge and guidance and counselling. At the same time, in the objective aimed at facilitating the integration of young people into working life, vocational training can also

[28] See Jones, n. 24 above, 15.
[29] Cf. Lyon-Caen and Lyon-Caen, n. 11 above, 271.

include instruction equivalent to compulsory schooling.[30] In the objectives that the ESF shares with the other Funds, the aids are for: education systems (Objective (1)) training and research and development in regions whose development is lagging behind (Objective (1)), regions in industrial decline (Objective (2)) and rural areas (Objective (5b)).

Apart from this, the set of actions and aid programmes financed by the ESF must, as prescribed by Regulation 2084/93, respect the principle of equal treatment for men and women.

b. Expenditure

It has already been stated that the ESF is a financial instrument of the EU in the service of the achievement of economic and social cohesion which grants financial subsidies rather than loans. The ESF does not, however, finance the totality of the expenditure deriving from the actions in which it takes part. The fund´s intervention is subject to a dual principle: first, the principle of co-financing or sharing of economic burdens between the fund and each Member State as a result of the implementation of projects in which the former takes part; and secondly, the principle of prior determination of expenditure in projects granted ESF funding.

The principle of co-financing will be discussed later. As concerns the second principle, in accordance with the provisions of Article 2 of Council Regulation (EEC) 2084/93, the financial contributions of the ESF may assist only towards expenditure deriving from: (1) the remuneration and subsistence and travel costs of beneficiaries of the actions or aid programmes described in the preceding section; (2) the preparation, operation, management and evaluation of those actions; and (3) employment aid granted under arrangements existing in the Member States.

The nature of this expenditure is defined and agreed within the framework of partnership. Indicative average amounts for such expenditure are determined jointly by the Commission and each Member State concerned, taking into account the type of vocational training involved.

7. Performance

a. Governing Principles

In 1988, the European Community started a series of reforms.[31] Among these was the reform of the structural funds, through which it was intended to

---

[30] See Reg. 2084/93, n. 16 above, Art. (1)(1)(b).
[31] Which were part of the so-called 'Delors deal', and which the President of the Commission presented in a document entitled *Reussir l´Acte Unique* ([1988] OJ L185).

double their budget and achieve a better use of the resources available. As a result of this reform, the Framework Regulation passed that year (2052/1988) stated a number of operational principles, which the 1993 rules have consolidated. These principles are: concentration, co-ordination, complementarity, co-financing, and partnership.

Concentration, to which we have already referred indirectly, entails the selective grouping of the objectives assigned to the structural funds. In Objectives (1), (2) and (5b), it is geographical concentration, so the performance of the Funds is restricted to certain geographical areas; in Objectives (3) and (4), however, it is functional concentration.[32] Directly linked to the principle of concentration is that of the co-ordination of all the structural funds, both with one another and with the other financial instruments in the Community. Co-ordination manifests itself in, among other aspects, the appropriation of the available resources, the distribution of financial contributions, the elaboration of Community support frameworks, and the implementation of integrated operational programmes.

The principle of complementarity, in its general sense, means that Community operations are conceived as a complement of or contribution to national operations, giving them added value. It is therefore advisable for each Member State to maintain, within all the areas involved, a level of public structural or comparable expenditure equivalent to the one in the previous programme. As concerns the ESF directly, the principle of complementarity implies, consequently, that the employment policy implemented by means of this Community instrument has to be seen as a support policy for national policies, not as an independent policy. The principle of complementarity explains the system of co-financing of the aid programmes granted by the ESF. It also explains the principle of partnership, which defines a decision-taking process undertaken by the Commission, the Member State involved, the national, regional, or local authorities involved and, where appropriate, the eonomic and social partners designated by each State, in a context of co-operative criteria and not 'bureaucratic or administrative'[33] procedures. Thus, a whole array of authorities and bodies act as partners in the preparation, financing, implementation, and, later, monitoring and evaluation of Community actions, making them 'une affaire de tous, chacun étant responsable á son niveau'.[34]

b. Operational Functioning

Following the above description of the principles that inform the actions of the ESF, we list here the formal arrangements for its operation:[35] (1) it is the

[32] Cf. J. Ginderachter, 'La réforme des Fonds Structurels' (1989) 327 *RMC* 272.
[33] Cf. Martín Valverde, n. 2 above, 39.   [34] Cf. Giniderachter, n. 32 above, 277.
[35] See Council Reg. (EEC) 2082/93, esp. Chs. IV–V. There is an in-depth description of these operational arrangements in M. Colina Robledo, *et al.*, *Derecho Social Comunitario*, (Ed. Tirant lo Blanch, Valencia) 1991), 186 ff.

responsibility of the Member States to submit to the Commission their plans for the implementation of actions within the framework of the objectives; (2) After the plans have been assessed, the Commission establishes a 'Community support framework', following the principle of consultation based on partnership; (3) preferably within the framework of the plans produced, the Member States, or the appropriate authorities designated by them, submit their applications for financial assistance from the ESF, upon which the Commission decides; (4) payment of the financial assistance may take the form either of advances or of final payments at the end of the project.

13

Employment policy

MARK FREEDLAND[1]

In the course of the 1990 Chorley Lecture, on the subject of the Social Charter in Britain, Bill Wedderburn offered the reflection that: '[t]he European Community's Social Charter of Fundamental Rights has appeared at a moment when the transnational economy puts national laws in a new frame'.[2] That observation is still at least as pertinent as it was in 1990; and nowhere is it more applicable than to the field of employment policy. The initial purpose of this chapter is to try to assess the development and present direction of employment policy in and of the European Union, and, picking up on that observation of Bill Wedderburn's, to describe the way in which employment policy forms part of the transnational economy of Europe.

The further, and more ambitious, purpose of the chapter will be to explore the relationship between, on the one hand, the employment policy of the European Union and, on the other hand, the body of measures and doctrine which we identify as European Community employment law. In the course of doing so, we shall draw upon some aspects of regulatory theory, such as the distinction between hard and soft law, the distinction between government by *imperium* and government by *dominium*, and the distinction between economic and social regulation. It is hoped by those means to place the discussion of European-level employment policy and employment law in a context of European constitutional development. It will be suggested that, so far as the European Community is concerned, the development of employment policy and employment law has become significantly intertwined with regulatory and constitutional development.

These purposes will be pursued by a discussion which will proceed in the following stages. First, we shall try to identify what we mean by European Community employment law and how far the two are inter-related. Secondly,

---

[1] I am much indebted, for comments on the first draft of this Ch. to Gráinne de Búrca, and, among the editors of the symposium work, Paul Davies and Silvana Sciarra. I am also much indebted to the European Documentation Centre of the Bodleian Law Library Oxford, and in particular to Elizabeth Martin, for help with access to sources. I have also benefited greatly from discussions with Christopher Docksey and George Kintzele of the European Commission; but neither they nor any of those cited above are in any way responsible for the views stated here.

[2] Lord Wedderburn, 'The Social Charter in Britain: Labour Law—and Labour Courts?' (1991) 54 *Modern Law Review* 1, reprinted as ch. 11 of Lord Wedderburn, *Employment Rights in Britain and Europe* (Lawrence and Wishart, London, 1991).

we shall consider the development of European Community employment policy as it stood at the time of the recent White Papers on Growth Competitiveness and Employment and on Social Policy. In a further section we shall look at the significance of those White Papers for employment policy. We shall then discuss the specific area of vocational training policy in which the relationship between Community employment law and employment policy has been developing in a largely unnoticed way. We shall conclude with some general suggestions about the theoretical and practical status and possible future of EC employment policy generally. So we begin with some definitions, some taxonomy, and some theory of European-level regulatory activity in the field of employment law and employment policy.

1. Employment Law and Employment Policy Convergence and Divergence

We should start by identifying some working definitions; this is a necessary preliminary to considering in detail how far European Community employment law (ECEL) and employment policy (ECEP) converge or diverge. We can take as crude working definitions on the one hand the idea of ECEL as representing the body of European Community law which is directly concerned with the employment relationship, whether at an individual or at a collective level, and on the other hand the idea of ECEP as referring to the collection of policies or policy measures which are directly concerned with the creation and maintenance of employment (including policies and measures concerned with training). As thus stated, the notions of ECEL and ECEP might appear convergent; we need, however, to explore the reasons why there is in practice a greater divergence between ECEL and ECEP than one might in theory expect.

Definitions of areas of law, like most operations of drawing boundaries, are apt to be controversial. This is particularly true of labour law or employment law. (I am using these terms interchangeably here, although I recognize that this is itself debateable.) One is likely to define the subject differently according to whether one has a collectivistic or an individualistic agenda. One's definition may also vary according to whether one's preferences are interventionist or abstentionist, or (in a different frame of reference) whether they are regulatory or deregulatory as the current terminology has it.[3]

These difficulties, which we know to be considerable in the context of national labour law systems, are compounded in a European Union context,

---

[3] Bill Wedderburn offers a significant recent contribution to this discussion in Wedderburn, *Labour Law and Freedom* (Lawrence & Wishart, London, 1995), Ch. 10—which is at once a recognition of how the shift of focus from national to European labour law serves to widen the conceptual as well as the geographical frontiers of the subject, and, on the other hand, a warning against a loss of attention to the traditional concerns of labour law.

where there is a continuing and sharp debate about how far policy-making and law-making should occur, on the one hand, at the level of the Community-wide institutions and, on the other hand at the subsidiary levels, especially that of the Member States—the debate about Community federalism, no less. The existence and the profundity of that debate are so evident as to require no elaboration here;[4] what deserves emphasis is the extent to which employment issues have become central to that debate. It is no exaggeration to say that at the time of writing, which is during during the 1996 Intergovernmental Conference on the Treaty of European Union, most people would single out employment issues, together with monetary issues, as the main focal points of that whole discussion.

That statement might occasion some surprise in the form in which I have just put it. If, however, one substitutes the words 'social policy issues' for the words 'employment issues', the proposition becomes, I suggest, much more recognizable, and indeed irrefutable. This brings us to an important point about terminology which has not been sufficiently addressed, and which enormously complicates the discussion of the relationship between employment law and employment policy in the European Community. This is that, in European Community parlance, the term 'social policy' has very largely come to mean 'employment-related social policy'.[5] The same thing is true of the use of the word 'social' in the terms 'Social Action Programme', 'Social Dimension', and latterly, of course, 'Social Chapter', 'Social Protocol', and 'Social Agreement'. The use of this terminology has the result that the body of policy upon which the employment-related legislative, administrative, and judicial activity of the European Community is based has tended to be described as social policy rather than as employment policy.

We then find that the term employment policy, not being used to describe what has come to be known as social policy, comes to be used for the different purpose of describing the policy agenda relating to job creation and maintenance, and the maintenance or enhancement of employment skills by means of vocational training. As we shall see in more detail in the next section of this Chapter, there is a complex set of issues surrounding the relationship between EC social policy and EC employment policy in their respective meanings as just described. Employment policy as thus identified is clearly not synonymous or co-terminous with social policy. Should we view it as a sub-set of social policy? In one sense we should; but there are, as we shall see, reasons for

---

[4] It may, however, be useful to refer to J. H. H. Weiler, 'The Transformation of Europe', 100 *Yale LJ* 2403 (1991) as one of the major starting points for the pursuit of that debate in terms of legal and constitutional theory.

[5] This use of terminology, reflecting, at least French and Italian usage (*droit social*, *sozialrecht*) and deeply embedded in the history of labour law in civilian legal systems, is now current in British academic legal usage; compare, for instance, 'European Union Social Policy Law' in Erica Szyszczak, 'Future Directions in European Union Social Policy Law' (1995) 24 *Industrial Law Journal* 19.

thinking that employment policy does not fall wholly within the sphere of social policy. In short, the relationship between EC social policy and EC employment policy is complex and elusive—especially given the extent to which the proper scope of each of them is politically controversial and politically contested.

All this is symptomatic of the fact that, both at the level of terminology and at a deeper ideological level, there is no single clear or accepted policy agenda for employment law in the European Union. We are quickly confronted with this reality when we approach the questions whether we have such a thing as European Community employment law (ECEL) and, if so, what is its content. In these circumstances, it has been natural to adopt a primarily positivist approach as the best way of side-stepping those difficulties.[6] Such an approach asks in what aspects of the employment relationship do we find intervention at EC level which is clearly of a legal character, that is to say consists of specific legislative measures or judicial adjudication.

In other words, this approach defines ECEL according to what Treaty Articles have been agreed upon and what directives have been issued, or according to which measures have been the subject of litigation in the ECJ— always given that we are talking about broadly employment-related legislation or litigation. It means that ECEL is viewed in terms of employment-related social policy that has taken a certain concrete form. So what is often assumed to be a substantive mode of definition of ECEL turns out on further examination to be in part a procedural one, depending upon the procedure used to give effect (whether partially or totally) to the norm in question.

This apparently descriptive and objective approach to defining the scope of ECEL produces some rather curious results. In particular, it suggests that ECEL is concerned only with a few rather eclectic sets of issues; with equal pay and treatment as between men and women,[7] rather than with discrimination in employment generally; with collective dismissals and acquired rights on transfer of undertakings,[8] rather than with the termination of the employment relationship generally; with particulars of the terms of the contract of employment,[9] rather than with the terms themselves; with consultation of

---

[6] This is not intended to level that charge at any particular writers; indeed, I would acknowledge the existence of serious attempts to proceed otherwise—see, for instance, Catherine Barnard, *EC Employment Law* (John Wiley and Sons, Chichester, 1995), and compare Brian Bercusson, 'The Conceptualization of European Labour Law' (1995) 24 *Industrial Law Journal* 3; *European Labour Laws* (Butterworths, London, 1996), esp. ch. 1, 14–24. Rather, this seems to me to be a path we all naturally tend to follow, especially when designing and teaching the EC component in employment law courses. Brian Bercusson seems to make that criticism of the views of Eliane Vogel-Polsky about the status of the Social Agreement (Bercusson (1995) at 80; but I doubt whether her views are directed to defining the scope of ECEL in the way that he implies.

[7] i.e. EC Treaty, Art. 199 and Council Dirs. 75/117/EEC, 76/207/EEC.

[8] i.e. Council Dirs. 75/129/EEC, 92/56/EEC, 77/187/EEC (and cf. 80/987/EEC (Insolvency of Employer)).   [9] i.e. Council Dir. 91/533/EEC.

workers' representatives on certain issues[10] rather than with collective representation and workers' organizations as a whole; with the work-related
implications of pregnancy,[11] rather than with those of maternity and parenthood more generally; and with working time and health and safety[12] rather
than with the quality of working conditions generally.

In advancing this argument, I am not underrating the tendency or potential
for EC employment-related measures to develop into a coherent or even
comprehensive system of ECEL;[13] on the contrary, I am drawing attention to
the danger that, by defining the scope of ECEL by reference to enacted
Directives, we may misinterpret both the present state of the art and its future
possibilities.

Moreover, the consequences of this mode of definition of ECEL are
decidedly significant in relation to ECEP. For ECEP tends in a special sense to
be implemented by means other than detailed Treaty Articles or regulations
or directives. As within national systems, we find that where employment
policies are the subject of actual legislation, that tends to consist of very broad
authorization to engage in public expenditure on job creation or maintenance
and on vocational training. At that level, the normative regulation is either
extremely loose or non-existent; there may be a formal proclamation of
principles, but these are unlikely to be very specific or exacting. Below that
level, there is further normative regulation, but consisting of (often informal)
administrative rule-making; schemes for the expenditure of Community
resources on employment policy measures are expressed in the form equivalent to what this author has described, at national level, as 'leaflet law'.[14]

Since in its nature, therefore, employment policy tends to be implemented
by means other than specific legislation or judicial creativity, the procedural
mode of definition tends to locate employment policy measures as beyond the
scope of ECEL. This may give rise to a kind of paradox; for it can be that the
closer a policy comes to the crucial areas of social and economic contestation
which lie at the heart of labour law—where many employment policy issues
are to be found—the less possible it is to achieve the political consensus
necessary to produce specific legal measures; and therefore the more likely
that policy is to be excluded from the scope of a labour law system which is
defined in formal, procedural, or source-based rather than subject-based
terms. It can easily be inferred that one of the purposes of this chapter is to

---

[10] i.e. the Dirs, cited at n. 8. Council Dir. 94/45/EC (European Works Councils) is of
more general import, but is, for the purpose of the present argument, an EC measure only
in a special sense as it is taken under the Social Agreement to the TEU, and so does not
extend to all Member States, i.e. does not extend to the U.K. Cf. however, n. 21 below.

[11] Council Dir. 91/533/EEC.

[12] Dirs. 93/104/EC; 89/391/EEC (the Framework Directive on Health and Safety at
Work).

[13] Compare Szyszczak, n. 5 above, and Barnard, n. 6 above.

[14] See e.g. Freedland, 'Labour Law and Leaflet Law: The Youth Training Scheme'
(1983) 12 *Industrial Law Journal* 25.

escape from the constraints of that mode of definition. We can draw upon arguments or distinctions both from within employment law theory and from the theory of regulation generally to help us to do that.

(a) Soft Law and Hard Law

No doubt some of the readers of the foregoing argument about the positivist definition of European Community employment law will have perceived that it draws on, even comes close to, the distinction between soft law and hard law. That is, indeed, a highly relevant and useful distinction for our present argument, though it does not, as will be seen, provide a conclusive answer to the question how should we think about the relationship between ECEL and ECEP. Admitting, then, that we cannot in a simplistic way consider ECEL and ECEP as divergent purely because ECEP gives rise to soft law rather than hard law, how far can that analysis nevertheless contribute to our understanding of the relationship between them?

We should begin by trying to identify what we mean by 'soft law', particularly in an EC context. Snyder has recently used the cryptic definition, 'rules of conduct which, in principle, have no legally binding force but which, nevertheless, may have practical effects'.[15] In their extremely important article on the subject of soft law in EC law, Wellens and Borchardt had offered the following very punctilious 'provisional working description' of the concept:

'Community soft law concerns the rules of conduct which find themselves on the legally non-binding level (in the sense of enforceable and sanctionable) but which according to their drafters have to be awarded a legal scope, that has to be specified at every turn and therefore do not show a uniform value of intensity with regard to their legal scope, but do have in common that they are directed at (intention of the drafters) and have as effect (through the medium of the Community legal order) that they influence the conduct of Member States, institutions, undertakings and individuals, however without containing Community rights and obligations'.[16]

Even before taking account of the 'marginal comments' with which those authors then expand that description, one realizes that defining or describing 'soft law' involves a studied compromise between ascribing legal force and denying legal force to the norms in question. This is an enterprise doomed to end in self-contradiction if pursued too rigorously, but which nevertheless can assist with our present discussion.

---

[15] Francis Snyder, 'The Effectiveness of European Community Law: Institutions, Processes, Tools and Techniques', ch. 3 of Terence Daintith (ed.), *Implementing EC Law in the United Kingdom: Structures for Indirect Rule* (Institute of Advanced Legal Studies/ John Wiley & Sons, Chichester and New York, 1995), 64.

(1995) at p. 64.

[16] K. C. Wellens and G. M. Borchardt 'Soft Law in European Community Law' (1989) 14 *European Law Review* 267, 285.

It will not assist us, as indicated earlier, if we try to use the hard law/soft law distinction as a simple technique for identifying the divergence between ECEL and ECEP. The attempt to depict ECEL as hard law and ECEP as soft law has some initial attractions but is scarcely viable. This becomes apparent if we use Baldwin's valuable breakdown of European Community rule-making in his recent treatise on regulatory theory and practice[17] This offers a classification of norms emerging from European Community activity as either primary, secondary, or tertiary rules. The primary rules are essentially the treaties founding the Community legal order; the secondary rules are the hard laws made within that legal order, embodied in regulations, directives, and binding decisions of the Council or Commission; the tertiary rules are the norms which do not qualify as primary or secondary rules, such as recommendations or opinions of the Council or Commission possessing 'no binding force'.[18]

We cannot satisfactorily locate ECEL entirely on the hard law side of that classification, because we can expect that almost any mainstream definition of ECEL would probably include some soft law within it. Those offering such a definition would be likely to accept the Charter of the Fundamental Social Rights of Workers[19] as part of ECEL, although that charter, being a declaration by a group of Member States not including all the Member States, is a good example of soft law.[20] They might also regard as part of ECEL any specific outcomes of the social dialogue which the Commission must endeavour to develop under Article 118b of the EC Treaty, or any Community collective agreements reached under the Social Agreement which Bercusson has described as giving rise to 'bargaining in the shadow of the law'.[21]

Just as we should not see ECEL as made up entirely of hard law rather than soft law, so also we should recognize that the legal component of ECEP does not consist entirely of soft law rather than hard law. There are, as we shall see, Treaty provisions and secondary measures such as decisions of the Council of Ministers implementing employment policies such as re-adaptation of workers in declining industries and promoting vocational training. Thus, the most important Community measure in the field of vocational training is the recent Council Decision 94/819/EC (the so-called Leonardo Decision), unquestionably a major piece of hard law.

One may ask why in those circumstances it is asserted that the distinction

---

[17] Robert Baldwin, *Rules and Government* (Clarendon Press, Oxford, 1995), ch. 8— 'Rules and the European Union'.

[18] See ibid. 220–30. The reference to absence of binding force is to EC Treaty Art. 189 which so enacts.

[19] The Community Charter of the Fundamental Social Rights of Workers adopted by the Heads of State or Government of 11 Member States at Strasbourg on 9 Dec. 1989 (ECFSRW).

[20] For discussion of the status of the ECFSRW as soft law, see Baldwin, n. 17 above, 229.

[21] Brian Bercusson, 'Maastricht: A Fundamental Change in European Labour Law' (1992) 21 *Industrial Relations Journal*, 177, 185. Cf. n. 10 above.

between hard and soft law has any utility in understanding the relationship between ECEL and ECEP. The answer is that admittedly it does not fully capture the divergence between ECEL and ECEP. However, the distinction between hard and soft law does illuminate the fact that, while ECEL has tended to be defined around focal points of a hard law nature, ECEP has tended to be expressed mainly in soft law. That is an important aid to understanding why ECEP has appeared to be a very marginal part of ECEL.

On the other hand, the hard law/soft law analysis also suggests bases of convergence between ECEL and ECEP as well as of divergence. It shows why ECEP can be regarded as having a significant legal content, albeit mostly in a soft form. Furthermore, the hard law/soft law analysis recognizes that the relationship between the two types is a dynamic one—in particular that soft law often has the potential to evolve towards hard law. This is especially true where there is a contest between institutions for the legitimacy of normative or regulatory power; soft law may represent the cautious advance of a central authority into disputed territory. There is no shortage of illustration of normative behaviour of this kind in the annals of the development of EC law generally or ECEL in particular.[22]

In fact, the hard law/soft law analysis is so suggestive of a dynamic from soft law to hard law that we have to be careful not to over-use it. It could easily lead us into the assumption that ECEP is simply a part of ECEL in the making. Such a view could easily represent a misreading of the signals about the general development of the European Union in the employment sphere. In order to understand the relationship between ECEL and ECEP in a way that is not tendentious, we need some other analytical tools.

(b) Substantive, Procedural and Promotional Standards

A very useful analytical tool of this kind is provided from within employment theory by Deakin and Wilkinson in their recent piece on transnational labour standards.[23] They distinguish between three types of normative (as opposed to descriptive) labour standards—substantive, procedural, and promotional standards. Substantive regulation consists of the insertion of particular levels of minimum protection into the employment relationship. Procedural regulation is concerned with the establishment of norms governing the process of bargaining about terms and conditions of employment. Regulation by means of promotional standards is 'designed to channel economic activity through the provision of public support services or subsidies, as occurs in the case of vocational training and worker placement'.[24]

---

[22] See Snyder, n. 15 above, 65–6 and compare 66–70 on 'structural reform'.
[23] Simon Deakin and Frank Wilkinson, 'Rights vs. Efficiency? The Economic Case for Transnational Labour Standards' (1994) 23 *Industrial Law Journal*, 289, especially at 290–1.
[24] Ibid. at p. 291.

This way of classifying labour standards is decidedly helpful in understanding the relationship between ECEL and ECEP. For it will be fairly readily apparent that, whereas ECEL consists very largely of regulation of the first two types, that is substantive or procedural standards, ECEP on the other hand generally takes the form of promotional standards—it is no coincidence that the examples of promotional standards given by Deakin and Wilkinson come from the area of employment policy.

It is also no accident, I suggest, that their argument about rights, efficiency, and transnational labour standards is really an argument about substantive and procedural standards rather than about promotional standards. Most of our tradition of discourse about employment rights, labour standards, and labour law relates to substantive and procedural standards rather than to promotional standards, both at a national and a transnational level. For reasons which have been touched upon earlier in this Chapter and which will be explored more fully later in this Chapter, we are not accustomed, or at least not fully accustomed, to thinking about promotional standards and employment policy measures as located in the mainstream of employment law.

One part of the explanation is touched upon, though not extensively explored, by Deakin and Wilkinson in the way in which they characterize the notion of promotional standards. For even in their brief explanation of what they mean by promotional standards, as quoted above, it becomes clear that those standards involve quite a different mode of regulation from that which is involved in substantive or procedural labour standards. Promotional standards depend upon quite a different relationship between the State and those whose behaviour it is wished to control or affect. We have already concluded that there is something different in issue here from the distinction between hard and soft law. We need to return to general regulatory theory, but to another aspect thereof, in order to seek a yet clearer understanding of this contrast.

(c) Employment Law as *Imperium*; Employment Policy as *Dominium*

The piece of regulatory theory so referred to is that in which there is developed the distinction between government by *imperium* (GBI) and government by *dominium* (GBD). The theory in question is principally or entirely that of Daintith.[25] Basically, his theory distinguishes between two ways in which governments may pursue their policy objectives; they may either use power in the sense of command (GBI) or they may use the wealth of government to create positive or negative inducements (GBD).

Both modes of government may be effected in whole or in part by legal measures; but the legal measures will tend to be of different types according to which mode is being employed. The paradigm of legal measures giving effect to GBI is that of command or rule-making; while the corresponding paradigm

[25] The theory is first developed in T. C. Daintith, 'Legal Analysis of Economic Policy' (1982) 9 *Journal of Law and Society* 191, and its current expression is to be found in T. C. Daintith, 'The techniques of government' in J. Jowell and D. Oliver (eds.), *The Changing Constitution* (3rd edn., Clarendon, Oxford, 1994).

for legal measures associated with GBD is that of authorization to government or its agents to gather in or to distribute wealth, and of definition of the conditions upon which those things can be done. Daintith's main aim or concern in developing this theory is to build in to the discourse about government by law an equal awareness of the issues raised by GBD as of those arising in the area of GBI, the latter being the traditional and better established focus of attention.

This theory offers to throw an almost dazzling light upon the relationship between employment law and employment policy in the senses in which we have been using those terms in this discussion. For it will be clear that employment law exists mainly in the mode of GBI, while employment policy is implemented largely by means of GBD. Relating this to the classification of labour standards offered by Deakin and Wilkinson, we can say that, while substantive and procedural standards are in the realm of GBI, promotional standards are the very stuff of which GBD consists.

By applying the GBI/GBD theory to the employment sphere, we can hope to make in our specific area the very gains which Daintith aims to achieve in the more general field of regulatory theory and constitutional law. That is to say, we can perceive more clearly the theoretical continuity or association between employment law and employment policy, and the reasons why our conception of employment law should make integral inclusive links with employment policy. It will also enable us to argue that, just as the relationship between GBI and GBD is complex and mutable, so the relationship between ECEL and ECEP should be seen as a dynamic one. This is a theme which it will be sought to develop in relation to certain specific aspects of ECEP in the concluding section of this Chapter.

The foregoing argument may have helped to understand better the convergence and divergence between ECEL and ECEP. In particular, it may represent a way of meeting the threat that ECEP will be marginalized in the thinking of employment lawyers because of procedural or source-based perceptions that ECEP has little or no place in a legal discourse. However, it is extremely important not to claim too much for this kind of reasoning. There is a further set of issues about the nature of ECEP and its relationship to ECEL which we can only satisfactorily explore by looking at the history of ECEP in development of the European Community—though we may find that a different branch of regulatory theory is of assistance to us in doing so. We turn to that kind of inquiry in the next section.

2. The Scope and Development of Community Employment Policy

In the previous section, we explored ways of challenging a sharp procedural or source-based differentiation between ECEL and ECEP. We used this in order to indicate why ECEP measures should be seen as being an important component of ECEL. There is, however, a sense in which that discussion was an incomplete one. For we remarked at the outset of the discussion that the substantive definition of the policy agenda of employment law is a controversial and highly-charged matter, and this is as true of ECEL as of national labour law systems. In the previous section we took that discussion as far as, but no further than, remarking that in EC terms the policy agenda of employment law is generally identified as employment-related social policy, and that employment policy tends to be regarded as a sort of sub-set of that social policy. In this section we shall argue that an examination of the actual development of ECEP reveals a highly complex interplay of different, even competing, policy agendas.

In essence, that argument runs as follows. EC law and EC policy, probably in general and certainly so far as they relate to employment matters, are the subject of two main types or realms of discourse, which we can identify as economic policy and social policy. European Community employment policy exists in a third realm, that of labour market policy. We should not, however, regard labour market policy in an EC context as a third distinctive type of discourse, but rather as a realm which is contested between the two established discourses of economic policy and social policy. In order to understand that contestation it is necessary to look in detail at the development of labour market policy; but before doing so it will be useful to sketch in a background about the discourses of economic policy and social policy both in terms of regulatory theory generally and in terms of the history of the EC in particular.

The growing body of literature on regulatory theory supports a distinction between social regulation and economic regulation which may contribute to the understanding of the distinction between economic policy and social policy which is being argued for here in an EC context. This literature, perhaps best exemplified by Ogus' recent treatise on regulation,[26] concerns itself not with regulation of human behaviour generally but more specifically with regulation of productive and distributive activity in society.[27] Discussion of this area of regulation tends to be organized around a distinction between social and economic regulation which is drawn in various ways but broadly treats as economic that kind of regulation which is concerned with creating and sustaining efficient, non-monopolistic, and competitive production systems or markets, while classifying as social the kind of regulation which addresses societal or not immediately commercial concerns such as consumer protection, protection of the environment, or protection of health and safety.[28]

---

[26] Anthony Ogus, *Regulation—Legal Form and Economic Theory* (Clarendon Press, Oxford, 1994).

[27] Ogus, Ibid. 1, adopts Selznick's notion of 'activities that are valued by a community'; but the focus seems to be more specifically upon *business* activity valued by a community.

[28] Ogus, ibid. 4–5, suggests that social regulation 'deals with such matters as health and safety, environmental protection and consumer protection' while economic regulation

The utility of this distinction seems to consist in its contribution to the precision of analysis of both the ends and the means of regulatory activity. For Ogus, for instance, the distinction is helpful in organizing a discussion of whether we can use economic theory to identify 'rational' regulation; he concludes that we may wish to use different sets of arguments in relation to rational social regulation on the one hand and rational economic regulation on the other.[29]

I suggest that this distinction between economic and social regulation translates not precisely but nevertheless very helpfully into a corresponding broad distinction between, on the one hand, EC economic regulation supported by an economic policy discourse, and, on the other hand, EC social regulation supported by an social policy discourse. The translation is imprecise in that, for instance, EC social regulation is more employment-oriented than is the general category used in regulatory theory—although I wish to stress that, despite the fact that I am writing from an employment perspective, I do not assert that EC social regulation and social policy are *exclusively* employment-oriented.

The transposition of the social/economic distinction from regulatory theory generally to EC regulation in particular is nevertheless extremely helpful, because of the way in which it implies the existence of diverse policy discourses supporting diverse types of regulation—an economic discourse concerned with trade-based or market-based goals, and a social discourse concerned with human-rights-based or communitarian goals. To state it in the most direct (and therefore no doubt simplistic) terms, the contrast is between regulation in support of a free-market-led conception and regulation in support of a citizenship-led conception of the European Community.

The argument advanced in this section is that an awareness of the central importance of this dichotomy between economic policy and social policy is enormously helpful in understanding the development of ECEP, and its

'applies primarily to industries with monopolistic tendencies'. Of the sources cited by him in support of this distinction, Graymer and Thompson (LeRoy Graymer and Frederick Thompson, *Reforming Social Regulation—Alternative Public Policy Strategies* (Sage, Beverley Hills, 1992), writing from the American perspective from which this distinction largely originates, say (at 9–10) that while economic regulation 'relates primarily to those efforts by government to correct or offset problems related to monopoly practices in the free-market economy', 'social or protective' regulation deals with a 'much more diffuse set of concerns' of which the major instances are water quality, air pollution controls, consumer product safety and occupational health and safety. Swan (Dennis Swan, 'The Regulatory Scene: An Overview', ch. 1 of Kenneth Button and Dennis Swan, *The Age of Regulatory Reform* (Clarendon Press, Oxford, 989), 4–6, has a three-part classification into anti-trust policy, economic regulation, and social regulation. The combination of his first two categories corresponds to the notion of economic regulation used by Graymer and Thompson, while his conception of social regulation, described in terms of control of 'externalities', is very close to theirs, though with the interesting addition of discrimination in access to jobs.

[29] Ogus, n. 26 above, 338–41.

relationship to ECEL. I suggest that the awareness of this dichotomy in fact enables us to organize our analysis of ECEP, and even to some extent of ECEL also, by locating them in relation to that dichotomy. In broad terms, the argument runs as follows.

As we remarked in the previous section, there has perhaps been a general tendency to assume that the development of ECEL depends largely or entirely on the ability of the EC to evolve a distinctive social policy competence. Implicit in that assumption is the view that the discourse upon which ECEL depends and to which it seeks to give practical effect is that of social policy.

A more sophisticated line of analysis exists which recognizes that the evolution of ECEL has always depended upon the possibility of legitimating ECEL in economic policy terms as well as in social policy terms.[30] This is a possibility which is made the more attainable by the fact that the proponents of economic policy have felt the need to be able to lay claim to a social legitimation. Hence the discourse of EC social policy often invokes the economic notion of 'social dumping', while the discourse of EC economic policy often claims that the area of market integration which it seeks to create is a 'social space' as well as an economic one. The protagonists of ECEL have had to seek allies in both territories, and have had to depend on the elaborate diplomacy existing between them.

That more sophisticated line of analysis tends towards the recognition that ECEL has always been and is likely to continue to be crucially constrained by this need to operate on two fronts. The proponents of this view of ECEL have begun to demonstrate how this tension can issue forth in direct conflict between the market integration rules of the EC (giving effect to EC economic policy) and the labour laws of Member States (giving effect to social policies of which EC social policy is ultimately an aggregation).[31]

So these arguments point to the existence, in the area of ECEL, of a substantial contested zone between EC economic policy and EC social policy. It is not necessary or appropriate in the compass of this Chapter to seek to establish how large that zone of contestation is.[32] For it is clear that, however

---

[30] See, particularly, Paul Davies, 'The Emergence of European Labour Law', ch. 10 of WilliamMcCarthy (ed.), *Legal Intervention in Industrial Relations: Gains and Losses* (Blackwell, Oxford, 1992); and compare Deakin and Wilkinson, n. 23 above.

[31] See, for a most significant presentation of this argument, Davies, 'Market Integration and Social Policy in the Court of Justice' (1995) 24 *Industrial Law Journal* 49; and compare A. Lyon-Caen, 'Droit social et droit de la concurrence: Observations sur un rencontre'; in *Essays in Honour of Professor Jean Savatier* (PUF, Paris, 1992), and Gerard Lyon-Caen, 'L'infiltration du droit travail par le droit de la concurrence', *Droit Ouvrier*, Sept. 1992, 313.

[32] It is, however, worth pointing to the Commission proposal for a Dir. on the Protection of Posted Workers (COM(93)225 final–SYN 346 [1993] OJ C187/5) as coming within this area of contestation; cf. Davies, n. 31 above, 73–5. The issues underlying this proposal are highly complex, but can be seen in terms of the question whether the EC economic policy of guaranteeing freedom of provision of services (as embodied, for this purpose, in EC Treaty Arts. 57 and 66) entitles inter-State entrepreneurs to undercut

large or small that zone may be, EC employment policy falls squarely within it. The remainder of this section consists of the application of this idea of contestation to particular aspects of EC employment policy and particular measures taken in pursuit of EC employment policy.

Before we can satisfactorily undertake that inquiry, however, it is important to clarify in one respect what we mean by the distinct discourses of EC economic policy and EC social policy. By asserting the existence of two distinct discourses, we are in danger of implying that each of the discourses is internally resolved and harmonious, and points unequivocally in a single direction. That is very far from being the case. Each of the two discourses is internally contested between competing tendencies, the nature of which we shall attempt very briefly to indicate.

So far as EC economic policy is concerned, it is useful to think in terms of two competing tendencies which are best identified in Snyder's analysis of two EC ideologies of competition.[33] One ideology is a neo-classical one in which the role of the EC is to create and maintain an entirely free and unconstrained single internal European market. Another ideology is a more co-ordinative one in which the role of the EC is to provide a framework for the negotiated adjustment of different market structures existing within the Community. In the terms of an analysis pursued in another EC context by Tim Frazer,[34] proponents of the former ideology would be more likely to concentrate on *free* competition, while proponents of the latter ideology would be more likely to see themselves as concerned with *fair* competition.[35]

So far as EC social policy is concerned it is perhaps harder to disentangle competing tendencies, but we might be able to identify two divergent approaches. One approach is built upon the aims and priorities of labour law systems (including that of the ILO) and social security systems. The other approach depends rather on more general notions of non-employment-specific human rights and claims to freedom from various sorts of discrimination, especially, though by no means solely, gender discrimination. The former approach will tend to concentrate on labour standards and social protection,

minimum labour standards imposed by Member States in pursuance of their social policies. (For a different, though not inconsistent, perspective upon this proposal, see n. 35 below.)

[33] See Francis Snyder, *New Directions in European Community Law* (Weidenfeld and Nicholson, London, 199), especially 72–8 ('Competing perspectives').

[34] See Tim Frazer, 'Competition Policy after 1992: The Next Step' (1990) 53 *Modern Law Review* 609 and 'The New Structural Funds, State Aids, and Intervention on the Single Market' (1995) *European Law Review* 3, 8–10.

[35] This would be another way of analysing the issues at stake in the debate about the proposed Posted Workers' Dir.—see n. 32 above. The notion of 'economic and social cohesion', the strengthening of which was identified as a Community objective by EC Treaty Art. 3(b) as inserted by the TEU, is contested between these ideologies (as well as between economic and social policy), but would seem to be more reflective of the ideology of fair competition.

while the latter approach will be more likely to focus on human rights and conceptions of citizenship.[36]

The existence of these divergences within each discourse does not, however, discredit the identification of the two discourses. It is hoped, on the contrary, that the recognition of these divergences makes it more feasible to assess a number of lines of EC policy development in terms of the two discourses, and to recognize how EC employment policy develops not on the outer margin of social policy discourse—as we have tended to assume—but at the central point where the discourses of social and economic policy intersect.

(a) The Collective Dismissals Directives as Employment Policy Measures.

It will be useful to begin by looking at an example of measures normally regarded as mainstream social policy measures, but which appear in a different light when considered as employment policy measures. The example is that of the Directives on Collective Dismissals of 1975 and 1992[37]—of which the first Directive, that of 1975, is much the more important. We have tended to view this Directive very much as a measure within the traditional agenda of labour law—as being concerned primarily with workers' rights relating to termination of their employment, and with mechanisms of collective representation or, at least, consultation. Of course, the Directive does have those dimensions, and is an important measure in those terms. It can also, however, be seen as an employment policy measure, in fact as an attempt to create a more controlled approach to economic dismissals than had previously existed. In this conception, the 1975 Directive is at least as much concerned with the influence of the State over collective dismissals as with the rights of the particular workers concerned.

There are indeed various particular features of the 1975 Directive which are more readily explicable from the employment policy perspective than from the workers' rights perspective. We can better understand the lengthening of the normally required consultation period as the scale of the

---

[36] By identifying two divergent approaches, I do not intend to imply that particular writers can be straightforwardly classified as taking one or other approach. In fact, many exponents of labour law seem to internalize the tension between the two approaches when writing about EC developments. Bill Wedderburn shows himself keenly aware of this in 'European Community Law and Workers' Rights after 1992: Fact or Fake?' (1991) 13 *Dublin University Law Journal* reprinted as ch. 8 of Wedderburn (1995), n. 3 above), which is a powerful plea not to allow the promotion and protection of collective bargaining to be neglected in the pursuit of a more broadly human-rights-based approach, as in his view the Action Programme on the Community Social Charter threatened to do. It is significant that the reprint of that piece in Wedderburn (1995), n. 3 above, has an 'Appendix on the Maastricht "Social Chapter"' in which he speaks of 'the impoverishment of the social dimension' (at 285), and seems to be referring especially to the failure to fulfil the hopes for the development of European collective bargaining which had been raised by or as a result of the Community Social Charter.

[37] Council Dir. 75/129/EEC amended by Council Dir. 92/56/EC.

dismissals gets larger, and also the importance attached to the prior notification of impending redundancies to the public authorities of the Member
State concerned. This latter requirement was intended to exert some pressure
on all Member States to require State permission for collective dismissals—as
some Member States (most notably France) at that time did, though as the
United Kingdom even at that time determinedly refused to do. It would also
be fair to say that the central requirement of consultation with workers'
representatives was at least as much directed towards avoiding or minimizing
the adverse labour market effects of collective dismissals as towards securing
industrial democracy in relation to such dismissals. The two aims are not
incompatible with each other, but it is nevertheless possible to identify
priorities as between them.

By the time that the 1975 Directive came to be revised by the 1992
Directive, the emphasis can probably be said to have shifted towards workers'
rights. Many of the Member States' requirements of State permission for
collective dismissals had been relaxed or abandoned in the course of the
1980s, and the part of the 1975 Directive concerned with notification of State
authorities was scarcely the subject of any attention by 1992. Nevertheless, we
can clearly observe a considerable degree of priority accorded to labour
market considerations in what is probably the central provision of the 1992
Directive, namely that of Article 2(4) which ensures that the 1975 Directive
applies although the redundancy decision is taken not by the employing
enterprise itself but by another undertaking which controls it. This initiative
towards ensuring that the Directive has a trans-national dimension reflects a
growing concern about the ability of multi-national corporations to, as it
were, play the labour market on an inter-state basis within the European
Union, trading on differences between national labour conditions and labour
laws—in this instance, national labour laws governing the trans-national out-
reach of consultation requirements.[38]

In assessing the policy basis for these measures, it is useful to remind
oneself of Bob Hepple's contemporary assertion that 'the origin of the 1975
Directive lies clearly in the "economic liberalism of the Treaty directed
against disparities in the conditions of competition"'.[39] It is on the face of it
surprising to see this measure, which has generally been seen as a product of
interventionist social policy, being characterized as based in economic liberalism. Bob Hepple did not mean that the measure was grounded in economic
liberalism generally but in the particular economic liberalism of the Treaty of
Rome which opposed itself to disparities in the conditions of competition. So

---

[38] See Leslie Dolding, 'Collective Redundancies and Community Law' (1992) 21 *Indus-
trial Law Journal* 310, 312, referring to the EC Commission Report, *The Impact of the
Internal Market by Industrial Sector: The Challenge for the Member States* (European
Community/*Social Europe* 1990).

[39] Dolding (1992), n. 38 above, 311 quoting Bob Hepple, 'Community Measures for
the Protection of Workers against Dismissal' (1977) 14 *Common Market Law Review*
489.

the Collective Dismissals Directive is thereby identified as a direct off-shoot of the particular free-market enterprise which is at the core of the whole original European Economic Community project. That is an analysis which is readily endorsed by the argument of this chapter; it is the kind of point that we seek to make by emphasizing the extent to which EC employment policy measures are informed by economic policy as well as by social policy.

We can see that analysis as helpful in identifying the role of the European Community in relation to the labour market. From its inception the EC has faced choices about the structure of its labour market, and in particular whether its labour market should be structured by considerations of economic policy or of social policy. As the strains placed on the Community by economic social and political pressures increase, so there is a perceived need to re-examine those choices, and to resolve the equivocations which are tolerable in easier times. The necessity to choose, and as a result some degree of actual choices, is present throughout. It will be useful to consider how this argument applies to some of the major areas of Community employment policy activity.

(b) EC Employment Policy and the Coal and Steel Community

The foregoing argument certainly applies strongly to the institution which provided both the pre-history and the initial foundation for the Treaty of Rome, namely the European Coal and Steel Community. The Treaty of Paris of 1951 which established that Community proclaims its combination of economic and social objectives if anything more prominently than the Treaty of Rome, and contains specific commitments which make it evident that it is as much concerned with employment policy as with controlling the product markets in coal and steel. One of the most important provisions of the Treaty of Paris has been Article 56, which provides for financial aid to workers in the coal and steel industries, and which has been the basis for a long history of provision of readaptation aids and benefits consisting of severance payments, training and mobility allowances, short-time working payments, and early retirement pensions and benefits.[40] Should these be seen as economic policy measures or as social policy measures?

I suggest that in relation to the ECSC readaptation scheme, as in relation to the many other EC and Member State schemes responding to decline of production and employment in traditionally labour-intensive industries and sectors, three analyses or policy profiles are possible:

1. Such a scheme might reflect a strong economic policy thrust—often thought of as 'active manpower policy'—by concentrating on ensuring

---

[40] See generally William Rees and R. Barry Thomas, *Study of the European Communities Readaptation Aids in the Coal and Steel Industries* (European Community, Luxembourg, 1988) 10–29, 'C. The Readaptation Aids System'.

re-employment and retraining of the relevant workforce, by making substantial resources available for those purposes, but by confining the use of resources to those purposes.

2. Such a scheme might, on the other hand, reflect a strong social policy thrust by concentrating on the violation of rights or legitimate expectations of the workers affected by industrial decline. Where there was that sort of policy thrust, such a scheme would be more likely to identify the need for re-employment or retraining in terms of the rights or the legitimate expectations of the workers concerned, but would be less likely to make the financial support of those workers conditional upon the contingency of specific retraining or re-location opportunities being available for those workers.

3. A third possibility is that such a scheme represents a combination of or compromise between these economic and social policy thrusts, in which weaker versions of both the economic and social policies involved in models (1) and (2) are reflected in measures to reduce the resistance of employers and the workforce to industrial closures, and to palliate the immediate absolute or relative hardship suffered by the workforce.

It should be made clear that this set of models is not advanced as representing all the possible responses to industrial decline which EC employment policy could or does offer. On the one hand, there is a strand of EC economic policy which argues for or seems to require a severely abstentionist response to sectoral or regional industrial decline. On the other hand, there is equally a strand of EC social policy which seeks to accord to State authorities or to workforce representatives a strong voice in deciding how to manage the outcomes of industrial decline. Those possible, though more polarized or extreme, lines of EC economic and social policy are, however, unlikely to inform schemes such as the ECSC scheme. With that observation, we can use this set of models to draw some further conclusions both about the ECSC measures in particular and about this kind of EC employment policy measure more generally.

An account of ECSC readaptation aids in terms of that set of models might run as follows. In its inception, the scheme was probably intended to conform to the first, strong economic policy model. That fits in with the original aims and objectives of the ECSC, and with the stance of the EEC towards traditional heavy industry in the foundational phase of the Communities and the early period of their development—the 1950s and 1960s. The scheme will then have come under the influence of the second model in the active social policy period of the 1970s. There will however have been a gravitation towards the third model which was completed during the 1980s. This will have left the scheme in an amorphous condition, vulnerable as such to the de-regulatory thrust coming from some Member States with increasing force during the later 1980s and 1990s.

The foregoing evaluation of that particular scheme tells us a good deal about the working of this kind of employment policy measure in the EC generally. Income support schemes and severance payment schemes of that kind are capable of being highly contentious, especially when pressure is placed upon them in recessionary conditions; readers familiar with the history of U.K. employment legislation will immediately recall the arguments about the objectives and efficacy of the redundancy payments legislation. The tensions and difficult choices which give rise to those arguments are, if anything, heightened when the debate acquires a dimension of power allocation between a central federation and Member States. Member States tend to become suspicious that their particular interests are not receiving adequate consideration, or that there is not sufficient adaptation to their local labour market. This effect may become acute when the availability of the benefits or aids is made conditional upon matching action by the Member States concerned. That then becomes a very direct question about willingness to engage in State support for workforces in beleaguered industries. The U.K. Government, having continued to make use of and match contributions to the EC Readaptation Benefits Scheme for Iron and Steel Employees from 1974 to 1994 then terminated its participation in the scheme[41] on the grounds that it was not very effective in assisting redundant steel workers to re-enter the labour market and had not proved very good value for money.[42]

We can usefully relate this analysis of the ECSC Re-adaptation Aids Scheme to our discussion in the previous section of the nature and typology of EC employment policy measures. For the Readaptation Aids Scheme is a classic example of a *dominium* type of measure, in that it deploys the resources of the ECSC to achieve the policy objectives of the ECSC, and by so doing engages in its own kind of normative regulation of the practice of employers and of the governments of Member States. The Scheme fully typifies Daintith's model of government by *dominium*, in that the legislation in which it is embodied is of a loosely textured facilitative kind, authorizing the use of resources for broad policy objectives and leaving the effective regulation to be achieved by administrative rule-making and executive practice.

In an EC context, that administrative rule-making and that executive practice necessarily consist of or involve elaborate and less than fully transparent dealings between the central authorities of the EC and the governments of Member States as well as with employers, training institutions, and trade unions. There is a real risk that even strongly formulated policy objectives imposed on such a scheme at its inception or generally at EC legislative level

---

[41] The European Communities (Iron and Steel Employees Re-adaptation Benefits Scheme) (No. 2) (Scheme Termination) Regs. 1994, S.I. 1994/141.

[42] Hansard HC 6 Ser. Vol. 230 Written Answers col. 804 (29 Oct. 1993).

may be diluted or even subverted in the course of those dealings. That perhaps explains a gravitation towards the third model of normative indeterminacy reflecting compromise between weakly expressed policy objectives. If such a tendency does exist, we should be aware of it when fitting *dominium*-type employment policy measures into our understanding of EC employment law. It is emphatically not a reason for deeming such measures to be outside the purview or concerns of EC employment law.

(c) EC Employment Policy and the Social Fund

In order to complete this argument about the pattern of development of EC employment policy, it is necessary to carry it through to areas which are the subject of separate treatment elsewhere in this symposium volume. As I do not wish to trespass far into the territory of my co-authors, I shall make the discussion a brief one at this point. I would, however, give an incomplete and distorted account of my subject if I failed to refer to the employment policy aspects of, first, the EC Social Fund and, secondly, (in the following sub-section) the EC Principle of Freedom of Movement of Workers.

It is, I suggest, fully appropriate to think about the Social Fund as an instrument—some might say the most important single instrument—of EC employment policy. The Social Fund is indeed in a sense formally dedicated to employment policy objectives. This is the nature of the set of commitments expressed in Article 123 which states that:

> In order to improve employment opportunities for workers in the [common market/ internal market[43]] and to contribute thereby to raising the standard of living, a European Social Fund is hereby established in accordance with the provisions set out below.

That commitment was reinforced and elaborated in 1988 by the Council Regulation which defined five priority objectives for the structural funds.[44] (It is now customary to treat the structural funds as a group. They consist of the Social Fund, the Regional Development Fund and the Agricultural Guidance and Guarantee Fund) These objectives included:

2. assisting the regions . . . (including employment areas . . .) seriously affected by industrial decline;
3. combating long-term unemployment;
4. facilitating the occupational integration of young people'.

If we thus regard the Social Fund as in one sense at least an instrument of employment policy, it is useful to try to analyse it in terms of our dichotomy between economic policy and social policy. It is not obvious that we have to think of the Social Fund in terms of social policy simply because of its name.

---

[43] As originally formulated/ as amended by TEU.
[44] Council Reg. 2052/88/EEC.

The language of the objectives as stated in 1988 is if anything more that of economic policy. We may detect some shift into the discourse of social policy in the 1993 re-definition of Objectives (3) and (4), though even then the language remains at least in part that of economic policy. Those Objectives are now expressed to be:

3. combating long-term unemployment and facilitating the integration into working life of young people and of persons exposed to exclusion from the labour market;
4. facilitating the adaptation of workers of either sex to industrial changes and to changes in production systems'.[45]

This does involve some shift of emphasis further towards the legitimate expectations of individuals in the labour market or facing exclusion from it.

However, rather than trying to extract too much from linguistic deconstruction, it is probably better to view the employment policy aspects of the Social Fund as analogous to the ECSC Readaptation Aids Scheme (on the grand scale), and as therefore best analysed according the three models which we applied to the latter scheme. I think we find a comparable tendency to gravitate towards a combination of relatively imprecise economic policy and social policy objectives. We certainly encounter, again I think on the grand scale, the same set of characteristics, including the same risks of lack of transparency, which we associated with the typology of the *dominium* mode of government. We return to this discussion later in this Chapter in the contexts firstly of the White and Green Papers relating to employment policy, and secondly of the particular development of vocational training policy.

(d) Freedom of Movement of Persons and Employment Policy

In the previous two subsections we have been concerned with measures or instruments of employment policy in relation to which the dichotomy between economic policy and social policy, although discernible, has not been very sharp. When we turn to considering the principle of freedom of movement of persons in employment policy terms, we find that the dichotomy becomes much more decisive. Indeed, we find that the two discourses of economic policy on the one hand and social policy on the other give rise to two quite distinct, even contrasting, accounts of why and on what terms we should regard the principle of freedom of movement of persons as part of EC employment policy.

At one extreme, we can see the principle purely in terms of an economic policy of market integration. We can view this as an employment policy if we associate it with the view that the aim of creating and maintaining high levels of good quality employment is best achieved within a trans-European labour

---

[45] Council Reg. 2081/93/EEC.

market free of internal barriers restricting labour migration. Such a view might actively oppose the harmonization of labour standards or the indirect social costs of employment on the ground that such harmonization would negate the competitive process which it was the very purpose of the principle of free movement of persons to stimulate.

At the opposite end of the spectrum, the principle could be interpreted according to a strong version of social policy. It could be seen as a personal right for the worker and his or her family to enjoy throughout the Community a favourable regime for employment and family life constructed around employment. Such a right could be interpreted, on an extreme view, as a right to combine the favourable aspects of the employment and social regime in the worker's Member State of origin with those of the Member State in which he or she chooses to seek work. This sort of approach views freedom of movement of persons as a contributing to an employment-led conception of EC citizenship. From that perspective, freedom of movement of persons is part of an emphatically social interpretation of EC employment policy.

There are some important concessions to this approach in the Community law of free movement of workers, for example in Article 7 of Regulation 1612/68, which, as well as guaranteeing migrant workers equal treatment with that of nationals of the host State in respect of any conditions of employment, includes the provisions that the migrant worker 'shall enjoy the same social and tax advantages as national workers' and 'shall also, by virtue of the same right and under the same conditions as national workers, have access to training in vocational schools and re-training centres'. Building on similar starting-points Craig and de Búrca have recently argued for the potential of free movement of persons to develop a substantive content for EC citizenship.[46]

Nevertheless, one must not lose sight of the fact that the principle of free movement of workers is, at least in terms of its origins in the foundations of the Common Market, far more obviously a measure of free market economic policy than of human-rights-based social policy. Rather than constructing a set of hypotheses about the way in which the principle of free movement might be used as an instrument of positive employment policy, it will be more useful to consider the impact on that development of the policy debate which was conducted through the medium of the Green and White Papers of 1993 to 1994.

---

[46] Paul Craig and Gráinne de Búrca, *EC Law—Text, Cases and Materials* (Clarendon Press, Oxford, 1995), 707–11.

3. Employment policy in Community Law after the Green and White Papers of 1993 to 1994

So our discussion has shown how the questions of what is the employment policy of the Community, and what is its role in Community employment law, identify issues fundamental to the future development of the European Union. That set of issues was central to those which the Commission sought to address by means of the policy debate which gave rise to the 1993 Green Paper, *European Social policy Options for the Union*,[47] the White Paper, *Growth, Competitiveness, Employment—The Challenges and Ways Forward into the 21st Century* also of 1993,[48] and the White Paper, *European Social policy—A Way Forward for the Union* also of 1994,[49] In this section we shall attempt to assess the impact of that policy debate upon the development of EC employment policy. The argument will be advanced that the impact consisted in bringing about a convergence of economic policy and social policy upon employment policy issues. It will be considered whether that was a positive or a negative development.

In its initial stages, this policy debate—which had been provoked by Jacques Delors as President of the EC Commission in an effort to ensure a positive EC response to recessionary pressures upon the social and political economies of the EU and its Member States—had two quite distinct aspects, an economic policy aspect and a social policy aspect. In fact the first two of the three policy documents in question conform very exactly to the dichotomy between economic and social policy which has been depicted in the previous section.

Thus, the *White Paper on Growth Competitiveness and Employment* is straightforwardly a discussion of EC economic policy in the face of declining levels of growth, competitiveness, and, above all, employment, especially high quality employment. In fact its central proposals were for a kind of New Deal economic policy response to unemployment, that is to say a public works borrowing programme to develop trans-European infra-structure 'networks' in areas such as transport, energy, and advanced information technology.[50] There is a strong element of job-creation running through these and indeed all the proposals and arguments of this White Paper.

The *Green Paper on Social Policy Options* was equally firmly cast in the mould of social policy discourse. Unemployment was only the third of its expressed starting points, the first two being the fact that 'the present Social Action Programme is reaching its natural end' and that the entry into force of

---

[47] COM(93)51. See Bob Hepple, 'Green Paper: European Social Policy—Options for the Union' (1994) 23 *Industrial Law Journal* 18.

[48] Published as EC Bull., Suppl. 6/93.

[49] COM(94)333.

[50] For a useful description and evaluation of the White Paper and its proposals, see the editorial comments at (1994) 31 *Common Market Law Review* 1.

the Treaty on European Union had 'opened up new possibilities for Community action in the social field, particularly by giving a stronger role to the social partners'.[51] The agenda and approach of the Green Paper reflected the whole range of tendencies of EC social policy discourse,[52] and displayed a high level of commitment to quite boldly stated social ideals, even if there was a paucity of practical proposals for securing their practical implementation and compliance with the standards thus laid down.

The third policy document, the White Paper on European Social Policy (the *Way Forward White Paper*), has an interesting and not immediately obvious relationship with the other two. It appears to be simply deciding the outcome of the social policy debate opened up by the Green Paper. Further examination suggests, however, that it really represents the outcome of both the social policy and the economic policy debate. This White Paper weaves the rhetoric of both policy debates into a single discourse which is really about employment policy first and foremost, and only secondarily about social policy. The central emphasis is on the creation and preservation of employment.[53] To the extent that this White Paper is about social policy as such,[54] its version of social policy is one which expressly draws on principles of economic policy as formulated in the earlier *White Paper on Economic Policy*. Why did that shift of focus occur, and should we regard it as a positive development?

As with so much of the discussion of the development of EC employment law and policy, the explanation has to be sought in two dimensions. The one dimension is that of employment-related politics; the other dimension is that of the politics of EC federalism. The *Way Forward White Paper* is symptomatic of a degree of retrenchment in both dimensions as compared with the progressiveness expressed in the *Social Policy Options Green Paper*, which reflected the Delors policy thrust within the EC Commission generally.

Here our argument about the different tendencies within the respective discourses of economic policy and social policy becomes crucial to understanding the significance of the *Way Forward White Paper*. The merger of the two policy debates about economic policy and social policy into a single policy statement about employment policy permitted a degree of selection between different policy directions within each debate. Within the economic policy debate there was a powerful line of rhetoric about the importance of deregulation and flexibility to effective job creation policies. Within the social policy debate, there was a line of rhetoric in which very broad notions of social justice and citizenship are asserted, perhaps at the expense of more concrete notions of social protection. In both debates, there is a theme about

[51] *Green Paper*, at 6.
[52] Compare *Green Paper*, Pt. V, 87 ff.—'Listing of Questions'.
[53] Thus its Ch. 1 is entitled 'Jobs—The Top Priority'; this had no counterpart in the *Green Paper*.
[54] Particularly, therefore, in Chapter VI—'Social policy and Social Protection—An Active Society for All'.

the importance of subsidiarity to the effective development of employment-related social policy. The *Way Forward White Paper* constitutes an employment policy amalgam in which those lines of rhetoric are far more dominant than in either of the two policy documents from which the amalgam was made up.

The subsequent employment-related policy pronouncements and measures both of the Commission and of the Council strongly support this notion of a convergent employment policy discourse reflecting a compromised version of the inputs from the economic policy debate and the originally more vigorous social policy debate. In June 1994 the Commission decided to introduce two new Community human resource initiatives, one concerned with employment and Development of human resources (called Employment) and one concerned with adaptation of the workforce to industrial change (called Adapt). They were the subject of two consecutive Commission Communications which identified these initiatives as being a direct follow-up to the *Growth White Paper*.[55] Indeed, the first of the two Communications identified the objectives of the Adapt initiative in a way which exactly reflects and follows the discourse of competitiveness and flexibility which is to be found in that White Paper. The second Communication, on the other hand, identifies objectives for the Employment initiative which come from a social policy discourse, namely those of promoting equal employment opportunities for women, improving the employment prospects of the disabled and other disadvantaged groups, and promoting labour market integration of young people. As these initiatives were essentially guidelines for the employment-related grant-making and programme-supporting activities of DG V (the Directorate-General for Employment, Industrial Relations and Social Affairs), this really marks the formulation of an important part of the employment policy of DG V in terms of the liberal economic policy elements of the *Growth White Paper* and the anti-discrimination elements of the *Way Forward White Paper*.

It would seem that a distinctly similar approach equally shaped the conclusions, about future EC social policy, of the European Council meeting in Essen in December 1994, as expressed, for instance, in the Council Resolution on European Union social policy of 6 December 1994.[56] The same essentially cautious set of attitudes and policy prescriptions is evident in the Commission Communication of March 1995 setting out the Commission's

---

[55] Commission Communications 94/C 180/09 and 94/C 180/10 [1994] OJ C180/30, 36.

[56] Council Res. of 6 Dec. 1994 on certain aspects for a European Union social policy: a contribution to economic and social convergence in the Union (94/C 368/03) ([1994] OJ C368/6). Note, for instance, how para. 8 reaffirms values of competitiveness derived from the *Growth White Paper*, and how para. 17 demands respect for the principles of subsidiarity and proportionality in EU social legislation.

Medium Term Action Programme for 1995–7[57]—which is the social policy programme whereby DG V seeks to implement the *Social Policy White
Paper*.

However, it would be both naïve and unnecessarily negative to let that be
our sole conclusion about the significance of the White and Green Papers for
the development of Community employment policy and its role in Community employment law. It would be naïve, in that we should of course
expect a debate to be conducted, at the level of public pronouncements, in
terms which are rhetorical rather than specific. We should also not be
surprised that it is sought to present deregulatory and re-regulatory policies as
capable of sitting comfortably alongside each other. The differences of
wording and nuance between these policy pronouncements may turn out to be
more important than immediately appears; they may be the basis of progress
towards a more positive fusion of the discourses of economic and of social
policy into a single discourse of active employment policy.

A conclusion in those terms would also possibly be unnecessarily pessimistic, in that it would neglect some possibilities for the future role of
Community employment policy in Community employment law. The combining of the discourses of economic and social policy into a discourse about
employment policy does result in a consistently positive approach to the
importance of vocational training. In the next section we shall explore the
possibilities resulting from that approach by looking at the development of EC
vocational training policy.

5. The Role of Vocational Training Policy in EC Employment Policy

A vivid illustration of the theories which have been advanced in this Chapter
about the nature and problems of EC employment policy is to be found in the
treatment of vocational training. In fact one has a growing sense that, so far as
EC employment policy is concerned (in the sense of policy directly concerned
with the creation and maintenance of high quality employment), vocational
training policy is, if not the only card game in town, then at least the one
where the stakes are high enough to be interesting. The first part of this
section will consist of showing why and in what sense we can expect vocational training policy to be the main focus of EC employment policy. The

---

[57] Communication from the Commission to the Council and the European Parliament
and to the Economic and Social Committee and the Committee of the Regions (COM
(95)134) published by EC DG V as *Social Europe* Supp. *1/95*. Note how the first three
sections are devoted to employment policy before the programme moves on to the areas of
employment-related and general social protection. The cautiousness of approach is well
demonstrated by the Annex on pending proposals in the social field, many of which are
shown as 'to be withdrawn'. No doubt that list has to be understood in the context of the
elaborate politics of choosing between legislating under the EC Treaty and legislating
under TEU Protocol No 14 (the Social Agreement), upon which it is not intended to
comment here.

second part will argue that this makes it specially important to determine the policy direction of EC vocational training measures, and will attempt an assessment of what those policy directions seem to be.

The reasons for the prominence of vocational training policy within EC employment policy are to be found partly within the politics of employment policy in particular and partly within the politics of EC development in general—those two areas being, as we have argued earlier, increasingly intersecting ones. Within the discourse of employment policy there are both positive and negative reasons for prioritizing vocational training policy.

On the positive side, vocational training policy seems to lie within a relatively highly consensual area of convergence between economic policy and social policy, such as we identified in the previous section as the territory claimed by the *Way Forward White Paper on Social Policy*. It has always been politically difficult to deny the generally ameliorative nature of vocational training policy, both in economic and social terms (though we shall suggest later in this section that we should be concerned about an over-readiness to assume that vocational training policy is straightforwardly beneficial in a policy-neutral sense).

On the negative side, vocational training policy seems to be relatively successful in avoiding the stigma which is apt to attach to many kinds of employment policy measures on the ground that, viewed as economic policy, they amount to crude employment subsidies which distort competition or that, viewed as social policy, they attempt to gratify unrealistic expectations in the nature of claims to a right to work. Again, we shall point to reasons for not being over-ready to see vocational training policy measures as free and safe from these objections: but as the EC economy or its constituent economies come to seem less and less able to be successfully propped up by particular job subsidy operations, and as it therefore comes to seem more and more important not to offer unsustainable promises of unconditional opportunities for employment, so the search intensifies for employment policy which avoids those appearances of futility, and so the temptation increases to view vocational training policy as the best path along which to seek to make progress.

In terms of EC policy more generally, vocational training policy has for the above set of reasons seemed a good area for Community development and the strengthening of the power base of the central EC institutions, particularly the Commission, both in the general spheres of economic and social policy and in the special areas of employment and education. One can make that assertion without necessarily implying that the Community is intent on a central-ist federalizing process, or that the Commission is engaged in self-aggrandizement; it may be simply that vocational training policy seems so readily to find a central place in most accounts of the aims and objectives of the Community as a whole.

Moreover, for reasons explored earlier in this Chapter in terms of regulatory theory, vocational training policy seems a good area for the development of the normative potential and methodology of the central Community institutions. This is despite the fact that normative authority is hotly disputed, both in the employment sphere and in the educational sphere and especially where they intersect, and as between central Community institutions, national governments, and sub-national institutions of employment, education, and training. This means that claims to jurisdiction over vocational training are doubly contested both vertically down the institutional hierarchy (in terms of subsidiarity) and horizontally between employment institutions and education institutions (in terms of areas of competence). Nevertheless, the fact that vocational training policy can be implemented partly by soft law rather than hard law, and largely by *dominium* government rather than *imperium* government, has enabled significant progress to be made against those heavy odds. We shall seek to give a brief account of that without becoming too enmeshed in the considerable intricacies of EC law-making.

It is perhaps ironic that the aspect of EC law and policy relating to vocational training which receives most attention in accounts of EC social policy law and EC law generally is in fact the aspect which is of least interest to us in making an assessment of the development of EC employment policy. As we observed in an earlier section, rights to vocational training have been an important component in the development of the EC principle of free movement of workers (and also in the EC Treaty general prohibition on discrimination on the grounds of nationality within the scope of application of the EC treaty, which complements the principle of free movement in this context). Various rights to education and training conferred by or under that principle or that prohibition are, by various particular formulations, confined to vocational education or training. So there are important decisions concerning the question of what constitutes vocational education or training and how that is to be distinguished from other kinds of education.

Although that discussion is undoubtedly interesting and significant, its outcomes do not tell us very much about the nature or development of EC vocational training policy as part of EC employment policy. That is because, hitherto at least, the principle of free movement as it applies to the provision of vocational training has not been seen as creating Community-wide entitlement to general levels and standards and types of vocational training; rather, the principle of free movement has been seen as having the more limited purpose or effect of entitling those exercising a right to move into a Member State to the benefit of the vocational training provisions made for the nationals of the State in question. In other words, the relative adequacy of vocational training provision as between Member States has not in any significant way as yet been brought into question or sought to be regulated under the banner of free movement of persons.

So far as regulation of vocational training provision within and as between Members States is concerned, a much more significant area of normative activity is that which is created by the EC treaty provision for implementing a Community vocational training policy, originally contained in Article 128 which was replaced by Article 127 of the EC Treaty as amended by the TEU. The normative power created by Article 127 was exercised in an important EC measure, Council Decision 94/819 establishing an action programme for the implementation of an EC vocational training policy. That action programme is styled the Leonardo da Vinci programme, and that measure has become known as the Leonardo Decision. The remainder of this section is mainly devoted to an explanation of it and an assessment of its significance.

The Leonardo Decision can be explained as representing the legal source for a potentially far-reaching assertion of a greater degree of regulatory control on the part of the Commission over vocational training activity within the Community. What was the basis for that assertion of extended control? The original Article 128 required the Council to lay down general principles for implementing a common vocational training policy 'capable of contributing to the harmonious development both of the national economies and of the common market', and the Council produced a decision to fulfil that requirement in 1963.[58] This set forth ten principles and included the recognition that 'the freedom of choice of occupation, place of training and place of work which is the fundamental right of every person should be respected'. All this sounded impressive; but the fact remained that Article 128 could be seen as, and was in due course interpreted as, authorizing the laying down of general principles for implementing a policy as opposed to the actual implementation of such a policy.[59] Moreover, Article 128 was set among the Social Fund provisions of the Treaty rather than among the Principles or Foundations of the EEC, and tended to be viewed as dealing with principles for the administration of the Social Fund rather than with more generally applicable principles.

The provisions of Article 127, which replaced Article 128 as the result of the TEU, seemed at once better and worse than those which had gone before. On the one hand, the Community now had a competence in respect of vocational training policy which was free-standing from the Social Fund, part of a separate chapter in the revised EC Treaty. Moreover, the duty was now actually to implement a vocational training policy. However, the protagonists of subsidiarity seemed to have been in the ascendant. The actual function of Community vocational training policy was declared to be that of 'support[ing] and supplement[ing] the action of the Member States, while fully respecting the responsibility of the Member States for the content and organisation of vocational training'. And the measures which the Council was to adopt in pursuit of the objectives of Article 127 were to exclude 'any harmonisation of the laws and regulations of the Member States'.

---

[58] Council Dec. 63/266/EEC [1963–4] OJ Spec. Ed. 25.
[59] Cf. Barnard, n. 6 above, 93–4.

The new Directorate General of the Commission, DG XXII, to which was entrusted this new body of competence in the fields of education, vocational training and youth, nevertheless pressed on to the point that the Leonardo Decision was duly enacted at the end of 1994. There are, as we have indicated earlier, reasons for thinking that despite the restrictedness of its Treaty base,[60] that Decision with its 'common framework of objectives' may acquire greater normative significance than its 1963 predecessor with its ten principles ever did. We can draw in two particular ways on our earlier discussion of regulatory theory to substantiate those reasons.

First, we can see the Leonardo Decision as a good example of a hard law measure which is being supplemented by important soft law measures. The Commission (in fact DG XXII) has produced two documents by way of implementation of the Leonardo Programme which are classic examples of soft law in the making. The first is the *vade mecum* of the Leonardo Programme which provides guidelines as to how the different strands of the programme will relate to each other, and as to how the Common Framework of Objectives will be interpreted and applied. The second is the Promoters' Guide[61] which develops those guidelines still more specifically into the form of guidance to applicants for funding as to how projects should be framed and presented in order to meet the criteria of the Programme.

Although the discourse of these documents is purportedly descriptive, there leap out from the pages some propositions which (though couched in the bureaucratic oracular style which has been elevated to an art form in this context) have a decidedly normative sting. For example, the *vade mecum* adds the criterion that projects applying for funding are expected to 'contribute to overcoming outdated conventions or compartmentalisation of actions and facilitate the transfer of innovation'. It will be highly important to know what employment practices are either favoured or disfavoured in the application of that criterion.

The second way in which we can make use of regulatory theory to understand the importance and potential of the Leonardo Decision is by considering it as a powerful example of government by *dominium*, and as an illustration of the capacity of government by *dominium* to acquire regulatory power and authority. In particular, by thinking about the Leonardo Decision as government by *dominium*, we can identify an important process of transformation of the normative status and effects of the common framework of objectives which it lays down.

This transformation occurs in three stages. The Leonardo Decision, being

[60] The legal base for the Dec. was, moreover, controversial in so far as it represented a choice which limited the role of the European Parliament in the legislative process, thus raising the set of issues associated with the *Comitology* case, Case C–70/88, *European Parliament* v. *Council* [1990] ECR I–2041; see Craig and de Búrca, n. 46 above, 452–455.

[61] For the full text of the *vade mecum* and the Guide see Internet code http:// www.cec.lu/ec/comm/dg22/leonardo.html.

essentially a *dominium* measure in the sense that it provides for the application of EC resources to achieve the goals of the EC in relation to vocational training, is in the first stage directed inwards to the EC itself. That is to say, the EC establishes and specifies its own power and authority to deploy its resources for particular purposes in a particular way. The formulation of a common framework of objectives is thus legitimated as a structuring by the EC of its own activities; it is formulating, as it were, its own standing orders.

At the second stage, however, it is in the nature of government by *dominium* that this normative structuring is addressed outwards to those whose behaviour is controlled or affected by the deployment of the governmental resources in question. We can see this happening in relation to the Leonardo Decision when the *vade mecum* and the Promoters' Guide make it clear that the funding of vocational training projects under the Leonardo Programme will be conditional upon compliance by those projects with the common framework of objectives.

There is also, in this instance, a fascinating case of the normative structuring being attempted to be addressed laterally to another centre of EC activity in the same field. The Leonardo Programme is the responsibility of DG XXII, operating within the objectives laid down by the Leonardo Decision. Another very significant base for EC funding of vocational training activities is the set of Community employment and training initiatives for which DG V is responsible, in particular the Adapt and Employment initiatives operating within the objectives identified by the Commission communications which introduced those initiatives.[62] Each of those measures commits the Commission to ensuring 'complementarity' between the Initiatives on the one hand and the Leonardo Programme on the other. A highly crafted note from DG V and DG XXII[63] sets out the understanding between them about how complementarity is to be achieved. It reveals an effort, presumably emanating from DG XXII, to establish the Leonardo Objectives as universally applicable across the whole range of measures covered by the note—as a common set of objectives in the sense of being common to all three programmes.

This takes one on to the third stage of transformation of the status of the common set of objectives—a stage about which one has to be more tentative than in relation to the two earlier stages, but which is nevertheless a realistic development to anticipate. It is, I think, a feature of government by *dominium* —we may wish to think of this as a dynamic towards government by *imperium*, but on the whole I prefer to regard it as a tendency within government by *dominium*—that the prescriptions or propositions emerging from it may be generalized and endowed with enhanced authority until they assume full

---

[62] See n. 54 above.
[63] EC Commission, DG V and DG XXII, *Note on Complementarity between the Leonardo Programme and the Community Initiatives, Adapt and Employment* (Brussels, 1995).

normative regulatory status and are recognized as part of a body of law or legal rules. This process can include, but is not confined to, the hardening of soft law into hard law.

The discourse and dynamics of EC law lend themselves especially well to this sort of transformation; the whole notion of *acquis communautaire* identifies an inclusive conception of a body of law capable of being expanded in precisely this kind of way.[64] One must, of course, be careful to handle this kind of discourse in such a way as not to pander to the ambitions of EC expansionists or exacerbate the fears of the sceptics. Nevertheless, I think we can reasonably expect a third stage of development whereby the common framework of objectives comes to be regarded as part of the body of EC law which gives effect to EC vocational training policy.

However interesting such speculations may be, it is in my view more important for labour lawyers to identify the employment policy implications of these developments than to reach conclusions about their juridical status or their contribution to the general constitutional development of the EU. The assessment in policy terms is apt to be neglected because it is often, and I think in this instance, more difficult to make than the juristic evaluation. There are nevertheless some points which can usefully be made.

We have seen that there is some degree of contestation for the job of formulating the objectives of EC vocational training policy. Let us assume, however, that the Leonardo Decision succeeds in setting the tone for and indicating the main thrust or direction of EC vocational training policy, so that the Leonardo common framework of objectives becomes the main reference point. We may feel that we will thereby have acquired an enlightened and unexceptionable set of goals for vocational training policy. There are commitments to promoting life-long adaptive training on the one hand, and to giving all young people in the Community a guarantee of at least one, if not two, years' initial vocational training leading to a vocational qualification. There are also commitments to combatting a wide range of discriminations or exclusions to which vocational training programmes may be subject or to which they may contribute. It might be felt that this reflects a social policy

---

[64] The term *acquis communautaire* is used to mean the whole body of Community law or norms; it figured, for example, in the discussion of what legal regime would be applicable to a less than complete set of Member States acting together under the Social Agreement, and of what impact their normative activity would have upon the law of the Community itself. The concept, although extensively used, is inadequately defined or even discussed; it is significant, however, that in the recent Commission White Paper on the preparation of the associated countries of Central and Eastern Europe for integration into the Internal Market of the Union (COM(95)163—3 May 1995), a distinction is drawn between the whole *acquis communautaire* the adoption of which by the associated countries would be left to eventual accession negotiations, and, by contrast, a more limited body of Community legislation identified as indispensable to the successful operation of the single market, with which those countries would be required speedily to comply (see especially paras. 3.1–3.9 for the articulation of this distinction and its application to the social policy area; compare also the Annex on social policy and action).

discourse which better implements notions of EU citizenship than the liberal economic policy discourse which is more evident in the texture, for instance, of the Community Employment Initiative.[65]

Nevertheless, there are some residual worries. If the Leonardo Decision does become the canon of EC vocational training activity, it will mean that EC vocational training policy is being fashioned and developed in the policy community of education, training, and youth, rather than in the policy community of employment, industrial relations, and employment-related social policy—the respective spheres of DG XXII and DG V. We may have concerns that the policy community of employment and industrial relations is more captive to the discourse of flexibility and competitiveness than it used to be. But we might also apprehend that the policy community of education and youth training might be less attuned to or concerned with certain employment policy implications of vocational training measures than we would ideally wish.

To be specific, I suggest that there is a risk that, from the perspective of education and youth training, it may seem overridingly important to ensure that vocational training is provided for all groups in society, and especially all young people, and hence justifiable and necessary to provide training which responds to the dictates and pressures of deregulation in the labour market. This may result in an under-awareness of or under-concern with the un-doubted potential of vocational training arrangements to contribute to the erosion and undermining of labour standards. Admirable though the Leonardo common framework of objectives is in many ways, it makes no obvious concessions to the case for ensuring the protection of labour standards either by identifying rights of individual trainees and trainee workers to minimum standards, or by creating collective protective mechanisms for those standards. That is perhaps an appropriate point at which to turn to the attempt to draw some general conclusion about the state of EC employment policy.

6. Conclusion—EC Employment Policy: Its Present Status and Possible Future

At the end of the 1980s, the *Oxford Review of Economic Policy* conducted an assessment of economic integration and the role of the European Community. Among the papers published as part of that assessment was one by Gatsios and Seabright, two Cambridge economists, on the topic of regulation in the European Community,[66] which attempted to distinguish the circumstances in which national governments in Europe might have something to gain from transferring regulatory powers to the Community from the circumstances in which such a transfer might be against their interests. They suggest that the

[65] See n. 55 above.
[66] Konstantine Gatsios and Paul Seabright (1989), *Oxford Review of Economic Policy*, No. 2, 37.

possible benefits of such transfers are to be assessed in terms of credibility, co-ordination, and costs, and that credibility is by far the most important of those three. While suggesting that there may be great gains in credibility if inter-State co-operation over economic policies is formalized by transfer of regulatory power to the Community, the authors are concerned to point out the risks attached to such transfers. They suggest that the most serious danger is due to the fact that European regulation typically involves an agreement by Member States to co-operate on some of the many policies they undertake, but not on all. Gatsios and Seabright apply their arguments to, indeed base their arguments on, a wide range of areas of Community activity, and reach differential conclusions as between those areas. For example, they see environmental regulation as good on most tests, but public procurement and State aids as suffering from serious credibility risks.

They do not, however, consider how their arguments bear upon the area of employment policy; it is interesting to try to work out how they might do so. I suggest that they would see risks to credibility as being at least as great in this area as in the high risk areas which they do identify. This would both explain and reinforce the reluctance which clearly exists in relation to transfer a major regulatory power to the Community so far as Employment policy is concerned.

We may, however, as employment lawyers interested in the role of Community law, be able to contribute something to the very useful discussion which these economists have embarked upon. For their discussion is largely cast in terms of relatively hard choices between retention of regulatory power at national level and its transfer to the executive or administrative organs of the Community. The development of and juristic thinking about Community law in general, and perhaps about Community employment law in particular, suggests less stark alternatives. In particular, the idea seems to be gaining ground that Community policies might be effectuated, not so much by means of assumption of regulatory powers, but rather by being translated into adopted principles, which would authorize and require a critique of national action and practices.

There are increasing indications that the European Court of Justice is prepared to assume the role of applying such a principled critique to the legislative and administrative action of Member States.[67] This seems to be possible not just in the sphere of securing fair competition and achieving market integration, but also where the Court can draw on principles derived from formally adopted statements of human rights, and, in the employment field, especially where they can identify principles proscribing discrimination and requiring equal treatment between groups or types of persons.

It is of course highly ambitious to suggest that developments of this kind

---

[67] See Craig and de Búrca, n. 46 above, chs. 7–8, *passim*.

might extend to the field of employment policy.[68] Nevertheless, this Chapter will conclude with the suggestion that this is a discussion which might be worth undertaking. Such a discussion could be initiated, perhaps even given some degree of focus, by asking whether there is emerging, from the area of debate and Community development which it has been sought to identify in the course of this Chapter, a sufficient body of agreement about employment policy goals and priorities to sustain some possible development of Community employment law along these lines.

Even if the immediate answer to that question has to be a negative one, this may still be a profitable line of inquiry. Within the area of employment policy, we might think of the particular field of vocational training as one where there is a potential for development of this kind, especially with the common framework of objectives created by the Leonardo Decision as a possible starting point. One feels emboldened to conclude with a suggestion of this positive kind when one is writing by way of tribute to and friendship towards one of the truly progressive jurists of our time in the field of labour law.

[68] See, for a most interesting contribution to this debate, Silvana Sciarra, 'European Social Policy and Labour Law—Challenges and Perspectives' Collected Courses of the Academy of European Law, Vol. IV, Book 1, Kluwer 1995, 307 ff.

Index

Lightning Source UK Ltd.
Milton Keynes UK
UKOW01n1106100817
307044UK00012B/254/P